JOCK:
THE LIFE AND
TIMES OF
JOHN HAY WHITNEY

BOOKS BY E. J. KAHN, JR.

JOCK:
THE LIFE AND TIMES OF JOHN HAY WHITNEY

By E. J. Kahn, Jr.

DOUBLEDAY & COMPANY, INC., Garden City, New York
1981

A small portion of this book appeared, in considerably different form, in *The New Yorker*.

Library of Congress Cataloging in Publication Data

Kahn, E. J. (Ely Jacques), 1916–
Jock, the life and times of John Hay Whitney.

Includes index.
1. Whitney, John Hay. 2. Capitalists and financiers—
United States—Biography. 3. Ambassadors—United
States—Biography. 4. Philanthropists—United States—
Biography. I. Title.
CT275.W5553K34   973.9′092′4   [B]   AACR2

ISBN: 0-385-14932-8
Library of Congress Catalog Card Number 81-43052

FOR BETSEY, SARA, AND KATE

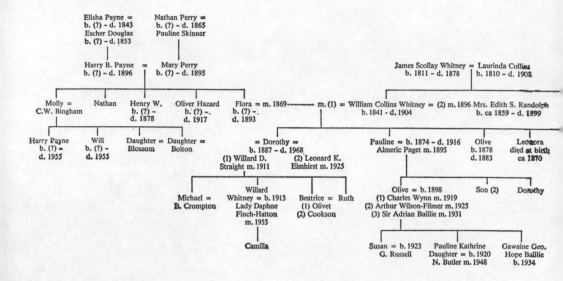

Elisha Payne =
b. (?) – d. 1843
Escher Douglas
b. (?) – d. 1853

Nathan Perry =
b. (?) – d. 1865
Pauline Skinner

Harry B. Payne =
b. (?) – d. 1896

Mary Perry
b. (?) – d. 1895

James Scollay Whitney = Laurinda Collins
b. 1811 – d. 1878   b. 1810 – d. 1908

Molly =
C.W. Bingham

Nathan

Henry W.
b. (?) –
d. 1878

Oliver Hazard
b. (?) –.
d. 1917

Flora = m. 1869 ———— m. (1) = William Collins Whitney = (2) m. 1896 Mrs. Edith S. Randolph
b. (?) –.   b. 1841 – d. 1904   b. ca 1859 – d. 1899
d. 1893

Harry Payne
b. (?) –
d. 1955

Will
b. (?) –
d. 1955

Daughter =
Blossom

Daughter =
Bolton

= Dorothy =
b. 1887 – d. 1968
(1) Willard D.   (2) Leonard K.
Straight m. 1911   Elmhirst m. 1925

Pauline = b. 1874 – d. 1916
Almeric Paget m. 1895

Olive
b. 1878
d. 1883

Leonora
died at birth
ca 1870

Michael =
B. Crompton

Willard
Whitney = b. 1913
Lady Daphne
Finch-Hatton
m. 1955

Beatrice = Ruth
(1) Olivet
(2) Cookson

Olive = b. 1898
(1) Charles Wynn m. 1919
(2) Arthur Wilson-Filmer m. 1925
(3) Sir Adrian Baillie m. 1931

Son (2)

Dorothy

Camilla

Susan = b. 1923
G. Russell

Pauline Kathrine
Daughter = b. 1920
N. Butler m. 1948

Gawaine Geo.
Hope Baillie
b. 1934

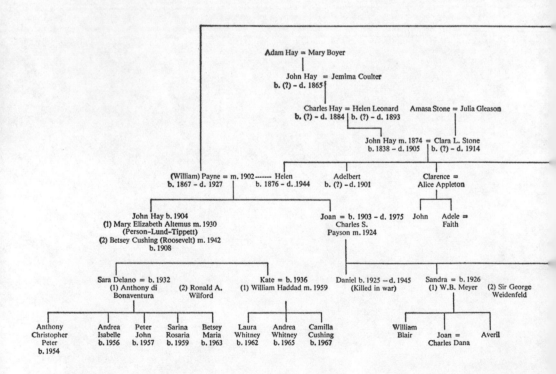

Adam Hay = Mary Boyer

John Hay = Jemima Coulter
b. (?) – d. 1865

Charles Hay = Helen Leonard
b. (?) – d. 1884 b. (?) – d. 1893

Amasa Stone = Julia Gleason

John Hay m. 1874 = Clara L. Stone
b. 1838 – d. 1905   b. (?) – d. 1914

(William) Payne = m. 1902 ——— Helen
b. 1867 – d. 1927   b. 1876 – d. 1944

Adelbert
b. (?) – d. 1901

Clarence =
Alice Appleton

John Hay b. 1904
(1) Mary Elizabeth Altemus m. 1930
(Person–Lund–Tippett)
(2) Betsey Cushing (Roosevelt) m. 1942
b. 1908

Joan = b. 1903 – d. 1975
Charles S.
Payson m. 1924

John

Adele =
Faith

Sara Delano = b. 1932
(1) Anthony di   (2) Ronald A.
Bonaventura   Wilford

Kate = b. 1936
(1) William Haddad m. 1959

Daniel b. 1925 – d. 1945
(Killed in war)

Sandra = b. 1926
(1) W.B. Meyer (2) Sir George
                Weidenfeld

Anthony
Christopher
Peter
b. 1954

Andrea
Isabelle
b. 1956

Peter
John
b. 1957

Sarina
Rosaria
b. 1959

Betsey
Maria
b. 1963

Laura
Whitney
b. 1962

Andrea
Whitney
b. 1965

Camilla
Cushing
b. 1967

William
Blair

Joan =
Charles Dana

Averil

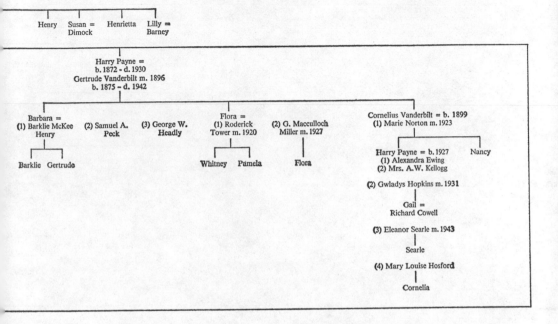

Henry   Susan =   Henrietta   Lilly =
         Dimock   Barney

Harry Payne =
b. 1872 - d. 1930
Gertrude Vanderbilt m. 1896
b. 1875 - d. 1942

Barbara =   Flora =   Cornelius Vanderbilt = b. 1899
(1) Barklie McKee   (2) Samuel A.   (3) George W.   (1) Roderick   (2) G. Macculloch   (1) Marie Norton m. 1923
Henry   Peck   Headly   Tower m. 1920   Miller m. 1927

Barklie   Gertrude   Whitney   Pamela   Flora   Harry Payne = b. 1927   Nancy
                                                                                           (1) Alexandra Ewing
                                                                                           (2) Mrs. A.W. Kellogg

                                                                                           (2) Gwladys Hopkins m. 1931

                                                                                           Gail =
                                                                                           Richard Cowell

                                                                                           (3) Eleanor Searle m. 1943

                                                                                           Searle

                                                                                           (4) Mary Louise Hosford

                                                                                           Cornelia

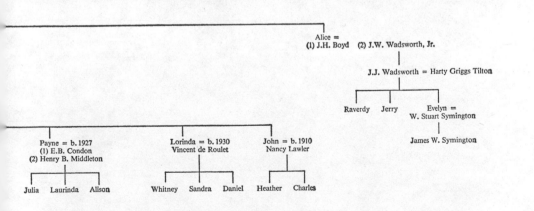

Alice =
(1) J.H. Boyd   (2) J.W. Wadsworth, Jr.

J.J. Wadsworth = Harty Griggs Tilton

Raverdy   Jerry   Evelyn =
                    W. Stuart Symington

Payne = b. 1927   Lorinda = b. 1930   John = b. 1910   James W. Symington
(1) E.B. Condon   Vincent de Roulet   Nancy Lawler
(2) Henry B. Middleton

Julia   Laurinda   Alison   Whitney   Sandra   Daniel   Heather   Charles

AUTHOR'S NOTE

There are certain disadvantages to writing a biography of a living person. It is hard to summarize a life that is still in progress; there are aspects of biography that, like those of history, do not fall sharply into focus until the present has become the past. Biography most frequently begins where obituary leaves off.

There can also be advantages, however. To have ready firsthand access to an individual and his thoughts and feelings is an opportunity of inestimable value. By the same token, to have access to the subject's relatives and friends while their memories are fresh, rather than merely to sift through musty records, has much to be said for it. Oral histories, where they exist, are research lodes that can be rewardingly mined; but one can't ask questions of them.

I have been fortunate, accordingly, in having known John Hay Whitney for thirty years, and in having had numerous chances over that time span to delve with him into the details of his singular life. Beyond that, he has opened to my prying scrutiny his voluminous and tidy files. Without his generous co-operation, and that of his family and friends and business associates, this book could hardly have been written. Jock Whitney, though, has had no editorial say about the contents of my work.

Over these three decades, I have talked about Whitney to numerous people—some now dead—who have crossed and influenced his multi-faceted path. They have in many instances been unstinting with their recollections and impressions; but what I have culled from the information they have shared with me is wholly my own choice and responsibility.

I would be remiss in not here thanking those without whose assistance I could never have hoped to undertake this book. I am grateful, then, in strictly alphabetical order, to Eddie Arcaro, Fred Astaire, Ted Atkinson, Harry W. Baehr, Walworth Barbour, Edward L. Barlow, Mrs. Tracy Barnes, Nathaniel Benchley, Jonathan B. Bingham, Louis Faugeres

Bishop, W. Scott Blanchard, George H. Bostwick, Philip Boyer, Jr., Kingman Brewster, Jr., Katharine Brown, Mary Morrissey Case, Marshall Cassidy, Henry Chauncey, Jr., Peter J. Christensen, Jr., Mr. and Mrs. Averell Clark, Arthur J. R. Collins, John Sherman Cooper, Charles F. Deshler, René d'Harnancourt, Christopher di Bonaventura, Florence Dickerson, Robert J. Donovan, Jack Forrest, Seymour Freidin, Mrs. Alexander Frere, B. H. Friedman, John M. Gaver, Sr., A. Bartlett Giamatti, Archibald L. Gillies, Lord Harlech, Richard Harwell, Mrs. Clarence Hay, Isabel Hill, Phyllis Horan, Lee W. Huebner, Henry B. Hyde, Flora M. Irving, William H. Jackson, Jacob K. Javits, Mrs. Edward G. Kellett, John S. Kelly, Bernard W. Kieran, Richard Kluger, Ed V. Komarek, Roy Komarek, William S. Lieberman, Fred Lundy, Russell Lynes, Frank MacShane, David McCall, John McClain, Tex McCrary, Lady Alexandra Metcalfe, Flora Whitney Miller, William J. Miller, Alice Leone Moats, Nancy E. Opdyke, William S. Paley, Samuel C. Park, Jr., James Parton, Joan Whitney Payson, John S. Prescott, Esther Raushenbush, Charles H. G. Rees, John Rewald, Kathryn A. Ritchie, Nelson A. Rockefeller, Anna M. Rosenberg, Benno C. Schmidt, Daniel M. Selznick, David O. Selznick, Irene M. Selznick, Gordon Simmons, Red Smith, Carlos F. Stoddard, Jr., Lady Daphne Straight, Frank S. Streeter, Frank Sullivan, Cyrus L. Sulzberger, Herbert Bayard Swope, James W. Symington, Walter N. Thayer, Franklin A. Thomas, Whitney Tower, Jeremy Tree, Alfred G. Vanderbilt, Richard C. Wald, Stanley Walker, John L. Weinberg, Sidney J. Weinberg, Philip S. Weld, Betsey Cushing Whitney, Kate R. Whitney, Sara R. Wilford, Langbourne M. Williams, Marguerite Williams, John H. Wright, Lord Zuckerman, and Lester Zwick.

And not least of all, foremost in order of importance, to Jock himself.

E.J.K.
New York, N.Y.
15 June 1981

CONTENTS

FOREWORD

Although he was never the sort to brag about such matters—nor, indeed, to brag at all—John Hay Whitney enjoyed at least one uncommon distinction. Both his grandfathers, William Collins Whitney and John Hay, were esteemed statesmen who at one time or another were considered to be of presidential caliber; both became Cabinet officers. Inheritance—of genes, of names, of tall good looks and princely bearing, of lofty social standing and political influence, and of enormous wealth—figured importantly in the long and busy and mostly merry life of the twentieth-century Whitney who nearly from birth was known as Jock.

In fact, Whitney was more often addressed as Jock by race-track touts and journalists than by his closest friends and relatives. His wife, the former Betsey Cushing Roosevelt, used the ubiquitous nickname only when she was mad at him, which was seldom; the rest of the time she called him Johnny.

On his own, Whitney became a protean man of means. From boyhood he was a devout worshiper of the printed word; during the most challenging decade of his life he presided over the flickering fortunes, and ultimately the demise, of the much-lamented New York *Herald Tribune*. As a sportsman, he was the only polo player ever to grace the cover of *Time*, and his stable of race horses was among the world's fleetest. As a political figure, he ranked high in the councils of the Republican Party, and high in the circle of Dwight D. Eisenhower's personal friends. As a diplomat, he spent four years as the United States Ambassador to Great Britain's Court of St. James's. As a philanthropist, he grandly nurtured hospitals, museums, and educational institutions, serving for nearly two decades as a Fellow of his alma mater, Yale University; through his own foundation, he sought to enhance the quality of life in social strata far removed from his own. As a collector, he amassed one of the finest accumulations of paintings in his era. As an investor, he founded one of the earliest and most innovative venture-capital firms in his country. As a

Broadway and Hollywood angel, he was in large measure responsible for bringing *Gone With the Wind* to the screen.

By breeding and rearing, Jock Whitney led a sheltered, even pampered life, but he strove incessantly to attain a common touch. When one of his horse-racing assistants worried about conferring the slangy name "Fuzzbuster" on a yearling because Mr. Whitney probably would not know what the word meant (a fuzzbuster is a device installed in motor vehicles to warn their occupants against radar traps, and the colt was born of a mating between No Robbery and Clear Road), the co-proprietor of the Greentree Stable put that doubt swiftly to rest.

Whitney's own doubts were more consequential. Born himself into a carefree way of life that was on the whole impregnable, he was persistently nagged by a sense of owing some debt to society, by a search for the true dimensions of that obligation, and, above all, for a constant pursuit of what, for want of a better word, could be called excellence. As a young man he had believed that people from "advantaged groups"—to one of which he emphatically belonged—could and perhaps should take things pretty much as they came along. As he matured, that attitude began to bother him; he wanted to become an instrument for change. Tradition was always meaningful to him—at the Groton School, he used the same napkin ring that his father had used there before him—but tradition did not make him hidebound, or even particularly conservative.

He was a tolerant man. He went along when his deputies at the John Hay Whitney Foundation proposed underwriting research by a pair of radical economists whose findings seemed unlikely to advocate, or even abide, the perpetuation of the free-enterprise system that had nurtured and sustained him. He had, at work and at play, myriad employees, but he could rarely bring himself to fire any of them. He kept on one airplane pilot who persistently declared that the weather was too bad to fly; and kept on another, an aviator who was hair-raisingly intrepid, and who had the unsettling habit of landing aircraft on their noses. Similarly, he retained the marginal services of one office employee whose inability to attend to his duties was sadly explained, upon his death, by the disclosure that his desk drawer contained little beyond empty one-drink whiskey bottles.

Whitney was a German prisoner of war in 1944, and during that ordeal was amazed to perceive that among his fellow American captives there were precious few who, like him, were under the impression that they had gone into combat for a noble purpose: to rid the world of fascism. After the war, as owner of the *Herald Tribune,* he refused to give special treatment to the New York Mets, even though they were owned by his only and much-loved sister; and he refused to play up the Congressional campaign of a son-in-law (who lost); but he felt so strongly that a re-

sponsible newspaper proprietor should have political views and express
them that, although a lifelong Republican running a long-time Republican newspaper, in 1964 he spurned Barry Goldwater and, while neutrality might have been the easier way out of his dilemma, ran an editorial
headed "We Choose Johnson."

What does a man blessed with vast resources do with all that money?
What does having all that money do to the man? One of Whitney's partners in the postwar venture-capital firm called J. H. Whitney & Company
once said, trying to analyze the senior partner's complex character, "Jock
is caught in a terrible conflict between the discipline required to do all
the things he feels he should do and the alluring demands of his legions
of interests and friends. If he isn't tied up with some hospital or museum
or Yale meeting, someone is bound to be calling him up and telling him
about the best shooting here or the best fishing there or the best horse
race or the best show, or the best seat for the best show. Still, he man-
ages to do surprisingly well, all in all, at being around when he's really
needed."

Whitney, for example, was one of a handful of directors of a large corporation who were invited by its president to a lunch at the Union Club
in New York for an influential out-of-town industrialist. "On the appointed day," the corporation president later said, "one of my directors
got in touch with me at ten in the morning and said he wanted to go to a
ball game that afternoon, and would it matter to me if he skipped the
lunch? The party happened to mean so much to me that I had even
worked out a seating chart for it, but that director was important to me,
too, so I bit my lip and said no, it wouldn't matter. At ten-thirty, another
director, a downtown banker, called to say that it had started to rain,
and the Union Club was an awfully long way from Wall Street, and I
wouldn't mind if he didn't make the trip, would I? I was fit to be tied,
but I said no, I wouldn't mind, and consoled myself with the thought
that Jock was coming. At eleven, Jock telephoned and said he was terribly afraid he couldn't make it; his mother-in-law was gravely ill and he
had to go over to the hospital. I said that in that event, of course, he
shouldn't bother, and this time I really meant it. But Jock went on to say
that if he could possibly get away for a few minutes he'd drop in. And,
by golly, he did. Whenever I hear the expression 'noblesse oblige,' I
think of Jock that day."

John Hay Whitney, who never *had* to do a lick of work in his entire
life, once mused wryly, not long after his seventy-fifth birthday in 1979,
that he couldn't think of a single material object that he had ever craved
but had had to forgo because he couldn't afford it. His father didn't have
to work, either, and never did. Jock could have gone through life like
that. But even as a schoolboy he began to sense that being very rich and

very popular—for it is hard to be the one and not also the other—was not the stuff from which happiness, his happiness, anyway, could be made. He was a playboy for a while and a redoubtable one; the wild oats he sowed were strewn from coast to coast and across an ocean. But he tired of that in due course. He could not abide the second rate—not in horses, not in paintings, not in wines, not in clothes, not in women, not in anything. He was never embarrassed about his especially good fortune—a very great fortune—and he almost always relished his legacy of affluence. But how he shaped it and how he shared it, generously, with many others was significant. For history could well judge him to have been one of the last of a unique species of American.

E. J. KAHN, JR.

LIST OF ILLUSTRATIONS

JOCK:
THE LIFE AND
TIMES OF
JOHN HAY WHITNEY

I

The Largest Estate
Ever Appraised

The bride was the daughter of President Theodore Roosevelt's Secretary of State.

The bridegroom was the son of ex-President Grover Cleveland's Secretary of the Navy.

The young man and young woman who would become John Hay Whitney's parents were married, in Washington, D.C., on February 6, 1902. Few of the one thousand guests invited to the Church of the Covenant at noon that day for the wedding of Payne Whitney and Helen Hay could imagine there being any more elegant social occasion in the nation's capital for the rest of the year. President Theodore Roosevelt was there. So were all the members of his Cabinet, the justices of the Supreme Court, the ranking military and naval officers of the country, and the entire diplomatic corps. The bridegroom's father, William Collins Whitney, almost didn't get in. He arrived without his invitation, and a policeman at first wouldn't believe he was who he said he was; that sentry said he had already been approached by enough people who professed to be related to the nuptial pair to populate a good-sized city.

The church was festooned, practically inundated, with white roses and lilies. One of the many newspapers that from coast to coast were following the romantic event with intensity ran the headline: "Greenhouses to Be Ransacked for Decorations." After the ceremony the truckloads of flowers that had been transported to the church were, at the bride's behest, distributed among local hospitals.

The couple who stood before the flower-decked altar were both twenty-five. Among Payne's eight ushers was his older brother Harry, whose own marriage in 1896 to Cornelius Vanderbilt's daughter Gertrude had been the high-society acme of *that* year. Helen had just two attendants—her sister Alice and Payne's young sister Dorothy. According to the society reporters, who professed to know all about such matters, it was Dorothy's first outing in a long dress.

Helen—slender, straight-backed, brown-eyed, brown-haired—had come in on the arm of her celebrated father, John Hay; he had been secretary, friend, and biographer of Abraham Lincoln. Four years earlier, while her father was serving as President McKinley's Ambassador to the Court of St. James's, Helen had been presented to Queen Victoria. Her Majesty, whose criteria were stiff, had admired her bearing. The London *Times* had soon afterward reported Helen's engagement to her father's secretary. When she returned to Washington, the papers there reported that she was being assiduously courted by the First Secretary of the Austrian legation. On neither occasion had any troths been plighted. Still the public evidently liked to be kept informed of her comings and goings, real or fancied. An adjective several newspapers used to describe the general reaction to her wedding was "agog."

Payne—tall, clean-shaven, grey-eyed, brown-haired—was debonair as ever in his cutaway. The New York *Herald* proclaimed him "an example of perfect young manhood." John Hay had written a friend two months previously, about his son-in-law-to-be, "He is a thoroughly good fellow . . . and we are all very fond of him. So this event, so vital to our happiness, which I have dreaded for a good while, comes to us with a gentle aspect after all." Some of the newspapers expressed amazement that Payne, who presumably could have delegated the routine task to some underling, had actually applied for his marriage license in person. He had also betaken himself to an art gallery and purchased a painting of a young man by Sir Joshua Reynolds for which Helen had been overheard to profess a hankering. Among Payne's costlier gifts to his bride—he had earlier hand-picked the diamonds that flanked the huge emerald on her engagement ring—was a diamond necklace that, along with some of her other presents, had been on display two days earlier for callers at her parents' home on Lafayette Square to gawk and gasp at.

The ceremony was a cheerful happening in what for Helen's family had otherwise been a dreadful year. Secretary Hay's son Adelbert, a classmate at Groton of the bridegroom and later Payne's roommate at Yale, had followed his father into diplomacy and, soon after graduating from college in 1898, had been posted to the British colony of South

Africa. Del Hay had escaped unscathed from the Boer War but then, returning to New Haven for a class reunion in 1901, had toppled from a window to his death. He was much on the minds of the principals at the church; it was he who had introduced the young couple to one another.

Because of Adelbert's death, the Hays had been in deep mourning. Helen's mother, for the first time in eight months, forswore black on the wedding day and appeared in a white-corded silk gown, one that the Indianapolis *Sentinel* somewhat snidely observed was "almost identical" to that of the President's wife. The bride had designed her own dress, of heavy white silk with a simple V neck. The material was so rich, a society reporter insisted, that the dress could stand up without anyone inside it. The bride's veil was of tulle; the orange blossoms affixed to it were fresh, rushed up from Florida. There were more orange blossoms, along with white orchids, in her bouquet. It was the first time so far as anyone knew that any American bride had carried what was known as an English shower bouquet, which trailed downward over the hand holding it. Helen had had one like it when she was presented to the Queen.

Leaving the church for the wedding breakfast at her parents' house, Helen was stopped by Teddy Roosevelt, who addressed her as "Mrs. Whitney." On hearing her new name for the first time, Helen "blushed most prettily," said one eavesdropping reporter, "and her attendants laughed delightedly at her confusion over the matron's title thus conferred upon her by the Chief of the Nation."

The Roosevelts were among the very few non-family members at the wedding breakfast. The President proposed the first toast, "To the health, happiness, and long life of the bride." Then John Hay toasted the Roosevelts. Then Payne's best man, Eugene Hale, Jr., toasted Secretary and Mrs. Hay. At each table setting there was a white satin box with the bride's initials on the outside and a souvenir piece of wedding cake within. The breakfast, catered by Rauscher's, consisted of crevettes parisiennes; consommé de volaille en tasse; mousse d'homard batelière, sauce crabes d'huîtres; filets mignons aux champignons frais; croustades à la moelle; riz de veau en chartreuse; petits pois à l'anglaise; cailles à l'estouffade; salade duchesse; glace fantaisie; café; Moet & Chandon Brut Imperial; and, anticlimactically, Apollinaris water.

The new Mrs. Whitney was at once accorded the honor, by those few observers of the social scene who cared, of having succeeded the former Miss Hattie Blaine—who had been married in Washington to Truxton Beale while *her* father was Secretary of State—as the bride who received the most and grandest wedding presents. It is not inconceivable that in the ensuing eight decades no one has displaced Helen Hay Whitney from the top of that particular honors list. The Theodore Roosevelts gave her a four-foot antique mahogany clock and two flanking vases. The 1898

Yale varsity crew, which the bridegroom had captained, gave her a loving cup. The best man gave her four solid gold plates. Among her other gifts were a tiara of diamonds and pearls and a diamond and ruby brooch (that diamond was three and a half inches in diameter) from her father-in-law; a string of matched pear-shaped pearls from one of her husband's sisters; an Empire clock from Senator and Mrs. Mark Hanna; a silver service from the Whitelaw Reids; a Japanese porcelain vase from Senator and Mrs. Henry Cabot Lodge; a spray of sapphires from the Harry Whitneys; a sterling silver punch bowl and matching compote dishes from the Andrew Carnegies; another loving cup from the Richard Harding Davises; and three Maxfield Parrish paintings from Maxfield Parrish. Mrs. Vanderbilt, Helen's sister-in-law's mother, gave her a sapphire brooch, the principal stone one inch in diameter, and a lesser Vanderbilt a bracelet of pearls and turquoises. Lord and Lady Pauncefote—he was the dean of the diplomatic corps—gave still one more clock. The German Ambassador gave a repoussé silver punch bowl, the French Ambassador an etching by Mueller; the Chinese Minister a bolt of precious silk.

Helen's mother gave her a silver chest containing one hundred and eighty-five pieces of sterling; and from one source or another the bride ended up with a solid gold coffee set, crystalware (each glass bore her initials, in gold) to strain the capacity of a royal pantry, silver spoons enough to accommodate five hundred at tea, and enough parasols with jeweled handles to furnish the most forgetful of mortals a lifetime of shade. The Denver *Daily News* devoted an entire page to the wedding and its appurtenances, and the Kansas City, Missouri, *Star* ran an editorial describing the bridegroom as a "fine manly young fellow" and the bride as a young woman who "fills his heart through and through with all that he desires, and he is the realization of her fondest dreams." That state of affairs, the editorial rambled on, "made the wedding of Helen Hay and Payne Whitney just like hundreds of other weddings which take place every day in this broad land. The houses and the yachts and the tiaras and the necklaces are mere incidents. They were not any more vital or essential than the doilies and the tidies and the cake-baskets and the pickle casters which were bestowed upon the rural brides of Kansas or Missouri. . . . Love is the same, youth is the same, hope is the same, romance is the same, the world over. A bride without a gem with which to bless herself and in dove-colored cashmere, may be as radiant and as beautiful and as happy as one in satin and laces and diamonds, and with houses and lands for her dowry. Herein is the principle of justice in the human scheme made manifest."

There was one member of the wedding whose appearance was bound to cause a stir among all who knew anything about the social world in which the Hays and the Whitneys serenely moved. That person was the bridegroom's maternal uncle, the feisty, impulsive, imperious Oliver Hazard Payne. William Whitney had named every one of his six children, in part, after Uncle Oliver, and with good reason: Oliver was one of the world's richest bachelors. Oliver doted on his sister Flora, Will's first wife and the mother of his children. Following Flora's death, Will had remarried; and his erstwhile brother-in-law and close friend Oliver had been monumentally offended.

Oliver Payne and Will Whitney had been roommates themselves at Yale and had pulled oars in the same crew; but at the time of the wedding five years had passed since the two onetime brothers-in-law had exchanged a civil word. Although they shared the same table at the wedding breakfast, it was a relief to all others present that the table was a large one and they were seated as far apart as possible.

In the cascade of wedding gifts, nobody was going to outdo Uncle Oliver, who by then had come to consider himself to be standing *in loco parentis* to his dead sister's children and especially to the bridegroom Payne. Oliver wanted that relationship to be unarguably clear. He gave his nephew's bride a pearl and diamond brooch and a diamond necklace worth—in 1902—a hundred and fifty thousand dollars. (The John Hays did not put that one on home display with Helen's other gifts. Until vows were exchanged, it was stored for safekeeping in a State Department vault.) Oliver gave the bridal couple an Italian Renaissance town house in New York, at Fifth Avenue and Seventy-ninth Street, which he had Stanford White design. (White's own wedding present was a bronze replica of Augustus Saint-Gaudens' nude Diana; the original perched atop Madison Square Garden.) Uncle Oliver also gave them, *en passant*, a yacht, a private railroad car, and fifty thousand dollars in cash. For their honeymoon—Helen embarked on it in a black silk cloak lined with ermine—he made available a splendid plantation he owned in southwestern Georgia, and eventually he would give them that, too. Perhaps never again in history, as it turned out, would any newlyweds have so indulgent a rich uncle.

Years later, when that bridal couple's son Jock (a modest and self-effacing man) was mustered out of service in the Second World War as a full colonel, he issued a jesting "final and only order of the day" to the employees who handled his voluminous business and financial affairs. In it he said that "since I am not running for office, do not intend to live in the South, and have never been mocked by an appointment to the staff of the Governor of Kentucky, there is no effective reason for continuing use of my wartime title of Colonel." Mister, he said, would do.

His great-uncle Oliver Payne, by contrast, clung to the rank *he* had attained in the Civil War—lieutenant colonel in the 124th Ohio Volunteer Infantry—until his death, at seventy-seven, in 1917. When his kinfolk referred to "the Colonel," there was no question to whom the respectful allusion applied. (Oliver had previously had the nickname Ol, but it was seldom used except among a few Rockefellers who had known him when he was young.) By the same token, there were numerous uncles perched on various limbs of the Whitney and Hay family trees, but there was only one "Uncle."

Periodically throughout their childhood, Jock and his older sister Joan were escorted into Uncle's New York town house to pay dutiful calls. They could never get out quickly enough. What they remembered best about the then old man was that he had a small, bristly, tobacco-stained mustache, and that when they were presented for the ritual avuncular kiss they got scraped. "I will never forget that mustache," Whitney would say some seventy years later. He also recalled, not without awe, that Uncle's front door was upholstered in fine green leather.

Uncle could by then have afforded double doors made of emeralds. A native of Cleveland, Ohio, Oliver Payne was born in 1839, the second son of Henry B. Payne, who could claim collateral descent from a *Mayflower* passenger. Payne *père*, who had studied law alongside his cousin and friend, Stephen A. Douglas, was profitably into the coal and railroad businesses; he supervised the construction of Cleveland's municipal water works and was prominent in Democratic politics. Toward the end of his life he was successively a member of the House of Representatives and of the United States Senate. Before that, during his party's 1860 national convention held at Charleston, South Carolina, he had been the spokesman for the Democratic faction that opposed slavery and hoped nonetheless, but in vain, to prevent the party from splintering over that issue. When the Civil War broke out, the senior Payne, too old to fight, devoted himself to raising funds to fit out the Union troops from Ohio.

His son Oliver was not too old to go to war. After being sent east to boarding school, at Andover, he made the then routine move from that campus to Yale, matriculating at New Haven in the fall of 1859. He quit college in 1861 to accept a commission in the 1st Battalion of the Yates, Illinois, Sharpshooters. After participating in, and surviving, five battles (he was wounded at Chickamauga), with a promotion in rank close to each of the five, he returned to Cleveland at the end of hostilities. There he met up with John D. Rockefeller and joined that eminence in founding the Standard Oil Company, of which Oliver Payne became treasurer. He had a flair for handling money and made much of it in oil, tobacco, the Northern Finance Corporation, and Singer sewing machines. His name would never become a household one like Morgan or Harkness or Gould—or Rockefeller—but he was their financial peer. He was a bachelor all his life, apparently fonder of his sister than of any other female.

In 1884 he moved to New York (meanwhile having arranged for his older brother to become Mayor of Cleveland), where in due course he would establish the Cornell University Medical College with what for him was a readily manageable gift of $4,350,000. He was neither miserly nor austere. He treated himself to an oceangoing yacht (bachelor or no, he christened it *Aphrodite*), which, while not quite the size of J. P. Morgan's celebrated *Corsair*, could and did traverse the Atlantic in ease and comfort.

Uncle Oliver was a sturdy branch—though a non-breeding one—on the maternal side of Payne Whitney's multiple-limbed family tree. Nowhere did Oliver more enjoy sojourning—and enjoy being called "Colonel"— than at his Georgia plantation, which would later become one of his grandnephew Jock's favorite homes. The Thomasville place was called Greenwood. Oliver was known as "Colonel" there even though he had, of course, been a Northern colonel. His wartime service was less a local irritant than it might otherwise have been because Thomasville, a cotton-growing town before the Civil War, had not been damaged by the Yankees. During the last couple of weeks of the war, it had harbored five thousand Union prisoners who'd been hastily moved from Andersonville when the South feared that General Sherman was going to raid the Andersonville encampment and release its inmates. Thomasville lore has it that some of the captives who were briefly held there became so enamored of the region that they later voluntarily returned as vacationers. Whatever their motives, a good many Northerners began spending winter holidays in Thomasville around 1890. It was a mecca then much like Miami a generation later, and it had attributes that few other resorts could boast—some of the nation's finest quail, dove hunting in its pine woods, and a testimonial by the eminent physician Sir William Osler that tuberculosis victims would find its air as bracing as that of Saranac Lake in the Adirondacks.

Thomasville, a terminus of the Savannah, Florida & Western Railroad, was twelve miles from the Florida border, two hundred and sixty-seven miles south of Atlanta, a thirty-six-hour Pullman ride from New York. Many of the early nomads, the senior John D. Rockefeller and Senator Mark Hanna among them, were from Cleveland. At Hanna's urging, President McKinley sojourned there, too. At first, the visitors would put up at big Thomasville inns like the Piney Woods Hotel, and lease land outside town for bird shooting. Then they began buying acreage and building elaborate winter homes. One called his property Cleveland

Park. There were Hannas all over the place, and still are. Mark's brother Melville bought his estate in 1891, and eight years later persuaded Oliver Payne to follow suit.

Oliver's main house at Greenwood had been built over a nine-year stretch, starting in 1835, by an émigré from Savannah named Thomas Jones. Its massive timbers, kiln-dried for four years, were hewn from local longleaf pines. Four Ionic columns graced its façade, over each of them a frieze with laurel wreaths hand-carved with a pocket knife by the English architect John Wind, whose credentials were impeccable: upon graduating from the Queen's School of Fine Workmanship in London, he had received a diploma signed by Her Majesty Victoria herself. That, the Colonel may have reasoned, was a cachet that mere money couldn't buy. Stragglers from Sherman's army had set the house afire in 1865, but a couple of furloughed Confederate soldiers in the neighborhood had doused the blaze. When Oliver bought the then thirteen-hundred-acre place, he invited Stanford White down to look it over, with a view toward altering the residence. The architect refused (although he did import some Italian marble statues to enhance the gardens), on the redoubtable, if redundant, ground that it was "the most perfect example of Greek Revival architecture in America." The Colonel nonetheless subsequently tacked two flanking wings onto the main building, and while he was at it installed a golf course and a hundred-thousand-dollar garage that could, and not infrequently did, house twenty automobiles.

In the foyer just inside the main door, he enshrined a bust of Lafayette. The marquis had had most of his landholdings in France confiscated during that country's revolution. In gratitude for his services during the American one, Congress had authorized him to select some public lands for his own. He had picked a chunk of Florida, close to the Georgia border and to Thomasville, and although he and his heirs had ultimately disposed of it all, he was still something of a regional war hero. Accordingly, Oliver Payne had honored him in his entranceway, and the marquis's marble head came to have a functional use; when the Colonel returned from a bird shoot, he would hang his hat on it. So, in his day, would Payne Whitney—and so, in his (no man to flout a family foible), would Jock.

Uncle Oliver was—insisted on being—a dominant figure on the mother's side of the bridegroom's family. There were plenty of illustrious personages on Payne's father's side, too. One of them was believed by some Whitneys to be William the Conqueror. (In tracing their ancestry back to the eleventh century, the latter-day members of the clan had to make some broad assumptions as to just who begat whom in the twelfth.) That William, in 1066, bequeathed some land in Hertfordshire, near the

Welsh border, to one of his deputy conquerors, whose purported descendants were more or less indisputably known in 1242 as the de Whitneys. Their village in Herts was eventually called Whitney-on-Wye. The name "Whitney" was supposed to have derived from "white water," and there was plenty of that in their bailiwick. The river Wye overflowed its banks in 1730 and inundated the local castle, the church, and the cemetery, burying many Whitney graves under a thick carpet of mud.

In 1959, more than two centuries after that family catastrophe, Jock Whitney, while United States Ambassador to the Court of St. James's, visited the spot and gratified the community's one hundred and fifty latter-day residents with a subscription to the refurbishment of their modest town hall. (His grandfather William had earlier contributed a stained-glass window to a new church that had gone up ten years after the eighteenth-century flood.) "I just went to Whitney-on-Wye to seek out our forebears—our roots," Jock Whitney said afterward. "I didn't realize I'd anticipated Alex Haley's *Roots*. The senior resident escorted me to the edge of the Wye where the original family manse probably stood. And while I was standing there, an enormous salmon sprang up out of the water as if to bid me welcome. It was a very moving experience."

The Whitney forebear who forsook the then relatively placid Wye and emigrated to the Massachusetts Bay Colony, in 1635, was John Whitney, who settled in Watertown. He did well there in business and was active in community affairs, serving at one time or another as town clerk, town constable, and selectman. He had five sons, and their scions spread across the continent. (Genealogists have further contended that John Hay Whitney and Eli Whitney were cousins—extremely distant ones—and indeed that both were kin, even more remotely, to Edward III of England.) One descendant who stayed in New England was James Scollay Whitney, born in 1811, who at the prodigious age of twenty-four was a brigadier general in the 2nd Brigade of the Massachusetts Militia. He ran a general store for a spell, went on into cotton milling, banking, and insurance; and at his death, in 1878, was president of two rewarding enterprises, the Metropolitan Steamship Company and the Boston Water Power Company. On the side, he was for six years just before the Civil War—he, too, like Henry Payne, was outspokenly against slavery—in charge of the National Armory at Springfield; and later he was designated Collector of the Port of Boston. General Whitney, as he was regularly known, had five children, among them William Collins Whitney, who became Oliver Payne's roommate at Yale.

The social observer Lucius Beebe, a Yale classmate of Jock Whitney, once characterized Jock's paternal grandfather William in a phrase that would have been no less applicable, in due course, to the grandson. "Mediocrity in Whitney was unthinkable," Beebe said. William Whitney, born in 1841 at Conway, Massachusetts, bequeathed to his heirs another *Mayflower* connection: his mother, Laurinda Collins, was a certifiable descendant of the Pilgrims' Governor William Bradford. With Will Whitney's father's military background, it was reasonable that the son should have aspired to West Point. But his parents talked him out of that, and he went to Yale. He rowed on the varsity crew; he was tapped for Skull and Bones. By the time he was graduated, in 1863, he had so far abandoned the notion of pursuing the martial life that instead of, like Oliver Payne, going to war, he entered Harvard Law School. On getting his degree, he obtained a law clerk's job in New York City and helped draft a bill that set up a Metropolitan Fire District and had the effect of sapping the political strength that Tammany Hall's Boss Tweed had derived from members of volunteer fire companies who were among his staunchest henchmen.

As Will Whitney matured, he drifted away from the law—though he put in a stint as corporation counsel of New York—and divided his considerable energies between business and politics. He prospered in both. He consolidated the surface transit of Manhattan into the Metropolitan Street Railway Company. He organized the New York Gas & Electric Light, Heat, and Power Company and, after a spirited battle with a forerunner of Consolidated Edison, sold out at a handsome profit. He was an early admirer and supporter of Grover Cleveland. When Cleveland first ascended to the White House, after the election of 1884, he invited Whitney to be his Secretary of the Navy. Whitney took over a fleet in dismal shape; it boasted not a single vessel that could stay at sea a single week. He proceeded to modernize the American navy, and he was generally credited with having made it strong enough and self-sufficient enough to assume and carry out its responsibilities later in the Spanish-American War. (The first naval vessel built at the Newport News, Virginia, shipyard was a ninety-foot tugboat named, after the Secretary's youngest child, the *Dorothy*.) Whitney himself was often mentioned as a likely presidential candidate in 1892, but he begged off and busied himself instead helping to bring about Cleveland's unprecedented re-election. Henry Adams predicted to John Hay that Whitney would succeed Cleveland in the White House, but Will's candidacy did not progress much beyond the distribution at the 1896 Democratic convention in Chicago of some "Whitney for President" buttons.

Though in his youth noted for solemnity—his boyhood friends called him "the Deacon"—in middle life Whitney exhibited a more fun-loving streak. He acquired the reputation of making money faster, and disposing of it faster, than any man of his day, and that was in an era of spectacular big spenders. He lavished a good deal of his outgo on real estate. At his death, he was the unembarrassed owner of seventy thousand acres in the Adirondacks (including fifty-two lakes), of eleven thousand acres near Lenox, Massachusetts (including a wild-animal preserve), of five thousand acres on Long Island (including a covered race track), of three thousand acres at Aiken, South Carolina (including a court-tennis pavilion and a house with twenty-four guest bedrooms), of three thousand acres in Kentucky (including a stud farm), and of a shooting box in England. His Aiken place had a lilting name—Joye Cottage, at the confluence of Easy Street and Whiskey Road. He went into horse racing in 1900, importing the expert jockey Ted Sloan from England. When Sloan won the Brooklyn Futurity in Whitney's colors, the joyful owner reached into his pocket and gave his rider all the cash he had on him—nine thousand dollars. Then, evidently feeling that pourboire was inadequate, Whitney dug into another pocket and gave Sloan his gold watch. The following year, Whitney exported himself to England, leased a speedy horse named Volodyovski (known among English punters who had trouble with its whole name as Voly or Bottle o' Whiskey), and with it won that country's coveted Derby. By 1903, Whitney had emerged as the leading money winner—$102,569 was enough then to earn that honor—of the American turf. The prestigious Whitney Stakes, an annual feature of the August race meet at Saratoga, was initiated in his honor.

Whitney had kept in touch, after leaving New Haven, with his Yale roommate, Oliver Payne, who would often visit New York on business. On one such trip, in 1868, Oliver introduced Whitney to his sister Flora.

Flora Payne was an anomaly among the young ladies of her time. At eighteen, she had betaken herself from Cleveland to Cambridge, Massachusetts, to attend the seminary for young ladies that was being conducted there by Professor Agassiz, the naturalist; Radcliffe College would eventually sprout from this academic seed. Flora had traveled widely abroad, even to places such as North Africa, with which few sophisticated New Yorkers of William Whitney's circle had firsthand acquaintance. Oliver Payne thought she would make an ideal wife for his old roommate, and his matchmaking instincts were sound. William and Flora were married in Cleveland, on October 13, 1869, and they began housekeeping on a sumptuous scale. Among *their* many wedding presents was a Park Avenue town house that the bride's brother Oliver thought would be a suitable setting for domesticity. William and Flora grew fond of their home but felt obliged to move out of it when, ten years later, the Colonel decided that they deserved yet more spacious digs and conferred on them a much larger house, at Fifty-seventh Street and Fifth Avenue, which he bought for seven hundred thousand 1879 dollars. The young wife's father, Senator Payne, was not niggardly himself; on the birth of Flora's first child he gave her a million dollars.

In New York, the William Whitneys were notable, in a time of elegant at-homes, for their glittering soirées. But it was when her husband became Secretary of the Navy and they moved temporarily to Washington that Flora Whitney became a fixed star in the firmament of American hostesses. Her champagne flowed so freely and generously—she was credited with receiving over sixty thousand guests in her four years in Washington—that one branch of the Women's Christian Temperance Union passed a resolution denouncing her; that censure was somewhat abated by the concurrent dedication to the Navy Secretary's wife of a John Philip Sousa Marine Corps march entitled "La Reine de la Mer."

The Whitney mansion on the outskirts of Georgetown had several much-talked-about features. There was a European chef. There was a Negro maid who spoke French and interpreted for diplomats when they came to call. There was a ballroom so vast that a contemporary annalist of social affairs observed with awe that one could roast a whole ox in its fireplace, or turn a two-horse wagonload of hay around inside it without grazing a wall. It is not known whether either feat was ever attempted, which may have been just as well: the ballroom walls were upholstered in brocaded satin.

Flora Payne Whitney had six children. One died at birth. One, testimonially named Olive after Flora's doting brother, died at five, of diphtheria, while the family was in Paris. The oldest who survived, Pauline, married an English gentleman, Almeric Hugh Paget, whose doubly titled father—General and Lord—was for many years a member of Parliament and equerry to Queen Victoria. The youngest child, Dorothy, born in 1887 when her mother was forty-five, was married first to Willard Straight, a foreign-service officer in China, later the representative there of J. P. Morgan, and later still the founder of the *New Republic;* after Straight's death, she married Leonard K. Elmhirst and they established Dartington Hall, the celebrated center of progressive education and modern dance in England.

William and Flora had two sons, both of whom were given the middle name Payne, as were their sisters. Their uncle Oliver liked that. He was further repaid for his many kindnesses by having a suite of rooms set aside for him in the Whitneys' New York town house, before the Colonel moved east and acquired one of his own. William and Flora's first son, Henry Payne Whitney—known as Harry—was born in 1872. The second son, William Payne Whitney—known originally as Willie—came along four years later.

Both brothers were in their twenties when their mother died, of heart disease, in 1893, at the age of fifty-one. Her widower husband was a year older. It was considered meet, in those conventional days, for bereaved husbands of Whitney's class to observe three years' mourning. In 1896,

William Whitney informed his family of his plan to remarry. His bride-to-be was Edith Randolph, the daughter of a Baltimore physician of proper social standing, and the widow of an English army captain. Just how his two sons felt about this turn of events is not documented, although it was clear that Harry (the older and thus in Uncle Oliver's apparent view the more important) was concerned; but Oliver Payne's reaction was strong, outraged, and explicit. On April 6, 1896, he sent a handwritten note to his brother-in-law that began with a curt "Dear Whitney." It went on:

I have been down to the club alone and while there have given your last letter a great deal of thought, and have seriously considered just what I ought to say to its suggestions. It was my idea—in which you agree—that we should have, for Harry's sake, relations at least of formal friendship & courtesy. You go further and suggest that we should try to cultivate relations of real friendship. I know that this would be much more satisfactory to Harry and the other members of the family and I have asked myself the question many times, whether this is possible. I could not, even if I tried, successfully act a part which I did not honestly feel. If you are willing to give me your assurance that you have definitely and finally abandoned the intention of marrying Mrs. Randolph—I believe that I could honestly say that I would on my part make the effort you suggest. This would accomplish two things. It would give Harry, in itself, the greatest happiness you could confer upon him and relieve him permanently of his greatest anxiety. It would also furnish the only solid basis of a really reunited family—and I should then hope that we might all have such relations, as would really mean some things to all. Under such circumstances I would pledge my best efforts in the direction you indicate. Can we both do this for Harry and the family? I should not be a successful hypocrite, even if I tried the role, and it is better that I should not try. So I have written you this in all honesty, believing that this, and nothing less, is the only real solution of the matter.

It had been long apparent to the entire family that Oliver Payne expected to leave his substantial estate to his beloved sister Flora's progeny. (Whenever the Colonel added something like a hunting lodge or greenhouse to his Georgia property, he would exclaim, "Oh, this'll be lovely for the children!") But now Uncle was putting his nephews and nieces on an awkward spot. He was letting them know in his customary no uncertain terms that if their father went ahead with his proposed marriage to Mrs. Randolph there was no middle path they could walk. Should they wish to remain in Uncle's favor, they would have to turn against their father. As for the Colonel himself, if and when the wedding took place, he would have nothing further to do with his old friend

Whitney. The children—even young Dorothy, aged nine—would have to declare themselves.

The eldest son, Harry Payne Whitney, despite misgivings, declined to forsake his father. William Payne and Pauline wavered, and finally tilted in Uncle's direction—tilted so far, indeed, that William soon dropped his patronymic first name and from then on elected to be known, as he is now almost exclusively remembered, as Payne Whitney. When Helen Hay married him in 1902, though, while she was willing enough to be called Mrs. Payne Whitney, she called her husband Willie. (In June 1904, writing his sister Dorothy from Ellsworth, Maine, where his son Jock would shortly be born, Payne said that his daughter Joan had just called him Willie and had thereby shocked her nurse. Whether the nanny had been upset by the use of a first name or of *that* one Payne did not disclose.)

Will Whitney ignored Oliver Payne's threats and married Mrs. Randolph anyway. None of his children attended the ceremony. The newlyweds' life together was brief. The second Mrs. Whitney took a bad spill while horseback riding in 1899 and soon died of her injuries. The family rift persisted and ran deep. Will Whitney had not attended the graduation from Yale in 1898 of his son William Payne—by then mainly called Payne. Colonel Oliver Payne, in pointed contrast, did attend; so solidly had he entrenched himself as a surrogate father that when young Payne Whitney came down from New Haven to spend weekends and holidays in New York, he stayed at his uncle's house. (How it must have galled Uncle, when Payne married Helen Hay, that protocol required Oliver to sit in a pew directly behind the bridegroom's real father; and that, as a further irritation, Will Whitney had marched down the aisle of the church arm in arm with his stepdaughter, Adelaide Randolph!)

Will Whitney lived on till 1904, but the Colonel was uncompromisingly unbending. For all that Will had been his college roommate, his intimate friend, and his brother-in-law, he refused to go to his funeral. William Whitney left half of his estate of $22,906,222 to his loyal son Harry, three tenths to Dorothy, and a mere one tenth apiece to Pauline and Payne. One of Pauline's daughters, Dorothy Paget, a well-known horsewoman of her generation, bought a yearling in 1936 and named it Colonel Payne. The horse never amounted to much, which might have pleased her mother.

At the Colonel's death, in 1917, he had the last word. After a few bequests such as a million dollars each to the Lakeside Hospital in Cleveland, to the New York Public Library, and to Yale, and twenty-five thousand dollars each to his sailing master and to his accountant, Oliver Payne bequeathed to Payne Whitney nearly all his residual estate—about fifty million dollars, plus odds and ends like the big Georgia plantation.

Payne's brother Harry, who in friendlier days had been handsomely treated by the uncle (when Harry had married Gertrude Vanderbilt, the jewels that Oliver gave the bride were costlier than those from her own father), was cut off with nothing but a single painting. One can only speculate how the bristly Colonel would have reacted to the destiny of that work of art. The painting was J. M. W. Turner's *Juliet and Her Nurse,* a portrayal of St. Mark's Square during the Venice Festival of 1836. Colonel Payne had acquired it for a few thousand dollars in 1901. When in 1942 it passed into the hands of Gertrude Vanderbilt Whitney's daughter Flora, it was worth about eighty thousand dollars. When Sotheby Parke Bernet auctioned it off for Flora in the spring of 1980, it fetched $6,400,000—the highest price paid up to then for any painting anywhere.

As for Payne Whitney's legacy from his uncle, so shrewdly did the nephew build upon the sturdy foundation the Colonel had laid down that in 1924—twenty-two years after his marriage to Helen—Whitney's federal income tax came to $2,041,951, which was exceeded that year only by the levies imposed on Henry Ford and John D. Rockefeller. And when Payne Whitney himself died in 1927, his net assets, before the comparatively modest inheritance taxes of that era, were computed at $178,893,655—the largest estate that had ever been appraised in the history of the United States.

2

The Plunger
and the Poet

Jock's father, Payne Whitney, was born on March 20, 1876. He grew
up somewhat in his older brother Harry Payne's shadow. Harry was the
family pet; Payne the plodder, the sluggard, the fat little boy toddling
after his leaner, lither sibling. Within the family, obviously, there was
never any confusion about their identities. (Harry was the bright one,
the one who made Phi Beta Kappa, the one with the higher handicap at
polo.) It was not always so with the general public. The Whitney brothers and their kinfolk were much written about in the days when the comings and goings of society personages were faithfully chronicled; Payne,
for instance, was dangerously stricken with appendicitis in 1921, but the
first published announcements of the affliction attributed it to his perfectly healthy brother. The two were reared in heady affluence, but their
parents made some attempts to imbue in them a sense of balance. (Later,
when Payne's own son was growing up, Payne told Jock that *he* never
owned a dinner jacket until he got married, and that when he was court-
ing his future wife he was on such a skimpy allowance that he could
never buy her any flowers showier than carnations.)

Like his brother, Payne Whitney prepared for college at Groton. Their
father, who was wont to complain after leaving Yale of that institution's
"narrowness and stupidity," had grown fond of Cambridge, Massachusetts, while at law school. He wanted his sons to go to Harvard. Their

mother Flora had been educated at Cambridge, too, but she favored Yale. She was a strong-minded woman, and so was her indulgent brother Oliver. Harry Payne and Payne both went to Yale. (Payne Whitney did ultimately obtain a Harvard law degree himself, but he never intended to practice; he reasoned that a legal background would better enable him to confront the many attorneys with whom it was apparent even then that anyone destined to come into a fortune was surely also destined to vie.)

At Yale, Payne was a reasonably big man on campus—especially big in one respect. During the Depression of 1893, despite the allowance he considered scant, he ran a personal financial-aid program, helping out classmates whose families had been hard hit. He was tapped for Skull and Bones. Following his father's example, he went out for rowing, and as a senior he was elected captain of the crew. After his graduation, in 1898, his loyalty to Yale rowing was unflagging. Attendance at the annual Yale-Harvard races off New London was for him almost ritualistic, and agreeable: he would sail to the scene either on his brother Harry's yacht or aboard his own. He was a member for most of his life of the Yale graduate crew committee. He provided genteel housing for the undergraduate crewmen on the eve of the big Harvard races, in an accommodation at Gales Ferry called the Whitney Cottage. His name would be further emblazoned upon Yale athletics after his death; his widow and children gave the university six million dollars for the erection of one of the nation's most imposing calisthenic shrines—the Payne Whitney Gymnasium, designed by John Russell Pope. Under its spreading Gothic roof were facilities for swimming, basketball, squash racquets, golf, polo, handball, wrestling, fencing, boxing, and, it went without saying, dry-run rowing.

Payne Whitney never had a job, in the conventional sense. Nor did he ever have to worry about not having one. As early as 1903, just two years after leaving law school, he became a director, by virtue of his robust holding of its shares, of the Great Northern Paper Company; two years after that, by virtue of its being the repository of much Whitney money, he became a trustee of the United States Trust Company, which has ever since been a Whitney family bank. In due course, he was a trustee also of the Metropolitan Museum of Art and of the New York Public Library, whose reference department was on the point of collapse in 1923 when three benefactors—Whitney, John D. Rockefeller, and Edward S. Harkness—shored it up with a six-million-dollar emergency contribution.

On May 10, 1927, only a few days before Payne Whitney's death, the New York *Sun* carried an editorial entitled "This Punctual Spot."

The meeting was called for 4 o'clock [the text went]. At one minute before the appointed hour the attendant closed the doors. As he did so he took notice that all the chairs were occupied.

The room and its furnishings were in taste with the architecture of the building. A long table occupied the center of the room. Lewis Cass Ledyard was in the chair set for the presiding officer. At his right hand was Cardinal Hayes. Next to the Cardinal sat J. P. Morgan, then came Payne Whitney and George F. Baker, Jr. At the table's end was Elihu Root and next to him Vincent Astor and Henry Walters. The engineering profession was represented by William Barclay Parsons and the law by two former Justices of the Supreme Court, Morgan J. O'Brien and Samuel Greenbaum, and by John G. Milburn and Frank L. Polk.

At a sign from President Ledyard Mr. Whitney arose and proceeded to read the report of a committee of which he was chairman. It was the monthly meeting of the trustees of the New York Public Library. Every man was on time.

They had hard-hitting editorials in those days.

Payne Whitney was also a governor of the New York Hospital. Its wing for mental patients has been known since 1932 as the Payne Whitney Psychiatric Clinic; to most twentieth-century New Yorkers, "Payne Whitney" means a place, not a person. The clinic has an outpost in Westchester County. After Payne's death, his son Jock succeeded him on the board of governors. The governors met once at the suburban branch, which was temporarily short of funds; they debated selling off some adjacent real estate, which they weren't using and which seemed likely to command an attractive price. "Maybe that's the sensible thing to do," Jock told the board, "but it would probably make my father turn over in his grave. Father used to come out here and play golf with the patients." The governors resolved to find the cash they needed from some other source.

Polo and various racquet games headed the list of Payne Whitney's other sports. He belonged to a lot of clubs, sporting and social, urban and suburban, but he found them insufficiently exclusive. In the 1920s, accordingly, he bought an East Side brownstone in Manhattan and converted it into a really private private club, called the Meeting House. It had fewer than two dozen members, no officers, and, inasmuch as Payne Whitney was defraying all its expenses, no dues. His brother Harry and other polo players of the era belonged to it; so did the writer Finley Peter Dunne. (The author of *Mr. Dooley* was sometimes described as the court jester of Payne Whitney's dinner table.) So did the architect Samuel Adams Clark and the broker Eugene Hale, Jr., who had been Payne's best man. In his will, Whitney left each of these three companions half a million dollars; while alive, he had given each of them, whose resources were markedly inferior to his own, about a million more. At his death, he also instructed his executors to destroy an accumulation of I.O.U.s from another old crony that added up to half a million.

Payne Whitney was a high-spirited gambler and, for a while, a heavy drinker; when he gave up alcohol and switched to coffee, he imbibed so much of that that it was a wonder to some of his family and friends that he could ever fall asleep. He refused to play bridge, one of his favorite sedentary sports, for more than half a cent a point with people who he suspected could not afford as easily as he could to lose; however, with adversaries like Harold Vanderbilt, the guru of contract bridge, he would and did compete at the then astronomical level of ten or twenty cents a point. At the race tracks, he was a notorious plunger—according to the sportswriter Toney Betts, the biggest bettor ever. Betts had it that Whitney dropped a quarter of a million dollars on the first five races at one track one day but nonetheless managed, before the afternoon was over, to come out sixteen thousand ahead. No matter how his luck was running, Whitney would always tell his family that he had just about broken even. At the tracks, he had his own betting commissioner, a mysterious figure named Lester Doctor, who fancied being called "the Doc." Doctor would busily shop around among bookmakers to obtain the best possible odds for his patron and was well rewarded for his assiduousness. Whitney's son more or less inherited the Doc, to whom, Jock would say in the 1950s, he had over the years now and then "slipped a few bucks"—thus modestly alluding to the more than one hundred and fifty thousand dollars he had lost by guaranteeing an ill-fated brokerage account that Doctor had set up, and poorly gambled with, at the start of the Depression.

When Payne Whitney, following his father Will's example, married his Yale roommate's sister, he acquired a father-in-law who was at the summit of a long, varied, and eminent career. As Secretary of State under Presidents McKinley and Roosevelt, John Hay would have his name appended to a number of notable treaties—the Hay-Buneau-Varilla, for instance, which gave the United States the Panama Canal. It was Hay who was largely responsible for his country's open-door-to-China policy after the 1900 Boxer Rebellion. While that uprising was in progress, Secretary Hay told a friend in Washington, "Minister Wu came by this morning and stayed for two hours, at the conclusion of which Wu was Hazy, and Hay was Woozy." Hay's great-grandson James W. Symington liked to quote that quip along with a Hay riposte uttered the year before, just after the Spanish-American War: "Dealing with Cuba is like trying to carry on a polite conversation with a squirrel in your lap."

John Hay was born at Salem, Indiana, in 1838, but his doctor father soon moved to Warsaw, Illinois, in Pike County, and raised his children there. Warsaw had once been called Spunky Point, which John thought a much preferable name; referring to the change, he wrote to a friend, "I hope every man who was engaged in the outrage is called Smith in Heaven." In an autobiographical speech before the Ohio Society in 1903, he said:

> "When I look back on the shifting scenes of my life, if I am not that altogether deplorable creature, a man without a country, I am, when it comes to pull and prestige, almost equally bereft, as I am a man without a state. I was born in Indiana, I grew up in Illinois, I was educated in Rhode Island, and it is no blame to that scholarly community that I know so little. I learned my law in Springfield and my politics in Washington, my diplomacy in Europe, Asia, and Africa. I have a farm in New Hampshire and desk room in the District of Columbia. When I look to the springs from which my blood descends, the first ancestors I ever heard of were a Scotchman, who was half English, and a German woman, who was half French. Of my immediate progenitors, my mother was from New England and my father was from the South. In this bewilderment of origin and experience, I can only put on an aspect of deep humility in any gathering of favorite sons, and confess that I am nothing, but an American."*

Back in 1314, for exemplary services rendered during the Battle of Bannockburn, King Robert Bruce had made one Hay—Gilbert Hay—the Hereditary Great Constable of Scotland. In a later battle, that of Flodden Field, in 1513, the clan had been grimly thinned; ninety officers and men named Hay perished there while fighting for King James IV of Scotland against England's Henry III. (Jock Whitney was not especially interested in genealogy, but it pleased him once, on a drive through Scotland, to come across a stone marker dated "A.D. 1753" and inscribed, "The Right Hon Lord Charles Hay Comdg the 33 Regt built this road from here to the Spey.") The world was smaller in John Hay's time than in his grandson's, and public affairs were much more personally conducted. In an undated penciled note Hay scribbled to his daughter Helen while he was Secretary of State, he told her, employing titles of respect rather than consanguinity, "Your poor old Daddy has got a sick world on his hands to take care of. Uncle Henry [probably Adams] in Paris is hugging himself black and blue with delight over my troubles. Things are horrible in China. The poor Ninth Infantry was Uncle Leonard's [Wood] regiment, of which he was so proud and fond."

John Hay Whitney never knew either of his illustrious grandfathers. Jock was born in 1904, the year Will Whitney died. John Hay died in

---

* Asked on another occasion what era he would have liked most to live in, Hay replied, "The twentieth century," and, asked where, he said, "Everywhere."

1905. To the grandson, the maternal grandfather was more consequential than any of his relatives on his father's side, including the redoubtable Colonel Payne. Whenever Jock would refer to "Grandfather," he meant his grandfather Hay; when he meant his father's father, he said, "Grandfather Whitney." From early manhood on, John Hay Whitney proudly wore Hay's signet ring. The office desk from behind which Whitney managed his multitudinous affairs had belonged to John Hay. "I suppose there is in me a preponderance of Hay genes," Jock once said. "Grandfather Whitney was active in public life, but he was primarily a businessman, not a statesman. My own inclinations, ever since I started to have any, have been, like Grandfather's, more in the direction of the humanities than of economics." He told a schoolgirl inquiring about his forebears that both grandfathers were "powerful factors in the development of this country. One devoted all of his life to diplomacy and the arts. The other mixed statesmanship with business—for which I'm very thankful." In the drawing room of Jock's principal residence one table top would always be occupied exclusively by framed photographs of royalty; the only commoner whose likeness was enshrined there was John Hay.†

John Hay had gone to Brown University and had graduated in 1858. The John Hay Library there, built in 1910 with funds donated largely by Hay's friend and admirer Andrew Carnegie, contains most of Hay's papers. Hay went into law instead of the ministry because, as he once jested, "I would not do for a Methodist preacher, for I am a poor horseman. I would not suit the Baptists, for I dislike water. I would fail as an Episcopalian, for I am no ladies' man." He studied law in a Springfield, Illinois, office that was shared by his uncle, Milton Hay, and by Abraham Lincoln. John accompanied Lincoln to the White House, as the President's secretary. After Hay's death, his surviving children, going through some of his belongings, came upon the first and second drafts of the Gettysburg Address. The children public-spiritedly sent them along—the repository at Brown did not yet exist—to the Library of Congress.

Hay was, of course, in collaboration with John Nicolay, one of the assassinated President's earliest serious biographers. On his own, Hay became a writer of some renown in other areas. There was a novel of social criticism entitled *The Bread-Winners*. There were several collections of dialect verse—*Jim Bludso, Pike County Ballads, Little Breeches*. Tallulah

† Archibald MacLeish, who in 1964 was living in General James Whitney's home town of Conway, Massachusetts, wrote Jock then wondering if he'd be interested in knowing that the residents were rehabilitating an old church where his great-grandfather had worshiped. Jock wrote back that he would be glad to help out, adding, "I am aware and proud of my New England roots, although as I'm sure you know, I'm more of a Hay man myself."

Bankhead would recall in her memoirs that her father, the United States Senator from Alabama, recited from *Little Breeches* so often when she was a girl that until 1934 she had always assumed he had written it. She herself, she said, could recite those verses in her sleep. She was disillusioned upon being summoned from London that year to act in a play that Jock Whitney, a gold-winged Broadway angel of the decade, was shepherding toward Broadway. "Back in the thirties I had a great crush on Jock Whitney," she confessed, to the surprise of no one who had seen the two of them together. The reciprocator of her affections, after listening to one wakeful Bankhead recitatif from *Little Breeches*, bet her that the lines she was declaiming were not, as the actress insisted, the product of her father's pen but rather of his grandfather's; and he pulled down a copy of the book from a nearby shelf to prove it. "Jock had caught me with my quotes down," Tallulah breezily conceded.

On a more serious level, John Hay spent five years, after Lincoln's death, on Foreign Service assignments in Paris, Vienna, and Madrid; and five more years, starting in 1870, as an editorial writer. He worked chiefly for the New York *Tribune,* which then belonged to Whitelaw Reid. When Reid went abroad on a leisurely honeymoon in 1881, Hay took over as editor *pro tem.* He liked to call the *Tribune* the "G.M.O."—short for "Great Moral Organ." Along Newspaper Row, Hay himself was called both "the jocund Hay" and, inevitably, "Little Breeches." He reached the summit of his diplomatic career when, in the spring of 1897, President McKinley dispatched him to the Court of St. James's. Hay's stay in London prompted him to observe afterward, "There are three species of creature who when they seem coming are going, when they are seen going, they come: diplomats, women, and crabs." Queen Victoria, whose Diamond Jubilee was celebrated during Hay's tour of duty, herself observed that he was "the most interesting of all" the envoys she had known; and in a sixty-year reign she had been exposed to quite a few. Henry James went even further and described the American mission, during Hay's tenure, as the keystone of the arch of permanent Anglo-American friendship.

In 1875, John Hay had married Clara Stone, whose father Amasa, still another Clevelander, was a wealthy bridge builder. (Amasa Stone contributed dramatically to that element in Jock Whitney's character that shrank from any deviation from high standards. In 1884, overcome with remorse when an iron bridge he had overhauled outside Ashtabula, Ohio, collapsed and caused eighty-four deaths, Stone shot himself.) Clara and John Hay had four children. Cleveland was their main year-round residence, although, as the paterfamilias was fond of pointing out, he was often to be found elsewhere. The Hays and their close friends the

Henry Adamses later built adjoining homes in the nation's capital, across from the White House. Thus, the Hay-Adams Hotel. John and Clara spent many summers at Lake Sunapee, New Hampshire, where they built an enormous house on a thousand-acre farm. That would become, in 1973, the John Hay National Wildlife Refuge, a gift to the federal government from the widow of Hay's anthropologist son Clarence. (Life in the refuge proved to be too wild; in 1978, some youthful vandals knocked the head off a marble satyr that, installed in a garden by the Hays in 1903, had molested no one for seventy-five years.)

John Hay hoped, vainly, as it turned out, to attract to Lake Sunapee a colony of his Midwestern friends. He was staying there, in June 1905, when he died. He had never wholly cheered up in the four years since his son Adelbert's tragic fall from the class-reunion window. "Moral integrity and a sense of humor will carry you a long way," Hay had written Whitelaw Reid in 1901; "but when your sense of humor fails—woe unto you! Mine, I fear, is on the wane. There can be few things funnier than sixteen Senators wrangling over a $2,000 consulate. But it has ceased to be funny to me—and that is a bad symptom." Early in the marriage of Helen Hay to Payne Whitney, the young couple would sometimes visit New Hampshire to try to lift her father's spirits, usually after taking in the August races at Saratoga Springs. Hay did manage some wry smiles at his son-in-law's antics. There was no golf course at Lake Sunapee, but Payne Whitney, not wishing to have the fine edge of his game dulled by even a few days' abstinence, would bring along his clubs anyway and, with prodigality that his less well endowed in-laws never ceased to chuckle at, spray practice balls irretrievably into the surrounding forests.

By the time Adelbert Hay had introduced his Yale roommate Payne Whitney to his older sister Helen, she had already cut quite a social and literary swath. Born in 1876, Helen Hay had boarded at the elegant Masters School, in Dobbs Ferry, New York. While John Hay was in London, she often stood in for her mother—who had two younger children to attend to—as her father's hostess. Like her father, Helen was a poet. She had her first collection of poems printed, at his expense, in 1898. It was diffidently entitled *Some Verses,* and it was dedicated to John Hay, who wrote a friend at publication time, "I can't help thinking they are very good." The young author's name was familiar by then to readers of society columns on both sides of the Atlantic; but the Brooklyn *Eagle,* presumably with tongue in cheek, declared, "There is nothing in the book to indicate whether the volume is the work of a daughter of our Secretary of State or whether she is connected [she wasn't] with Henry Hanby Hay, the well known poet and Shakespearean scholar. It may well be that the author is in no way related to either." The *Eagle* was on the whole well disposed to her effort; the Portland, Oregon, *Bulletin,* on the other hand, wrote sharply of one of her lines—"Kiss me but once, and in that space supreme my whole dark life shall quiver to an end"—"Is it to be understood that the legitimate recipient of that kiss was around somewhere with a gun?"

Meanwhile Helen, in the fashion of well-bred young ladies of the day, was doing Good Works: she was reading some of her poems to the inhabitants of the Pavilion for the Blind at the Library of Congress. From then until 1910, Helen brought out nine other collections of her work, all but that first one published by recognized houses. Among her further titles was a 1905 volume, put out the year after her son was born, called *Verses for Jock and Joan.* Typical of that offering was "Loneliness," presumably written for Jock:

> It isn't very nice to be
> a little boy alone;
> I walk about, and have my tea,
> and sometimes throw a stone.
>
> And all the pleasant games I make
> Are games that two must play;
> I'd really like to share my cake,
> Or give some toys away.
>
> I'd like to wear an emperor's crown,
> Then sternly I would send,
> And order all the boys in town
> To come and be my friend.

Jock and his sister, whose lifelong nickname within the family was Mouse, may have been especially pleased, when they were old enough to read, by one of the rhymes in a 1907 volume of their mother's called *The Bed-Time Book,* which a reviewer for the Cleveland *Plain Dealer* acclaimed "about as good verses for children as have been written." Helen's home-town adulatory critic was probably not aware that one of the poems in that volume, entitled *Uncles,* was rather pointedly evocative of Uncle Oliver Payne:

> The Uncles come at tea time,
> They laugh and pull my hair.
> They hide in corners and they make
> Loud noises like a bear.
>
> Then mother says "Kiss Uncle, Mouse,
> And toddle off to bed."

Most times I do, but some times don't
And cry and hide my head.

Some Uncles they have whiskers,
    They scratch me in the face;
And mother says, "What ails the child?
    My dear, you're in disgrace."

There are two kinds of Uncles—
    I wish there was but one.
The Uncles who have whiskers,
    And the Uncles who have none.

After her marriage, living on Long Island, Helen Hay Whitney had a small study built apart from the main residence, and there she would sequester herself, away from children, guests, and servants, and compose verses. There were, among other books, *Sonnets and Songs, Herbs and Apples, The Rose of Dawn*, and *Gypsy Verses*—the last dedicated, in 1907, to her sister-in-law, the sculptor Gertrude Vanderbilt Whitney, with the peculiar phrase "because she is my friend." Gertrude, the founder of the Whitney Museum in New York—Juliana Rieser Force, who ran that institution after the sculptor's death, was employed as Helen Whitney's social secretary when she met Gertrude—would jot in her diary two years later, about Helen, "She had had every advantage both from a worldly standpoint & an intellectual one. Her husband in the same strata of life was full of charm, clever, a first-class sportsman. . . . There was only one dissimilarity in their tastes. He did not like intellectual people and she did not like sports. . . . Had she not married she would have drifted into literary company."

On the earlier appearance, in 1901, of *The Rose of Dawn*, which was subtitled "A Tale of the South Sea"—"The little isle seemed now a sleeping maid/Kirtled in green, the beach her snowy breast/Veined with the purple brooks that sought the sea"—Theodore Roosevelt sent the author's father a handwritten commentary from the White House that went:

It gave me half an hour's rest and real pleasure; it was good to forget the harsh, grimy facts of life as it must be lived in the realm of actual workaday effort, and see the palms, and the slow surge of the sea, and the tropic dawn over the lush tropic beauty; and through it all the brown little men and women living their evanescent glorious moment—of love and hate. I am glad I have known both! Life offers much, and in many different shapes, and it is good to have done what one can with it, before going out into the "limitless twilight."

Helen instilled in her children an early love of language (Joan later ran a shop that specialized in children's books) and a fondness for intellectual exercises. A favorite word game that the three of them played required the condensation of the classics of juvenile literature into a telegram ten words long. Joan Whitney Payson would contend in her fifties that as a result she had never been able to compose a wire of nine or eleven or any other number of words but precisely ten; Jock was less permanently shackled by their mother's disciplined pastime. Helen herself, though she all but stopped writing about the time that a third child was born to her in 1912 and died in infancy, never lost her interest in literature. It pleased her when people like Ernest Hemingway came to call. The story goes that she told him his works were mostly potboilers, and that he concurred. That incident may be apocryphal, as may also be the *mot* once attributed to Dorothy Parker—what *mot* was not?—that she would rather have her name inscribed in Helen Whitney's autograph book than on a tomb in Westminster Abbey. Helen was indisputably a friend of Rudyard Kipling; among the memorabilia in her Long Island home was a framed holograph of some rhymes especially written for and affectionately inscribed to her by him. In a library whose contents consisted almost entirely of first editions, she also proudly housed Keats's letters to Fanny Brawne. Of all the paintings Helen owned, she was especially fond of an 1885 John Singer Sargent portrait of Robert Louis Stevenson, and she asked to have carved on *her* gravestone that poet's "Home is the sailor, home from the sea,/And the hunter home from the hill."

Helen also collected cookbooks, on a prodigious scale; the set of them that she gave to the New York Public Library is one of the world's greatest. For a New York Hospital benefit, she donated some recipes dating back to the sixteenth century; a relatively modern one was for Banbury cake, as concocted by Queen Victoria's own pastry chef. Helen specialized in cookbooks even though there is little reason to believe that she ever went into a kitchen except to give orders. She led the life of a grande dame, but with a redeeming touch of moderation: however fancy a gown she might select from her wardrobe to wear to one of the formal balls she was forever attending, she would not leave her home in it unless and until her children had appraised and approved it. The musicales she gave as part of her own splendid at-homes featured performers like Josef Hofmann, Kreisler, and Paderewski. A lifelong baseball fan, she also entertained Babe Ruth, and at lunch one day was delighted at his deft catch of a roll she pitched across the table. Her conversation, poet or no, often had an earthy ring. Her father's motto, *"Quod habeo desidero,"* was usually translated "I desire that which I have." Helen's English version was "I like what I got." She had a private railroad car to ride around in when she wished to inspect the world outside; and she could feast her eyes at home on the blossoms of ten thousand rosebushes that graced her grounds. The displays her gardeners annually prepared for the International Flower Show at the Grand Central Palace won many prizes. She was endowed with worldly goods that Midas might have envied, but at times she seemed not altogether to grasp how well off she was. When her husband would say occasionally that the moment might not be propitious to buy this island or that yacht, she appeared to take his observations to mean that she couldn't afford a new dress.

Such clouds of doubt, however, rarely darkened Helen's acquisitive horizons. One rainy day in the spring of 1911 she got bored and bought a race horse named Web Carter. She boarded it initially at August Belmont's stables. She was glad that Belmont charged her only for the horse's feed. Payne Whitney thought she was crazy and called the animal's exercise boys the Web Carter Extermination Society; but when he sensed that she really cared about her new hobby he indulgently gave her, for Christmas, a hundred-and-fifty-acre horse farm in New Jersey. She won her first race, a steeplechase, in 1912. In pointed contrast to her husband, she would never bet more than five dollars on any race. In 1942 she became the first woman stable owner to be the leading money winner in the United States. Eddie Arcaro was long her jockey. She ended up usually referred to on the sports pages, and elsewhere, as "the First Lady of the American Turf."

Over the years, Helen's Greentree Stable won two Kentucky Derbies and at least one running of every other major stake race in this country. After she won her first Derby, in 1931, with Twenty Grand, her son Jock, by then twenty-six and a horse owner himself, knew she would be asked to utter a few words on the radio, and he inquired what she had in mind to say. "I'll say the best horse won," she told him cheerfully. At less ecstatic moments, though, she had a philosophy about racing that she sought to impart to her children. "One of the most difficult things for me," Jock would say after her death, "has been to follow a precept that was given to my mother, when she first started racing, by John Madden, the famous old trainer. He said to her, 'One thing you must learn is to lose as if you like it, and to win as if you're used to it.' I have found myself on occasion, unfortunately, winning very vociferously. In England, once, I had a horse, Sir Lindsay, that was coming to the last fence in the Grand National head to head with the favorite. I was standing on top of the stand at Aintree, and with what would have been perhaps one tenth of my normal volume at home, I screamed, 'Come on, Sir Lindsay!' Everybody within earshot stopped looking at the race and turned around to stare at this outlandish loud American raising his voice."

3

Nice If You
Can't Afford Pewter

When word came from the coastal resort of Ellsworth, Maine, that a male child had been born there, on August 17, 1904, to Helen Hay Whitney, Theodore Roosevelt sent a note to his Secretary of State. "I only wish his last name was Hay," the President wrote.

At birth, John Hay Whitney did not bear the whole name that would become widely known on society and sports pages, in political and gossip columns, in diplomatic correspondence, and in both the inscribed and unsung annals of philanthropy. The infant's name was recorded by the town clerk of Ellsworth, at the parents' instruction, as John Oliver Whitney. To anyone acquainted with the familial travails of the Payne Whitneys, their original choice of "Oliver" as a middle name for their first son and presumptive heir was as clear as the crystal on their tables. It is less certain why at the baby's baptism, ten months later, at Christ Church, Manhasset, he was invested with the middle name he bore contentedly ever afterward.

Whatever the reason for the switch might have been, there was never any doubt in Jock's mind that it had not come about without Oliver Payne's approval. "Very few things were ever done in my family that were not welcome to the Colonel," Jock would say in later years, "so it couldn't have been done against his wishes." He never did ask his parents to explain why they had changed their minds. His older sister Joan, a girl who acted out many boys' fantasies by becoming the owner of a major-league baseball team, did once explain why he had happened to be delivered in the state of Maine, a territory that their parents, though as peripatetic as any social lions of their age, did not regularly frequent. "It was perfectly obvious," Joan Whitney Payson said. "That's where Mother's doctor spent his summers."

Of all the stately residences the Payne Whitneys would move in and out of while Joan and Jock were growing up, their mother often seemed most comfortable in Colonel Payne's big Georgia enclave, where she and Payne had spent their honeymoon. Uncle had spared no expense in fitting it out. When after his death the Payne Whitneys took over the establishment, Helen thought it would be nice to have some old vases that were lying around converted into table lamps. She changed her mind on being informed they were all Ming. She held no brief for slavery—indeed, in her will she set up a trust to provide for all her servants as long as they lived—but there was an ante bellum aspect to some of the divertissements she and Payne would put on there for their Northern guests: the plantation darkies, as they were then unexceptionably termed, would sing spirituals for the masters and mistresses, and field hands with names like Chittlin' Jones would engage in fisticuffs for the postprandial delectation of what he termed the white folks.

Georgia was a place to visit, though, only for a couple of winter months. There was also the five-story residence at 972 Fifth Avenue that Uncle had had built as one of his wedding presents. Sheathed in granite, its broad main staircase and its bathtubs carved of white marble, it stood in a companionable neighborhood. There were Phippses to the north, Dukes to the south. The newlyweds adorned this nest with such trimmings as a hundred-thousand-dollar sixteenth-century millefleurs tapestry; three Isfahan carpets worth, not long after the turn of the twentieth century, thirty thousand, twenty thousand, and twelve thousand dollars; seven polar-bear rugs; and, to Helen's special delight, a plaster group of sculptures Rodin had once made for Robert Louis Stevenson. There were watercolors by Blake and Rowlandson; oils by Romney and Raeburn; pastels by Manet and Degas; assorted works by Monet, Pissarro, Renoir, and even Rembrandt.

And then there was Greentree, the Long Island estate that Payne had bought for Helen in 1904. It sprawled across a nearly six-hundred-acre slice of Manhasset. Payne's brother Harry—by then a luminary of the Long Island polo set, a ten-goal man whose formidable Meadow Brook team was called the Big Four—had taken over their father's place, only twenty minutes from Greentree by car, at Old Westbury. The main residence *there*, which was later readily convertible into a country-club clubhouse, had an entrance hall so long and so wide that during one of

Harry and Gertrude's parties the lawyer Devereux Milburn, another of the Big Four, excused himself from the festivities, went out and found a horse, came back in upon it, and galloped up and down the spacious corridor without hitting any wall, or any person.

The Payne Whitneys' nearby enclave, though wrongly proportioned for indoor equitation, was unarguably one of the great residences of America. Visitors who knew the stateliest homes of England pronounced themselves amazed at it. John Hay Whitney's adopted daughter Kate, who was Franklin Delano Roosevelt's grandchild, once took her children, who unlike her had no youthful acquaintance with the White House, on a tour of that commodious establishment; after inspecting it, they pronounced it nice enough, but hardly on a par with Greentree. It was quite possible to hold a fund-raising dinner for one hundred and fifty people under part of the Greentree roof without disturbing the family under another part of it. The estate was comparatively modest in scale when Payne Whitney acquired it, but he made extensive alterations and additions. He bought adjacent land from some of the old families in the neighborhood—Schencks, Brinkerhoffs, Kissams, Mitchells. He bought the nearby shops of a plumber, a blacksmith, a grocer, a butcher, and a harness maker. He bought a hotel, and he bought the village playground. The playground had long been used as a baseball diamond by the teenage members of the Manhasset Field Club. Unaware of any change of ownership, they came around to play one day and were unceremoniously shooed off by Whitney's superintendent. The aggrieved boys staged a sitdown protest in a Greentree driveway just as Payne was being chauffeured along it. He asked what the trouble was and, on being apprised, invited the boys to call on him that evening. When they did, he said they could use the playground whenever they felt like it, and offered further to equip them with new uniforms. They declared to a man, or to a boy, that whenever he felt like running for President they would vote for him.

For his estate gateposts, Payne obtained some huge stones that had been carried into Manhasset Bay in the winter of 1900 by a schooner that got stuck in the ice there for three months. (The estate already had within it Shelter Rock, the largest rock on Long Island, near which Captain Kidd was rumored to have buried some of his pirated treasure.) Payne built garages that eventually sheltered twenty-eight of his vehicles, including four Rolls-Royces. It was said that one of his chauffeurs earned a rascally extra ten thousand dollars or so a year by slightly cheating his employer on gasoline bills. There were stables and kennels and outdoor pools with swans, three grass tennis courts, and a nine-hole golf course. When Payne and his friends were ready to play a round, the host would ring a bell and summon a flock of caddies who awaited his bidding in a little golf house near the first tee. They were among Green-tree's army of two or three hundred employees.

A foresighted man, Payne Whitney anticipated the onslaught of Prohibition by having an underground wine cellar constructed alongside one of his parking lots. He stocked it so copiously that its contents sufficed almost exactly until Repeal—there was even enough champagne on hand for a big coming-out party for his daughter Joan in the early twenties and enough spirits, too, to see Jock through college. While Payne's son was at Yale, and almost everybody else was having to make do with bathtub gin, Jock was treating his friends to the real thing, of English-import quality. Perhaps hoping to achieve a sort of balance between sacred and profane, Payne planned at about the same time he laid in his cellar to erect a private chapel, which was just about the only facility his home lacked; and he imported a thirteenth-century stained-glass window from France for that lofty purpose. But that was as far as that project ever got, and in 1934 Helen gave the surplus window to Christ Church in Manhasset.

Whitney *père* was an aficionado of court tennis, that arcane game fancied also by Henry VIII and the monarchs of France. Payne could indulge in that regal indoor sport, in New York, at the Racquet & Tennis Club. In 1914, however, he had decided it would be more convenient to have a court of his own at Greentree. So he had a two-hundred-and-fifty-thousand-dollar annex attached to his house. The tennis court, which Whitney staffed with a full-time pro, was unveiled, with background music provided by the Brown Brothers Saxophone Quartet, on January 10, 1915. The New York *Times* called the annex "the most costly and elaborately appointed structure of its kind in the world."

Among the elaborate appointments adjacent to the court, which had red felt thrones for spectators, were an indoor swimming pool, a gymnasium, a Turkish bath, and a chamber called the Big Room that could serve as a movie theatre. Between the Big Room and the court were a series of bedrooms that Payne—and his son Jock after him—made available to stray bachelor friends who stayed the night. There were dressing rooms at these transients' disposal equipped with white flannels, shirts, boots, spurs, breeches, jackets, linen, swimming suits, dinner clothes, a rubbing table, a bar, and one of the most complete assortments of toilet articles and lotions ever assembled under a private roof. A man who often availed himself of these amenities recalled once that he hardly ever shaved at his own home. "Shaving was always much more fun at Greentree," he said.

Practically every inch of wall space along the corridors threading the annex was covered with trophies or sporting prints or other specimens of athletic art. The oar with which Jock would stroke the freshman crew at

Yale was eventually impaled there, only a few hundred feet from a pedestal upon which perched a Herbert Haseltine bronze of a much younger Jock astride a pony. The outside world got a glimpse of this in 1917, when his aunt, Gertrude Vanderbilt Whitney, borrowed it for a show she put on at her Greenwich Village studio, the forerunner of her museum—an exhibit she entitled "To Whom Shall I Go for My Portrait?" The Payne Whitney side of the family often went to Haseltine, who seemed at times in his career to be almost on retainer from them, but not necessarily for portraits of themselves. The English sculptor immortalized Twenty Grand in bronze for Helen Hay Whitney. He did the same for John Hay Whitney's English horses Easter Hero and Royal Minstrel, and his American Tom Fool. During the Second World War, when the Nazis were closing in on Paris, Haseltine was working in a studio there on yet another commission for Jock—a bronze portrait, à deux, of Whitney's favorite dog and his favorite polo pony. Haseltine barely got out ahead of the enemy. After the war, it developed that his assistant, before hastily abandoning the premises himself, had taken away and hidden just one of Haseltine's pieces—the job he was doing for Whitney. The piece duly ended up in the commodious Greentree annex.

Payne Whitney used the annex to play bridge in, too. His wife, who had not much taste for that game, kept aloof; her friends believed that she was not allowed to enter that largely male preserve without special permission, though her daughter Joan, a gifted cardplayer, could come and go at will. (Joan gave up bridge after her marriage, in 1924, to still another Yale oar, Charles Shipman Payson. A woman with a hot competitive streak, she quit because, while sitting at one card table across from her husband, she feared that if she didn't quit she was going to try to smite him with an ashtray for some alleged misplay or other.) Payne Whitney would die in the annex, at a relatively youthful fifty-one, from a heart attack suffered while playing court tennis. In his memory, his widow and children initiated an annual court tennis tournament, with teams invited from the few oases where the old game flourished: New York, Philadelphia, Tuxedo Park, and Boston, where the first American court had been built, in 1876. (There were never more than a dozen courts in the United States, and by the middle of the twentieth century only a single private one was still in use—the Whitneys'.) Jock was not as adept at court tennis as his father, never having played it as a boy, but with Ogden Phipps he did win the Payne Whitney Memorial Cup doubles in 1945. Allison Danzig, of the New York *Times*, the dean of racquet-games writers of that day, reported that "Whitney started off in nothing less than sensational fashion. . . . In the final game of the love set [it was 6–0, 6–4] he brought the house down [it was his house] with his exploits. . . . The crowd shook its head in amazement, the Boston pair blinked unbelievingly and Whitney was having the time of his life."

At the grand opening of the Greentree annex in 1915, the eminent racquets player Jay Gould and one hundred and forty-five other gentleman guests—"probably the largest aggregation of sportsmen ever assembled," according to the *Times*—were joined for a ceremonial group photo by the host's ten-year-old son Jock, a blue-eyed, dark-haired, pudgy boy with protruding ears. Jock (who had been accoutered for earlier portraits, as late as the age of three, in a white bonnet and long white dress, a getup indistinguishable from that sported by his sister) did not look overwhelmed by the company or the occasion. He was used to crowds of important people, more to those, actually, than to gatherings of his contemporaries.

The children of the very rich did not have to be especially protected, at the turn of the century, against kidnappers or other violators of security. Nonetheless, as his mother's poem "Loneliness" suggested, Jock had a rather isolated childhood. Strangers made him uneasy. "When my sister and I were little," he said in adulthood, "we hid behind the window curtain to see who was arriving, and if it was someone new, we ran away." He moved in a phalanx of servants. Most of the homes of most of the people his parents consorted with had plenty of help. Jock played soccer, at Greentree, on a team otherwise composed—the pun is inescapable—of footmen. One of these was so conscientious about looking after the boy that he would often spend his nights on a chair outside Jock's bedroom door. Thus attended, day and night, Jock grew up without having to pay much heed to the small details of ordinary living that preoccupy and plague most people. In later years, whenever he had to go anywhere, there was a car or a train or a plane or a yacht standing by to take him there, and someone to remind him that it was time to get aboard. (He had one secretary who would insert little red flags in his pocket diary bearing reminders like "Tomorrow is your wife's birthday.") Even so—or perhaps because of that—in adult life he found it difficult to abide anybody else's tardiness. His own life was so meticulously arranged that he found slipshoddiness all but incomprehensible.

Once, after Jock had taken in some races at Saratoga with his friend John S. Kelly, a onetime professional football player known far and wide as "Shipwreck," they flew to Long Island in Whitney's private plane. There was, unprecedentedly, no car to meet them at that airport. Whitney wondered how they would ever get to Greentree. Kelly said, according to his possibly embellished account of the incident, that there were vehicles in general use called taxicabs, and forthwith commandeered one. A taxicab! It was kind of a lark for Jock, riding in one, and when they reached Greentree he had the driver pull up not at his front door but at his garage, where half a dozen or so chauffeurs were idling in the sun. The chauffeurs, sensing that something had gone dreadfully amiss, leapt to their feet. Whitney, after making certain that they were aware of the unconventional situation, spurned their hoarse offers to drive him up to the house, and to their further mortification continued on by taxi.

Wherever the Payne Whitneys migrated—to Thomasville in January, to Aiken in the spring, to Saratoga in August, to various New England resorts in other warm months—they traveled with a retinue, often in their own Pullman. In 1958, doing research for one of his books about trains, Lucius Beebe wrote Whitney from Nevada to inquire whatever had happened to Jock's parents' old private car. Jock replied that his sister Joan had it parked somewhere, and he added, "It was my idea of heaven when I was young enough not to care how thick the dirt. It was always too hot to live in, but in those days what fun to wipe the sweaty face and exhibit with pride one's black handkerchief." Whitney did not add that there was probably some servitor within hailing who could quickly have supplied him with a clean handkerchief.

Some summers, the family stopped by the vast camp that Payne's father, William Whitney, while gobbling up real estate, had acquired in the Adirondacks. The Harry Payne Whitneys had taken over that outpost; it had been expanded by 1910 to an eighty-five-thousand-acre watering hole. Assigned once in prep school to compose an autobiographical essay, Jock recalled that he had first fallen in love up there, with a girl who did not notably reciprocate—conceivably because she was playing first base on a local team and he was consigned to right field, the usual position allotted to the most inept participant in any such youthful contest. He never forgot her; years later he named a horse after her. In his theme—it earned him a B plus—Whitney recounted the two most memorable incidents of his Adirondacks sojourns: the time he tried to stroke what he took to be a black and white kitten that turned out to be a skunk; and the time, during a thunderstorm at night, when he woke to find his room full of flying bats.

The acknowledged ringleader among all the Whitney children who congregated in the Adirondacks was Jock's first cousin, Harry Payne's son Cornelius Vanderbilt Whitney, who was known in boyhood as Sonny, a sobriquet he was never able to shed. Sonny Whitney was five years older than Jock, and was for years Jock's idol. The younger cousin would sit entranced while the older one read stories to the other children, and Jock would admire the skill and assurance with which Sonny conducted sailing classes for the rest of the Whitney flock. In later years Sonny and Jock would become somewhat estranged; it may have stemmed in part from their fierce rivalry in the 1930s, when they were captains of the country's two foremost polo teams.

In boyhood, however, Sonny, in Jock's admiring eyes, could do no wrong. C. V. Whitney, as Sonny preferred to call himself, went to Groton and Yale ahead of his cousin. While at New Haven, he rowed on the varsity crew. He was much more widely publicized when, in 1920, aged twenty-one, he was sued for breach of promise by a young woman described as a chorus girl by the newspapers that had a field day with the story. The aggrieved party wanted a million dollars to forgive and forget. Harry Payne Whitney wouldn't bail out his son. Payne Whitney thought it was worth a million to get the whole affair over with, and put up the money for his nephew. The then sixteen-year-old Jock had been found guilty at Groton, while Sonny was the talk of the tabloids, of some minor schoolboy trespass; and one of Jock's masters said to him sternly, "If you're like this now, what will you be like when you get to be Sonny's age?"

"Just like Sonny, I hope," said Jock.

As John Hay Whitney and Cornelius Vanderbilt Whitney matured, their paths often crossed—in joint motion picture and aviation ventures, for example. They crossed so often that people who didn't know them found it difficult to distinguish the one from the other. *The New Yorker* twice took editorial note of the confusion: first, in 1929, when one of Otto Soglow's manhole cartoons had a disembodied subterranean voice calling up to the sidewalk, "No, Joe, Jock's father was Payne Whitney"; and again, in 1941, when Geoffrey T. Hellman entitled a Profile of C. V. Whitney "The Man Who Is Not His Cousin."

Christmases were usually celebrated at Greentree. On the big day, one of Jock's aunts by marriage, Alice Appleton Hay, would recall with awe, the living room there—a large room by any standards—was so full of gifts for Joan and Jock that it was hard to move around in, "and that despite the fact," Mrs. Hay added, "that there were servants cruising around picking up paper and twine as fast as the kids could unwrap. Whatever there was for a child to have, Joan and Jock seemed to have got it. I kept wondering what on earth there was I could give them myself, and finally settled on simple things like books." Jock's own earliest memory of being more blessed with material goods than most people went back to a day when his parents took him to a department store to buy some toy he craved. He didn't recall what it was, but he did recall that after getting it his covetous eye lit on a handsome and probably expensive tricycle, and that he expressed a greedy yen for that, too. "I remember that my father gave it to me without wincing or protesting," he said. "I was absolutely staggered."

In the years that followed, Whitney learned to look upon his imposing ownership of worldly goods with equanimity, if not wholly without an appreciation of their existence. After he became the squire of Greentree, he had a guest for lunch, and they felt like having a beer. Presently a footman appeared, bearing two mammoth sterling silver tankards, each with the capacity of a couple of quarts. The guest, after managing to hoist his massive flagon to his lips, made some admiring comment on the treasure out of which he was sipping. "Yes," said Whitney, good-naturedly reversing the kind of lament a poorer man might have uttered. "These are pretty nice to drink out of if you can't afford pewter." He was accustomed to the best of everything, and he would sometimes demand it. Shipwreck Kelly recalled a Florida fishing trip in the course of which Jock and he stopped off at a roadside restaurant for dinner. It took quite a while for Jock to find a wine on the premises that he considered fit to drink, and almost as long to find a wineglass thin enough for him to be willing to drink out of. At Greentree, there were never such problems; Kelly maintained that once he picked up a wineglass there and cupped it in his big athlete's paw and it crumbled into shards.

Payne Whitney did make some halfhearted attempts to keep his son's attitude toward money in proportion. He would tell Jock periodically that while it was obvious he would always have more than his share of things, if he ever started throwing money around ostentatiously, his access to it would be severely curtailed. Being a very rich little boy, the father warned, entailed having responsibilities toward others relatively less well endowed. The agreeable condition also had frustrations. When much later, for instance, Jock Whitney had a town house under construction in Manhattan, he enjoined his interior decorator to have installed directly inside the front door a large chest into which children could throw things; as a boy himself, he ruefully remembered, there had never been such a receptacle inside any of the entrances to any of his homes in which he could fling a glove or a bat or a pair of skates.

Payne Whitney was far from being a nagging father, but he did like every now and then to give advice. Once he overheard his teen-age son being offered ten strokes by a golfing opponent. Jock said that was too much, he'd take seven. Payne drew him aside and said, "Son, never turn down an advantage." In his teens, however, Jock, not unlike other young men at that stage of life, did not always listen to his father. Jock would confess to Frank Sullivan, the squire of Saratoga, that on his seventeenth birthday he had bet a thousand dollars with the bookmaker Johnnie Walters on the horse Color Sergeant. He had liked the name. Also, the horse belonged to his uncle Harry. Color Sergeant all but got left at the post, but pulled himself together and somehow managed to win by a nose. "The young man sure gave us a hot one today," Walters had said to Payne Whitney afterward. Payne was furious, because as far as he knew his son didn't *have* a thousand dollars. (When Sullivan turned seventy-five, in 1967, Jock arranged to have a race named after him at Saratoga. The venerable writer was elated. His very first job, he wrote Jock, had been as a dipper boy in the betting ring at the track there— "Best job I ever had"—and he was so honored at the institution of the Sullivan Stakes that he had bet two dollars on each of the eight horses entered in it; he wanted to be sure to have a winner. He didn't even mind ending up behind; the horse that came in first—C. V. Whitney's Hail the Queen—paid only $6.20.)

Children of the well to do, when Jock was a boy, were routinely entrusted to the custody of governesses. He had many, who loomed large as surrogate parents. At the age of three or four, he would recall much later with much remorse, there was one nanny who was looking after him in Paris—people like the Whitneys not infrequently turned up in Paris, or London, or wherever—in an apartment overlooking the Bois de Boulogne. At noon, a hurdy-gurdy man would appear on the street below, and, after he had cranked out a few songs, the governess would throw him a coin. One day when the governess' back was turned Jock had grabbed the handiest coin—a gold one, the nurse's entire weekly wage— and had imitatively tossed it down, and had leaned out to watch it roll shinily into a gutter, and had leaned too far, and was clinging to the window sill by his fingertips when the nurse hauled him back in. She might have had second thoughts about it had she known the form of his bounty.

When Jock was ten or eleven, there was another governess, of the old-fashioned no-nonsense school, who had the peculiar notion, when it was his wish to, say, read a book, that instead he should put on boots and go out hunting.

Almost ever since he could talk, Jock had been afflicted with a stutter. This nurse tried to straighten him out by kicking him whenever he opened his mouth and halting sounds emerged. On hearing of this form of therapy, his parents fired the woman, but when Jock's sister told them that he stuttered even more after her departure, they begged her to come back, and to his dismay she did. In the long run, her return proved ineffectual. The stutter persisted, and had lasting side effects; for instance, though he had gifted stenographers at his beck his entire adult life, Whitney shied away from dictation, preferring to scribble the most inconsequential of messages in his own not easily decipherable hand. The stutter was never psychoanalytically explored. Payne Whitney had great faith in doctors, but psychiatry was not much in vogue when Jock was growing up. The physicians whom his father consulted on the boy's behalf, to little avail, included one who put a woman friend of the Whitneys on a stiff ulcer diet until it became clear—fortunately, before too late—that she differed from the physiological norm only in that she was pregnant.

Overweight, stuttering, awkward—the young Jock had his burdens. Incredibly, he had dental problems, too, and his parents seemed to do nothing about that, nor did any of the governesses. On top of that his eyes were weak. Doing homework in a moving car while commuting between Manhattan and Long Island may have been one cause of this; another may have been that the governess who made it a practice to kick him also disapproved of his reading in bed, so that Jock, whose mother had instilled in him a hearty appreciation of the written word, too long pursued that pleasure under a blanket, with a flashlight illuminating the pages. From his early twenties on, accordingly, he had to wear glasses, usually dark-rimmed ones. He switched to the rimless sort when he arrived in England as American Ambassador, in part because, when he had visited that country as a young man, the cartoonists there had poked fun at his spectacles. Many American comedians of that time—Groucho Marx, Harold Lloyd—wore dark-rimmed glasses, and to the English cartoonists any American thus decorated was *per se* an object of mirth, as indeed were, to most Americans of the era, all Englishmen with monocles.

As a boy, though, Jock could see well enough to help out his mother during the August races at Saratoga, where his birthday presents annually littered the floors of the Whitneys' mansion. The house was next door to that of Chauncey Olcott, who would sometimes have John McCormack as a guest. After lunch, the two Irish tenors would expedite digestion by singing loud duets, to the enchantment of a claque of two —Joan and Jock Whitney, who would sit out on their lawn and savor the free concert. The youngsters probably deserved that interlude, because at dawn—Jock eight or nine, his sister a year and a half older—they would head straight to a training track and scrutinize Helen Whitney's horses in their early morning workouts. (At six or seven one morning, a veterinarian confided to the Whitney offspring that a dollop of Benedictine would perk up a sluggish race horse marvelously. Feeling dispirited himself later that day, Jock remembered the prescription and thus dosed himself, with predictable results.) Jock would clock all of the horses, and Joan would handicap them, and later they would solemnly advise their mother on which entry she should place her customary five-dollar bet. Their father had more experienced sources of intelligence to consult. "I've got horse-clocking in my blood," Jock would say years afterward. "It's as much of my inheritance, really, as Greentree."

4

Who Would Want to Eat
an Egg That Just Gets By?

Payne Whitney, much of whose life was contentedly dedicated to competitive sports, did not take to the notion of his only son's merely observing horses from the sidelines, and being relegated, when baseball positions were being assigned, to the ignominy of right field. The boy had to be slimmed down, for one thing, the worried father judged; and, for another, he needed some expert athletic instruction. That conclusion was, in a way, the father's most important legacy to the son, aside from money. Payne was trying to demonstrate to Jock that whatever one did, one could derive the most satisfaction from it (one's father could, too) if one did it as well as one's body and mind could be trained to do it. So a pro soon materialized to teach Jock golf, and another pro for tennis, and another for swimming, and another for shooting. (William S. Paley contended grumpily years later, after a losing session at a billiard table, that Jock had no doubt had a pro to teach him bottle pool.) "Although I admired and respected my father," Jock would say, "I was never truly close to him, perhaps because he was always hiring surrogates to teach me things I'd rather have learned from him himself." (There were also piano lessons, but Jock abandoned them because—possibly to his father's satisfaction—they conflicted with elementary school baseball practice.) Jock had had his own Shetland pony when he was five but had never shown much equestrian prowess; for expertise in that, Payne Whitney turned the boy over, at twelve, to his uncle Harry, who spent a good part of his life in the saddle, alternating between polo and riding to hounds.

Harry Payne Whitney presently invited the lad to tag along with the Meadow Brook Hunt. A groom inadvertently assigned Jock to a mount that was a good enough jumper but loathed dogs; at the sight of one, it would go berserk. As soon as the hounds were brought around, the horse bolted, bearing its rider to a ridge above a road where the rest of the hunters were waiting for the pack. Jock would probably have been thrown off and tossed square on top of his uncle Harry's head had not a tree branch dislodged him first. The commotion attracted his uncle's attention. "What's the boy doing on a rogue horse like that?" Harry Payne Whitney demanded. He ordered up a fresh steed. That was all right with Jock, but the replacement had an erratic gait—attributable, it later developed, to blindness. Jock Whitney always liked to give people, including his uncle Harry, the benefit of every doubt. "The horse was only blind in one eye," he would charitably say, later, whenever the educational experience was brought up.

But Jock was still, in his father's concerned view, too stout. To pare him down, a new expert was brought in—Tommy Shortell, the boxing instructor at the Racquet & Tennis Club. Payne Whitney made it clear to Jock that the object of his boxing lessons, quite apart from weight reduction, was to enable him not to push anybody else around but to be able if necessary to defend himself against aggression. Jock surprised him. Shortell taught him so well that not only did his pupil slim down, but he became a genuinely promising prizefighter. His tutor, pleased with the protégé's progress, entered him in a city-wide boxing tournament, the forerunner of the Golden Gloves, at the old Madison Square Garden, but Jock was dissuaded from appearing there by his father, who felt that a good thing was on the point of being carried too far. Jock subsequently won the heavyweight championship at Groton, in a competition his family considered more suitable.

Jock's appreciation of boxing had been turned on along with his aptitude for it, and it could not easily be extinguished. In the 1920s and '30s, when it was fashionable to take in the Friday night fights at Madison Square Garden, he was often to be seen rooting at ringside. In 1921, when Georges Carpentier was preparing for his heavyweight championship set-to with Jack Dempsey, the French challenger established a training camp on Long Island just half a mile away from the perimeter of Greentree. Jock, his sister, and his mother were escorted to the camp one day by Philip Boyer, a skillful society boxer himself and one of Payne Whitney's intimates. (Boyer was one of those for whom Payne, in his will, forgave all debts.) Carpentier, who spoke no English, was having lunch with three dazzling young ladies whom Boyer, who had been around, could identify as Ziegfeld Follies girls. The Frenchman's manager confided to his admirers as they approached this decorative training table that the boxer had earlier gone fishing, and Helen, as a conversational gambit, meant to ask him if he had made a good catch that morning and to say, "*Avez-vous fait une bonne pêche ce matin?*" But instead, she came out with "*Avez-vous fait un bon péché ce matin?*"—a rather brazen sexual inquiry. There was instant hilarious rapport except among the chorines, who were not fluently bilingual and looked puzzled.

Jock subsequently befriended Gene Tunney, and twice called on him when he was getting into shape for Dempsey bouts. At one of Tunney's training camps, in the Adirondacks, Whitney and Tunney posed for a gag snapshot—the shirtsleeved amateur ostensibly driving a left to the pro's unguarded midriff, while Tunney affected helplessness. Another time, the two of them did actually spar, but delicately. When a third party asked Jock afterward how he had made out against the champion, he replied, "Gene was very careful." In 1934, Whitney's old instructor, Tommy Shortell, introduced him to still another heavyweight, a teenager who Shortell thought had promise—a six-foot-four, two-hundred-and-fifty-pound behemoth named Abe Simon, whose *curriculum vitae* was more diverting than that of most run-of-the-mill pugilists. Simon was fond of classical music, raised canaries, and was the son of a Hungarian émigré who, while farming in the old country, had managed by adept grafting to coax eleven varieties of fruit from a single tree. Shortell invited Jock to the Racquet Club to watch his new protégé perform. Simon took one belt at the club's sandbag, which thereupon split open at the seams.

Whitney was impressed, having frequently pummeled that bag himself, and he hastened to introduce Simon to Tunney. The by then ex-champ suggested that Simon go a couple of exploratory rounds with an established boxer, and, to ascertain whether Abe could take a beating as well as he could presumably give one, quietly offered the sparring partner fifty dollars for every time he knocked the fellow down, and a hundred dollars for a knockout. Simon fought three rounds with this eager adversary, while Whitney and Tunney looked on with rising interest, and not only remained on his feet but grew progressively stronger.

Jock was then backing Broadway shows and, for tax purposes, setting up separate corporations to finance each production. To back Abe Simon, whom by then Whitney had judged to be a "pugilist extraordinary," Tunney and he incorporated an entity called White Hope, Inc. They gave Simon five hundred dollars for signing up with them, put him on a weekly training allowance of thirty-seven dollars, and put his career in the accomplished hands of the promoter Jimmy Bronson, who ordered the young man, as a starter, to lose weight. Occasionally, Simon would work out in the Greentree gymnasium. Interrupting one such session to catch his breath, Simon wandered out into a garden, clad only in shoes, trunks, and sixteen-ounce practice gloves. He came unexpectedly upon Whitney's mother, who was sunning herself in a lawn chair. Helen Whitney was a lady capable of meeting almost any situation with grace, and although she'd had no intimation that a sweaty, half-naked giant was at large on the premises, she smiled gamely as he approached her and held out her hand in welcome. "Pardon my glove," said Simon, and took her hand.

By 1936, Simon had won a couple of fights, both by knockouts, but he looked bulkier than ever. He came to call on Whitney one day at an office Jock then had at 230 Park Avenue. Tunney, retired from the ring, had an office in the same building. Whitney took the fighter upstairs to weigh him on Tunney's scales. Abe tipped them at two hundred and sixty-five. He had tried manfully to reduce; the trouble was, he was still growing. Tunney and Whitney regretfully released him from their contract with him and dissolved their corporation, although in the end it might have proved not too bad an investment. For, under new management, Simon got as far, in 1941, as lasting thirteen rounds with Joe Louis. He retired from boxing soon afterward and became a liquor salesman. "An awfully nice big fellow," Whitney would recall.

Amidst all the Payne Whitneys' peregrinations, their children had to be formally educated. When Jock was a toddler, Miss Chapin's, a fashionable academic beginning for girls who would end up at finishing schools, also admitted boys, but only through the first grade. That co-educational experiment was soon aborted, because, as one obituary of the headmistress put it in 1934, "years ago, Miss Chapin had a number of small boy pupils who caused so much trouble that she dropped them from the school." Whether young Whitney was in any way responsible for the change is not known (though it may be significant that he filed the obit), but he did cause one minor commotion at Miss Chapin's graduation ceremonies when he was a first-grader. His sister was also enrolled there, and Joan was on the official program, designated to recite "*Mon Ami Pierrot.*" She had scarcely finished and curtseyed to polite applause when there was a shrill voice from the audience. "Miss Chapin, I can say a piece, too," Jock piped up. (He had a lisp then to complement his stutter.) Whereupon he marched onstage and delivered the whole of "The Village Blacksmith." He got so much bigger a hand for his impromptu declamation than Joan had that she would maintain forty years afterward that she determined that awful day never again to make a speech in public.

Starting with second grade, Jock attended St. Bernard's, which prepared boys and boys alone for high school—in its case, nearly always for topflight New England boarding schools. St. Bernard's had been founded in 1904, the year of Jock's birth, by John Card Jenkins, whose father had been an English chaplain in Belgium; the school's name derived from the fact that in Brussels the Jenkins family had lived on the Rue St. Bernard. By the time Whitney was enrolled, in 1913, Jenkins was running it in partnership with Francis Tabor, whom he had met at a soccer game on Staten Island, and the school had moved from two earlier sites to East Ninety-eighth Street, between Fifth and Madison avenues. One of the Messrs. Jenkins and Tabor's shared headmasterly traits was cruelly suppressed by Prohibition: at lunch every day, while their wards sipped milk, they would indulge in beer sprinkled with salt. It was a school densely populated by sons of the rich, many of whom were disgorged each morning from chauffeured Rolls-Royces. Jock's allowance was twenty-five cents a week. He amplified that, after the move uptown, by urging other boys whose parents expected them to get there by public transport to ride in *his* Rolls-Royce, and by exacting from each delighted passenger a nickel a day. On the other hand, young Whitney often treated the less affluent to soft drinks at a neighborhood soda shop.

At St. Bernard's, Jock was invited to join an exclusive fraternity called, no one can now remember why, the B.B. Club. The officers of the club presently concluded that ensuing initiations into its fold could most comfortably be held at the Whitneys' Fifth Avenue establishment, where new members had to crawl out onto a window ledge of Jock's fifth story bedroom and drop paper bags filled with water on passersby below. Fortunately, the Payne Whitneys had wide window ledges. Jock was at first embarrassed to have to ask his schoolmates into a home that, even though most of them were more than decently domiciled, was manifestly superior to what they were accustomed to; he would hustle neophytes to the top story and hope that en route they had not espied the ground-floor ballroom.

Academically, he was a fair student. (Not that that mattered much; there was hardly anything he could have done to keep him out of Groton short of adulterating the heads' beer with cayenne pepper.) What remains on record is that in the spring of 1913, Jock's first year at St. Bernard's, when the passing grade in some subjects was a curious 25, he achieved a mere 30 in arithmetic and in drawing, and a 40 in "general knowledge." (In neatness and conduct, over the next few years, his performance was also only so-so. He required extra tutoring in arithmetic one year, and wrote his mother during that ordeal that on top of everything else he had had to stop using "Gee" because his teacher "gives us sums for every gee we say.") It was the custom at St. Bernard's—it still is—to put on a Shakespearean evening each winter, with an all-student cast. In December 1916, Whitney's last year there, *Hamlet* was the offering. It had been apparent since Miss Chapin's that Jock, stutter notwithstanding, was stage-struck. He was elated when he was given the title role. But it was soon taken away; he was deficient in arithmetic at the time, and was accordingly demoted to Claudius and the First Gravedigger. "Whitney took the part of the King exceedingly well and spoke excellently," declared the school publication, the *Budget*.

Ordinarily, the *Budget* was entirely student-written. An exception to this policy was the publication in its 1916 summer issue of one more poem by Helen Hay Whitney, entitled "To the Masters of St. Bernard's School":

> "Only a seed, a bulb," the careless say,
> "Only a cutting"—and they turn away.
> Being so blind they do not see or guess
> How the bright bloom and ardent loveliness
> Of all the garden's pride lies in that husk,
> Promise and proof, as dawning holds the dusk.
> Promise—but not for these, the careless ones,
> But for the gardener who bears the suns
> And rains of effort for the perfect flower
> Not by a moment's toil, not by an hour,
> But patiently and brave, as one who knows
> The weary work whereby such glory grows.
>
> Only a schoolboy, uncouth, lazy, wild
> —Bulb, cutting, seed—more hopeless seems the child,
> Those who lack wise and inner vision view
> Merely the ugly shell of all things new.
> Rough as a colt, the boy with eager eyes
> Fares to a "football goal" of destinies.
> Steady must be the hand and calm the brow
> That guides the stumbling feet through why and how,
> Losing himself. How fierce the irksome fret
> To know the Doric singing, and forget
> And dream the future, *now* perfected *then*.
> These are the patient gardeners of men.

On arriving at St. Bernard's, young Whitney had special reason to be glad his father had engaged Tommy Shortell to teach him fisticuffs. It was the school rule then that every student take up either boxing or fencing, and to some boys the alternatives seemed to be ludicrous; one told his father that street urchins were forever robbing him of his nickels and dimes and that he couldn't very well hope to fend them off by carrying a sword around wherever he went. Those boys who, like Jock, espoused pugilism would be placed on either side of a chalk line on the gymnasium floor, and anyone who stepped back would be declared a loser. After a while, most students learned the knack of standing toe to toe and pretending to flail away at one another, but without landing any telling blows.

St. Bernard's had an annual Sports Day, an intensely competitive occasion of great import to the boys and their nurturing parents. The first time Jock took part in one—it was held, in 1913, at the Livingstone Cricket Club, on Staten Island—he finished a creditable second in a Sub-Junior Sack Race, thus barely missing a chance to walk off, or stumble off, with a cup donated by his mother. By the spring of 1917, he had advanced athletically to the point of winning a baseball bat on Sports Day, and the erstwhile right fielder had become so much more proficient at that sport that he was captain of the school nine. The *Budget*, however, which had earlier said of his football skills, "Whitney played well at times, but was never in his place," elected in its 1917 summer issue to sum up that spring's sports calendar with "There was great difficulty in choosing a Captain of this year's Baseball Team, and ultimately J. H. Whitney was elected, and it was hoped that he would have most influence in inspiring the team and getting them to practice and play in a proper sporting spirit. Our expectations have not been altogether realized."

Notwithstanding that farewell low blow, in later years Whitney remained fond of, and loyal to, St. Bernard's. Thanks to his mother's and his largess, the school's most coveted student award, given yearly to the boy regarded by his masters as outstanding in work, play, and conduct, is the Payne Whitney Honor Award, a large, two-handled, sterling silver Tiffany trophy. (The recipient was entitled to retain possession for one year; a long-gone holder of this reward for exemplary moral behavior, though, never returned it; so St. Bernard's, not wishing to inform the Whitney donors of such egregious misfeasance, had Tiffany make up a replica.) In 1974, the school conferred on John Hay Whitney its St. Bernard's Associates Award—its highest honor for an alumnus. By then, Jock had demonstrated in numerous ways his reciprocal affection for the institution: not only had he contributed handsomely to its various fund drives, but he had engaged as steward for his office mess a man who had retired from St. Bernard's after serving its boys their lunches for thirty-two faithful years. Whitney could not attend the award ceremony, but his steward, Jack Forrest, could, and favored the guests with a few impromptu remarks. On the occasion, the *Budget*'s bygone reflections on Whitney's baseball prowess were quoted, but slightly out of context; the only words cited were "most influence in inspiring the team and getting them to practice and play in a proper sporting spirit."

The First World War was under way when the thirteen-year-old Jock Whitney arrived, in the fall of 1917, at Groton School. Military training was an extracurricular activity for the older boys; they drilled with equipment given to the school by Payne Whitney, Groton '94. Even in peacetime, Groton in some ways resembled a martial encampment. The students slept in cubicles of barracks-like austerity. Their reveille was at 5:45 A.M. They took cold showers. Most of them came from wealthy backgrounds—it did not surprise a teacher there to be handed a theme that began, as did one of Jock's, "Foxhunting seems to me to be one of the finest sports existing in this country"—but no boy in the lower grades was allowed spending money, while on campus, of more than a quarter a week, and a nickel of that had to go into the church collection plate each Sunday.

All the boys were under the absolute command of Groton's legendary Rector, the Rev. Endicott Peabody, a benevolent despot who for Jock, as for many a boy before and after him, became something of a father figure, alternately feared and respected. The mother of another student, a Whitney neighbor on Long Island, came to lunch at the school one day, sat next to the Rector, looked around, and said to Dr. Peabody, "That's Jock Whitney down there, isn't it?" The Rector nodded. "Well, you must have a pretty hard time keeping *him* in order," the visitor prattled. She went on about some of Whitney's colorful escapades at Manhasset, a recital that Jock described in a letter to his father as more tragic than funny. "For Heaven's sake train these North Shore friends of yours a little better!" the boy wrote. "The Rector almost blew up." Jock was sure during the remainder of that edgy lunch "that the Rector would be grouchy and sore when I next saw him. But he wasn't at all, and has been darned nice ever since." Dr. Peabody had died by the time Whitney named one of his stallions Groton and one of its offspring The Rector.

Dr. Peabody regularly kept in touch, by handwritten notes, with his boys' families, especially with fathers who had once been his boys themselves. Thus, soon after Jock settled in, not altogether auspiciously—he stood thirtieth in a class of thirty-five and had been cited nineteen times for tardiness in a couple of weeks—the headmaster wrote Whitney *père*, "He behaves well & is learning the ways of the school—except in punctuality."

Payne Whitney was less concerned about lateness than about athletics. "I am terribly keen to know what position they are making you play on your football team," he wrote his son on September 28, 1917, apparently taking it for granted that *some* position would be available. "Do work hard at it. Whatever position you play put your mind at it all the time, and see if you can't work out by your brain some way to beat the other fellow who is not using his head."

As the Groton years rolled by, Whitney even started arriving at assigned destinations more or less on time, but there were still petty problems. Writing in February 1920 to his mother, who was basking in the southwest Georgia sun, he said, with juvenile jocundity, "You smell the sweet scent of flowers while all the scent I get is being sent to the Rector every so often." That same month, though, he was pleased to be able to write to his father, who had remained in New York, "The Debating season has been going wonderfully for our side, the Demosthenes. We have won every debate so far and the only one in doubt is the next one, and of course the one after that. The latter is mine. I have already spoken a couple of times, but my main speech doesn't come until a week from this Thursday. I wish, if you possibly had time, that you'd write me the points that you told me, and any more. The argument is 'Resolved: that the prohibition of intoxicating liquors should be modified to allow light wines and beer.' We have the pro." It is not known how Payne Whitney, who not long before outfoxed the drys with his consummate wine cellar, responded; but it might have been more challenging if his son had had the con.

Jock would reflect in later years that, having gone to boarding school at so young and impressionable an age, he had perhaps been more influenced at that stage of his life by schoolmasters—as by governesses before that than by his parents. One Sunday, the Rector had preached a sermon about an egg. It was an egg of marginal edibility, an egg a hair away from rotten. "Who among you boys would want to eat an egg that just gets by?" Dr. Peabody had thundered from his pulpit. Jock, though he had made a football team all right, perceived himself to be that borderline egg. He was indisputably just getting by, and the Rector seemed to be glancing his way. He did not particularly mind the analogy. But then he was given a "sitdown"—an after-hours chat that was largely a remonstrative monologue—by one of the masters, a dedicated disciplinarian whose habit it was to prowl around the dorms in sneakers, hoping to catch boys with lights on after bedtime. That master lectured Jock long and hard about what high expectations his family had for him and how he, the dubious egg, was letting them down. "I changed completely," Whitney recalled, "and nobody could have been more astonished at the transformation than I was. I'd been a very poor example of a student until that master showed me the error of my ways."

There are watershed moments in all lives. For Jock Whitney, that master's sulphurous chastisement was certainly one. Up to then, he had been in large part a hesitant little rich boy, always getting by, sometimes only just getting by, as lax as he was likable. Without making any

conscious decisions about the matter, he seems at that point to have resolved to strive afterward to change his image—rather, change his actual
self. There would be lapses—plenty of them, in the hedonistic 1920s—but
once he had achieved an awareness of debatable ways he set forth, if for
a while somewhat haltingly, on a path that would later be adjudged by
his peers to be consistently uphill, and in the end commendably high.

As his family and he had known all along that he would have no trouble being admitted to St. Bernard's or to Groton, so did he know that,
barring some unimaginable dereliction, he would make it on to Yale. But
he began to want to make something of himself. By the end of his senior
year at Groton, he was even climbing academically; he ranked thirteenth
in a class of twenty-two.

The highest distinction any boy could aspire to at Groton was to be
chosen—by the members of the two upper forms and of the faculty, subject to the Rector's approval—senior prefect of the student body. Payne
Whitney had had that accolade bestowed on him in the spring of 1893,
and in the spring of 1921 Jock was notified that he'd been named senior
prefect for the following year. That august title imposed responsibilities
upon its bearer: it was a Groton tradition, for instance, that the senior
prefect-designate should spend a few summer weeks, before he assumed
office, as a counselor in a Massachusetts camp for underprivileged boys
from Boston. Jock's assumption of that duty was made less onerous than
it might otherwise have been by his enjoying the use of one of his father's fancier motor vehicles—a custom-made three-seater, with a sort of
couch in the rear in case an occupant wanted to stretch out while in
transit. So well did Jock wear his prefectural mantle after the fall term
got under way that, on the eve of the Christmas holidays, Dr. Peabody
called his boys together for a special announcement. Despite the football
team's having come out behind in its annual confrontation with its
archrival St. Mark's, the Rector declared, because of the praiseworthy
behavior their senior prefect had instilled in his schoolmates, the entire
student body could have an extra two days' vacation.

Payne Whitney made one stipulation while his son was at Groton. He
dearly hoped that Jock would, like him, one day stroke the varsity crew
at Yale—an educational distinction that, in Payne's view, all but eclipsed
any other—but although the Groton crew rated respectably in prep
school circles, the elder Whitney would not let his son try out for it.
Payne did not want Jock to learn rowing from an amateur. That the particular amateur coaching Groton's shells happened to be Dr. Peabody
himself was, to Payne, irrelevant. The Rector did not hold a grudge because of the senior Whitney's appraisal of his oarsmanship. In March
1926, for instance, Peabody wrote Payne about a situation that had him
worried. Groton scarcely had room, he lamented, for the sons of its grad-

uates, let alone outsiders, and so he wanted to start a spillover school for worthy boys whom fate had not blessed with the right antecedents. Peabody had found an estate in North Andover, Massachusetts, around which he believed a fine new school could be constructed, and would Payne help him out? One hundred and fifty thousand dollars, the Rector thought, would suffice for start-up money.

Thus came into being the Brooks School, which opened its doors in the fall of 1927. Its first headmaster was Frank Davis Ashburn, who had been Groton's senior prefect just before Jock; one of its first teachers, later also headmaster, was Jock's classmate Arthur Milliken. Payne Whitney died that year, but Jock continued to support Dr. Peabody's spillover school, and he served on the Brooks board of trustees for thirty years. He had special reason to be grateful to Arthur Milliken. In Jock's junior year at Groton, as a tackle on the football team, he was supposed to run downfield under punts and hurl himself upon the receiver. Toward the end of *that* fall's game against St. Mark's, Whitney was exhausted, and when it came time for Groton to kick, he asked Milliken to exchange positions with him. It was late in the afternoon, the skies were darkening, and the action on the field was hard for the spectators to follow. The Groton kicker got off his punt, and the Groton right tackle leapt off the scrimmage line, tore downfield, and tackled the St. Mark's receiver so viciously that he fumbled. Groton recovered the ball, and, thanks to that jarring tackle, went on to win the game. The spectators cheered loud and long—and mistakenly—for Whitney. It was the least Jock could do after that to support Brooks School—all the more so because, owing in no small part to Milliken's admirable performance in his stead, Whitney was named an outstanding prep school lineman of that season.

1. Portrait of Payne Whitney by Raymond P. R. Neilson. (Eric Pollitzer photo)

2. *Typical of the insatiable interest of the American press in the forthcoming marriage of Helen Hay to Payne Whitney was this full-page spread on January 26, 1902, in the* Daily News *of Denver, Colorado—a city to which neither the bride nor the bridegroom had any particular ties. Payne is shown at the lower left, and Helen's late brother Adelbert, Payne's Yale roommate, at lower right. Directly beneath the bride is portrayed the redoubtable Colonel Oliver Hazard Payne, here characterized, not unreasonably, as "The Fairy Prince."*

3. *Jock's mother, Helen Hay Whitney, on her wedding day in 1902, with her attendants: her sister-in-law Dorothy (l.) and her sister Alice (r.).*

4. *Helen Hay Whitney's residence at Lexington, Kentucky.* (Bradley Studio photo)

5. *Helen Hay, when she was presented to Queen Victoria at the Court of St. James's in 1898.*

6. *Jock's father, Payne Whitney, at Yale, in his varsity crew sweater.* (Brown Bros. photo)

7. *Payne and Helen Whitney modeling, as it were, the fashionable hats of their day.*

9. *John Hay, Jock's grandfather, in 1902, when he was President Theodore Roosevelt's Secretary of State.* (J.E. Purdy photo)

8. *One of the biggest plungers of his era, Payne Whitney (c.) confers at the track with his personal betting commissioner, Lester Doctor (l.), and the celebrated polo player Larry Waterbury (r.).* (Brown Bros. photo)

10. *William Collins Whitney, Jock's paternal grandfather.*

11. *Helen Hay Whitney with her children when Jock, at about two, was still in skirts.*

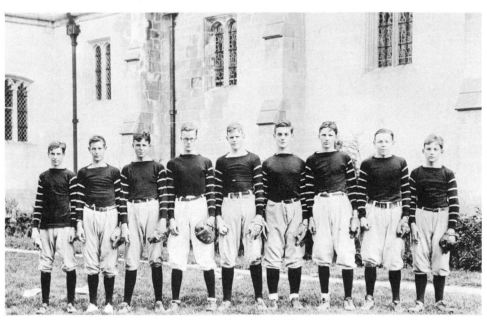

12. *The Groton baseball team. Jock is fourth from right.*

13. *The Groton School constituency in 1922. The Reverend Endicott Peabody, the headmaster, is in the center of the picture, with Senior Prefect J. H. Whitney on his left.*

14. *Jock is also fourth from right here, on the Yale junior varsity crew.*

5

I Had So Much So Young

Never having had to wear rags, except as a *Hamlet* gravedigger, and having from birth been fairly well assured of lifelong riches, in young manhood Whitney hardly resembled a Horatio Alger character. Yet there was something Algeresque about his determination to succeed as an actor despite his stutter. There was a difference, of course, between declaiming other people's lines and having to evolve and enunciate one's own. Notwithstanding, as at Groton he had squared off against his speech impediment by debating and also by performing in school plays, soon after entering college in the fall of 1922 he continued to show a lively interest in the theatre. "From St. Bernard's through Yale," he would say in later years, "I would always play a part whenever anybody would let me on a stage. After Yale, unfortunately, nobody ever gave me an opportunity to do anything theatrical except invest."

It was rare for a Yale freshman to wangle a role in the annual production of the university's vaunted Dramatic Association, then directed by Monty Woolley, among whose own memorable subsequent opportunities was the embodiment of the title role in *The Man Who Came to Dinner*. In Whitney's freshman year, Woolley cast him as Belzanor, the captain of the palace guard, in a winter Dramatic production of *Caesar and Cleopatra*. "His flute-like voice was felt to be a distinct innovation," a campus critic observed. It was an abbreviated part that called for an abbreviated costume. The barelegged freshman appeared in it at, among other auditoriums, the Heckscher Memorial Theatre in New York City. Belzanor's parents were in the audience. Payne Whitney was especially pleased when, in an entr'acte, another old Yale oar rushed up to him, beaming, and said, "Congratulations! What a fine pair of legs for crew!" Next, Jock wangled the part of the Town Crier in *Playboy of the Western World*, and because this was his second Dramat show, he was elected—the first member of his class to be so honored—to membership in the Association.

By then the eighteen-year-old freshman stood just over six feet tall and weighed one hundred and seventy-five pounds, five pounds more than his Groton fighting weight. He did not box at Yale, but his proportions were splendid for rowing. He had his father's clean-cut good looks and his mother's regal posture. By then, too, Payne Whitney was ready— eager—to have his son embrace the sport that the father had denied to him at Groton. Whatever the soundness of that restrictive strategy, within a month after enrolling at Yale and sweeping his first oar, Jock was stroking the freshman shell, which set a new record for the two-mile upstream course at New London, Connecticut. His sophomore year, he rowed on the junior varsity. His only unsettling moment came when he learned that his sculptor aunt wanted to do a statue called *The Rower*, wanted him to pose for it, and wanted to immortalize him in the nude. He kept making up excuses to stay away from Gertrude Vanderbilt Whitney's studio, and after a while she lost interest in him as a model.

In Jock's junior year, he was stroking the varsity eight when he came down with rheumatic fever. After he had recovered, he was told by his doctor to give up rowing for a year. Upon receiving this shattering intelligence, Payne Whitney—who evidently had no qualms about the fact that a brother of his uncle Oliver Payne had died young as a result of an injury sustained while rowing at Yale—went into conference with the Yale crew coach, the celebrated Ed Leader. (Perhaps contrite because he had deprived Groton of Jock's rowing services, Payne Whitney gave that school a special sort of present one Saturday in 1924. He arranged for Leader to spend a day there helping Dr. Peabody with his coaching chores.) They appealed jointly to Jock to drop back one class, so he wouldn't lose a year of crew and thus, in all probability, forfeit his chance of becoming—like his father before him—varsity captain. Jock was fond of rowing, but not to the extent of forsaking his classmates for it. He stuck with them and, as a result, when he was allowed to row again his senior year, got only as far as stroking the junior varsity. The university awarded him his major "Y" anyway. Two years later, while in London, he reciprocated by shipping to New Haven, as a mascot for the crew, a pedigreed English bulldog, which brought it such good luck that the football team adopted it, too, in preference to other available bulldogs. It became Handsome Dan VII in the succession of Yale mascots.

In his senior year, Jock was on his class's book committee—also the senior prom committee—and for the 1926 yearbook he wrote "The Class in Athletics," which, he emphasized at the outset, was not a history but a review. There was a good deal about crew, understandably, in his critique. Referring to the varsity shell that would take to the water that spring after the yearbook was finished, he said, "The members of our Class who are now candidates are Captain Kingsbury, about whose chances there seems to be very little doubt, Russell, Crosby, Waterman, and Whitney. To them all we wish the greatest success, especially to the last named (see signature at close of article!)." He was signing himself then "John H. Whitney." He did not include therein an episode that may be apocryphal but that has become a legend among Yale archivists. The story goes that while Jock was rowing he went to a barber and asked to have his hair cut very short. "You know, like Hindenburg's," Whitney said. Memories of the First World War were still fresh in the minds of older men. "I won't give you anything called a Hindenburg cut," the barber is said to have replied. "But since you're having it cut like that for crew, why not call it a 'crew cut'?" And thus, in Yale lore, did the English language acquire that particular phrase.

Like his father, Jock remained a perennial devotee of rowing (he was a judge at the 1956 Olympic crew trials), and especially of Yale rowing. Now and then, on feeling obliged to spur on his office staff, he would say it was no time to rest on their oars—as have many employers said, of course, who never had occasion themselves thus literally to relax. Jock, too, served for many years on the Yale Graduate Advisory Rowing Committee. He gave the Yale crew a motor launch, in 1960, which was christened the *Payne Whitney;* and that same year he arranged with Spyros Skouras, of Twentieth Century-Fox, to have first-run motion pictures shipped to Gales Ferry for the delectation and distraction of the Eli oarsmen nervously awaiting the big Harvard race under the roof that Payne Whitney had provided a generation before. Jock continued to do that ever afterward; Bo Derek in *10* was among his selections to help the 1980 crews relax. (Earlier, Whitney *fils* had furnished divertissement of another form for the edgy oarsmen, ferrying Abe Simon up there for boxing exhibitions.) More than fifty years after receiving his "Y," Jock Whitney was still responsive to the demands of Yale rowing. "Well, that saves me a thousand dollars," he remarked, not altogether happily, on learning that the Yale varsity had lost to Harvard in 1978. It seemed he had pledged that sum toward the Yale boat's expenses to the Henley Regatta, should it have won and gone.

One went to college even then, of course, to get an education. In the light of Jock's earlier academic record, it did not startle his parents—he was young, after all, and was going through a gradual transformation, not a resurrection—that at Yale he flunked freshman math. Despite that failure, the average of all his marks was a shade better than his classmates' average. English was his best subject. He would soon join the Elizabethan Club, a haven for undergraduates with literary interests. He wrote a couple of book reviews for the student literary magazine. He became one of the "pundits" of the legendary Yale professor William Lyon Phelps—an élite group of bookish underclassmen. Billy Phelps gave them gold charms in the shape of a one-inch Buddha as evidence of their proficiency and good taste. Whitney's average was manifestly improved one term when he earned a 95 in Phelps's contemporary drama course, an achievement that was apparently not too taxing. In later years one of his classmates, Carlos F. Stoddard, Jr., teasingly reminded Jock that *he* had got a 98, whereupon Whitney retorted, "Well, Stoddard, you read the plays."

By the time Jock matriculated at Yale, he had also become proficient in another gentlemanly sport. He had begun playing polo while still at Groton. His family spent summers then on the Massachusetts North Shore, and he wore the colors of the Myopia Sea Gulls, a team based in Ipswich. He did not try out for polo at Yale—there was a conflict with crew—but during his summer vacations he galloped around with various pickup intercollegiate teams that competed around New England. In the summer of 1925, when some of his more serious-minded contemporaries were earnestly debating the pros and cons of the Scopes trial under way at Dayton, he traveled to Colorado Springs for some polo matches, accompanied—how else would Payne Whitney's young man be expected to go west?—by five polo ponies, a riding horse, and a manservant. His father, elated at Jock's increasing show of interest in horses, gave him two thoroughbred yearlings as a twenty-second-birthday present.

That anniversary—celebrated, as had become customary, at Saratoga in August—was all in all a more serene occasion for Jock than his twenty-first had been. His father had promised him some stocks and bonds to mark his entrance into adulthood, and to celebrate that anticipated windfall Jock had spent his birthday eve gambling at the Arrowhead Inn. When his sister Joan poked her head into his room the following morning to extend a natal greeting, she muted it by adding, "Are you in trouble!" Jock thought she was referring to his having patronized the casino, which hadn't troubled him a whit; indeed, on the floor alongside his bed was a pile of money he had won and, in the flush of auroral victory, hadn't yet even counted. It turned out, though, that his parents had just come across a story in a New York newspaper relating in lively detail how he had taken the glamorous and notorious Peggy Hopkins Joyce for a moonlight cruise aboard his mother's yacht. It was a caper not much different in principle from any zesty young man's borrowing his parents' automobile to take a girl friend for a spin, but a yacht and a Whitney and a Peggy Hopkins Joyce made up a spicy editorial treat.

The Yale class of 1926 is remembered fondly in New Haven because it was the one that argued loudly and successfully for the abolishment of compulsory chapel. It also helped prick the myth that among Yale final clubs Skull and Bones stood high above all others, and that not to belong to that arcane body was, for anyone who had the chance, akin to playing on a junior varsity team. Payne Whitney had been a Bones man, and when the traditional Tap Day came along in the spring of his son's junior year it was assumed that Jock would routinely continue the family tradition.

In the 1920s, newspapers not only peeked into the cabins of private yachts but regularly ran the names of all the society folk attending their practically non-stop round of balls. In similar fashion, the New York press covered events like Tap Day, reporting faithfully how Yale's five hundred juniors gathered around a particular oak tree in the hope of having their shoulders thumped by recruiters filling sixty vacancies in four senior societies. Thus the *World* was on the scene on May 14, 1925, to chronicle the solemn festivities for posterity, and it was able to favor its readers with a startling development. "The throng of student onlookers gasped in amazement," the paper reported, "as John Hay Whitney of New York and Edmund Cottle of Buffalo ignored taps for Bones. Both later accepted elections to Scroll and Key."

There were a number of reasons for Whitney's choice, none of them in his view amazing. He felt Bones was a ridiculously secret society, and anybody who joined it practically had to get down on his knees and confess to a legion of sins. Also, unlike the protagonist of Owen Wister's *Stover at Yale,* Jock couldn't have cared less about Bones's prestige—or what Key men have called over the years "alleged prestige."

On the other hand, Whitney was impressed with some of his forerunners at Yale who'd been attracted to Key: Cole Porter, Wilmarth Lewis, and, especially, Louis Stoddard and Watson Webb, two of the four members of the first United States polo team ever to beat Great Britain. Beyond that, Jock knew in advance that among his classmates who were going to take Key if they got the chance, as they did, were his good friends Henry C. Potter, the president of Dramat, and Carlos Stoddard, the chairman of the *Daily News;* and the captains of the football, baseball, and hockey teams. And then there was crew. Who at Yale did not know that, of the shell that had won the gold medal in the 1924 Olympics, five of the eight oarsmen had ended up in Scroll and Key?

Edmund Cottle, who with Whitney chose Key over Bones, was a Big Man on Campus—Student Council representative and halfback on the football team. Three of the original members of the class of 1926 who would later become celebrated never made it to that Tap Day at all. Lucius Beebe—whose New Haven peccadilloes included leading a student revolt against the food in Commons (Jock and all his classmates were fined fifty cents apiece for broken crockery)—was encouraged by Yale to switch to Harvard. Herbert Prior—later Rudy—Vallee (he spelled it Vallée then), a transfer from the University of Maine, left New Haven to play the banjo at the Savoy Hotel in London. He returned to Yale in due course and became leader of its band, but by then he had been assigned to the class of 1927. Then there was Curtis Arnoux Peters, Jr., who belonged, as did Whitney, to a small private social group called the Bulldog Grill, which entailed no ceremonial tapping; the members had organized it themselves. Peters was in New Haven only briefly, departing in June 1924, but before he left had made himself known as a gifted saxophonist. He played in a dance band conducted by still another classmate, Benjamin J. Cutler.

Shortly before graduation, Cutler was chosen "Most to Be Admired" by his classmates. Stoddard won "Done Most for Yale" hands down. "Most Popular" was Frederic A. Potts, who became president of the Philadelphia National Bank. "Most Gentlemanly" was Elliott Schieffelin, who went into teaching. Whitney received not a single vote in any of those categories, or, when it came to that, in "Most Original," "Best-natured," "Most Modest," or "Best-looking." But he ran away with "Greatest Social Light," and scored a creditable fourth in "Most Versatile" and a fifth in "Most Likely to Succeed." While the class of 1926 was at it, it voted Mussolini "Biggest World Figure of Today." Far in his wake were Calvin Coolidge, Mahatma Gandhi, and George Bernard Shaw.

Ben Cutler went on, practically forever, as a musician, becoming the leader of a society dance band that officiated at thousands of coming-out parties and other such rites of passage. Curtis Arnoux Peters became Peter Arno. Only five years out of college and already an established cartoonist, Arno got involved in a musical comedy about divorce. It was to be called *The Road to Reno,* and he was to provide not merely his by then glittering name but also the stage sets. Looking for a suitable backer, Arno approached his classmate Whitney. Jock was mildly impressed on hearing that Claudette Colbert and Victor Moore had been lined up for the production, but his ears pricked when he was told, almost as an afterthought, that a rising young singer would also be in the cast—Bing Crosby. "That got me," Whitney would say afterward. He had become a slavish Crosby fan. Crosby could be heard weekday evenings, from seven to seven-fifteen, on radio over the Columbia Broadcasting System; the crooner was one of the more soothing weapons William S. Paley was using in a strident effort to make his fledgling CBS competitive with the older and solidly entrenched National Broadcasting Company. Whitney would not accept a dinner invitation that conflicted with the fifteen minutes he piously devoted to Crosby each evening. (Twenty years later, he had the same fanatical addiction to Tallulah Bankhead's radio program; if then he was unable, during the months she was on the air, to avoid sitting down to dinner at seven o'clock of a Sunday evening, he would take a portable radio to the table with him.)

Whitney was overjoyed at the prospect of being permitted to invest in his idol's vehicle, and put up eighty-five thousand dollars to that end. Then things started going wrong. Colbert came down with appendicitis and had to withdraw from the cast. Moore, too, fell by the wayside. But the most awful intimation of impending disaster came at an early rehearsal, with Jock in blissful attendance, when it turned out that without a microphone Crosby couldn't be heard beyond the fourth row of the orchestra. This was at a time when amplification was taboo in the legitimate theatre. So Crosby was out of the show. Eventually there was little left of the original notion save Arno's scenery. Even the title had vanished, replaced by *Here Goes the Bride*. The comedy team of Clark and McCullough had become the stars. Accomplished as they were, they were not up to the task of salvaging the venture. Whitney had loyally stayed with it, to the extent of going on the road for pre-Broadway tryouts and coming through with an additional fifteen thousand dollars to bolster the producers' sagging finances. It was all to no avail. The New York premiere was so mournful an occasion that almost none of Whitney's friends had the heart to turn up for a gala opening-night party Jock threw at the Starlight Roof of the Waldorf-Astoria. The show folded after seven performances, a calamity that, if at considerable expense and inconvenience, nevertheless strengthened Whitney's belief in Crosby's indispensability. When Crosby went into horse racing, in 1935, the first horse he bought was Whitney-bred. The animal was named Zombie. It was too well named; like *Here Goes the Bride*, it was a flop.

In 1948, Whitney was brooding about what to do to improve sales of the Minute Maid Corporation, one of the frontrunners in the frozen orange juice derby. Minute Maid was the outgrowth of a wartime entity first named Florida Foods and then Vacuum Foods. A government agency called the National Research Corporation had organized the company to make dehydrated orange juice powder for the armed forces. The orange juice project was announced on April 12, 1945, a day otherwise memorable because of the death of Franklin Roosevelt. Funds for the construction of a big dehydration plant in Florida were authorized one hour before the atom bomb fell on Hiroshima. With the end of the war imminent, the government lost interest. The company came into private hands, and it was floundering along when Whitney bought heavily into it. Minute Maid was in the process then of switching from a powdered concentrate to a frozen one, and for a while Whitney subjected his business associates to long tasting sessions in his office. At one meeting, a tin can of orange mush was ceremoniously ushered into a Whitney conference room. Nobody had a can opener. One of Jock's business associates borrowed a screwdriver and a pair of pliers from a building maintenance man, wrestled the can open, filled a glass with its contents, and deferentially handed the potion to Jock, for the first judicious sip. "Tastes a little tinny to me," Whitney said.

Sampling the product was not enough. It had to be sold. Whitney had kept in touch with Crosby. The two of them played golf together when they happened to be in the same part of the world. Now it occurred to Jock that Bing might be amenable to plugging the drink on the radio, in return for being let in on a deal with a potential capital gains feature. Crosby was readily agreeable. He was made a director of Minute Maid—"a rather juicy enterprise," he called it in a ghost-written memoir—and received a fee of fifty thousand dollars. Moreover, he was allowed to buy two hundred thousand shares of Minute Maid common (Whitney had more than twice as many) at ten cents a share only shortly before less vocally endowed investors were obliged to pay as much as ten dollars a share for it. The singer ended up vastly multiplying that twenty-thousand-dollar investment.

For two years, Crosby spent fifteen minutes on the radio every weekday morning alternately singing popular tunes and singing the praises of Minute Maid. The performances were transcribed, and there was a new transcription daily. Whitney was able to arrange with CBS's Paley—who by then had become another golfing crony and, more important, his brother-in-law—to have Crosby's testimonials carried over selected stations of Paley's network immediately preceding the morning Arthur Godfrey program, to which almost every clean-living American was presumed to be tuning in. Crosby proved an irresistible huckster. It took a couple of million boxes of oranges a year to slake the massive thirsts he spawned. Arthur Godfrey was so impressed that he soon worked out a lucrative deal himself with another orange juice company.

Whitney encouraged all his friends and associates, even those whose diets called for grapefruit or baked apple, to drink Minute Maid at breakfast; and because a good general must always set an example for his troops, he consumed twice as much as anybody else. That was not difficult. He had an enormous appetite, and as a trencherman would sometimes be compared by awe-struck friends to Henry VIII, though they would hasten to add that Whitney had much better table manners. One of them, half in jest, once gave Whitney a dinner plate the size of a serving platter. His wife thought it most practical, and served him lunch on it every Sunday, while the rest of the family ate off conventional-size china.

Whenever Whitney formed a real attachment to something, whether it was a pet dog, a reconstituted beverage, or a university, it was usually rock-hard. His relationship to Yale was typical. It stood to reason that any private institution dependent for its existence and expansion on the alms of its wealthier alumni would hold out a hand to someone with his resources. But the vigor with which Whitney grasped that out-stretched palm—and kept filling it nearly to overflowing—probably sur-prised even Yale. His friend Carlos Stoddard, who had taken Billy Phelps's drama course with Whitney, went to work after graduation for the Yale Development Office. How agreeable for someone in a job like that to be on such terms with such a classmate!

Another Yale man who was in the right place at the right time was its treasurer from 1910 to 1942, George Parmly Day. In the 1920s, Day was also president of the Yale University Press, which he had co-founded, and had a guiding hand in most of the university's publications. During the summer of 1928, Day invited Whitney, then just two years out of college, to work part time for the quarterly *Yale Review*. Whitney gladly ac-quiesced. He had had a yen to get into some phase of publishing, and his mother was enthusiastically supportive. The neophyte was not paid for his efforts, but that was irrelevant, inasmuch as he had already come into a formidable inheritance. Indeed, one of his first editorial achievements was to put up the prize money for a thousand-dollar *Review* competition for articles on national or international affairs. Among the judges he cor-ralled for this contest was an old family friend, Elihu Root, who, re-sponding that summer to young Whitney's "almost pathetic eagerness to have you accept," said that "it is a special pleasure for me to do some-thing which will please the son of your father and mother and the grand-son of your grandparents." (Earlier, Root had written a letter on Jock's behalf when he was applying to Oxford, and a generation before that had collaborated, in 1904, with John Hay on a pro-Theodore Roosevelt political tract entitled *The Republican Party—A Party Fit to Govern*.) In September, Dean Wilbur Cross of Yale, later the governor of Connect-icut, asked Whitney to become an assistant editor of the *Review*, and in that honorific, though still unremunerative, capacity he was able to add to its roster of contributors some of the talented friends he had by then acquired on his own—among them Robert Benchley, Dorothy Parker, and Donald Ogden Stewart.

So effective a procurer did Whitney become of manuscripts of the sort the *Review* did not ordinarily attract that he was asked in due course to solicit Albert Einstein, in Germany, for an article about his newfangled theory of relativity. Whitney was able to report to his superior editors in the summer of 1931 that "Dr. Einstein expects no payment for the *Review* article . . . is prepared to write it and will welcome suggestions." The piece never materialized. Whitney's embrace of the *Review* was all-encompassing. He surprised a young Englishwoman with whom he'd waltzed in London by sending her a subscription. At home, he so unflaggingly pestered his friends and relatives to subscribe that Barklie McKee Henry, then married to one of Jock's first cousins, remarked that he was delighted to perceive that Jock was working his way through college by selling magazine subscriptions. One of the few times Whitney had to disappoint his publishing associates at Yale was when George Day, who was also running the Yale University Library, asked him in 1932 to obtain for its stacks the manuscript of Thornton Wilder's *The Bridge of San Luis Rey*, which had come out five years earlier. In that instance, Jock reported back his impression that the author, Yale '20, felt that the manuscript was not worth preserving. It was indicative of the mounting complexity of Whitney's life that he had to skip one scheduled meeting with Wilder because it conflicted with the semi-finals of a polo tournament.

Yale's nurturing of Whitney's interest in its publications turned out rewardingly for the university. In 1927, he established a seven-hundred-and-fifty-thousand-dollar endowment fund for the University Press, in his father's name. Ever since, public libraries across the nation, without having to dip into their acquisition funds, have been receiving copies of nearly all Yale University Press publications, each bearing a bookplate reminding readers that Payne Whitney was a member of the Yale class of 1898. From that time on, there was scarcely any group at Yale that did not look to Jock Whitney for succor. The Library Associates, the Episcopal Church, the Golf Course Fund, the polo team—they all considered him fair game, frequently competing in *their* eagerness for his acceptance of their blandishments with other fervently beseeching campus organizations. The smallest contribution Whitney ever made to Yale was one dollar. That was to defray a fine for a parking ticket he received one day while visiting New Haven on philanthropic business. It was characteristic of the reciprocal affection that had grown between Whitney and Yale that he didn't have to pay for the summons directly. His dollar was to reimburse the president's office, which on hearing of his transgression had hastened to pay the fine on his behalf. It was rare that Whitney turned Yale down cold. Once, though, he did. In the 1940s and '50s, he had a secretary, Isabel Hill, who had earlier served in that capacity for both Condé Nast, the *Vogue* man, and Clare Boothe Luce. Mrs. Hill, Jock's elder by sixteen years, was extremely protective of him and was also of an authoritative disposition. Whitney had a young employee named Frank Streeter, who would in time be entrusted with handling most of Jock's personal financial affairs. Mrs. Hill summoned Streeter to her office one day, handed him a begging letter she'd decided to reject, and said, "Here, you take care of this." It was a request from James Babb, then the Yale University librarian; and the secretary may have asked Streeter to draft the turndown because she knew Streeter was a Harvard man. Babb had hoped Whitney would make it possible for Yale to acquire a fine collection of Texas memorabilia that had just come on the market. Mrs. Hill further instructed Streeter to write a letter, for his employer's signature, which began with something like "Dear Jim: I'm afraid this one is really not within my range of interest. . . ." But, as the secretary may or may not have known, it was certainly within Frank Streeter's range of interest: it was his father's collection. Yale did eventually come into the collection, but through other channels.

In 1973, in a letter to a high school student who was applying to Yale and hoped for a character reference, Whitney reflected on how much the university had meant to him, and to his father before him. "None of us ever really left the place," he said. So close did he remain to his alma mater all his adult life that when he was asked by the *Saturday Review of Literature* in 1951 to write a critique of William F. Buckley, Jr.'s scratchy *God and Man at Yale,* he asked the president of Yale whether or not he should take on the book. "My greatest concern is that I might even have to read it," Jock wrote to Whitney Griswold. Griswold told him to decide for himself. Whitney left the controversial work alone—at least in print. Privately, at a New Haven meeting on November 2, 1951, of a body called the University Council on which Jock was then serving, he scribbled a penciled note to Griswold entitled "Random Thoughts for a Happy (formerly) Humanist":

> Is the honor and distinction of your great office worth the burden of the corpus alumnus?
> The infamous Buckley has revealed one thing to me which is clearly an indictment of Yale over the past 30 years: and that is the number of men who have graduated from this place without *any* knowledge of the liberal tradition which was offered them here.
> Almost the entire group should rise in fury. Whereas from every side I get weak and sinister doubt.
> Granted the times are in joint for the machinery of reaction, and so I shouldn't be shocked at this special noise.
> But it seems to me so clear that only in the humanities is the infra-red light for the fog of this day. What I meant to say was—I feel for you, Mr. President.

Yale, like Harvard, had long had a largely self-perpetuating Corporation, whose Fellows constituted its supreme governing board. Harvard

also had a Board of Overseers, a lesser but still prestigious body of
alumni watchdogs. In 1947, Griswold had initiated a Yale Council, pat-
terned roughly on the Harvard Overseers. Whitney was made a member
of the first Yale Council. He was designated, logically enough, chairman
of its Committee on Publications. In 1954, he would receive the Yale
Medal Award, conferred annually on a true-blue Eli during Alumni Day.
The year after that, there was a yet higher honor: he became a Fellow of
the university. "I have had lots of commiseration about this being the
end of my spare time," he wrote President Griswold in December. The
Fellows usually met in New Haven. Not all of Whitney's pilgrimages up
there took overly long. Juan Trippe, the head of Pan American Airways,
was a fellow Fellow; and in the days when helicopters were permitted to
fly on and off the roof of the Pan Am Building in mid-Manhattan, Whitney did once hitch a chopper ride.

Whitney came to admire the calmness and steadfastness with which
Griswold handled such sticky situations as the reluctance of Yale's undergraduate admissions people to accept sons of alumni just because they
were sons of alumni; and their concurrent orneriness about accepting
otherwise not terribly qualified prospects just because the football team
was short of cornerbacks or running guards. (Yale never seemed to lack
for gargantuan tackles and towering ends notwithstanding.) Whitney
and Griswold (Yale '29, a freshman when Jock was a senior) became
close friends. When Whitney was posted to London as American Ambassador in 1957, he confided to Griswold his concern that, aside from day-
to-day politics, the British were paying too little attention to American
affairs. Why, United States history had been dropped, even as a mere
elective course, at Oxford. By 1959, still in London, Whitney knew that,
when his tour of duty there was over, he would be returning home to
publish the New York *Herald Tribune*. He wrote Griswold then that he
would work *at* the newspaper but *for* Yale. (One of the worst indignities
a Yale alumnus could have inflicted on him he stoically suffered while
Ambassador; in that job one had to take the most stinging blows without
flinching. On July 4, 1958, after playing host to four thousand guests at
an embassy party, protocol required Whitney to move along to the Dorchester Hotel, where the American Society was holding a banquet; and
where, according to a reporter for the *Daily Express* who had clearly
never visited New Haven and sat at the tables down at Mory's, Whitney
had led the assemblage in singing "Harvard's 'Whiffenpoof Song.'")

With Griswold's blessing, Yale had conferred an honorary Master of
Arts degree on Whitney in 1956. In 1963, the university president gave
his Fellow an even rarer token of thanks for past services: a set of special
Yale buttons. In his grateful acknowledgment of them, Whitney said he
planned to have them affixed to a jacket he generally wore to breakfast.

(Griswold probably wore the same suit coat to breakfast and lunch, but then he had not grown up with a valet.) When, a few months after that, Griswold died of cancer, Jock wrote his widow that "in these last two years I had come to realize that I have never in my life been more drawn to anyone. I felt deeply his leadership and his glorious spirit, and I looked forward eagerly to every chance to be with him. This may not be a naughty world, but it is mostly pretty grim, and Whit shone a light on it that gave it always renewed meaning and joy. At Yale we will try to do the things he wanted so much, but it won't be easy and it will *never* be the same."

On being graduated from Yale, the twenty-two-year-old Whitney decided to spend a year at Oxford, studying history and literature. His father asked around among English friends what kind of spending money the lad would require. Payne Whitney was duly informed by William Waldorf Astor that three hundred and ten pounds should adequately cover Jock's out-of-pocket needs, exclusive of clothes, travel, horses, and hunting outfits—which Viscount Astor evidently regarded as essentials. He did not include the cost of a valet. That was a Whitney essential. It would have been well-nigh unthinkable for Jock to have gone anywhere then for more than a couple of days without taking along one of the most faithful retainers with whom any mortal had ever been blessed. This was Edgar Woodhams, who had joined the Payne Whitney ménage in 1913 as just another soccer-playing footman and, after taking a leave of absence to serve as a pilot with the Royal Canadian Air Force in the First World War, had returned to tend to Jock. Edgar was an indifferent valet. He never seemed to pack the right clothes. When his young master took off for a weekend, as often as not he would have to borrow a pair of riding boots or a black tie from his host. But Edgar's devotion to Whitney was touching, and abiding. In 1961, long retired and living in Florida, Woodhams heard that Whitney was ill and bedded down at the New York Hospital. The onetime valet knew that his former boss was chairman of the board of governors of that institution and was thus presumably assured of reasonably good patient care; nonetheless Edgar, though in his seventies, offered to rush north and serve as an auxiliary male nurse.

Whitney was somewhat depressed as he set sail for Oxford in the fall of 1926. The allowance his family had put him on, while ample by Astor standards, seemed to him rather inhibiting; it wasn't large enough, for one thing, to permit him to take along the horses his father had given him that summer. Aboard ship, however, he won a couple of distance-run auction pools, and with that windfall was able to buy two horses in England, a hunter and a steeplechaser. Riding the steeplechaser, he entered a point-to-point race at Oxford called the Grind. This was his first competitive endeavor as a gentleman jockey, and so discouraging that he let it be his last, too. The horse was speedy enough, but it appeared not to know when it was approaching fences—it kept going through them instead of over them. Handicapped by poor vision himself, Jock seemed constantly to be saddled with horses similarly afflicted. This mount, he was shocked to learn from the vet he took it to after the race, was all but totally blind in *both* eyes.

At Oxford, Whitney was affiliated with New College. His fellow students included Hugh Gaitskell and Alan Lennox-Boyd, both of whom would later become prominent in English public life. Thirty years after their joint stay at the university, by which time Lennox-Boyd was Colonial Secretary, Gaitskell Leader of the Opposition, and Whitney United States Ambassador, Jock was invited by the Oxford University American Association to make a nostalgic return to his old digs. New College dubbed him an Honorary Fellow, and he was the honored guest at a luncheon in its Great Hall. Sitting at the High Table, he was told by the Warden at his side, "This must bring back many days of memory." In truth, Whitney couldn't explicitly recall ever having eaten there; at Oxford, a waiter had brought most of his meals to his valet, and Edgar had relayed them to his room. Later on that reunion day, Whitney was further honored with a tea party in what was supposed to be his old room, but he didn't recognize the surroundings and wasn't sure his hosts had picked the right chamber.

Whitney's confusion may have stemmed from the fact that while he was enrolled at Oxford he didn't spend too much time on campus. There were a lot of girls in London, and a lot of parties, and it was rare that one of the former did not beseech him to escort her to one of the latter. He was often thought of then as one of the two most eligible young single men in the British Isles. The other was the Prince of Wales. They were not unalike. In Frances Donaldson's 1974 biography, *Edward VIII*, the author has the Prince saying to a daughter of Mrs. Dudley Ward, "And he told her that in his own childhood he had never known love. There were servants, he explained, who seemed to love him, but he could never forget that this might be because he was heir to the throne." Being heir apparent to Payne Whitney had been much the same thing.

The pair of social lion cubs had met, briefly, under circumstances that Whitney would remember with admiration. "I was out with the Leicestershire Hounds one day," he later reported to a Stateside friend, "riding my only horse. Sounds like hard times, but at the moment I happened to have only one hunting horse, a grey one. As we came to a fence, I heard a crack in front of me, and the horse took a stumbling step. I dismounted to look at his legs, while the rest of the field tore off at full cry after the pack. I was feeling my horse's legs when a chap I'd not yet met pulled up alongside me and said, 'Is he all right?' It was the Prince of Wales, who, seeing a fellow rider in trouble, had stopped out of kindness. The horse was all right, and I couldn't help feeling that day that the Prince was, too."

Even better than the Prince Jock knew his long-time friends the Metcalfes. Lady Alexandra—Baba to her intimates—was something special. She was half American, the daughter of Mary Leiter, a department store heiress from Chicago (whose name, as it happened, had been linked with that of Jock's Whitney grandfather before Will married Mrs. Randolph); and of Lord Curzon of Kedleston, a Viceroy of India. Baba married Edward Dudley Metcalfe, an Irishman who was a captain in the Indian army when the Prince of Wales visited India in 1921. Metcalfe, who had acquired the nickname "Fruity" at a time when a man could be thus apostrophized without sniggering, was an accomplished polo player and was assigned in India as temporary aide-de-camp to His Royal Highness; it was one of the officer's duties to arrange polo games for the Prince in Bombay. Fruity Metcalfe became the Prince's closest friend; he was best man, after Edward VIII's abdication, at the erstwhile King's marriage to Wallis Simpson. Baba Metcalfe, then and later, was one of London's most prized dinner guests, and from Oxford on one of Jock Whitney's dearest British friends.

On one of Whitney's pleasure-bent excursions from Oxford down to London—he had acquired a car, and Edgar usually drove him, having become adept at proceeding with unabated speed through dense fogs—Jock stopped by the Empire Theatre to call on Fred Astaire, who with his sister Adele was starring in George Gershwin's *Lady, Be Good!* Whitney and Astaire had met in New York while Jock was more or less studying at Yale. (As a child, Whitney was once taken by his father's friend Philip Boyer to call on Vernon and Irene Castle. "They had a police dog whom they would like to demonstrate attacking and mauling a man wearing protective clothing," Jock recalled. "When things had calmed down, Irene came out in a flowery gown, and began singing. She croaked like a raven. It was very disconcerting.") Astaire was five years older but, like many of the then acquaintances of the youthful Whitney, was impressed with his maturity. "Jock was up to everything that was going on," Astaire would say later. "He had a great willingness to appreciate life, and he enjoyed it very much. Doing anything with Jock was fun to do." Astaire, who enjoyed rating his friends' dancing skills, once credited Whitney with performing the Charleston more slowly than anyone else he knew. (On Astaire's speed chart, George Raft was fastest.)

Now, in London, early in 1927, Fred and Adele were finishing up their run. The night they closed, the Prince of Wales gave them a party at St.

James's Palace. Whitney tagged along with the Astaires. At some early morning hour, Fred confided to His Royal Highness that the American-at-Oxford was an expert dancer and might, if suitably coaxed, give a demonstration of the latest dance craze in the United States—the Black Bottom. The music was stopped. The floor was cleared. The drums rolled. Whitney took center stage. He was only barely familiar with the Black Bottom, but it was exciting to be offered a chance to perform without having to open his mouth. He resolved this time not to have his friend Astaire or anyone else belittle him for his slowness. He had executed two or three top-speed movements when Astaire shouted, "Look out, Jock, the floor is beginning to sag!" Whitney glanced down, lost his at best shaky balance, and—"to deafening cheers," Astaire would subsequently recount—fell flat on his face.

It was the kind of rollicking incident that people who went to London parties in the twenties would long savor. More than thirty years after his pratfall, when Whitney was his country's envoy to St. James's, he heard that Astaire was coming to London and scribbled a cable to him: "One of the days of your stay will be July Fourth which will give me the opportunity to repay an old favor by inviting you to dance the Black Bottom for our three thousand guests on that day." Jock's secretary, Isabel Hill, changed the number, with mother-hen meticulousness, to "four thousand" before transmitting the invitation. Astaire went to the party but refrained, possibly because of the thousand extra guests, from essaying so much as a soft-shoe shuffle.

Whitney was larking it up in London in gentlemanly fashion—tailored suits from Hogg and Davies, blue shirts with white detachable collars from Eldridge—when his father was stricken on his indoor tennis court in May 1927. Helen Whitney was having lunch in New York City, and although on receiving the news by phone she obtained a police motorcycle escort and made the drive to Manhasset in a record thirty minutes, she arrived too late. (In deference to the family's stature in the horse-racing world, the flags at Belmont Park and Churchill Downs were lowered to half staff that afternoon.) Helen put in a call to Oxford. The porter at New College who answered it said Mr. Whitney had gone up to London. It became an Oxford legend that Jock's mother said the porter should stay on the line until her son could be located, and that the phone call lasted forty-eight hours. (The American Telephone & Telegraph Company had no way of ascertaining, fifty-three years later, whether or not this was true. If it was, the call would have cost seventy-five dollars for the first three minutes and twenty-five dollars for each additional minute—$72,000 altogether. The same call in 1980 would have cost $11,664, though the figure probably ought to be adjusted for inflation.)

When word finally reached Jock, he caught the first westbound steamship. He got home too late for the funeral. "I didn't realize until then how much I adored my father," Whitney would say years later, "and one of the very real regrets of my life was that I didn't have a chance to tell him that before he died. I guess demonstrativeness was not our family style. I remember one Yale-Harvard boat race at New London, my junior year, when I'd been ill and couldn't row. My father and I were there together, and one well-wisher in the crowd, seeing me, yelled, 'Let's give a long cheer for Whitney, who should have been stroking the crew today!' At that my father did something very unusual; he put his hand on my knee and squeezed it. That's something I've always remembered."

Jock did get back in time for the reading of his father's will. Payne Whitney's estate was so large, it took two years for all its figures to be juggled to the satisfaction of all concerned. In those two years, with the stock market booming, the estate increased in value by $52,721,270, largely by inertia. In 1930, it burgeoned further, thanks to a tax refund of $16,329,217 from the state of New York. (The following year, an Albany songwriter sued the estate, in vain, for $44,900, maintaining that he had composed a ditty entitled "Pretty Rose, Pretty Rose," which Payne Whitney had promised to buy from him, and that Payne had paid only one hundred dollars on account.) At one point in the tangled reckoning Payne's estate was said to be worth $194,328,514.

The residual estate, finally pared down to $178,893,655, was divided into three hundred shares. Helen Whitney and the two children were to get one hundred and ninety-two. Charles Shipman Payson, Joan's husband, became instantly a wealthy man in his own right; he got five shares, worth nearly three million dollars. More than sixty-seven million dollars was allotted to Payne's favorite philanthropies. Yale University received five shares also, and Groton two. The New York Hospital was enriched by twenty-two—about twenty million dollars. Various household servants were awarded fifty thousand dollars apiece—more than enough, those days, to ensure lifelong comfortable security. As for Jock and Joan, it took no skill in higher mathematics for them to realize that, although their shares were not fully to be doled out until they reached the age of forty, each of them would, as soon as the estate was settled, inherit at least thirty million dollars outright—with more to come, presumably, upon their mother's death. At twenty-two, Jock had changed overnight from being a very rich man's son to being a very rich man himself. "I had so much so young," he would later reflect.

From that spring of 1927 on, for more than half a century, Jock had to bear the not entirely unenviable burden of enormous wealth. The actual handling of money was never especially taxing for him. Payne Whitney had had a Wall Street office that kept tidy tabs on all his financial affairs, and at the start Jock simply let his father's functionaries carry on, guided in their operation by the senior and junior Lewis Cass Ledyard, pillars of the downtown law firm of Carter, Ledyard, & Milburn. Some wealthy families—the Rockefellers, the Phippses—had offices that looked after the whole tribe's interests. There was never a central Whitney office. Jock never had more than one small safe deposit box himself, and it never contained a single bond or stock certificate; such tangible assets were always superintended for him by attorneys, trust officers of banks, accountants, and others. Some of these intermediaries between him and his resources would conscientiously furnish him daily, on occasion even hourly, reports on how various securities of his were faring on the stock market, but he rarely glanced at these bulletins. He trusted people.

That, in his position, was fairly rare. Some extraordinarily rich men, and women, seldom take people they deal with at face value; instead, they are forever beset by worry about what low ulterior motives their associates may have in seeking out their friendship and their patronage. "One marvelous characteristic of Jock," his brother-in-law Paley once said, "is his utter lack of suspicion of other people. I've often wondered how that came about. When you have that much money, you're apt to be suspicious all the time of others' motives." The proprietor of CBS added quickly that Jock was not above thoroughly enjoying the luxury he could afford. Once when Whitney was under the weather, his brother-in-law called on him at Greentree, was ushered into the master bedroom, and found Jock looking at an NBC program on television. Paley said there was a much better show on *his* network. "Where's your clicker?" the visitor asked, naturally assuming that Jock would have a remote-control device at bedside to switch channels. Jock pushed a buzzer and a butler instantly materialized to make the change. His butler was his clicker.

Like many another man of far more than modest means, Whitney rarely had much pocket money on him. There were always subordinates around who could give him practically instant access to whatever petty cash he might require. At the Polo Grounds one autumn afternoon, he won a bet on a football game from his sometimes hard-pressed crony Shipwreck Kelly. As they were leaving the stadium and Kelly reached for his wallet, to pay off, he discovered his pocket had been picked. Both men agreed that the thief had shown good judgment: there was usually more cash to be found on Kelly than on Whitney.

Jock would sometimes mock his singular good fortune. At parties in the 1930s, when it often happened that guests would take turns at entertaining each other, it was his habit to render an old song that went, in part, "Gee, but it's tough to be broke, dear/It's not a joke, dear, but a curse." Everybody knew that he was just kidding. If one was a close enough friend, one could kid him, too, about his wealth. One very close friend for many years was John McClain, who was the New York *Sun's* ship-news reporter in days when it was customary for the press to interview transatlantic passengers debarking at Manhattan piers. Jock might have taken umbrage if anyone but McClain, covering one arrival of the *Aquitania* in his "On the Gangplank" column, had remarked that within a fifteen-foot area of Pier 54 he had spotted J. P. Morgan, Helen Hay Whitney, and her son, and had wondered how much that part of that dock might at that instant have been worth per square foot. McClain left the actual figure up to his readers' imagination.

Another long-time Whitney friend, Alfred Gwynne Vanderbilt, who had never been within fifteen miles of poverty, once exclaimed of Jock, without jealousy or rancor, "He really travels first class." Whitney himself at times seemed unaware of how stylishly he existed. "In spite of what may appear, we really lead very simple lives," he once told a friend. The evidence did not always support that kind of testimony. Whitney's scale of life may have seemed to him to be relatively austere—and compared with that of his parents it probably was—but to others it never ceased to be impressive. Once, playing softball at Greentree on a baseball diamond he'd had superimposed on three lawn tennis courts, Whitney, pitching for his team, observed casually that some lemonade would certainly taste good. He was overheard by a lurking servitor. "During the next inning," another participant in the game said afterward, "there were men on second and third, the tying run was at the plate, and Jock was just winding up to pitch when all of a sudden we had to stop, because of the most outlandish parade I'd ever seen. Down the left-field foul line came three footmen, staggering under the weight of three giant silver trays with crystal bowls full of lemonade on them."

One of Jock's friends liked to cite an evening when he arrived at a Whitney home for an appointment and was told by a butler that Mr. Whitney was dressing, and until he put in an appearance, would the guest care to look at an evening paper? The visitor said he would. A moment later, the butler reappeared with *all* the evening papers. Jock customarily carried on in a great big way himself. When reminded that it was time to order new pewter mugs for the winning team in the Payne Whitney Memorial court tennis tournament, he would order a dozen. When informed that a tobacconist had in stock a brand of cigars he relished, he would order five hundred boxes. Playing golf one day with Fred Astaire, Whitney drove off the first tee into the woods. Jock uttered an obscenity, one that any other golfer might have used in the exasperating circumstances. But what struck Astaire as significant was that Whitney uttered it in the plural.

Whitney took his golf very seriously. He believed that having the right equipment had a lot to do with one's success on the course, and Bill

Paley, who often played the game with him, maintained that Jock owned more clubs than any other golfer on earth. "Every couple of weeks he'd get a new set and then have a pro come and give him a special lesson with them," Paley said. "I once wandered into a back storage room at Greentree where Jock kept just some of his golf clubs and saw twenty-five or thirty complete sets."

Even in his twenties, Whitney realized that his uncommon wealth would impose on him uncommon responsibilities, and for the rest of his life he would keep wondering how he could best allocate both his money and his time toward meeting them. His friend Nelson Rockefeller—who was in much the same gilt-edged boat—believed that throughout Jock's life one of his problems was that he never had time to concentrate sufficiently on any single thing that interested him. "Jock can helpfully project himself into situations where human values are involved," Rockefeller once said. "That's a useful factor, because traditional business groups tend to follow prestige leadership, and if prestige leadership, like Jock's, is aware of social values and problems it can be effective. Jock has always been on the constructive, liberal side of things and hasn't been afraid to say so, and he has always been close to the category of intellectuals, although most people wouldn't think of him in those terms. But competition of interests is his greatest problem."

Whitney himself once said, in a self-analytical mood, "My difficulty is that I was always either too young or too old to take the lead in anything, to be an initiator. I was always just a participant in things." Still, he had strong feelings about what somebody like himself should or should not participate in, and how he should comport himself. René d'Harnoncourt, the long-time director of the Museum of Modern Art, in the history of which Whitney played a prominent role, once said of Jock, "He carries his wealth, as he does his liquor, like an English gentleman. Also, he is one of the few people I've ever known who at the same time is utterly sure of himself and terribly shy. Once he phoned and asked me to help out with some project about American Indian art he was interested in. That was a speciality of mine, and I was the logical person for him to have called on. After all, he was chairman of the board of the museum and I was its employee. But that elegant shyness of his almost made him sound embarrassed to have brought the subject up. I guess he wanted to make damned sure that I was aware that he would understand it if I turned him down."

Whitney fretted constantly about whether he should or should not agree to participate in this or that proposed undertaking, and whether, once involved, he was getting involved *enough*. "Jock has a great emotional need to be useful," it was said of him by Anna Rosenberg, whom for many years he kept on retainer as a public relations adviser and consultant. Whitney never fretted much, though, about the likelihood that fortunes like his own were becoming more and more difficult to hand down from one generation to another; nor did he entirely agree with social historians who suspected that, income and inheritance taxes being what they became in his lifetime, his species had not much hope for survival. "I suspect that the Rockefeller boys won't leave their children destitute," he once said, modestly omitting himself from speculation. "In any event, it's hard to tell whether the era of large fortunes is really over. They're being whittled down all over the world, of course, not for any valid reason—since sharing the wealth has been seen to be ineffective insofar as improving the economy is concerned—but simply in line with a general social trend. If the momentum of the whittling-down process were to be severely stepped up, then obviously the ultimate act of total confiscation would soon result. It seems to me perfectly possible, however, that if the owners of inherited wealth employ it to some socially useful end, the trend not only may cease to accelerate but may even decelerate, with the result that large fortunes would continue to be perpetuated. And if that should happen, they can do a couple of jobs that will otherwise have to be done by the state: they can provide the capital both to keep businesses going and to take care of voluntary philanthropic work. I believe that the entrepreneur, no matter what the source of his money, can be a valuable member of society."

Whitney always realized that a number of people felt bitter about him because of the source of his money. "It's easy to understand," he said, "how a guy who has to survive by scratching every penny out of the ground and hanging onto it with his fingernails would resent somebody like me, who has a great deal of money through the accident of birth. But the guy resents just as much somebody who has amassed a great deal of money by working his head off. And nine times out of ten that self-made man, when the resentful guy tries to scramble up the ladder of success, will kick him down harder than someone like me will."

6

I Certainly Had a Lot of Fun

In the fall of 1929, the twenty-five-year-old Whitney's appetite for publishing, though neither as hearty as his taste for cakes and ale nor as readily appeasable, had been whetted by his flattering part-time association with the epicurean *Yale Review*. He was obviously under no compulsion to worry about earning a living. It seemed to him, however, that a full-time job in book publishing would be a useful springboard for whatever leaps he might choose to make in that general area. Accordingly, he offered his services to Nelson Doubleday, a family friend. Whitney was dismayed when Doubleday, who needed no outside financial backing, rejected him, with the advice that a man as well-to-do as he was had no business holing up in a single, narrow field of enterprise. W. Averell Harriman, whom Jock had bumped into on polo fields, thereupon offered him a job at the investment banking firm of Brown Brothers, Harriman; but Jock elected instead to throw in his lot with the rival company of Lee, Higginson & Co., one of the partners of which, Frederick Allen, had stroked the Yale crew that Payne Whitney had captained.

Jock was hired as a buzzer boy, and the news was considered epochal enough for the Paris *Herald*—which he would later own—to run it on page one, and, like so many other papers over so many years, to get the limbs of the Whitney family tree twisted up:

WHITNEY HEIR WORKS
AS $65-A-MONTH CLERK

(By Special Cable to the *Herald*.)

NEW YORK, Sunday.—John H. Whitney, who inherited $100,000,000 from his father, the late Harry Payne Whitney, is clerking in the banking firm of Lee, Higginson and Co. for $65 a month. Although he recently bought a Virginia estate for fox-hunting, he is punctually at his desk every working day.

He started in on October 12, 1929, less than three weeks before the stock market's Black Friday. During an unusual era of trading history, he was an unusual buzzer boy. He was living then, part time, in a bachelor apartment his father had built for him above a Whitney boathouse. He commuted to work, many mornings, on a seventy-two-foot, ninety-five-thousand-dollar yacht, which he had bought two years before and, in memory of his great-uncle Oliver Payne's flagship, named *Aphrodite*. Jock's galley was stocked with some of the cutlery and china from the Colonel's. One seagoing commuter whom Jock would daily leave in his wake exclaimed, "That boat of Whitney's is so fast it scares fish!"

At Lee, Higginson, Jock often spent his lunch hour not munching sandwiches with other buzzer boys but, rather, over at 14 Wall Street, discussing his own investments in deferential colloquy with the senior partners of Carter, Ledyard & Milburn. One venture about which Jock was more enthusiastic than his older mentors was the Aviation Corporation of America, to whose stock he had subscribed in the summer of 1928, at the urging of his cousin Sonny and with the encouraging concurrence of his valet Edgar. That small company evolved lucratively into Pan American Airways, on whose board of directors Jock served from 1931 to 1942, in the coming of age of aviation.

It was the elder Ledyard's stern and unbending counsel, however, that Whitney should have no part of an unctuous proposal made to Jock one day by his distant relative Richard Whitney, who suggested that the two of them pool their resources in a cozy investment partnership. Richard Whitney, then the vice-president of the New York Stock Exchange, had not yet fallen into the disgrace that would ultimately send him to prison, and Jock had no reason to doubt his probity. But even before Mr. Ledyard's warning, he had determined to have nothing to do with self-styled Cousin Richard: what had put Jock off as much as anything else was the gilded pig that the older Whitney—a somewhat porcine-looking member of Harvard's élite Porcellian Club—flaunted on his watch chain. Unlike other buzzer boys, too, Jock did not spend the contents of his first pay envelope, but kept it as a treasured souvenir of full-fledged gainful

employment. He also stashed away the first Lee, Higginson envelope he
was instructed to mail, with its two-cent stamp uncanceled. There was
no dereliction of duty; he addressed another envelope and bought another stamp out of his own treasury.

Whitney stayed at Lee, Higginson for about a year, ending up as a
fifty-dollar-a-week clerk in its statistical department. The firm had got itself deeply enmeshed in the common stock of Kreuger and Toll, the company run by the Swedish match king, Ivar Kreuger. One of Whitney's responsibilities, after his promotion, was to send out letters to Lee,
Higginson clients saying something like "It is our strong recommendation that under no circumstances should you dispose of your
Kreuger and Toll." When he tried to find out from one of his bosses what
was so good about that particular stock—which not long afterward
proved to be a disaster of disasters—the answers he got were so vague
and evasive that he concluded Wall Street was not an environment conducive to his healthy growth.

Whitney had meanwhile, though, come to repose great confidence in
the head of the Lee, Higginson statistical department, J. T. Claiborne, Jr.
Claiborne happened to be involved, on the side, in a proxy fight for control of the Freeport Texas Company, a sulphur-and-manganese-produc-
ing outfit that later was called Freeport Sulphur. The battle was being
waged under the command of Langbourne Williams, a onetime Lee,
Higginson junior employee whose father had founded Freeport Texas
but had lost control of it to bankers and other predatory types. Claiborne
urged his young clerk to support Williams, and Whitney obligingly
backed him with half a million dollars, a sum that markedly helped turn
the tide in Williams' favor. By the end of 1930, when Whitney departed,
without regret, from his first and only full-time job, he had been elected
to the Freeport board of directors. By 1934, having poured still more
capital into the struggling company, he was one of its major shareholders
and the chairman of its board. Freeport was to have its ups and downs—
an up when, during the Second World War, it produced one third of all
the manganese the United States required; a down when it signed a two-
hundred-and-eighty-four-million-dollar contract to provide the American
government with nickel from Cuba, shortly before Fidel Castro ascended
to power and made delivery impossible—but over the years his investment in the company proved gratifyingly rewarding. Langbourne Williams became one of his closest friends. Claiborne, the chief of the statistical department who had called the investment opportunity to
Whitney's attention, was rewarded, too: he became a partner, after the
war, in J. H. Whitney & Company.

"It was a very bold step indeed," Williams would write Whitney in
July 1973, "when, not quite twenty-six years old, you went counter to the

advice of your older advisers and joined the Freeport board." Williams did some heady recapitulating. The 23,650 shares of Freeport Jock had bought in 1930 for $591,250 had in the ensuing years been split eighteen for one. Even though fifty-three years later the stock was far from its all-time high, Whitney's holdings were still worth $10,482,862, and they had paid him dividends totaling $7,960,567. "I realize full well this is small potatoes," Williams added, but he thought Jock might nonetheless be interested in the summary accounting. Small potatoes it was indeed—ten million dollars then representing probably less than one twentieth of Whitney's tangible assets—but it was evidence of Jock's investing acumen that other associates of his (drinking their Minute Maid orange juice at breakfast) would often marvel at and have cause to be grateful for.

For John Hay Whitney, in those early days, life could never be all work and no play. He was one of the few buzzer boys of record who took holidays abroad. Even before his apprenticeship at Lee, Higginson he had become sufficiently interested in the English turf to invest in a racing stable there. His colors from the outset were watermelon-pink with black-and-white-striped sleeves and white cap—an ensemble picked by his mother, who had a dress she was fond of in that combination. All his life, Whitney professed to prefer the comparatively low-keyed scale of racing activities in England to the grander sort at home. English racing seemed to him to have quality, and class; the American racing scene often struck him as unacceptably tawdry. The difference, he once explained to a friend who rarely went to the track, was like the difference between shopping in a general store and shopping in a supermarket. (It is doubtful whether Whitney personally ever bought a can of dog food at either kind of establishment.) Whitney made such a splash in his very first year of English racing, 1928, that—along with older luminaries of the American turf like Joseph E. Widener, Walter Jeffords, and William Woodward, the chairman of The Jockey Club—he was invited to a dinner given by Marshall Field in honor of Captain Cecil (later Sir Cecil) Boyd-Rochfort, trainer to the royal family.

It was through Boyd-Rochfort, appropriately, that Whitney bought the topflight stakes horse Royal Minstrel. The seller was an excessively shy man who, after that animal had won a few big races, was appalled at the prospect of accruing the notoriety that such a horse inevitably conferred on its owner and was glad to get rid of it, for fifteen thousand pounds, before it attained any further fame. Whitney acquired Royal Minstrel chiefly for stud purposes, and the stallion did his work well. He was the sire of the dam of the fleet Devil Diver. More directly, he sired Singing Wood (out of Glade), a hundred-thousand-dollar Futurity winner for Whitney; and Time Step (out of Measure) which carried Whitney's silks to victory in the Victoria Cup at Newmarket, in 1940, beating the Boyd-Rochfort-trained favorite, Lord Portal's Ombro.

Another early racing acquaintance, whom Jock had met while at Oxford when both were riding with the Old Berkshire Hunt, was Jack Anthony, a onetime jockey turned trainer. In the latter capacity, Anthony had come up with three winners of the prestigious Grand National steeplechase. In 1928, he embarked on a protracted, never successful, effort to win a fourth, on Whitney's behalf. The horse that they thought could bring this off was Easter Hero, which until the advent of the Beatles was held by some residents of Liverpool to be the finest flesh-and-blood creature their community had ever bred. Easter Hero had no potential for stud. Like most English jumpers, he had been gelded, for the simple, practical reason that the thorny fences on many steeplechase courses were unfair to equine testicles. Jack Anthony got Easter Hero for Whitney from the Belgian financier Alfred Lowenstein. The horse had not long before botched a jump, landed in a ditch, and run up and down the ditch, causing a monumental traffic jam. Lowenstein was so mortified by the debacle that he refused to enter Easter Hero in any more races, and instead had the animal edify his lunch guests by performing in a show ring. That—so far as anyone could ascertain—mortified Easter Hero. On the whole, the horse survived the ignominy better than his first owner. Easter Hero joined Whitney's stable. Lowenstein fell to his death from the window of his own airplane. "Why a man with a horse like that should step out of an airplane confounds me," Whitney said years later.

In 1929, under Anthony's astute training and carrying Whitney's colors, Easter Hero won the Cheltenham Gold Cup. In that year's Grand National, the horse was the favorite, at nine-to-one odds, carrying top weight in a record field of sixty-six entries. Easter Hero was easily in the lead as he approached one of the last obstacles on the grueling course at Aintree. Then he twisted a plate on one hoof, and the plate cut another leg. He came in second to a hundred-to-one shot. To celebrate both the victory and the near miss, Whitney invited several dozen London friends to a banquet at the Piccadilly Hotel. The room was festooned with flowers in the twenty-five-year-old host's racing colors, and the waiters were outfitted in his silks. He engaged the quick-fingered conjurer Giovanni to entertain his guests, and Giovanni roguishly wandered around picking their pockets. At one point, the young American, feigning anxiety, grabbed the Cheltenham Gold Cup from a table and clutched it to his chest, lest the conjurer make off with *that*. The New York *Times*, which liked to keep its readers informed about such jolly goings-on abroad, called the party "one of the most elaborate and costly held in London since the war"—though in truth it was small stuff compared to a 1931 Joe Widener shindig at the Biltmore Hotel in New York, in the course of which live horses clattered into the banquet hall to divert the guests.

Over the next half century, Whitney would be on familiar, if not intimate, terms with thousands of thoroughbred horses, but there was none that could stir him as much as Easter Hero. "I realized even way back in 1929," Whitney said in 1979, "that I would never see his like again. Easter Hero was the kind of horse that really got your emotions involved. He had such a terrific personality. It was a great sight to see him doing anything—even exercising, at which times, if he couldn't lead a parade, he became almost unmanageable. The mere sight of him floating over a water jump in the Grand National would produce a roar from a crowd, and from me. The only flaw I could find in that great horse is that I was awfully young to own him."

Easter Hero tried to win the Grand National again in 1930, and again he looked like a sure winner. But this time a horse directly in front of him fell—a jumper owned, as it happened, by Jock's cousin Dorothy Paget. Whitney's horse swerved, and his jockey tumbled off, and that was that. Easter Hero ran in just one more Grand National, mainly because Jack Anthony was ailing and the trainer's doctor told Whitney a victory might have a tonic effect on his patient. The horse had competed the day before and was tired, and during that farewell race he was bumped broadside by a careening rival, but even so finished in a dead heat for first. "It was a truly gallant final appearance," Whitney recalled. He thereupon retired Easter Hero from competition and had him shipped to the United States, where Jock used him for a while as a hunter with the Piedmont and Middlebury Hounds.

But that did not work out particularly well. For one thing, Whitney was too heavy for his mount. For another, whenever another horse came up alongside Easter Hero, he would take off like a shot. "Once as I flew by the Master, top hat bouncing on my back," Whitney wrote a friend, "I could only apologize and say, 'Maybe you can stop him—I can't.'" Finally, the horse was put out to pasture in Kentucky, where he died, in 1948, at the patriarchal age of twenty-seven. Almost ever afterward, wherever Whitney had his principal business office, he had a 1936 Haseltine bronze of Easter Hero positioned so close to his desk that without stretching too far he could reach out and pat it.

When Whitney was in his late forties, he invited a friend to stay overnight at Greentree and said, "There're going to be some interesting people. We're going to talk most of the weekend." It was not always thus. In his twenties, he was an unabashed young man about town—in the view of some of his peers, an outright playboy. Asked once years afterward whether he had ever considered that sometimes opprobrious characterization applicable to himself, he reflected soberly, and replied, "I certainly had a lot of fun." He was given at all ages to understatement. He had in his heyday been well known to the proprietors of high-class restaurants and, during Prohibition, high-class speakeasies, often causing heads to turn by appearing at one boîte or another with a recognizable actress on his arm. It was not in Whitney's discriminating nature to date starlets. Among the ladies whose company he basked in, along with Tallulah Bankhead, were Paulette Goddard and Joan Crawford. "For a fellow with only one yacht," an envious contemporary of his once observed, "he sure has had a lot of girls in a lot of ports." Nearly three decades later, *McCall's* ran a feature entitled "The Most Attractive Men in the World," in the course of which a reflective Miss Crawford referred to Whitney as "A most attractive guy and one of the few Americans who seem to have mastered the European way of life."

Whereas in later years the kinds of organizations that attracted Whitney's time and energy were museums and hospitals, in the late 1920s and early '30s he was happy to be invested with the rank of commander in a Cleveland-based outfit called the Twentieth Century Crusaders, which mounted a knightly crusade to "substitute real temperance for Prohibition intemperance." One of the most popular Manhattan speakeasies of the twenties was the Puncheon Grotto, run by Jack Kriendler and Charles Berns—later the proprietors of the "21" Club—on West Forty-ninth Street. They had been given use of the premises by a member of the Yale class of 1920, Benedict Quinn, whose family had lived there; and some of Quinn's classmates were among the establishment's most faithful patrons. When Jack and Charlie were about to move to a new location, some of their regular clientele decided sentimentally to demolish the Grotto's sparkling accoutrements rather than have them demeaned by some plodding, law-abiding enterprise. Lucius Beebe, a onetime Yale '26 man who also knew the old place well, recounted in *The Big Spenders* how Whitney was accorded the signal honor of striking the first crippling blow at a twelve-foot mirror over the bar.

By the time the social circles Jock moved in became more or less institutionalized, in 1937, as "café society," *Fortune* proclaimed the group to have one hundred and seventy bona fide members, with, astride that élite heap, a "Regency Council" of seventeen. The Council consisted of, among others, Elsa Maxwell, the Herbert Bayard Swopes, and William Rhinelander Stewart. It went without saying that John Hay Whitney—along with four other Whitneys—was a member of that stratospheric group. (Indeed, *Fortune* maintained that Jock and his cousin Sonny had created café society because they were bored with Newport and Palm Beach society.) Jock no more cared how he rated in café society, though, than where he stood in society of the old order. (He stood high by any reckoning.) He would make his attitude emphatically clear in 1945, when he confounded some of his bluer-blooded acquaintances by insisting upon having his name deleted from the *Social Register*. This was a form of exile the satraps of the Social Register Association had always reserved the exclusive right to decree until Whitney, then an Army Air Forces colonel, had his secretary return unfilled an information blank for the 1946 winter edition, with the explanation that her boss wished no longer to be registered.

Whitney had decided, as he put it to a wondering friend, that "if you willingly go along with such a travesty of democracy as the *Register*, you tacitly subscribe to its absurd notions as to who is and who isn't socially acceptable." Before advising the *Register* of his desire to become an outcast, he conferred with his wife Betsey, and she and her daughters felt that they could probably lead adequate social lives without being in the *Register*. The family view was not immediately embraced by the *Register* people, who, in acknowledging receipt of the secretary's note, said, "The Association is reluctant to comply with this request, since names are not omitted from the *Social Register* unless for some good reason. . . . Will Colonel Whitney therefore kindly fill in and return the enclosed duplicate blank, giving his residential address and that of Mrs. Whitney for this winter?" Whitney thereupon replied:

> I have received your acknowledgment of my request that the names of Mrs. Whitney and myself be omitted from the *Social Register*. Your reluctance to comply need no longer trouble you, since the "good reason" which you consider a prerequisite for omission exists and is as follows: Mrs. Whitney and I want not to be included in the *Social Register*.

The Social Register Association gave in, and, according to Whitney, it later passed the word around that he and his family had been dropped "for good reason."

Quite a few of Whitney's sidekicks when he was young tended to be drawn less from high society, or even the café variety, than from the theatre, the movies, and journalism—the ship-news reporter and later public relations man John McClain, for instance, in whose honor Jock once called a horse The McClain. The Jockey Club, which has always been as protective of thoroughbred nomenclature as a lioness of her cubs, does not permit horses to carry the names of identifiable living persons, without their consent in writing. McClain, who was delighted to grant his, was himself, in the Whitney ménage, called Unc. He bore few other similarities to Uncle Oliver Payne; for one thing, the journalist was often broke.

In those circumstances, McClain was an exceptionally blessed friend, because he happened to be almost exactly Whitney's size. (Whenever they drifted apart in bulk, they would hold reducing contests to restore parity.) Now and then Whitney would order a suit from one of his London tailors that, on delivery, he would decide he didn't like. In one two-year stretch, he donated four brand-new discards to McClain. McClain was not ungenerous himself. Two Whitney suits that *he* did not much like he passed on to his father. (Some of the columnist's smaller-minded acquaintances used to advance the conjecture that his entire wardrobe consisted of Whitney's clothes. That was untrue; McClain had a number of thoroughly presentable outfits that he bought himself.) One warm night, while the two of them were shooting pool in the Big Room at Greentree, both men removed their suit coats and threw them over chairs. Whitney missed a fairly simple shot and, annoyed at his ineptness, whacked his cue across what he thought was his coat. There was a tinkle of breaking glass, followed by the discovery of a dented spectacle case in the breast pocket of the coat and the realization that he had whacked one of the garments he had given to McClain.

For nearly twenty years, one of Whitney's truly boon companions was a writer of far greater distinction than McClain ever attained, or even aspired to—Robert Benchley. It was a relationship that some outsiders found puzzling. Benchley was a wholly creative man, an indoors man, sedentary, non-athletic. If he had tried to row in a crew, he might have drowned. Also, he was fifteen years older than Whitney. As a result of that disparity—which never bothered either of them—Whitney's affectionate nickname for him was Gramps. Benchley's children liked that; they began calling their father Gramps themselves. (Whitney once dubbed a horse Gramps; The Jockey Club, unaware that a living person was involved, demanded no acquiescence from Benchley.) When in 1940 Benchley actually became a grandfather—the child was Peter, the author of *Jaws*—he sent Jock a telegram saying, "Now it's Gramps for real."

It was easy enough to understand why Whitney would be drawn to Benchley; the older man was an established figure in the publishing world Whitney hoped to get into himself, and he was as delightfully comical in person as in print. As for Benchley, he simply said, in a letter in the 1920s, "Jock Whitney is the finest young man I have ever met." He amplified that a bit a dozen years afterward, telling a reporter who was writing about Whitney in 1940, "The subject to his friends has the general approach, body displacement, and personal menace of a Newfoundland dog who might once have rowed on the Yale crew. Has a loud laugh, followed by 'that's marvelous' or 'I don't believe it,' followed by a loud laugh."

Whitney was introduced to Benchley by the humorist and playwright Donald Ogden Stewart, who for a while occupied a Greentree cottage called, in deference to Joan Payson's nickname, the Mouse Hole. Jock was a Yale undergraduate, and Benchley was acting in *The Music Box Revue*. There was a chorus girl in New York whom Benchley had taken under his amiable wing. He regarded himself as an educator of the young, and part of the curriculum he laid out for her was to meet some student who was not, in Benchley's view, a stereotype of Joe College. On learning that his protégée was in the chorus line of a show that was playing an out-of-town week in New Haven, he besought Whitney to make her acquaintance. Jock was to meet her in the lobby of a hotel near the railroad station and to identify himself by means of a boutonnière. It was a good thing that she was thus able to single him out, because he might never have identified her; he was looking for somebody flashily made up, and the girl in question was so demure-looking she might have been from Smith. When Benchley learned later of Whitney's surprise that not all chorus girls were stereotypical, he was enormously pleased: he had doubly contributed, he felt, to the education of the next generation.

If the word "groupie" had then been in vogue, it might have been used to describe Whitney as he happily tagged along, after leaving Yale, in Benchley's mirthful wake. That was the case mainly in New York. Outside the city, Benchley often happily tagged along in Jock's. Once when Jock was sailing to Europe, there was the usual bon voyage party at dockside. Benchley missed the all-ashore call, and to the delight of both of them accompanied Jock abroad. He had no passport, but John McClain was able to pull strings and get him into Europe and readmitted to the United States without censure or detention. Travel was more informal in those days.

Another time, by prearrangement and with a passport, Benchley joined Jock's entourage for a European tour by air. For that journey, Whitney chartered a First World War biplane with an open cockpit; nobody had ever toured the Continent before in that style. Benchley reported on his return that the co-pilot's seat—when he could persuade Whitney's valet to swap that perch for a seat in back—was one of the finest roosts he had ever known in which to recover from a hangover. On one leg of the jaunt, Benchley thought it might be tonic for his physical well-being if he exercised by standing up and running in place. He was delighted when Whitney leapt to his feet, seemingly the polite host joining his guest in a jog. The humorist was unaware that what had galvanized Whitney into action was his having noticed that an engine had conked out. Whitney was ostensibly collecting material for some *Yale Review* articles about the state of postwar Europe, but his research was traduced by Benchley's comicality. "I never stopped laughing from the time we took off till we got back," Jock said later. Harold Ross, the editor of *The New Yorker*, said that on their return Benchley had complained to him, no doubt in jest, that, while Whitney paid for the airplane, he didn't give his fellow traveler any pocket money.

In Ben Hecht's *Charlie*, a biography of his co-author Charles MacArthur, Hecht added a footnote to the Whitney-Benchley hegira. Whitney professed to have no recollection of the episode, but then he may have been laughing too hard to remember everything that happened on that trip. In any event, Hecht asserted that the two tourists, arriving in Italy and being told there had never been a live horse in Venice, filled a suitcase with horse manure and spread the stuff, one night, around St. Mark's Square. "The Venetians considered the horse shit the only miracle of the twentieth century," Hecht declared. All in all, it was good for Jock to have an older man along. En route, Benchley restrained him from making a pass at an alluring female impersonator. When asked years later how well acquainted he was with certain European cathedrals and museums, Whitney paused for a moment, smiled, and said, "I did most of my sightseeing at night."

There was a spell in the thirties when Benchley, in Hollywood, shared an apartment at the Garden of Allah with John McClain. Whitney would happily join them whenever he could think of an excuse to visit the west coast, which was often. Benchley did not, as a rule, care much about horse racing. Visiting Whitney once at Saratoga, the humorist was entrusted by his host with a lucky talisman, which he was instructed to hold during a certain race that Jock was eager to win. But at noon Benchley ran into his old friend Frank Sullivan, and the two of them repaired to a bar to exchange witticisms, and neither Benchley nor the talisman ever made it to the racecourse. In California, however, when he and McClain heard that Whitney had a thoroughbred that he had soured on and was willing to get rid of for a thousand dollars, the Garden of Allah residents impulsively purchased it. They called their joint proprietorship the Garden of Allah Stud Farms, and adopted some colors that seemed suitable—blue, red, and brown. The blue was because Whitney had gone to Yale, the red because Benchley had gone to Harvard, the brown because McClain had gone to Brown.

The new owners didn't know exactly what to do with their four-footed acquisition, but they were soon profitably delivered from their quandary: the horse won its first race under their stewardship and was claimed for fifteen hundred dollars. With his share of the profits, Benchley accompanied Whitney to a local gambling den, where they began losing consistently at a crap table. Suddenly Whitney picked up the dice, put them in his pocket, and said, "Come on, Gramps, we're leaving." Whitney had rightly sensed that the dice were loaded, and he demonstrated the following day that he was not going to let any crooked Hollywood gamblers put anything like that over on his friend and him. He phoned

Benchley and asked how much he'd dropped the night before. Fifty dollars, more or less, Benchley said. "Did you say five hundred?" Jock asked next. No, said Benchley, it was fifty. Five-oh. "You're sure it was only that?" Jock persisted. "There's a man here who's come at my invitation to buy back the dice for what we lost." Whitney's request might have been less rapidly acceded to had it not been for his still having the build, the mien, and the self-assurance of a heavyweight boxing champion.

In New York, Whitney was often to be found at Benchley's West Forty-fourth Street pied-à-terre, in the Hotel Royalton. When Benchley died, in 1945, his close friends were invited to help themselves to one souvenir or another from the room they knew so well. Jock looked around, spurned a proffered tie rack, and finally said shyly that if nobody objected he would like to have a bamboo curtain that separated the sleeping part of the room from the rest of the premises. He proudly carted the curtain back to Greentree, and when his wife asked where he had obtained that peculiar item of décor, told her quite accurately that it had graced Benchley's former habitat. He did not bother to inform her that Benchley had got it from Donald Ogden Stewart, who, his acquaintances had long been led to believe, had swiped it from a bordello in Marseilles. Betsey Whitney stashed it away somewhere in her commodious home, and it was never seen again.

There were dimensions to Whitney's complex life that in the view of such friends as Benchley were all but unfathomable. Reverent as Whitney felt toward the humorist, he was no less idolatrous of a man who moved in a totally different orbit—the polo player Tommy Hitchcock. "My feelings for Hitchcock remained hero worship long after that kind of emotion is supposed to stop beating in a boyish breast," Whitney once said. Hitchcock was a paragon sportsman, a man with marvelous co-ordination, stamina, and skill. Hitchcock revolutionized polo. He didn't believe, as did most other players, that long stirrups, a long bridle, and light handholds were *de rigueur*. He rode with a tight rein, and hard; yet, Whitney would observe wonderingly, he never cut a pony's mouth. Nor, unlike some competitors whose paths he crossed—George S. Patton, for instance—would Hitchcock deign to use spurs. He was one of a mere handful of American polo players (Harry Payne Whitney was another) ever to attain a ten-goal handicap—the highest there was. Hitchcock was generally conceded to be the best polo player of his era, and when in the mid-thirties he consented to play on a Greentree team Whitney captained (Greentree wore watermelon-pink shirts, like Jock's jockeys), Whitney's heart all but burst its bounds.

Whitney had played polo in a desultory fashion since prep school, but he began taking it seriously in 1929. He was not, like Hitchcock, a natural or graceful player, not even, when it came to that, an especially adept equestrian; and he pursued the game as diligently as he did chiefly because it was, along with a great many other things, expected of him, and because he was coming increasingly to demand diligence of himself. "I used to watch some of my contemporaries go off and shoot golf while our big matches were taking place," he said once, "and I thought they were being sacrilegious." At the time that polo predominated on his recreational agenda, Whitney did occasionally play a little tennis—usually with Hitchcock or their teammate Gerald Balding—but he thought of tennis simply as a form of exercise, like, say, push-ups, to help keep him in shape for polo. (Riding out from his New York office to a Long Island practice session in a chauffeured Rolls-Royce, he would take a secretary along and give her dictation; while he worked out, she would sit on the running board and type his correspondence, so that it would be ready for him to sign when he dismounted. That sort of thing was easier in the days when cars had running boards.)

Whitney played polo all over the United States, frequently traveling from match to match in a gaudy yellow and black Sikorsky amphibian called *Pegasus*, which he bought in 1928 for sixty thousand dollars and which was one of the first flying yachts in private service. In 1930, about to take off on one of his periodic jaunts to Europe, where he only dabbled in polo, he remarked offhandedly at Greentree that it was too bad he couldn't practice right there on his home grounds; even though the estate rambled over hundreds of acres, there wasn't a spot the size of a polo field that was smooth enough or clear enough of trees for him to knock a ball around without risking injury to himself or his ponies. (He had been struck in the eye earlier that year by a polo ball; fortunately, he wore shatterproof glasses while mounted.) He then sailed away, and was astonished while abroad to be advised that members of the Greentree staff, interpreting his wish as their command, had carved a polo field for him out of the side of a hill. It was undoubtedly the most velvety private polo field ever created, and it set him back two hundred thousand dollars. Whenever he played there in a match of any consequence, he would be rooted for by an intensely partisan claque of Greentree retainers, who would drop their assigned duties, flock to the field, and fill the air with proud, respectful cheers.

Whitney practiced hard and raised his handicap from a piddling two goals, in 1929, to six—his top rating—in 1936. He liked to say modestly that he got even that high largely because he could afford the best ponies. At one time, he owned a string of twenty, for one of which alone, an Argentinian horse named Chingolo, he paid fourteen thousand five hundred dollars. Most of his ponies came from Argentina. The only one he ever bred himself was a horse, by Teddy out of Free and Easy, that he named Princess Alice. If Alice Roosevelt Longworth, Theodore Roosevelt's daughter, had any objections, she never voiced them. She would probably have preferred a name like Rough Rider.

The 1930s were Whitney's golden polo years, and the years in which the game caught the public's fancy more than it ever had before or has since. (*Time* put Whitney on its cover in 1933, in polo clothes.) In 1935 and again the following year, Whitney's Greentree team won the United States open championship. His teammates were Hitchcock, Balding, and George H. Bostwick, the gentleman jockey widely known as Pete. Whitney played at back, and in that defensive position was not supposed to score many goals. He had a passion, however, for participating vigorously in anything that was going on around him; in consequence, he often found it intolerable to stick near his goalposts while the other players were wrangling at the other end of the field, and he was forever galloping down elatedly toward the opponents' goal. He was probably the most unflaggingly roving back in the history of the sport; in one notable match he tallied seven goals for his team, and Hitchcock, who was expected to do the better part of his side's point-scoring, only six. So exuberant a participant was Whitney that after one victorious match in 1935 he pressed a drink of champagne upon one of Hitchcock's ponies. Jock was fiercely loyal to his team. Before one Long Island match against a formidable aggregation captained by Winston Guest, Guest proposed a gentlemanly bet on the outcome—something in the neighborhood of a thousand dollars—and offered Whitney seven-to-five odds. Whitney was indignant. He refused even to contemplate the possibility that his team might be judged inferior to any other. He refused also to heed his father's advice never to spurn an advantage. He agreed to the bet, but insisted that it be at even money. He won the match and the bet.

Greentree's main rival was the Old Westbury team. Its captain was C. V. Whitney, Jock's first cousin and boyhood hero. Sonny, like Jock, was a good but never great polo player, and at his peak reached the same maximum handicap of six goals. Jock had Hitchcock as his prize asset, but Sonny had the only other two ten-goalers extant—Stewart Iglehart and Cecil Smith. The three of them, along with Michael Phipps, took the championship away from Greentree in 1937 and 1938, doing so the second time around despite Jock's accidentally braining Sonny with his mallet. After that shared four-year eminence, there were no further polo heights for either Whitney to scale. Besides, in 1939 war seemed likely to spread over Europe, and who knew where else? There were more important things to do than whack a wooden ball around like cavalrymen on their day off. Jock and Sonny both sold their strings of ponies and retired from active participation in the game, and big-time American polo pretty much ceased to exist. The costly Greentree polo field was planted with potatoes and alfalfa.

Whitney retained a mild interest in polo—for a while, he had a financial stake in *Polo* magazine—but he stuck to the sidelines. Twenty years after he laid down his mallet, when he was in London as American Ambassador, the Duke of Edinburgh kept asking him to play again, or at least climb upon a horse and act as referee, but Whitney demurred. It was rare that the Queen's husband would extend such an invitation; rarer still, perhaps, that once extended it would be regretted. But by then polo was as remote for Whitney as was Prohibition. Soon after leaving that London post, he received a letter from a fellow in Bechuanaland who reminisced about some of Jock's bygone polo exploits and inquired after the current state of the game in America. Whitney scrawled a reply to the effect that most of the players his correspondent had mentioned were dead—Hitchcock, for one, killed in a plane crash during the Second World War—and that in fact the game was about dead itself. "In England, however, it flourishes," he added, "if bad polo can flourish." Whitney's ever alert Mrs. Hill left out the last phrase when she was typing up the answer, because, as the secretary put it in a note to her employer, "What about Anglo-American relations when an ex-Ambassador to the Court of St. James's criticizes the Queen's husband?" And so Whitney agreed; and so went on record, at least in Bechuanaland, as stating without qualification that English polo was flourishing.

7

I Sure Thought We'd Never Make That One, Sir

While playing polo, in less exalted company, during his student days, Whitney had now and then crossed mallets with rivals from the upper-class environs of Philadelphia. Among them was a Bryn Mawr horseman named James D. Altemus. He came from a family that had had its good times and its bad. His father, Lemuel C. Altemus, was a stockbroker who around the turn of the century had helped introduce the Philadelphia Main Line to the refined pastimes of polo and fox hunting. The Altemuses had a summer place at Wernersville, Pennsylvania, a fashionable inland watering spot also frequented by Mrs. Frederic Austerlitz and her light-footed offspring, Adele and Fred Astaire. By 1911, Lemuel Altemus had lost most of his money and parted company with his wife Bessie—née Elizabeth Dobson—the daughter of a prosperous carpet manufacturer.

Bessie Dobson Altemus brought up Jimmy and his kid sister, Mary Elizabeth, who liked to watch her brother play polo with Jock Whitney and other young blades of the early twenties. She grew up to be one of the real beauties of her time—dark-haired, dark-eyed, olive-skinned, the belle of many a ball. (Also, in 1934, Queen Shenandoah XI of the annual Apple Blossom Festival at Winchester, Virginia.) It was carefully noted by society chroniclers that, during one of the Prince of Wales's terpsichorean jaunts to the United States, Mary Elizabeth Altemus was one of the few unmarried women he besought to dance with him, and that he had asked her twice. She was known as Liz. She was the familiar "Liz" of tabloid headlines before Elizabeth Taylor was born.

Liz loved animals. She was the only girl at Wernersville, to the best of local knowledge, who had a pet raccoon. A few years after that, it was a pet squirrel. Another time, a pet pig. She looked as ladylike as anybody, but she had a tough streak. She was one of the few female polo players of her set. She could hold her own at court tennis with many a male. She was a lovely luminary of the annual horse shows in Philadelphia and at Madison Square Garden in New York. After performing at the Garden, she would have a maid meet her in the basement, where the horses were stalled, and bring along her evening clothes, so she could change from her riding habit without any undue waste of time. A friend who went down there one night to congratulate Liz on her performance in the ring found her washing her face in a bucket that had oats floating on it. Some of her acquaintances thought she would have made an ideal wife for C. V. Whitney, who also hung around horse shows, but she never came any closer to Sonny than once naming a jumper Cornelius.

At the 1930 running of the Grand National, at Aintree, Mrs. Elizabeth Dobson Altemus Eastman, by then remarried, was proud and happy to be able to announce the engagement of her daughter to John Hay Whitney. Jock had courted Liz on both sides of the Atlantic, at one point competing for her favors with his polo-playing crony Gerald Balding. Liz's family having fallen on hard times, the young woman had no groom to saddle her horses for her morning canters. Whitney and Balding would vie to perform that chore for her. Neither was then a habitually early riser. If Balding got up at seven to provide grooming services, Whitney would drag himself out of bed the following morning at six to foil his rival. If Balding got up at six, Whitney would next get up at five. Balding needed more sleep, and Whitney had more stamina. He won the fair lady's hand.

The marriage took place on September 25, 1930, in the Church of St. James the Less, at Falls-of-the-Schuylkill, Pennsylvania. Dr. Endicott Peabody performed the service, as he so often did for old Grotonians. Jock was twenty-six, Liz twenty-four. The bride wore a two-hundred-and-twenty-five-thousand-dollar diamond necklace, a gift from the bridegroom's mother. Among Liz's attendants were Joan Whitney Payson and Adele Astaire. Among Jock's were his cousin Sonny; a couple of cousins on his Hay side, W. Stuart Symington and James J. Wadsworth, both of whom would later distinguish themselves in public affairs; a few Yale classmates; and such friends from the various facets of his life as Tommy Hitchcock and Donald Ogden Stewart. The best man, to the surprise of nobody who was acquainted with the Whitney of that time, was Robert

Benchley. Among the three hundred wedding gifts on eye-bulging display at the bride's nearby home were a George II silver fruit basket; a 1766 coffee urn; a 1782 silver tray; an 1805 silver plate; an 1834 patchwork quilt; the manuscript of Abraham Lincoln's last address. with annotations in the presidential hand; and the manuscript of Whitman's "O Captain! My Captain!"

Whitney's principal gifts to his bride were a check for one million dollars and a two-thousand-acre estate at Upperville, Virginia, in the foothills of the Blue Ridge Mountains. It was called Llangollen and was well suited to a young woman of athletic disposition. It had a gymnasium, a swimming pool, plenty of stables (complete with grooms), and, soon after the newlyweds moved in, a squash court. When Liz wanted to ramble around the property, she could do so stylishly in a fuchsia coach drawn by four pure white mules. The couple also had a suite set aside for them in the Payne Whitney town house on Fifth Avenue, and in 1931 they further acquired a summer home at Saratoga—a three-hundred-and-fifty-thousand-dollar, one-hundred-and-thirty-acre place that, while its main residence was a fairly modest ten-room establishment, had a mile-long private race track and stables that could accommodate sixty horses. Jock's August birthday parties there became high spots of the Saratoga social scene. He would always arrange for some first-rate professional talent to divert his guests. Joe E. Lewis was his pet importation. The gravelly-voiced comedian would use the occasion to try out jokes he planned to include in nightclubs the following season. Whitney was his litmus paper. If a gag made Whitney laugh so hard he turned red, it stayed in the act. Fortunately for Lewis, he could hardly open his mouth without sending Jock into paroxysms of glee.

Wherever Jock and Liz were in residence, she surrounded herself with animals. At one time she reigned over a colony of two hundred and fifty thoroughbred horses. They stayed mostly out of doors, but her houses were overrun with smaller creatures. A lady who spent a weekend at the Whitney place in Saratoga recalled that, when she arrived at the front door, she was greeted by a distraught butler tangled up in a pack of six large and howling dogs. "I thought for an instant I had descended to Hades and was being welcomed by Cerberus," she said. Visitors to Llangollen sometimes found it awkward to sit down; there seemed to be a dog in every chair. An Englishwoman who had spent many a weekend at the country homes of eccentric noblemen found Llangollen a bit much. "You'd walk into your bedroom and find a bitch whelping puppies all over the place," the visitor said. Jock's mother, a woman generally second to none in her devotion to animals, found it a bit too much when Liz, on a trip to the Whitney plantation in Georgia, was accompanied into Helen's spotless home by a couple of pet goats. It was a marriage made, if not in Hades, considerably short of Heaven; and it did not fare too well on earth.

Jock did not entirely share his first wife's fondness for livestock in wholesale lots, and, amid the profusion of her pets, he became deeply enamored of just one—a Jones terrier named Chillie, who was rarely far from his side. Chillie lived to be seventeen, and toward the end was blind and deaf and crotchety, but Whitney was fiercely faithful to him, so much so that some of Jock's friends joshingly called the dog's friend Strongheart. Chillie was buried, in 1948, in a canine cemetery at Greentree, alongside a dozen blue-ribbon dogs his master's mother had shown. On the terrier's tombstone Whitney had inscribed "The Real Ex-Champ." Chillie's grieving master had his pet twice further memorialized, in bronze, and for the rest of his life had just two portraits on his office desk—a photograph of his father and a statue of his dog.

Once in the 1930s, while at Upperville, Whitney got unbearably lonesome for Chillie, who happened unaccountably to be on Long Island. Jock phoned his mother at Greentree and had the terrier delivered by Rolls-Royce to Roosevelt Field and transported thence to Llangollen—which had its own air strip—in his Sikorsky plane. Commercial air lines did not then accept dogs as passengers. When one of Whitney's own planes was unavailable and he had to fly somewhere (he would often book two seats, one for most of his large body and the other for his legs), he would have a compliant secretary escort Chillie by train to their joint destination.

The first private pilot Whitney engaged, in 1928, who was supposed to fly him, in his sleek Sikorsky, to polo matches and other pressing engagements, was Wilmer Stultz. He had impressive credentials. He had just shepherded Amelia Earhart across the Atlantic. The following year, though, Stultz was killed while stunting over Long Island in an auxiliary Whitney plane, a small single-engined Waco Jock had bought to take flying lessons in. (Stultz's untimely end cooled Whitney's enthusiasm.) Not long after that, Edgar Woodhams, Whitney's Royal Canadian Air Force valet, who was himself the owner of yet another aircraft, told his boss that he'd be glad to pilot him as well as take care—to the extent that he ever had—of his wardrobe. Whitney was no less loyal to his manservant than was Edgar to him, and he accepted the offer.

Edgar was daring and fearless in a cockpit, but not particularly skilled. Whitney's next few years, accordingly, were crowded with unscheduled aeronautical acrobatics and the crumpling of metal. Once, taking off from an open field near Saratoga Springs in another small Waco that Whitney had purchased, Edgar misjudged his altitude and brushed some trees. "I sure never thought we'd make that one, sir," he said, cheerfully. Another time, coming down near Saratoga, he landed so maladroitly that two of his passengers spilled clear out of the plane—Chillie and Herbert Bayard Swope. The dog was unharmed, but the celebrated editor of the New York *World* suffered a crippling blow to his pince-nez, without which Swope felt practically naked. "We used to nose over with considerable regularity," Whitney reflected later, "but I was stuck with the situation, not wanting to hurt Edgar's feelings."

It was, all things considered, a rather extraordinary situation for Whitney or anyone else to permit himself to be stuck with. But Jock had made a commitment to Edgar and, by extension, to himself; it was part of Whitney's gentlemanly code that a pledge once made—to a bookmaker, a fund raiser, a musical-comedy producer, a valet, whomever—had almost sacredly to be honored. Over the years, Whitney had his share of abrasive bad bets and Broadway flops, but he never stepped out of a plane Edgar was piloting in less than one piece.

Edgar's navigation, too, was erratic. One afternoon, Whitney and William S. Paley attended a business meeting in Camden, New Jersey. Whitney invited Paley, with whom he was then only slightly acquainted, to fly back to New York with him. "You know," said Jock on the way to the Camden airfield, "my pilot's my valet, too."

"You mean you took your pilot and made him a valet?" Paley asked.

"Oh no," said Whitney, "I made my valet a pilot."

Paley's misgivings about the lift he'd been tendered intensified just before take-off. "The weather was so doubtful," the CBS man said afterward, "that I suggested we take a train. Jock was agreeable at first, but then Edgar gave him a look of such withering disdain that Jock said to me, 'You take the train. I'll fly.' Well, I didn't want to seem a poor sport, so I went along. I dozed off, and when I awoke, we were in the soup and Edgar was lost. Jock had his head out of one side of the plane and his valet had his out the other, both looking for the Newark Airport. All of a sudden, Edgar cried, 'I see it!' I was so relieved that I scarcely gave it a thought when, after we'd come down, we discovered we were at Floyd Bennett Field, on Long Island."

Edgar finally grounded himself after bumping into a mountain in New Jersey one day while he believed he was cruising, with Chillie as his only passenger, over a flat section of Long Island. They were both thrown clear, but lost track of one another in dense New Jersey woods. The dog turned up at a farmhouse a couple of days later and was in due course joyously reunited with his grieving master. When during the Second World War Whitney joined the Army Air Corps, some of his friends were relieved. They figured he'd be safer in combative flight than he'd ever been in Edgar's peacetime aerial custody. After the war, Whitney took on a pilot who himself had been in the Air Corps, and who was not a valet—he was required to look after only his own clothes.

Although a good chunk of Whitney's inheritance from his father was to be held in trust for him until, in 1944, he turned forty, Jock had enough loose cash at his disposal as a younger man to be able to take heady flyers in a wide assortment of ventures. Indeed, after leaving Lee, Higginson, in 1930, he became so active an investor that he never again felt the urge to seek conventional employment. He was still interested in, and indulgent toward, Yale publications. His not yet fully developed yearning to become actively involved in publishing was reflected by some of the investments he made in the thirties—not primarily in things like steels or oils or motors or utilities, though he had a fat enough port-folio of such run-of-the-mill holdings, but, rather, in a shelf full of maga-zines, among them (along with *Polo*) *Outlook* and *Newsweek*. Later, there would also be the *Scientific American*. Not all of these returned him much at the time in the way of dividends or, for that matter, in the way of capital. He sold his *Newsweek* stock in 1938, before that maga-zine had made much headway. *Outlook*, for its part, went bankrupt four months after he tried to shore it up with a hundred thousand dollars.

There was something unformed, inchoate, and also almost larksome about a few of Whitney's early investments. The unifying characteristic was his seeming determination not to follow well-trod paths but to blaze new trails. Like many pioneers, he had his share of setbacks. He took a licking on a company that proposed to refine sugar by some revolu-tionary process or other. He became the principal backer of an inventor who, anticipating the mounting perfidy of human beings, had obtained patents on a drain-plug lock, a snap lock, a cylinder lock, and an automo-bile gas-tank lock, as well as on a military jungle boot. None was ever manufactured. When the inventor died, Whitney inherited seven patents and one boot from *his* estate. Rich men like Whitney have functionaries in their employ who never throw anything away, lest someday somebody ask for it. After holding onto the single jungle boot for nearly twenty years, one of his assistants boldly junked it; if it had been part of a pair, it would probably forever have been tucked away somewhere in Whit-ney's files.

That jungle-boot-and-lock caper set Whitney back only about twenty-five thousand dollars, which was considerably less than the cost of many a yearling that went lame. Jock came off twice as badly in his very first investment fling after his father's death. While at Oxford, he had heard of a versatile tree, a species developed in England and kept practically secret by its originators. The tree was heralded by those who knew about it and had a stake in it as the harbinger of an economic revolution. Its bark was supposed to be a cheap substitute for hemp, jute, and sisal, its stem a substitute for the wood used in newsprint, and its leaves the tastiest and most nourishing cattle feed imaginable. Moreover, it was said to grow from a seed to a mature eight feet in a mere eighteen months.

Encouraged by the fact that such a tree seemed to be thriving in the royal gardens at Sandringham and had been endorsed by a director of the Bank of England, Whitney bought from its British guardians, Brotex Cellulose Fibres, Ltd., for a little over fifty thousand dollars, the American rights to some processes for separating its bark from its pulp. He set up a company called the American Brotex Corporation, and imported a leading agronomist at the University of London to watch over it. He had seedlings planted all over the United States, but mostly in Florida, North Carolina, and Georgia. The Georgia ones were embedded in the family turf at Thomasville, where they were assured of especially tender loving care. But nowhere could Whitney's arboreal henchmen find soil conditions that duplicated the hospitable ones at Sandringham. In the eighteen months during which their British prototypes had coaxed the tree to soar to eight feet, Whitney was never able to nurture one more than eighteen inches high.

Early on, as an investor, Whitney began to back stage plays. Like so many other aspects of his variegated life, that avocation had its ties to Yale—sometimes costly ones, as in the case of Peter Arno's *Here Goes the Bride*. One of his classmates at New Haven had been Alexander McKaig, who in 1928 wanted to produce a play called *Broken Dishes*. It was to be directed by still another Yale '26 graduate, Henry C. Potter, who had founded the Hampton Players, on Long Island, soon after leaving college. Hank Potter was even closer to Whitney than McKaig. Potter was a Scroll and Key man and had stroked the freshman crew Jock rowed on. Such bonds, for men of Whitney's mold, were all but unbreakable. To be sure, Potter had arrived in New Haven not from Groton but as a graduate of its then archrival, St. Mark's; men like Whitney could forgive such youthful indiscretions. Jock even pardoned Hank's young wife Lucilla for her unorthodox shooting style, when the Potters visited him at Thomasville, Georgia, in the winter of 1927. She had stumbled onto a covey of doves, had closed her eyes, had pulled both triggers of her double-barreled shotgun, had staggered backwards from the recoil, and had fallen down. So, miraculously, had two birds, one felled by each barrel. It was the kind of feat that less tolerant bird hunters might never forget and would rarely forgive.

Broken Dishes was memorable partly because Bette Davis made her stage debut in it, and no less so because it was the springboard from which Jock Whitney was launched as one of the legitimate theatre's most prominent and persistent angels. He relished that seraphic role. For one thing, from boyhood on, he had been smitten with acting. And as a

young adult, he had found the company of actresses agreeable. His angel's wings proved to be golden and widespread. Over a twenty-year
stretch, he would back some forty shows. By 1941, he would be acclaimed by one New York gossip columnist as "Park Avenue's gift to
Broadway." Actually, of course, Fifth Avenue deserved the credit.

In those days angels customarily underwrote larger pieces of a production than they would later. Productions were cheaper; a Broadway show
might be budgeted at twenty thousand dollars or less. In a few instances,
Whitney was a play's sole backer. More often, his sister went in with
him. Joan and Jock made their money available through a series of
ephemeral corporations—a precautionary device to protect them, in the
event of a catastrophe, from being held liable for more than the assets of
the particular companies involved—to which they gave such devil-may-
care names as Wild Cat, Pike's Peak, Whitplays, Hayplays, Jay Jay, Rab-
bitskin, and Undaunted. Once, bereft of inspiration, they called a corporation Plays, Inc.

Among the productions of which Whitney was a sponsor or co-sponsor
were *Gay Divorcee* (a logical choice for him; it starred Fred Astaire),
*Kind Lady, Whistling in the Dark, On Borrowed Time, Charley's Aunt,
A Streetcar Named Desire,* and *Dark Victory.* This last, produced at the
end of 1934, starred Tallulah Bankhead, who agreed to come over from
London for it, after having been mailed the script, on the receipt of a
cablegram from Jock that went, THIS REALLY IS WORTH YOUR WHILE AND
JUST YOUR DISH SO TAKE A LONG BREATH READ IT AND CABLE SOON STOP BY
THE WAY YOUVE BEEN GONE LONG ENOUGH LOVE.

As a theatrical backer, Whitney was by no means merely a foun-
tainhead of funds. He could not bear being consigned to behind-the-
scenes activity. If he was limited by his means and by his nature to serving merely as a participant in many ventures, he had a compelling need—
like a polo back hurtling upfield to try to score a goal—to be an all-out
participant. He would read scripts that came his way, attentively and critically. He would take eager part in casting decisions; he knew the Tallu-
lahs of his day better than did many a full-time producer or director. He
had assistants, of course. He always had assistants, whether to grease his
riding boots or his airplanes, or to cull his scripts.

To do this last, he recruited a knowledgeable young woman, Katharine
Brown, a literary agent, who scanned many of the plays submitted to
him. In the case of *On Borrowed Time,* which reached the Broadway
stage in 1938, Kay Brown read galley proofs of the novel of that name,
thought a successful play could evolve from it, and passed the proofs
along to Whitney. He could obtain an option on the dramatic rights to
the property, she told him, for a mere five hundred dollars; but he would
have to make up his mind by five o'clock on a certain afternoon. Whitney

went off to Saratoga and read the book. He was not able to reach Miss Brown by phone, however, until 5:07 P.M. on the stipulated day, at which time she informed him that he had owned the option for eight minutes. She had called the author's agent at four fifty-nine and had said, "Mr. Whitney likes it enormously." She had guessed right.

On Borrowed Time, whose principal characters were an old man, a little boy, and an apple tree, opened in New York with Whitney as its sole angel, but not without some of the tribulations so characteristic of, if not endemic to, the legitimate theatre. For instance, even after its New Haven tryout, then customarily an eve-of-Broadway engagement, the old man was recast. Kay Brown was resigned to the play's being a dreadful flop, and she was also miffed: she had initiated the whole production, and even told a fib to bring it about, but along the way had somehow got lost in the shuffle. Miffed? She was sore. Everybody had seemingly forgotten her. On the day before Christmas, a messenger brought her two packages from Whitney—the largest and smallest presents she had ever received. The bigger one consisted of a huge replica of a telegram from her to Jock predicting disaster, along with similar-sized blowups of rave reviews from the Times and the Herald Tribune. The smaller one was a jeweled clip that Whitney had had designed for her—a tree in diamonds, its pendant apples in rubies.

Jock later exhibited the same sort of imaginative thoughtfulness in 1948, when A Streetcar Named Desire, another of his investments (technically, the money was his wife's), completed the first year of its successful run on Broadway. Its producer, Irene Mayer Selznick, invited everyone connected with the show to an anniversary party, and she went to some trouble to buy appropriate commemorative gifts for all concerned. "'How odd!' I thought to myself," Mrs. Selznick said later. "'Everybody's taken care of except me! Maybe somebody will send me a telegram.' Then I went home to dress for the party, feeling horribly sorry for myself, and in my study, festooned with ribbons, I found a four-foot model of an antique streetcar that Jock had got for me, with 'Desire' beautifully lettered on its sides."

At times, Whitney seemed to give even more scrupulous care to small private beneficences than to the bestowal of a few million dollars on some university or hospital. Once, for instance, he got into a conversation with his Greentree Stable contract jockey, Ted Atkinson, about trees. Atkinson had not long before bought a house on Long Island, and he remarked sadly that the place was fine except in one respect: it didn't have on it any of three varieties of trees that he particularly fancied— blue spruce, red maple, and flowering dogwood. Whitney muttered something appropriately sympathetic, and Atkinson thought no more about it. The following Saturday, while the jockey was busy on Whitney's behalf at Belmont Park, a couple of trucks manned by gardeners from the Whitney place drove over to the Atkinson place, and when Atkinson got home, he found two blue spruces, two flowering dogwoods, and a red maple planted on his grounds, all neatly pruned and big enough to give a little shade to a small man. On another occasion, when an army comrade of Whitney's got married, Jock designed and had made up for the bride a jeweled brooch in the shape of a pineapple, which he sent along with the explanation that she had always reminded him of the way a pineapple tastes. The bride was charmed, and the bridegroom, though startled, was not offended.

Not long after becoming an angel, Whitney met an attorney who would figure prominently in his investing life. This was the New York lawyer John F. Wharton, himself a theatre buff. It was Wharton who, starting in the mid-thirties, was the catalyst in the formation of the Playwrights Company—that glittering producing organization whose other principals were Maxwell Anderson, S. N. Behrman, Elmer Rice, Robert E. Sherwood, and Sidney Howard. (Whitney, too, could have been a non-writing partner, but he begged off.) Wharton and Whitney together embarked on a long, convivial, and sometimes rewarding collaborative relationship. The lawyer looked after all Jock's investments in the entertainment world (and sometimes even kept track of his coast-to-coast bets), and his fees were easy enough to compute: he got two per cent of whatever Whitney got.

Carly Wharton, the attorney's wife, was a theatrical producer on her own. For a brief spell in the late thirties she and the actor Martin Gabel served as a joint sounding board for Whitney, filtering the flood of scripts that by then came pouring in on him from playwrights, producers, actors, directors, agents, and others aspiring to his aegis. The Wharton-Gabel team recommended to Whitney in 1939 that he—and his sister—get behind one comedy they particularly fancied, the adaptation by Russel Crouse and Howard Lindsay of Clarence Day's *Life With Father*.

It pleased Whitney to be reminded that Clarence Day had had the same paterfamilias as Jock's former Yale mentor, George Parmly Day. (Clarence had joined George in founding the Yale University Press, in 1908.) Still, brotherly love had its limits, all the more so when it was somebody else's brother: and at the outset Whitney was not especially disposed to get behind *Life With Father*. He had shown the script of the comedy to Robert Benchley, who, as the erstwhile drama critic of *The New Yorker* and a comic writer of high standing himself, had impeccable credentials to render a judgment on it. Gramps strongly advised his traveling companion against getting mixed up with *that* one. Jock and Joan prudently refrained from taking more than a part of the show, though a substantial share.

As late as the opening night in New York, on November 8, 1939, Benchley turned to Whitney during the first intermission and said, "See, we were right. It'll never go."

Life With Father went like a rocket. Its 3,213-performance run on Broadway set a record. Jock and Joan had each invested forty thousand dollars in it, and each was entitled to 31.58 per cent of the profits. By 1944, they had recouped their ante and also an additional $152,244 apiece. Their mother died that year, and they turned their interest in *Life With Father* over to the Helen Hay Whitney Charitable Trust, which Mrs. Whitney had set up to provide for her servants. Including her children's share of the proceeds from the movie sale of the play, the retainers' fund was ultimately enriched by about half a million dollars.

Most of Whitney's theatrical investments were in straight plays. He was fond enough of musicals, and rarely missed the première of one that opened while he was in New York; but his early misadventure with *Here Goes the Bride* had made him leery of putting money into them. When Billy Rose proposed in 1935, however, that Joan and Jock invest in a musical extravaganza with a book by Ben Hecht and Charlie MacArthur, with music by Richard Rodgers and Lorenz Hart, and with a cast that would include both Jimmy Durante and a live elephant, Whitney's resistance ebbed. The show was *Jumbo,* which would cost nearly a quarter of a million dollars to put on—in those days, an elephantine budget for any kind of stage offering. Rose, who liked to do everything on a grand scale, told Whitney cheerfully that if *Jumbo* flopped it would be the biggest flop in history. Whitney could not help admiring such panache.

The diminutive Rose had worked as a stenographer for the towering Bernard Baruch when Baruch was running the War Industries Board during the First World War, and the two men, so seemingly dissimilar in tastes as well as dimensions, had remained close. Baruch agreed to put twenty-eight thousand dollars into *Jumbo,* but, apparently not wishing to be publicly identified with such frivolous finance, let his friend and associate Herbert Bayard Swope pretend that the investment was his. Jock and Joan between them came up with more than one hundred and fifty thousand dollars. Rose and a handful of others shared the remaining burden. Rose rented the capacious Hippodrome Theatre, at Sixth Avenue and Forty-third Street, to house his spectacle, and he converted its stage into a circus ring. (Durante played a circus press agent, one of whose chief chores was to sing the praises of the elephant, whose name, fittingly, was Big Rosie.)

There were no fewer than twenty-one weeks of rehearsals in the big auditorium. Jock and Joan would frequently turn up with friends and picnic hampers and coolers of champagne to watch Rose try to whip his cumbersome production into shape. Whitney and Swope, who often also stopped by to see how everything was coming along, took to referring to the Hippodrome as "the club." Whitney usually referred to his real clubs —among them, to cite just a handful, the Yale, the Racquet & Tennis, the New York Yacht, the Knickerbocker, and the Links—by their various names.

Things kept going wrong. Rose chopped apart and discarded large chunks of the Hecht-MacArthur book, so he could squeeze more circus acts onto his stage. (Out of pique at the producer, Hecht later unilaterally rejected the only bid made for the motion picture rights—a quarter-of-a-million-dollar offer from Samuel Goldwyn. When Whitney inquired why the author had done that, Hecht replied, "Didn't you ever get mad at anybody?") On November 15, 1935, the night before the opening, there was a final dress rehearsal to benefit some charity. Jock drifted over to the Hippodrome at 1:15 A.M. and was surprised to find the show still running, hopelessly overlong. Rose performed some more surgery on *Jumbo* in the few remaining hours before its curtain officially went up, and the show got good enough notices to run for five months; but it never came close to breaking even. Whitney was not surprised. On opening night, Nelson Doubleday had come up to him in the lobby and had said, "Wonderful, Jock! It's a great success!"

And Jock had replied, "Success my ass."

Jock and Joan, when all the figures were eventually totted up, were together out about a hundred and sixty-seven thousand dollars. "You get an Arno show and a *Jumbo* and between those two you can establish quite a reputation for yourself in musical-comedy circles," Whitney said afterward. He continued nonetheless to invest in the theatre—*Life With Father* took a lot of sting out of some of his wounds—and until well into the 1950s, he continued to be besieged by importunate producers; but he did not believe that theatrical angels had, like other immortals, to go on forever.

At the start of the Second World War, the method by which profits on investments were taxed by the federal government was changed, with the effect that even though an investor in Whitney's income bracket— about the highest there was—could still lose impressive sums on failures, he stood little chance of netting much on successes. Whitney all but stopped making theatrical investments and was never much afterward a Broadway angel, or even a cherub. His interest in the romantic business, though, remained undimmed. In 1950, he asked one of the statisticians who worked for him to calculate how the returns from a five-thousand-dollar investment in *A Streetcar Named Desire*, made just before it opened, would have compared over a two-year stretch with the returns on a similar sum invested evenly in the thirty industrial stocks, the twenty railroad stocks, and the fifteen utility stocks used to compute the

Dow Jones averages. The report showed that Whitney's hypothetical investor would have made $797 in the industrials, $495 in the railroads, $1,044 in the utilities, and $8,005 on the play. But that would have been before taxes.

When one producer suggested in 1950 that Whitney underwrite a summer-theatre season, Jock told him—the fifteen-year-old memory of *Jumbo* painfully lingering on—"I am sorry, but I do not feel like investing any more money in theatres.at the present time, whether in circuses or barns."

8

Have I Gone Hollywood?

Whitney had been a devoted motion picture fan practically before there were fan clubs or fan magazines. Back in the days when Pearl White's endless perils gripped the nation, Jock, as a smooth-cheeked teen-ager spending summer holidays on the Massachusetts North Shore, contrived with his like-minded sister to see six different movies every week. There were three theatres within reasonable driving distance of their home, and each changed its bill twice weekly. By careful scheduling and the borrowing of a family automobile—unfazed by the technicality that neither was old enough to drive legally—Joan and Jock could take out a car and take in a film every afternoon except Sunday, when they allowed themselves a day off to rest up from their addiction.

By 1933, at twenty-nine, Whitney was more than old enough to have a driver's license (by then, he had a chauffeur) and had made something of a splash as an investor in the legitimate theatre. Now he cocked an inquisitive eye at the west coast entertainment industry. This time it was Jock who induced his cousin C. V. Whitney to join forces, along with Sonny's two sisters and, as usual, Jock's sister. Off to Europe once again that spring, Jock wired Sonny that he'd be back in the States on April 1, WHEN I EXPECT HAVE VERY INTERESTING PROPOSITION POSSIBLE BIG MONEY MAKER AT LOW RISK WITH ATTENDANT GREAT ARTISTIC SUCCESS OR HAVE I GONE HOLLYWOOD? Sonny was receptive. He had already gone Hollywood. He had invested in *King Kong*.

Jock's proposition had to do with a breakthrough development in moving pictures: color film. A chemical engineer, Herbert T. Kalmus, had invented a process called Technicolor, and he wanted financial backing. Whitney had asked John Wharton to look into Technicolor's potentialities, and the lawyer's initial reaction had been cooler than lukewarm. He reported back that another client had informed him that "colored motion pictures have never shown enough attraction at the box office to warrant any such increase in cost." But Wharton was not satisfied with second-hand information; he went out to California himself, saw a demonstration of Technicolor, and changed his mind. The Whitney cousins thereupon rounded up four hundred and fifty thousand dollars and set up a producing company which had the specific purpose of making films in Technicolor and which, after operating briefly under two chromatic names, Rainbow Pictures and the Spectrum Corporation, became known as Pioneer Pictures. Of all the concerned Whitneys, Jock stood out the brightest. "Pioneer Pictures," *Fortune* declared in October 1934, "*is* John Hay Whitney."

Jock and his associates hedged their bet on Pioneer's prospects. Just in case *their* color films failed and somebody else used Kalmus' process to better advantage, they bought three hundred thousand dollars' worth of Technicolor common stock—fifteen per cent of the shares outstanding. That turned out to be a profitable sideline. The stock increased tenfold in value. Meanwhile, Kalmus had invited Jock and Merian C. Cooper, who had produced *Sand, Grass,* and, most important, *King Kong,* to a showing of a screen test, in color, of Mary Pickford in the title role of *Alice in Wonderland.* Cooper was so impressed by that snippet performance that he agreed to join the Whitneys as their primary producer. Pioneer Pictures contemplated spending seven million dollars, over a four-year period, on the making of eight or nine full-length color films, and some of their ideas were majestic, *The Last Days of Pompeii* being among their more modest visions.

There were many proposals and many more screen tests: Katharine Hepburn as Joan of Arc, for one, and, for another, John Barrymore as Hamlet. It was the only time in history that that actor was ever captured in moving color as the soliloquizing Dane, and although nothing ever evolved from the test, prints of the footage would eventually be enshrined in the archives of filmdom, not to mention the Folger Shakespeare Library in Washington, D.C.; to project either screen test could only be done with Whitney's authorization. A few months later, Whitney, in New York, received a telegram from the Pioneer office in Hollywood: GARBOS AGENT OFFERS HER TO PLAY HAMLET STOP WILD IDEA BUT EXPLOITATION POSSIBILITIES ENORMOUS. Merian Cooper thought the idea was too wild to merit further serious consideration.

What troubled Whitney and his associates the most was that under the terms of their agreement with Kalmus they were obliged to produce *something* in Technicolor by June 1, 1934. They made that deadline, but barely, and at that with nothing more robust than a two-reel short subject about a winsome cockroach. Cooper had taken ill, and two stalwarts of the Theatre Guild back east—Kenneth Macgowan and Robert Edmond Jones—had gone west to pull *La Cucaracha* together. (So had Carly Wharton, who served as its scenic designer.) A print was flown to New York, just at deadline time, and on June 2, 1934, Whitney wrote to Jones, "The entire group of Pioneer directors saw it together and each one reacted in varying fashion, some goose flesh, some tears and some with loudly beating hands, but all with real enthusiasm. . . . Nothing so lovely has ever been seen in moving pictures and the most exciting part of it all is that this is really only the beginning." There seemed to be concurrence in Hollywood. Samuel Goldwyn saw *La Cucaracha* out there and announced that thenceforth thirty-five per cent of all Metro-Goldwyn-Mayer short subjects would be filmed in Technicolor.

After much debate, and the jettisoning of, among other dependable stories, *Ivanhoe* and *Rip Van Winkle*, Cooper selected *Becky Sharp* as Pioneer's first full-length Technicolor production. Whitney proposed Tallulah Bankhead for the title role; Miriam Hopkins got it. Among those tested for supporting parts—in this instance, that of Rawdon Crawley—was a moderately known English actor of whom Macgowan wrote to Whitney, "His features are a bit too irregular for the conventional handsome leading man, but he might do very well in costume pictures." So much for John Gielgud. Macgowan became the producer of *Becky Sharp* when Cooper's continuing indisposition made him unavailable. Rouben Mamoulian took over as director when Lowell Sherman, who had been signed up in that capacity, also got sick and died.

Becky Sharp was well enough received by the critics and did well enough at the box office, but its reception was all in all a disappointment to Whitney. He had a deal with Kalmus under the terms of which Pioneer Pictures was to receive additional Technicolor stock options for every full-length film any major company made using the process. But aside from a few MGM short subjects, there was no immediate show of interest in Technicolor, for the apparent reason that color film was almost one third again as expensive as black and white. So to protect Pioneer's options, Whitney had Mamoulian embark on another full-length color picture, a not especially memorable one called *The Dancing Pirate*. Among the few industry people to judge it at all noteworthy was the manager of the Grand Theatre in Pierre, South Dakota, who sent Whitney a handmade leather medal for having been responsible for the movie that in the view of that Midwest entrepreneur was the biggest box-office fizzle of the year.

The prospects of Technicolor would be further diminished by the outbreak of the Second World War. Whitney's confidence in the process, though, remained unshaken. He had been certain from the outset that someday all motion pictures—aside from those for which black and white was artistically preferable—would be made in color. By 1954, he was out of the movie business, so he could take only a pioneer's prideful satisfaction on learning that in that year four billion feet of 35-millimeter color movie film (some of it, of course, ending up on cutting-room floors) had been avidly purchased by the motion picture industry; and that the Academy of Motion Picture Arts and Sciences, the Oscar-awarding people, were seeking for their historic archives a print of *La Cucaracha*.

Among the Hollywood personages Whitney met in his early Pioneer Picture days was David O. Selznick. Selznick, two years his senior, had unassailable movie connections. His then wife Irene was Louis B. Mayer's daughter. Selznick had organized a producing company of his own, in 1935, called Selznick International Pictures, and the following year Whitney joined forces with him—Whitney as chairman of the board of Selznick International and east-coast manager of the enterprise, handling its commercial end; Selznick as president of the company and, out west, handling the artistic end. Selznick held forty-two per cent of the organization's stock. Whitney and his assorted kin held another forty-two per cent. The remaining sixteen per cent was divided among five individuals, including the financier John D. Hertz; the movie producer Irving Thalberg (who didn't want his employer, MGM, to know about that, put his shares in the name of his wife, Norma Shearer); a couple of investment-banking Lehman brothers, Arthur and Robert; and Selznick's brother Myron, a literary agent.

Over the next four years, Selznick International made ten pictures, including *Nothing Sacred, A Star Is Born, Little Lord Fauntleroy, The Prisoner of Zenda,* and *Rebecca.* During this stretch, Whitney worked just about full time for the company, though without drawing any salary or expense money; and he became so self-assured a movie mogul that, it was admiringly noted in entertainment circles, he could hold his own in occupational colloquy with any Schenck or Skouras, and socialize easily with any star or, if need be, starlet. "Jock had complete charge of the New York selling and financing end of the operation," Selznick told an acquaintance seeking clarification of their functions. "He was inordinately active for the chairman of a board. He handled the bookings and the advertising and the foreign distribution, and, equally with me, the acquisition of story properties and the major casting decisions. He was in effect exactly parallel to the New York head of any other picture company."

The only major problem for any of Selznick and Whitney's underlings was that it was sometimes hard to ascertain precisely in what place Whitney was at any given time. Kay Brown was working for them, recommending books or plays that they might usefully gobble up the screen rights to. "When you had a question for Jock," she said, "you almost always got an answer from him, but you never knew where it was coming from." When, typically, Selznick heard, in 1937, that the chairman of his board was on one of his periodic jaunts to London, the president urged him to call on George Bernard Shaw and pick up an option on *Candida*. Nothing came of that, or of a cable from Selznick to Whitney, at Claridge's, that same year, to the effect that Selznick had just seen a demonstration of something called television, that he thought it had imminent commercial possibilities, and that he would appreciate it if Jock would ascertain what England and Germany were doing about it.

Selznick was a man given to sudden and grandiose impulses, and Whitney learned to carry out all sorts of Hollywoodish missions for him without blinking. Once, when Whitney was in New York, Selznick sent him an urgent transcontinental teletype message requesting that he buy the steamship *Leviathan*, which was then languishing, unused and otherwise unwanted, at a pier in Hoboken, New Jersey. Whitney, who did not find out until later that his colleague had in mind doing a picture on the sinking of the *Lusitania* (Selznick had read an article about it that had got his creative juices flowing), unquestioningly set about trying to execute this formidable assignment. He had got as far as convincing a number of maritime men that he was out of *his* mind and ascertaining that it would cost fifty thousand dollars merely to have the *Leviathan* towed from New Jersey to San Francisco, where his partner planned to torpedo her, when Selznick abandoned the project.

While on the coast, Whitney often stayed at Selznick's home, and now and then, after finishing the day's business, the two of them would play Ping-Pong, making enormous bets on every game. It was understood between them that no money would change hands—that they would keep on playing until they were even. Sometimes they were obliged to paddle throughout the night to attain this sportsmanlike goal. Once, an acquaintance of Selznick's stopped by, after a late party, for a nightcap and strolled toward a room where what sounded like a buffalo stampede was in progress. Peeking in, he saw the two men facing each other across a net and heard one of them croak wearily, "Got to get some sleep. Two hundred thousand or nothing on this one." The visitor shrugged and moved on to the bar, certain that he had witnessed a scene epic even by the standards of that opulent community.

By most standards, the two partners were notably dissimilar. Whitney's patrician background contrasted sharply with that of Selznick, who came from Pittsburgh and was the son of a Russian-born jeweler. And yet while working together they became fast—even best—friends. David taught Jock half a dozen Yiddish words and phrases, and when Jock parroted them back east his polo-playing and horse-racing friends would kid him, nervously, about being part Jewish. The chairman and the president of Selznick International did not look at all alike—except, perhaps, for his jutting ears, Whitney could have posed for Arrow-collar ads, while Selznick was, as casting goes, well, ugly—but often they seemed to think alike. Sometimes the one would finish a sentence the other had begun, with no change of meaning. Both liked to pace while they thought. (Their Ping-Pong pacing was comparatively non-cerebral.) Whitney was by physique and experience the more athletic; but onlookers credited Selznick with being superior when it came to speed, maneuverability, and stamina.

Each partner hugely admired the other. "Jock is an extraordinarily able, well-balanced, objective, and conscientious man," Selznick once told an interviewer, "with a wonderful sense of obligation, both to his wealth and to the public interest. He's a real liberal, the kind of person leftists try hard to claim doesn't exist—a rich Republican who promotes every cause of the underprivileged and the minority groups. And he's exceptionally fair and generous in his business dealings. I've never known him to drive a hard bargain or take advantage of his position. And his loyalty to his friends is really something! During the 1940 presidential campaign, Jock took me to a dinner party on Long Island where Wendell Willkie was regarded without much enthusiasm and Franklin Roosevelt with outright malice. When the ladies left the table and the men began the inevitable political conversation, I thought I'd take F.D.R.'s side, just to brighten the atmosphere. Nearly everybody in the room turned savagely on me, and then suddenly and unexpectedly I heard a voice taking *my* side. It was Jock's voice. He was simply being loyal to a friend in need."

Jock and Liz never had any children. By the mid-thirties, it was becoming increasingly clear to their friends that they probably never would. Not all the friends knew why. The reason was perfectly simple: Liz didn't want to. The marriage, not exactly stable from the start, was growing increasingly shaky. Jock's visits to their big Virginia farm were scattered, as were Liz's to New York, where her husband was frequently to be seen in the loving company of a young divorcée and fashion editor, Louise Macy, whom he had met through Benchley and whose steady escort he became. (After Whitney was divorced and remarried, she married Harry Hopkins, President Roosevelt's grey eminence.) Never having had any children of his own, Whitney was pleased when various friends asked him to be their offspring's godfather. He served in that capacity—a non-religious service—for, among others, a daughter of his favorite cousin, the Englishman Whitney Straight, and sons of his Yale classmate H. C. Potter, his polo teammate Gerald Balding, and Shipwreck Kelly, among whose claims to fame were both having been an All-American football player and the first husband of the glamor debutante Brenda Frazier. By a later marriage, Kelly had a boy who was named at birth John Whitney Kelly, and who after Jock assumed his godfatherly role—which in this instance included paying the lad's way through school—was renamed John Hay Whitney Kelly. Shipwreck thus had good reason for the nickname he bestowed on Jock: Aga John.

It was indicative of the specialness of the relationship between Whitney and Selznick that Jock consented to be godfather to both his sons. They called him Uncle Jock, but they never called his second wife Aunt Betsey. "There's a strong sense of a single unit about Uncle Jock," Daniel Selznick, the younger of the pair, said. That Selznick *fils* was born in 1936, when Whitney was thirty-two; it was Daniel's lifelong impression that he and his brother Jeffrey were the first two small children their diffident godfather had ever actually picked up and held.

One time late in 1938, Whitney and Kay Brown happened to be going to London together on Selznick International business. In New York, just before departing, they had seen a Swedish film, *Intermezzo,* featuring a young woman they'd scarcely heard of named Ingrid Bergman. They were impressed, and so informed Selznick in Hollywood. He in turn urged them, while abroad, to try to obtain the rights to an English-language version of the film. It was characteristic of Whitney's conscientiousness in such matters that as soon as he reached London he betook himself to a drafty wharfside cinema at which a couple of obscure old Bergman films were playing. He wanted confirmation of his opinion of her worth. Selznick at first had demonstrated more interest in *Intermezzo* than in any of the actors in it, but on shipboard his emissaries received a cable from him instructing them to persuade the actress to visit Hollywood for a screen test.

Jock and Kay got so many high-powered messages from Selznick in the course of a normal week—nay, in a day—that this one, rather mildly couched, had little impact on either of them. Indeed, they forgot all about it until they were about to sail home. Then, they rushed to a phone booth and, with Miss Brown digging into her purse and Whitney into his pockets, came up with enough change to get through to Stockholm. But they couldn't get through to Miss Bergman; she sent word by an intermediary who answered her phone that, whatever it was they were calling about, she wasn't interested. They shrugged, hung up, and sailed home.

Selznick could not abide that kind of setback. When Kay Brown cabled him from mid-ocean that Jock and she had accomplished all their missions except to get hold of what's-her-name, he cabled right back that

Kay should stay on the ship, return to Europe, and sign up the actress, screen test or no. Whitney was allowed to debark.

Miss Brown soon arrived in Sweden, and Miss Bergman expressed her willingness to sign up. But by then Selznick had new worries. The name "Bergman" on a screen was all right, he guessed, in Europe, but for the United States of America? Maybe "Ingrid Berjman" would be better, or "Berriman." JUST TO COMPLICATE YOUR TROUBLES, he cabled Miss Brown in Stockholm, DO YOU THINK THERE WOULD BE ANY CHANCE GETTING BERGMAN TO CHANGE HER NAME STOP BETTER NOT BRING THIS UP UNTIL CONTRACT SIGNED BUT ONCE IT IS YOU MIGHT ARGUE ON SOMEWHAT UNATTRACTIVE AND EVEN SEMITIC SOUND OF NAME ON ANGLOSAXON AUDIENCE STOP WHAT IS HER MARRIED NAME AND WOULD THIS BE OF ANY USE TO US STOP LOVE.

Miss Bergman was then married—as the whole wide world would come to know—to Dr. Peter Lindstrom, a dentist. When she did duly put her name to a contract—her own name, despite all cajolery to the contrary—her husband's unattractive choice of professions also aggrieved the sensitive Selznick. He instructed Miss Brown to make sure, when she arrived with Bergman in New York and they were greeted by the press, that the actress describe her husband, should anyone ask about him, not as a dentist but as a professor. "I am serious about the dentist," Selznick wrote. "I can't think of anything so calculated to tear down everything we might do as a picture of her at home having her husband explain how he treated a very bad case of pyorrhea." And so, when a couple of months later *Screen Life* asked Miss Brown to look over a feature story on Miss Bergman that it had prepared, she replied, obediently, that "a change must be made when you speak of Dr. Lindstrom. He must not be called a dentist but 'professor.'"

When the person whom Kay Brown was by this time describing to friends—possibly to avoid any repercussions from Selznick—as "my little Swedish girl" landed, she rested up before approaching Hollywood at the Whitney place on Long Island. Jock looked out of a Big Room window at Greentree early one Sunday morning, and what he saw made him reflect that, whatever else happened from then on, Selznick International had certainly got itself involved with a very special sort of actress: out on the Whitney golf course was Mrs. Lindstrom, loping along with the loose, graceful strides of a Nordic cross-country skier. She turned out to be special in another respect, too. The nickname *she* presently and pleasantly conferred on Jock—only his adopted daughters would also ever call him that—was "Boss."

The official publication date of a first—and only—novel by an all but unknown author was set by the Macmillan Company for June 30, 1936. The book was Margaret Mitchell's *Gone With the Wind*. A number of readers for movie companies, Kay Brown among them, routinely received galley proofs in advance. Miss Brown got hers in May, and as soon as she had read them recommended in the strongest terms she knew that Selznick International buy the film rights. Miss Mitchell's price was reputed to be in the neighborhood of fifty thousand dollars, and no unpublished book had ever been sold for as much as that. Selznick, preoccupied in Hollywood with leading Marlene Dietrich through a labyrinthine production of *The Garden of Allah*, was unenthusiastic. He could not believe that any yet uncelebrated piece of fiction could be good enough to be that expensive. Miss Brown could not believe that if Selznick didn't snap up *Gone With the Wind* it would not soon be gone to someone else.

Whitney was on his way to California, and Miss Brown gave him the galleys to read en route. He was entranced. During a stopover in Pittsburgh, he wired the New York office of Selznick International to grab the rights at once. The office didn't, because Selznick, though Kay had been bombarding him with urgent messages, was still dubious. When Whitney, upon arriving in Hollywood, learned that no action had been taken, he declared that, if his partner wouldn't agree to buy the book for the company, he'd buy it on his own and give the company an option, if Selznick changed his mind, to buy it from him. "I didn't mind shelling out dough for a property I was sure I was going to make a picture out of," Selznick said later, "but in this case I was far from being sure. Jock, though, had enough courage and confidence for both of us." So Selznick capitulated.

"How in the hell could any rational person tell that *Gone With the Wind* was going to be so big a success?" an east-coast business associate of Whitney's mused afterward. "I once asked Jock to explain to me the mystery. 'Why did I decide to buy the book?' he said. 'It was easy. I read it.' "

Selznick International agreed on July 7 to pay fifty thousand dollars for the rights, and a formal contract was signed on the thirtieth. Miss Mitchell would later testily insist that it was the earlier date that counted. By the end of that month, the book had already become a roaring success, and she wanted the world to know, assuming that it cared, that she had sold the movie rights *before* the public embraced her work; otherwise, in her eyes, the world might think some Hollywood sharpies had put something over on her. She was not the easiest person in the world, Selznick International would come to realize over the next few years, to deal with.

David Selznick—D.O.S., as he liked to be known in the industry—at first estimated his production costs at a million and a half dollars, which was a lot to spend making a movie then, but only about a third of what it would eventually cost to make *Gone With the Wind*. Most of the necessary financing came in the form of loans from the Bank of America; its head, A. H. Giannini, joined the board of Selznick International. D.O.S. could hardly expect to shoot much film until he had a cast, and for more than two years—with the energetic help of press agents from coast to coast—the American public was posed the question: Who will play Scarlett O'Hara? Who will play Rhett Butler?

There was talk at the start of letting the public actually decide those weighty issues, by means of a poll. (John Wharton, not unmindful of Whitney's investment in Technicolor, proposed a supplementary question: "Would you rather see *Gone With the Wind* in color or black and white?") Whitney was opposed to a thus democratic solution of the throbbing question. He was certain from preliminary soundings that the public, given its head, would pick Clark Gable for its Rhett. But Gable was locked into an ironclad contract with Metro-Goldwyn-Mayer, and the chances of getting him seemed slim, if not non-existent. Margaret Mitchell, who was kept advised—chiefly through Kay Brown—of just about every small step taken or contemplated along the way, let it be known, surprisingly, that she didn't much care *who* portrayed her two leading characters: she told Kay that any competent actor and actress could handle those roles. The author was much more concerned about the casting of Ashley Wilkes (eventually Leslie Howard) and Melanie Hamilton (Olivia de Havilland). The author further told Miss Brown that most Southerners wanted Rhett to be played by, in order of preference, Basil Rathbone, Fredric March, or Ronald Colman; they disapproved of Clark Gable because he didn't look Southern or act Southern. The outside world was not made privy to these reservations.

D.O.S. was nervous. "Production costs kept mounting," he would say later, "and here we didn't even have a cast. What sustained me more than anything else during all this was Jock's unfaltering confidence. Practically everybody else was saying we were doomed to failure, that we were stuck with the biggest and whitest elephant ever. Jock kept saying, on the other hand, 'It'll be the best picture ever made.'" (Whitney's confidence didn't falter even after a couple of horses that he had named Tara and Scarlett O'Hara proved no great shakes at the track.*) Selznick's anxieties notwithstanding, by February 1938 he was already speculating about the possibility of a sequel to *Gone With the Wind*, assuming that Miss Mitchell would write a book from which one could be fashioned, or, failing that, a sequel based on acquiring the right to use the characters Scarlett and Rhett.

* Scarlett O'Hara was out of Gay Vixen, an appositely named mare to have had in foal at the time. Both fillies subsequently failed not only as racers but also as mothers.

Throughout that year, minor roles were being cast. In New York, Whitney and Miss Brown sat in a projection room at the Grand Central Palace day after day, scrutinizing tests that D.O.S. shipped east for their opinions, and keeping equally vigilant tabs on the sets, costumes, and props that the producer was assembling. It was typical of Whitney's concern about perfectionism and minutiae that at one point he complained to Selznick that a horse that was going to be ridden by Ashley had a cropped tail. Whitney felt the horse should have a full-length, free-swinging tail. Selznick came back with some scholarly research establishing that a Southern gentleman of the mid-nineteenth century could perfectly well have had a horse with a cropped tail. Whitney yielded.

Selznick International achieved a breakthrough late in 1937 when D.O.S. made a deal with Metro-Goldwyn-Mayer. With Whitney's concurrence, he sold MGM one half of the distribution rights to *Gone With the Wind* for $1,250,000 and the services of Clark Gable. That solved one big problem. But it did not entirely allay the industry's lingering misgivings about the project. For instance, Whitney and Selznick had a meeting soon afterward with their corporate director Robert Lehman and with Floyd Odlum, a wheeler-dealer of the era, who was connected with RKO Pictures. Odlum wanted Selznick International to take over RKO, with Whitney to serve as chairman of the merged enterprises, and Selznick as president and production chief. Matters seemed to be moving along swiftly and smoothly, and then all of a sudden, to Lehman's embarrassment, Odlum backed off. Whitney and Selznick were baffled, and also annoyed, inasmuch as no explanation was given them for the termination of the negotiations. It was not until years later that Odlum confessed to Selznick what the reason had been: the RKO people, he said, had liked everything about Selznick International except that it was stuck with *Gone With the Wind*.

One overriding question remained to be answered—the casting of Scarlett. The quest for an actress to fill that bill had begun late in 1936, and it lasted so long and assumed such proportions that Clare Boothe Luce was inspired to write a play, *Kiss the Boys Goodbye*, about the talent hunt. Isabel Hill, later Whitney's secretary, was the playwright's at that time; Mrs. Luce credited Mrs. Hill with verifying the accuracy of her Southern dialogue. The plot centered around the casting of a harebrained young Georgian named Cindy Lou Bethany as "Velvet O'Toole." The action took place at a weekend house party. One of the featured characters was a polo player named Top Rumson, who was "born with a silver bit in his mouth" and who described himself as a "Republican lousy with unearned increment"; during one scene he declared, "But I want to be more than—just—a gentleman. I want to *function* somewhere." That last was a remark John Hay Whitney might readily have uttered in the presence of Clare Boothe Luce.

The national and international publicity that the search for Scarlett engendered naturally did not displease the producers. Indeed, Selznick had cards printed up, for distribution to anybody who asked the question, that read, simply, "We don't know who the hell is going to play Scarlett." Selznick sent a batch of these to Whitney, but to Jock's best recollection he never passed a single one along. Before it was all over, the gossip columnist Walter Winchell would assert, without contradiction from D.O.S. or any other knowledgeable personage, that fourteen hundred young women had been interviewed and ninety of these actually tested. The known roster included Miss America candidates, debutantes, shopgirls, high school drama majors, cheerleaders, Junior Leaguers, and the more or less nubile daughters or younger sisters of just about anyone who thought he or she had influence. "I showed the pictures of my young hopefuls to Jock," Miss Brown wrote Selznick along the way, "and he thinks they're all frightful, but as I have said so often, he likes them all done up in cellophane." Margaret Mitchell reported to Kay Brown in March 1938, apparently not without satisfaction, that she herself had been reputedly considered for the glittering role.

Among the contenders for the honor who at one stage or another were fairly seriously visualized as Scarlett were Jean Arthur, Joan Crawford, Bette Davis, Joan Fontaine, Paulette Goddard, Katharine Hepburn, Miriam Hopkins, Norma Shearer, Lana Turner, and Loretta Young. Whitney, not surprisingly, put in an early recommendation for Tallulah Bankhead, upon getting wind of which the syndicated Hearst columnist Louella Parsons, whose impact on motion picture affairs was nearly as hefty as her girth, pronounced from on high that "if David Selznick gives her the part he will have to answer to every man, woman, and child in America." Selznick actually would have preferred Miss Bankhead to play Rhett's raffish friend, Belle Watling. Tallulah, after three screen tests, didn't get either part, which may have inspired the acerb statement in her memoirs that "Selznick and his aides kept looking in treetops, under bridges, in the Social Register and on lists of parolees in reformatories."

Even the White House got into the act. For the role of Mammy, the lovable Negro maid in the book, Mrs. Roosevelt proposed *her* maid, Lizzie McDuffie, who was also granted a screen test but, like Miss Bankhead, was dropped from contention.

There was still another Liz whose name cropped up, in her case, as a possible Scarlett—Liz Whitney. Jock's wife was never in his view a consequential challenger for the accolade, but there was some basis for outsiders' taking her chances seriously: she certainly had the right connections. She got as far as being one of thirty-one young women who were actually tested for the role of Scarlett. Though Mrs. Whitney was stunning-looking, oddly enough she photographed well only in still shots—as, somewhat to her husband's discomfiture, followers of Pond's cold cream advertisements were quite aware. Even so, she might have made a first-rate stunt girl in western movies. At Llangollen, their Virginia home, had she not once surprised a thief, leapt upon a horse, ridden him down, and trussed him up? She almost did appear in a western with Gene Autry. He may have been drawn to her because she had been credited with lancing her horses' boils.

Selznick hoped to unveil his Scarlett by the end of 1938, as a sort of Christmas present to the expectant public. D.O.S. was leaning, secretly, toward Vivien Leigh, and he knew that the English actress was available, provided that the United States immigration authorities would let her work. Miss Leigh's first test for the part was disappointing. But Selznick persisted, had her hairdo and make-up radically altered, made another test on December 22, and sent the footage to New York. Whitney and Miss Brown trudged off once again to the projection room where they had sat so often and stared at so many other putative residents of Tara. The room darkened, the projector whirred, and a few moments later Whitney, his eyes filled with appreciative tears, put his head down on the back of the seat in front of him and murmured, "Thank God." Then he looked over at Kay, to ascertain her reaction. She was crying too hard to say anything. Scarlett was set.

Selznick International formally announced Miss Leigh's selection on January 13, 1939, two and a half years after its purchase of the rights to the Mitchell opus. The choice was not universally popular. The United Daughters of the Confederacy, led by an outspoken woman who was also the director of the Georgia branch of the Robert E. Lee Memorial Foundation, protested. Not only was Miss Leigh not Southern, but she wasn't even American. It took Margaret Mitchell herself to persuade the Daughters to accept the Englishwoman, though she could never get them to abandon their conviction that the very character of Scarlett was, by the criteria they held dear, "thoroughly objectionable." If they had liked Scarlett more, they might have complained more. The author wanted Selznick International to make it clear, however, that she herself had had nothing to do with any casting—for nightmarish months on end, she lamented once to Kay Brown, she had had hundreds of would-be Scarletts literally encamped on her doorstep—and that she bitterly resented all stories emanating from Hollywood that intimated anything of the kind.

There were limits, though, to the extent of Miss Mitchell's co-operativeness. When D.O.S. thought it might help promote the film if the author would let Whitney buy her original manuscript, she replied that she had destroyed all of it that she could lay her hands on, and wouldn't think of selling any scraps she might have overlooked. It turned out that she had almost a fetish about letting her handwriting out of her hands. Selznick thought it might be nice, for instance, if Vivien Leigh and Clark Gable could have autographed copies of *Gone With the Wind.* The author said no. Whitney informed Miss Mitchell jubilantly that he had managed, not without difficulty, to obtain from her publishers the one millionth copy of her book to come off the presses, and would she inscribe that rarity for him? No. It would set a precedent, she explained. Since no other novel had ever sold a million hard-cover copies, it was hard to figure out what precedent she had in mind.

The motion picture version of *Gone With the Wind* was to be released in December 1939—that would make it eligible for the Academy Awards of the calendar year—but as late as November 24 D.O.S. was still fretful, and felt that the film needed more publicity than the enormous reams it had already received. Thus he wrote to the press agent Russell Birdwell, one of the chief drum-beaters for what Selznick was even before anybody saw the picture calling "the greatest theatrical attraction of all time":

> I have succeeded in persuading Mr. Whitney that he should associate himself publicly with *Gone With the Wind,* and overcome his long-standing resistance to personal publicity. . . .
>
> I am anxious, if possible, to associate Mr. Whitney with articles such as those appearing in *Life, Time, Look,* etc. Among the other things that I think should be brought out are . . . that he insisted *Gone With the Wind* should be made in its full length; that as chairman of the company, he refused to consider any offers to purchase it, even when these offers got up to the million dollar mark; that throughout the picture his faith in it never wavered; that he kept in touch with me by telephone almost every day as to its progress; and that never for a moment did he have any doubt about the outcome, or any worry about its cost, assuring the members of our Board at all times that he was confident of the final result, and that he would share responsibility for it; that every major decision was made jointly with him, including the one whereby we made the deal for MGM for release through them, and securing Gable. . . .

One thing Jock had done toward the very end was to approach the Motion Picture Producers and Distributors of America—the so-called Hays Office, which was empowered to confer or deny a seal of approval to movies, and which had a notorious aversion to four-letter words—on the very delicate mission of retaining in the film Rhett Butler's classic last words to Scarlett: "Frankly, my dear, I don't give a damn."† Whitney carried the day by pointing out to Hays that "damn" was a word in wide and even respectable use; why, Jock informed the astonished chief censor, he himself had seen it in the *Woman's Home Companion*. Hays not only granted his imprimatur but wrote to Whitney, just after the movie's première, that *Gone With the Wind* was "a milestone in motion-picture history" and something that Jock could be proud of for the rest of his life.

As indeed Jock was. He showed the film so often at his own home, at its full final running length of three hours and forty-eight minutes, that, although he enjoyed it hugely every time, some of his regular guests squirmed at the idea of sitting through it yet once more. For the rest of his life, there were two anecdotes that he hugely enjoyed reciting to, say, the Manchester, England, Chamber of Commerce abroad, or, at home, the Jockeys' Agents Benevolent Association. One story was about two goats grazing on the outskirts of a Hollywood movie lot, the one chewing on a print of *Gone With the Wind* and the other asking how it tasted, and the first goat responding, "Not bad; but it isn't as good as the book." The other story was a real-life incident, which took place in Hollywood when *Gone With the Wind* won a flock of Oscars: Jock had left his seat and had gone over to where David Selznick's mother was sitting and had said to her, "This is wonderful, but it must be old stuff to you," and Mrs. Selznick had replied, "No, it isn't. In fact, I don't usually come to these things at all. But this year it was fair." A story that Whitney himself did not relate, but that went the Hollywood rounds after the Academy Awards were distributed, had people out there dismayed because Margaret Mitchell had received scant mention during the ceremonies. Then at a party, the tale went, Selznick stood up, glass in hand, and said he wanted to propose a toast to the one individual without whom the great film could never have been made. As the assemblage began with relief to murmur the novelist's name, D.O.S. raised the glass and exclaimed, "Ladies and gentlemen—Jock Whitney!"

Gone With the Wind had a preview in Hollywood on December 12, 1939, and two formal openings within the week, one in New York and one in Atlanta. Selznick barely had the picture ready for those audiences. He sent Kay Brown a telegram at 5:32 A.M. on the twelfth that read, HAVE JUST FINISHED GONE WITH THE WIND. GOD BLESS US ONE AND ALL. He hadn't finished it. Whitney, who had flown to the coast for the preview,

---

† Forty years later, when the Ohio State football team, with its scarlet and grey colors, arrived at Ann Arbor for its annual game against the University of Michigan, it was greeted by a banner outside one fraternity house that read, "Frankly, Scarlet, you're not worth a damn." Michigan lost; whether a blocked punt or that flaunted taunt was the cause was hard to say.

thought the film needed trimming, and after an impassioned argument that any Groton School debating coach would have been proud to listen to, he convinced a grudging Selznick to shorten it by forty-five minutes.

For the New York première, Selznick International rented two theatres —the Astor and the Capitol—which between them could accommodate sixty-two hundred people. Even so, the demand for tickets far exceeded the supply, and at the last moment Whitney and Selznick, who had allocated themselves two hundred coveted seats apiece, were trying to buy still others from speculators who were outrageously demanding as much as five dollars for a single one. (The box-office price was $1.10.) Jock set aside one of his tickets, of course, for Robert Benchley, and another for the immigration official who had expedited Vivien Leigh's working papers. One place was reserved for J. Pierpont Morgan, who didn't attend, and another for Thomas Mann, who did. Kay Brown had two beseeching calls from men who identified themselves as long-lost cousins of David Selznick's. One proved to be a fraud and the other, D.O.S. declared on hearing about him, was a cousin he'd never much cared for and who, as far as the producer was concerned, could stay lost.

The major opening, however, was the one in Atlanta, on December 15. The première of *Gone With the Wind* was just about the biggest thing to hit that city since General Sherman. The city's schools were closed for three days, and when Miss Leigh and Gable arrived three hundred thousand Georgians poured out to greet them. Whitney, stifling his aversion to press agentry, had suggested to Howard Dietz, who was in charge of MGM's east-coast public relations, that the New York film critics be flown to Georgia for the historic occasion. Dietz, who knew the critics better than Jock did, vetoed the proposition; he feared it might provoke a drunken brawl. In Atlanta, too, tickets were scarce and fiercely fought for. The member of the House of Representatives for the First Georgia District was turned down, in part because, in the course of beseeching admittance from Selznick a month earlier, he had said he wanted to attend "to see if Miss Leigh performs as well as the Southern actresses we thought should have been given Scarlett's great role." The Franklin Delano Roosevelts, who through Warm Springs had gilt-edged Georgia connections, were invited but could not attend—possibly because the President had a war in Europe to contend with, possibly because Mrs. Roosevelt's maid hadn't passed muster. Whitney, resplendent in white tie and tails, sat next to Margaret Mitchell in the hand-picked audience.

Among Jock's Northern guests were the Charles Shipman Paysons, the William S. Paleys, the John Whartons, and the Herbert Bayard Swopes. It was a sign of those times that the hotel at which some of them stayed informed its guests in advance that there would be no accommodations for colored maids on its premises. It was a further such sign that a controversy had arisen over the contents of the souvenir programs for the gala première. Should these include a picture of the Negro actress Hattie McDaniel, who played Scarlett's Mammy, or should Mammy's likeness grace merely the programs to be distributed up North? Selznick put this weighty question up to the members of the cast, and they agreed unanimously that Miss McDaniel should appear on both.

There was one matter about which the Northerners and Westerners could do nothing: no Negroes, in or out of the cast, could attend the Junior League's *Gone With the Wind* World Première Ball, featuring Kay Kyser's orchestra and a bevy of local belles in ante bellum gowns. Whitney sat regally in a box with Vivien Leigh, Olivia de Havilland, the David Selznicks, and Victor Fleming, the film's director. Liz Whitney made the scene, but only as far as a dress-circle seat. Whitney judged a contest for the most striking costume. The Junior League reported afterward that some scoundrel had absconded in the commotion with two Scarlett pantalettes and a bustle. The souvenir program for the ball contained photographs of, among other regional idols of the hour, Robert E. Lee, Jefferson Davis, and David O. Selznick.

After *Gone With the Wind,* there were really no further motion picture heights for Whitney to seek to scale. Selznick thought there might be. He had not given up on the notion of a sequel. On January 8, 1940, he sent a letter jointly to Whitney and to Kay Brown, both of whom had expressed reservations: "I was under the impression that I was the artist, and you were the businessmen; but I have drawn no conclusion but the reverse each time I think about your fantastic attitude about the sequel. . . . The public wants it, and I want it, and what are three (the two of you and Miss Mitchell) against so many?"

Selznick went on to say that he would have preferred a Mitchell sequel, but if she remained adamant, he continued, "Other people have finished books for Charles Dickens and Robert Louis Stevenson, and I don't know why somebody can't finish the Rhett-Scarlett story by Margaret Mitchell if she doesn't want to herself."

Miss Mitchell, though, was as resolutely a one-movie woman as she was a one-book woman. She refused to have anything to do with a sequel even after Selznick sent her the Oscar *Gone With the Wind* won the following month as the best motion picture of 1939. The author told Kay Brown in a long, impassioned letter of rejection that the "stresses and strains" of the past four years had kept her not merely from thinking about writing a sequel but from writing anything at all; and that to authorize anybody else to undertake a sequel "would be a violation of all my own standards of honor, and it would also make me contemptible in the eyes of a great many people." Selznick reluctantly gave up.

By 1941, *Gone With the Wind* had grossed more than thirty-two million dollars at the box office, and its proceeds, of course, didn't stop there. Whitney did not reap any of the latter-day harvest. In 1940, Selznick and he had resolved, in order to obtain capital gains, to start liquidating their joint holdings. When the assets of Selznick International were being divided up, Selznick sold his interest in the movie *Rebecca* to Whitney for forty thousand dollars. (A year later, Selznick decided he wanted that one back, and Whitney let him have both their interests for more than double what Jock had paid for them, thus realizing a nice capital gain right there.) Whitney and his sister acquired most of Selznick's share of the distribution rights to *Gone With the Wind*, too, giving him half a million dollars for that. Jock and Joan kept their interest in the picture for a couple of years and then sold that to Loew's, Inc., to get another capital gain, rather than pay straight income taxes on whatever future revenue the picture might have brought them. If Jock had held on it would have had to gross thirty-five million dollars more before, in view of his top tax bracket, he could keep the equivalent of what he was able to net by selling outright.

There was a further, and final, liquidation of Selznick International in 1942. There were more complicated swaps of properties. Whitney paid the corporation fifty thousand dollars for Selznick's interest in half a dozen motion pictures. (Jock had already got full possession of *La Cucaracha*, which had great sentimental meaning to him. By 1960, he had twenty-six prints of the Technicolor short in storage, but because they were on nitrate film, and inflammable, theatres couldn't exhibit them.) For a matching fifty thousand dollars, Selznick acquired Whitney's interest in half a dozen others. Each laid out an additional five thousand dollars for a shelf full of literary properties they'd acquired along the way but had never made any use of. Selznick got fourteen titles, among them *Sex Duel, Talent Scout, Society Editor,* and *Let Fools Marry.* Among the fifteen Whitney ended up with were ones with less unpropitious names, though a few sounded close to home: *Café Society, Of Great Riches,* and *The Story of Richard Whitney.*

All told, Whitney had invested just under two million dollars in his various movie ventures, and when in 1948 his accountants finally added and subtracted the voluminous figures, they determined that he had ended up with a profit of $1,506,175, of which $1,128,800 could be attributed to *Gone With the Wind.* The net might have been a trifle larger had not he and Selznick, on dissolving their enterprise in 1942, generously donated fifty thousand dollars to an Atlanta charity of Margaret Mitchell's choice, and while they were at it given her an additional fifty thousand for her own benefit—thus in effect doubling their initial purchase price for her book. Whitney and Selznick also sent her a 16-

millimeter print of the film. Thanking Jock for the latter, Miss Mitchell said she had seen the movie of *Gone With the Wind* five and a half times by then, had liked it better each time she saw it, and while watching it would forget that she'd written the book in the first place. Twenty years later, Clark Gable's wife, hoping to give *him* a print as a birthday present, appealed to Whitney for assistance. The only print she'd heard of that was available had a price tag, she lamented, of thirty thousand dollars. Whitney couldn't help her out. He had one print that he had saved for himself, but that, clearly, was not for sale.

When it was all over, Whitney sent Selznick a special present, too—an oil portrait of D.O.S., edged in red velvet and framed in gilt, that depicted the producer as Rhett Butler, leaning against a Tara pillar, with some black slaves hovering deferentially in the background. Selznick hung it in the projection room of his Beverly Hills home, just above a statue of Jock Whitney dressed in polo habit. The two partners kept in touch after that but saw each other with increasing infrequency. Whitney had moved on to new interests. He was publisher of the New York *Herald Tribune* when Selznick died, at sixty-three, in 1965. Feelings between them had been briefly strained in 1960, when the Sunday *Tribune* ran a supposedly humorous comic strip attributed to "David O. Smelznick." D.O.S. hadn't thought that was funny at all, and neither had J.H.W., as Whitney's editors were sharply informed. The newspaper atoned for that posthumously, printing, at Jock's instigation and with his heartfelt concurrence, a farewell editorial that said, "David O. Selznick was one of that small band of film giants of whom it can truly be said that Hollywood—at its best—is their monument."

Not long afterward, Selznick's widow, the actress Jennifer Jones, sent Jock as a keepsake a gold watch and cigarette lighter that had belonged to D.O.S. In thanking her, Whitney wrote, "I was never to have a closer friend. He was pure joy."

15. *March 27, 1933, when Jock was twenty-eight.* (Reprinted by permission from **TIME**, The Weekly News-magazine; Copyright Time Inc. 1933)

16. *Jock's regularly assigned polo position called for him to stay back and defend his own goal. He sometimes found that hard to do.*

17. *Mary Elizabeth Altemus Whitney, more generally known as "Liz," Jock's first wife.* (Gray photo; courtesy of Whitney Tower)

18. Jock and Liz Whitney in the 1930s, at a polo match. (Freudy Photos)

19. The cousins many people could not tell apart: John Hay (Jock) Whitney (l.) and Cornelius Vanderbilt (Sonny) Whitney (r.).

20. *Willard Mullin, the longtime sports cartoonist of the New York* World-Telegram, *paid his special form of tribute to the competitive Whitney cousins on the eve of their 1938 championship polo match.*

21. *He was known to the literary and motion-picture worlds as Robert Benchley; to Jock he was "Gramps."*

22. *Jock's private DC-3 with the logo designed for him by Walt Disney.*

23. *Jock and David O. Selznick in Hollywood.*

24. *The Hollywood première, on January 5, 1940, of* Gone with the Wind. *Left to right: Olivia de Havilland, Jock, Vivien Leigh, Laurence Olivier.*

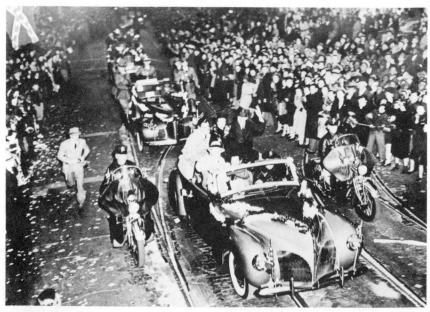

25. *Jock (at left in first car) during parade in honor of the Atlanta opening of* Gone with the Wind.

9

I'd Like You to Marry My Son

The Payne Whitneys, like other well-to-do society folk of their era, inherited or accumulated vast quantities of furniture and objets d'art, but they were not notable patrons of the arts in the sense of collecting fine paintings. They had their share of those, to be sure, but their tastes ran rather more to medieval tapestries and, in Payne's case, sporting prints. Helen had her Sargent portrait of Robert Louis Stevenson, but it was the subject that had attracted her to that one more than the artist. She was just as happy to hang a crayoned drawing Jock brought home from St. Bernard's on her walls as an old master. While her son was at Yale, he had exhibited a slightly more intense interest in art. College boys were different then. The wealthier ones might bring a string of polo ponies to school with them; they did not decorate their rooms with rock-group posters or *Playboy* centerfolds. Whitney could afford to, and did, liven up his walls with a few Whistler etchings, which were featured in a New Haven exhibit of student possessions. But he was mainly a sporting-print man then, too.

Jock's acquisitive attention was next drawn to early American portraitists: Thomas Sully, Francis Alexander, Matthew Jouett, Gilbert Stuart. (At one point, he may have owned a Stuart George Washington; he had one such, but its provenance was moot.) It was not until 1929, the year that the Museum of Modern Art was founded in New York City by friends of the Whitneys, that he began to assemble a collection of topflight paintings—mostly Post-Impressionist—that would be appraised fifty years later at more than thirty million dollars, and was, at a time when art prices were escalating wildly, mounting in value practically every month.

In 1930, the youthful Whitney was invited to join the board of trustees of the Modern Museum. He became its vice-president in 1937, its president in 1941, its chairman in 1946, and was named an honorary trustee for life in 1976. Throughout, he was one of its most persistent and prodigious benefactors. (In 1968, Whitney pledged one million dollars to a fund-raising campaign the museum then had under way but forgot to tell any of the people who implemented his philanthropic intentions about it, which made it difficult momentarily for them to cover the commitment. But they managed to scramble around in the thicket of his personal finances and scrape up the sum in question.) When Whitney took over from Nelson Rockefeller as the museum's president, he wrote, with characteristic self-deprecation, to A. Conger Goodyear, then the museum's board chairman, "I have never felt less fitted for any assignment in my life but will make a serious effort to avoid being drawn into revealing discussions with distinguished connoisseurs and/or collectors." As late as 1979, when art students and historians from all over the world were begging for glimpses of his Van Goghs, Derains, Matisses, Toulouse-Lautrecs, and other treasures, he would tell a friend, "Though I probably shouldn't say it about myself, I like to be honest—I like to be honest about everything—and I am bound to admit that I don't think of myself as a collector of art but more as an acquirer."

Some art connoisseurs tended to believe such oft-repeated self-appraisals were overmodest. René d'Harnoncourt, who became director of the Museum of Modern Art three years after Whitney assumed its presidency, once said of him, "I'm simply amazed by his general knowledge of art. You mention somebody to him whose name you wouldn't suspect he even knows and he'll not only be familiar with the name but with what work that person is currently doing. Jock's an extremely well-informed amateur."

Jock's parents bought a lot of art from Knoedler's, in New York. It was a gallery much patronized by high-society folk who then thought it *infra dig* to trade with Jewish dealers like Duveen and Wildenstein. (Andrew Mellon once took his young son Paul into Duveen's to look at a painting and, espying the proprietor, said to the boy, as if in a zoo outside a rare-animal cage, "This is a Jew!") Jock's sister Joan was fond of Knoedler's because she had an earthy sense of humor and *its* proprietor, Carmen Messmore, always had a ready repertory of traveling-salesman stories.* Whitney wandered into Knoedler's one day in 1929 and bought,

---

* In 1971, by which time Joan Payson was best known as owner of the New York Mets, Jock sought to cheer up Stewart Alsop, ill with leukemia, by recounting an inci-

for $165,000, the second—painted in 1876—of Renoir's three versions of
Le Bal au Moulin de la Galette. The first ended up at the Ordrupgard
Museum in Copenhagen, the third at the Louvre. A half century later,
Whitney's Renoir would be worth nearly two million dollars. He bought
it, he would always maintain, simply because he liked its looks. "My
taste was daring only to the extent that Impressionism was daring at the
time," he said. "As luck would have it, I've always had enough space to
hang pictures of importance that suited my taste."

Whitney was one of a syndicate of New Yorkers who in 1968 acquired
most of Gertrude Stein's celebrated collection of Post-Impressionist art.
The Stein works—thirty-eight of them, mostly Picassos but including one
Matisse and several by Juan Gris—had been in bank vaults in Europe
since their owner's death in 1946, languishing there because of a tes-
tamentary dispute between Alice B. Toklas, Stein's long-time mate, and
Stein's closest relatives, the offspring of a nephew. The Museum of Modern Art had tried to get Stein to promise it the collection while she was
alive, but she had reportedly said to Alfred H. Barr, Jr., its founding director, "You can be a museum or you can be modern, but you can't be
both."

In 1966, the art historian Bates Lowry, later the museum's director,
was tipped off in a phone call from England that the combative heirs
were close to a rapprochement and that the long-unseen Stein paintings
might be up for sale. Lowry and William S. Lieberman, then the head of
the museum's department of drawings and prints, betook themselves to
Pocantico Hills and had lunch with David Rockefeller, the chairman of
MOMA's board of trustees. Nelson Rockefeller, also a trustee, joined
them after lunch. It was agreed on then that six million dollars would
probably obtain the paintings, and that a handy way to accomplish this
would be to get six individuals to pledge a million dollars apiece—the
two Rockefellers and four others. The members of the pool would be expected, during or after their lifetimes, to give some of the Steins to the
museum. A phone call to William S. Paley, the president of MOMA,
sufficed to add him to the roster. Another phone call, and Jock Whitney
was lined up. Lowry was dispatched as an emissary to still another trustee, the Vanderbilt heir William A. M. Burden. When Burden said he
didn't have a million dollars lying around loose and Lowry thereupon
suggested that he borrow the money, Burden was indignant; he said he
had never borrowed in his life and wasn't prepared to sully that record.
By then, David Rockefeller, who could afford it, said he would take two

dent at the Metropolitan Opera. Just before the curtain went up, Whitney told the
columnist, the orchestra rendered "The Star-Spangled Banner," and in the brief hush
that followed, Joan's voice rang out loud and clear, "Play ball!" Alsop thanked Jock
for "a perfect letter for a very sick man."

of the six shares, and David got his financial mentor, André Meyer, to come in for the remaining one.

But exactly where was the Stein collection? Lieberman took off for Europe to track it down and finally found it in a London bank vault. All the paintings were in a single room, illuminated by a single bulb. Visibility was limited, but Lieberman could see enough to make an offer. He was especially impressed by a Gris collage of roses, which he was convinced had inspired Miss Stein's famous roseate lines. He got the lot. In December 1968 the paintings arrived in New York. They were unframed, and rather messy. Some had been smudged by smoke drifting year after year out of a Gertrude Stein fireplace. Lieberman propped them informally against a museum office wall, and David Rockefeller invited his allies over to inspect them. Like kids waiting their turn at a grab bag, the gilded quintet—the chairman of the Chase Manhattan Bank, the governor of New York, the doyen of Lazard Frères, the squire of Greentree, and (the emperor of CBS being sick) Paley's wife—drew lots to see who would have first pick. Whitney ended up with six Picassos—five still lifes and a portrait. "It was quite a way for all of us to get some marvelous pictures by the greatest modern artists," he said. "That sort of thing doesn't happen very often." ("What we paid for the works was almost a steal," Paley said later.) Lieberman was surprised that nobody put in a bid for the Gris collage of roses, but it had been dismembered in transit and, in scattered pieces, was not very appealing. The syndicate later had it reassembled and sold it to an outsider.

By 1978, Jock's Picassos were insured for $1,100,967 and, like most works of their era, were mounting in value almost daily. The remainder of Whitney's trove of paintings—among them eight others by Picasso, three by Braque, two by Cézanne, five by Degas, two by Manet, three by Monet, three by Matisse, five by Renoir, and two by Van Gogh—were insured that year for more than twenty-five million dollars, the most valuable one, at three and a half million, being Toulouse-Lautrec's *Marcelle Lender dansant le boléro dans "Chilperic."* The Toulouse-Lautrec had been acquired for the Whitneys by John Rewald, whom they had met shortly after the Second World War when, a displaced person, he had put on a big Bonnard show at the Museum of Modern Art. Not long afterward, Whitney and Rewald entered into an arrangement whereby the art historian would scout around for high-quality works that Whitney might like to add to his collection; on any that Jock bought, Rewald would get a five per cent commission.

Rewald spotted the Toulouse-Lautrec in Paris and was convinced his patron should have it. But the Korean War was on and Jock wanted to wait. True, the painting was expensive—it carried a one-hundred-and-twenty-five-thousand-dollar price tag at a time when one hundred thousand was about the most that anybody was paying for any painting—but Rewald was so confident of his judgment, he said if Whitney would buy it, he'd waive his commission. Jock agreed but soon afterward said he felt uneasy about their arrangement, and how would Rewald feel, from then on, about representing him on an annual-retainer basis? That was fine with Rewald. Over the next twenty-five years, he filled in what he perceived to be gaps in the Whitneys' holdings, until they had assembled perhaps the finest Fauve and Neo-Impressionist collections in the United States. In the process, Rewald naturally learned a good deal about their tastes. Betsey did not much fancy nudes; accordingly, Rewald would never even bother to call their attention to available Toulouse-Lautrecs if they were bordello scenes. When she jokingly let it be known—Rewald once said—that she thought the fish in a Matisse painting of a goldfish bowl Jock had bought were too naked, her husband gave the work to the Modern Museum.

The Whitneys pretty much stopped buying art when the prices began to rocket. One time in the sixties Rewald had a couple of Gauguin Tahitian still lifes sent over for their perusal. They were priced at three hundred thousand for the pair. Betsey liked them all right, but Jock was unenthusiastic and turned them down. The dealer who had them in tow not long afterward sold a single one of them in Paris to a Greek for four hundred thousand. Rewald couldn't help telling Whitney that he had let a real bargain slip through his hands. Jock didn't blink. He cared deeply about those paintings that appealed to him, not a whit about what other people thought any paintings were worth.

However Whitney felt about the value of art, the rest of the world was so hysterically engaged in pushing up prices that in the late 1970s there was scarcely a work in his possession that he could not readily have sold for at least ten times what he had paid for it. Whitney was by then an honorary trustee for life of the Museum of Modern Art—to its fiftieth anniversary fund-raising campaign, in 1979, he pledged a million dollars—and starting in 1961 he was also a trustee of the National Gallery, in Washington; its president, Paul Mellon, and Jock were principally responsible for the existence of I. M. Pei's new East Building. But when that spectacular annex was unveiled in 1978, Whitney did not feel well enough to be present. By then, moreover, he was unhappily aware that his attendance at subsequent trustees' meetings would at best be limited, so he resigned from the Gallery's board. At Mellon's instigation, Chief Justice Warren E. Burger, the Gallery's chairman, joined the other remaining trustees in a resolution of thanks that apostrophized Whitney as "a life-long connoisseur and astute collector of fine art" who had "a perceptive eye and awareness of what was best suited to add depth and lustre to the Gallery's collections." Whitney had by then tentatively resolved that many of his paintings—aside from a few earmarked for the Whitney Museum—would ultimately be divided among the Modern Museum, the National Gallery, and Yale. The Gallery would probably be getting, among other works, the Renoir that had started him on the collection road, and a Van Gogh self-portrait. The latter would be especially welcome. The collector Chester Dale had years back given the Gallery a Van Gogh self-portrait that had turned out to be a fake. But nobody had wanted to tell Dale the disquieting news while he was alive. So Whitney had it in mind to fill that particular untidy gap in the national treasury.

When in 1935 the Museum of Modern Art resolved to establish a film library, it was logical that Whitney, who was devoting the major part of his non-leisure time to motion pictures, should have been the trustee put in charge of that institutional offshoot. There was nobody else on the board who could so knowledgeably navigate in cinematographic waters. Indeed, Jock was the only person with movie connections whom Iris Barry and her husband Richard Abbott, the first directors of the library, had ever met. No other such repository for motion pictures then existed in the United States. Most movie producers did not seem to care much then what happened to their reels of film once theatres had lost interest in projecting them onto screens for profit. At Miss Barry's urging, Whitney went around to call on the bosses of various big Hollywood studios and told them—in some instances to their utter surprise—that they were dealing in an art form, that it was disgraceful that their works of art should be plain rotting, now that an eminent archive had been set up that would enshrine them forever; and wouldn't they please donate a print of their better pictures to the new library, plus a mite of maintenance money on the side? Whitney had a hard time persuading some of the moguls that any of their full-length oeuvre was worth preserving, let alone such scraps as the Barrymore screen test for *Hamlet*, which Whitney himself had added to the grateful Miss Barry's early acquisitions. The gentlemanly code of behavior to which Whitney was a lifelong subscriber precluded his disclosing the identity of the several Hollywood studio heads who turned him down flat. Some of their imperishable films thus in due course sadly perished.

For twenty years after its inception, Whitney was a moving force in the growth of the film library. Toward the start, he obtained for its then uncrowded shelves many of its proudest possessions—some D. W. Griffith prints, for instance, that he rescued from a warehouse that was about to junk them because nobody had paid the rent to store them; some pioneering William S. Hart westerns, some early Douglas Fairbanks, Sr., derring-do. When Barry and Abbott went to the west coast to solicit funds for their library from the movie industry, Whitney persuaded the often inaccessible Mary Pickford to give a reception for them at her home. Whitney was somewhat taken aback when Miss Pickford, who, while perhaps not quite as wealthy as he was, had amassed a tidy fortune, subsequently sent back east an itemized bill for her expenses (conceivably to save ink, she had put it in pencil)—an accounting that Whitney wryly described as "of some importance in detail, considering that it included the cost of the wood burned in Mary's fireplace."

Whitney resigned from the film library's board in 1955. He had just had lunch with two long-time acquaintances who were acknowledged Hollywood titans—one at Loew's, the other at MGM—and the reunion had depressed him, reminding him anew, he wrote a friend, of "my total loss of interest in this industry, this business, and the once fond hope I held of the possibilities of its medium. It's the mountainous inflexibility of their closed little minds which makes negotiation impossible and exhausts my patience." His patience had much earlier been stretched, if not quite snapped. Just before going into the army in 1942, Whitney had bade good-by to a couple of Loew's and MGM moguls of that day—Nicholas Schenck and Louis B. Mayer. On hearing the news, Mayer twirled his index finger around and then pointed it at Whitney's head in the conventional gesture to connote insanity. Schenck, for his part, couldn't comprehend why Whitney had sought a commission. "You've *got* a job," he said. Jock nodded, but said he wanted to get closer to the war than he otherwise could, whereupon the movie man shook his head in wonder and exclaimed, "A nice boy like you! What a shame!"

Through his mother's love of poetry, through his own affiliation with Yale publications, and through his agreeable social contacts with the likes of Robert Benchley and Donald Ogden Stewart, Whitney had long had a yen to get into publishing, and particularly into newspaper publishing. An opportunity to become at least peripherally involved presented itself in the summer of 1939, when Ralph McAllister Ingersoll began scouting around for backers of a new kind of daily newspaper that he wanted to bring out in New York City—a journal that Ingersoll seemed to visualize as a tabloid with a soul. John Wharton, whose advice Whitney had sought and benefited from in so many other ventures, introduced him to Ingersoll, who had the sort of credentials with which Whitney felt comfortable. Ingersoll had gone to Yale—though, he having been an august senior when Jock was a callow freshman, they'd had no contact there; he had been an editor at both *Fortune* and *The New Yorker;* and he had impeccable breeding. Moreover, the basic philosophy of his proposed paper, which he called *PM,* was to be "against people who push other people around." Whitney didn't like pushy people, either.

Whitney was further attracted by Ingersoll's determination to put out a paper that would carry no advertising and could thus be scot-free of commercial pressures. Whitney told friends that a prospectus Ingersoll had prepared for potential investors "breathed fiery hope into the local journalistic picture" and that *PM* would be a "truly impartial progressive and modern newspaper." Ingersoll estimated that he would need a million and a half dollars to get *PM* under way, and Whitney was glad to be able to furnish one tenth of that. Among seventeen other backers were Marshall Field III, Marion Stern (a Rosenwald heiress), Virginia Schoales (a Vanderlip heiress), Huntington Hartford (an A & P heir), Harry Scherman (of the Book-of-the-Month Club), M. Lincoln Schuster (of Simon & Schuster), and William Benton and Chester Bowles, the onetime advertising partners who would later both represent Connecticut in the United States Senate. To Whitney's added delight, he was permitted not merely to help underwrite the project but to participate in some of the nitty-gritty planning sessions: Ingersoll would carry dummies of future issues out to Greentree, spread them across the Big Room floor, and flatteringly solicit Jock's appraisal of them. Whitney liked what he saw and heard. He sent out letters to dozens of friends not previously identified with progressive causes urging them to become charter subscribers and to pay no heed to some of the scurrilous things that were already being bruited about the forthcoming paper, mainly intimations that it would have a left-wing bent; there had been so much gossipy speculation about Ingersoll's brain child, Jock wrote, most of it false, "that it has become practically the Scarlett O'Hara of journalism."

PM, a daily that if nothing else was sprightly, made its debut on June 18, 1940, but even before a single issue had come out, Whitney's ardor for it began to flag.† He had always been a Republican, though not up to then an especially active one; and he was bothered by the text of one promotional advertisement that Ingersoll sent over for his perusal. A presidential campaign was under way, and the ad was going to say that *PM* didn't trust Wendell Willkie and furthermore that its editors "see lit-

---

† Whitney had often been written up on sports pages and in society columns, but rarely in a national publication until—probably because of the phenomenal success of *Gone With the Wind*—he was featured in the May 1940 issue of the *American* magazine. By mid-June, the piece had inspired 1,207 personal letters to him, nearly all begging ones; and the *American* had invited him to go on an all-expense-paid, eleven-city promotional tour of the country in a private railroad car, along with an army officer, a Metropolitan Opera tenor, a fishing instructor, and—perhaps this was the bait—three models. Whitney declined (for one thing, he was sore because the magazine's editors had ignored some revisions he had suggested when he saw a galley proof; for another, he could have made the same trip in a railroad car of his own); and, while musing on the results of this exposure, wrote a friend, "I guess it is a lucky thing for me that I didn't go into the publishing business."

tle to be learned from the Republicans." Whitney felt constrained to write Benton, "I don't trust many people either, but I do believe that the two-party system promotes disaster less than any other that we know, and that it might not be sound to condemn one side when it is not yet proven it is incapable of improvement."

By publication time, Ingersoll had spent nine hundred thousand of his million-and-a-half-dollar grubstake; and while, by September, his circulation was close to the hundred-thousand mark, about one tenth of that consisted of subscribers who were already in arrears and were of dubious loyalty, and *PM* was operating at a thirty-five-thousand-a-week deficit. That month, Whitney nonetheless agreed, as did Field, to lend the struggling paper thirty-five thousand dollars, which could take care of a couple of weeks of publication but was far short of the additional two million dollars Ingersoll now calculated it would require to turn the corner. By then, too, a number of critics were saying loudly that the predictions about *PM's* political leanings had been confirmed. In the August issue of the right-wing *American Mercury,* for instance, Eugene Lyons had delivered himself of a bristling attack on the fledgling paper, accusing its staff of all sorts of sinister Stalinist affiliations. Abuse from such a biased source Whitney could stomach, but he was having misgivings of his own and was, as he put it to an acquaintance, "extremely discouraged by the obvious intention of the management to live up to as little of their original prospectus as possible." So he was not altogether sorry—though even people with a lot of money do not lightly relish losing any of it—when on September 24 Field offered to buy out all the other original investors for three hundred thousand dollars, a little more than one fifth of what they had put up. (In the spring of 1953, when Whitney's by then good friend Dwight D. Eisenhower was President, William Benton informed Jock that the F.B.I. had come around to inquire about him, because of his bygone connection with *PM.*)

In any event, by the time *PM* was launched, Whitney had other things on his mind. In the summer of 1940, when many of his friends—his brother-in-law Charles Shipman Payson conspicuous among them—were vehemently isolationist, Jock had already aligned himself with such interventionist causes as William Allen White's Committee to Defend America by Aiding the Allies, the Greek War Relief Association, the British War Relief Society, the American Field Hospital Corps, and the Defense Recreation Committee for New York City. At that time, as at the outset of the First World War, it was possible for civilians who hoped eventually to receive military commissions to pay for six weeks' training under the aegis of something called the Citizens' Military Training Camp, at Plattsburg, in upstate New York. Whitney betook himself there in July—along with such companionable citizens as Winthrop Rockefeller, Newbold Morris, Michael Phipps, and Angier Biddle Duke—hoping that should the United States go to war he would be an officer as well as a gentleman. Jock spent four weeks at Plattsburg, grappling with homework assignments for the first time since Oxford. He had felled a good many game birds in his time, but mostly with fancy shotguns; now, he had to learn how to take an ordinary rifle apart and put it back together again. Some quizzical photographers from newspapers he had no share in turned up one day and, unwilling to believe that the patrician John Hay Whitney could, like any plebeian, perform that feat, insisted that he do it before their cameras to prove his mettle. Whitney did not customarily enjoy that kind of notoriety, but it was a time of global sacrifice, and he obliged. The routine at Plattsburg, however, which entailed a good deal of marching and hiking, was by no means all warlike make-believe; it was strenuous enough for Whitney to lose eighteen pounds.

When Whitney had become vice-president of the Museum of Modern Art in 1937, he succeeded one of its founders, Abby Aldrich Rockefeller. Largely because of Jock's association with the museum, he got to know her son Nelson, four years his junior, and for the next forty years—in art, in philanthropy, in politics, in grouse shooting—their paths often crossed. The Rockefeller and Whitney families, though long financially linked— John D. Rockefeller, Sr., and Colonel Oliver Payne had been anointed with the same oil—had otherwise not been particularly close. The Whitneys were Long Island, the Rockefellers Westchester. The Rockefellers did not spend money the way the Whitneys did. They went to concerts more and to races less. Their women were plainer, their automobiles shorter. They did not object to rich folks' having fun (some Rockefellers had rather a good deal of it), but they often seemed prepared, at a moment's notice, to go en masse to church.

Yet because of the uncommon resources both families had at their beck there could not help being a kind of bond between them. Rockefellers and Whitneys could talk to one another openly and unself-consciously, without the reticence some very rich people inescapably feel in the presence of mortals less splendidly endowed. No Rockefeller ever had to wonder if a Whitney's companionship was proffered out of suspect motives; no Whitney, similarly, ever had to wonder if a Rockefeller might be professing fondness solely because of his money.

Indeed, money was a topic that rarely arose in the casual conversations of the ultrarich. (When it did, and they used shorthand terms common among them like "one," "two," or "three," it was hard sometimes to determine whether they were referring to thousands or millions.) Whitney was once asked, for instance, if in any of his many get-togethers with still another man of extraordinary means, Paul Mellon, they had ever discussed the special problem of being so well off. Whitney was astonished at the very notion that they might have. A Nelson Rockefeller or a Paul Mellon might request of a Jock Whitney a breeding share in one of his horses, or a few million dollars to bolster the exchequer of the National Gallery or Yale University (without the robust help of Mellon and Whitney both would be far scrawnier institutions), but that kind of talk related solely to the *allocation* of funds, the ample possession of which was taken for granted on both sides and was therefore not worth wasting time chatting about. And the possession of which, moreover, made it possible to talk about anything else without wondering what sordid, grasping notions might have inspired the words. Still, there were degrees of difference even among these members of the élite, and they had their own private hopes and jealousies. "Wouldn't it be wonderful," Whitney once told a non-rich friend, "if I could, someday, manage to give away more than the Rockefellers?"

Nelson Rockefeller regarded Jock Whitney as quite dissimilar from himself. "Jock was just a kid when his father died, after all," Rockefeller said when both men were in mid-life. "He had no family training, really, for handling his wealth, no pattern set for him. It was all easier for my brothers and me. I respect Jock for having moved as he has through the various cycles of his life. He's had to pull out of a lot of things that he got himself into. He's shown self-determination, has demonstrated evolution to a broader and deeper recognition of the opportunities and responsibilities of wealth." Rockefeller had looked on admiringly and appreciatively as Whitney helped build up the Modern Museum's film library, feeling, as Whitney did, that the importance of the motion picture in the contemporary cultural world had been much underrated and deserved broader and deeper recognition itself. So when in the fall of 1940 Rockefeller accepted an invitation from President Franklin Roosevelt to go to Washington and establish an Office of the Co-ordinator of Inter-American Affairs, he asked Whitney to join him and run its Motion Picture Division.

Europe was deep in war. It was important for England and France—as it would soon be for the United States, too—to keep as much distance as possible between Latin America and the Axis powers. One way of accomplishing this, Roosevelt felt, was to persuade the governments of South America, which had long been pretty much ignored or misunderstood by North America, that there was a strong hemispheric bond between the two. (The International Flower Show did its bit to emphasize this the following spring by announcing that its annual display would have a Pan-American theme; Helen Hay Whitney won another prize, this time for a tulip bed her gardeners had created in what were presumably Pan-American tones.)

South America liked movies, but the North American ones frequently shown there were not always welcome. It had once been the practice in Hollywood, for example, to depict all gigolos as Frenchmen, and after the French expressed resentment at this type-casting, the movie people had almost unanimously switched to Latin-American gigolos. Whitney managed right off to persuade the west-coast studios to portray gigolos of no recognizable national or geographical origin. The United States purveyors of newsreels—in the pre-television days, a consequential olio of current affairs, entertainment, and nonsense—had tended to overlook all events, no matter what their pictorial potential might be, that took place south of the border. Whitney cajoled these producers into sending camera crews into that largely uncharted territory.

Concurrently, he nagged the film library back at the Modern Museum into girding up for war service. On behalf of army intelligence, the library's staff began poring over old German—and later Japanese—films for clues to ethnic behavior. Among those called in to assist was Luis Buñuel, who was put to work analyzing Nazi newsreels. Whitney was happy to be able to say to his associates at the museum, in February 1941, in a speech entitled "The Museum's Place in National Defense," that the film library was about to append Spanish and Portuguese sound tracks to some of its most cherished documentaries.

Three months previous, he had convened a meeting of movie producers in Hollywood and in a speech there had urged them, in their treatment of Latin-American subjects, to accentuate the positive, to shoot more footage on location, and to export some of their glamorous stars to that deprived area on personal-appearance tours. "Process shots, gentlemen," he had told his audience, with what for him was unusual fervor, "are not the answer to Nazi propaganda!" Whitney's efforts to have motion pictures used for political ends came at just about the same time that other Americans—as they were later accused—were trying to use the medium to promote the cause of Communism. He cajoled MGM into making *The Life of Simon Bolivar* (starring Robert Taylor), Twentieth Century-Fox into making *The Road to Rio* (Alice Faye, Carmen Miranda), and Paramount into dispatching Dorothy Lamour on a seductive junket in the sarong-draped flesh. Perhaps his most widely esteemed feat was the recruitment to his crusade of Walt Disney, who produced, among other films overflowing with inter-American good will, a full-length animated opus called *Saludos Amigos,* some of the production costs of which were borne by the Rockefeller office in return for free prints to be distributed among United States embassies and legations in Latin America. A highlight of *Saludos Amigos* was a visit to Rio de Janeiro by Donald Duck.

Disney himself went there, too, accompanying Whitney on one of several jaunts Jock made south of the equator in the line of co-ordinating duty. (Later, Disney had one of his artists design a logo for Whitney to put on the nose of one of his airplanes: it showed Mickey Mouse pushing Donald Duck and his luggage on a wheelbarrow.) While in La Paz, Whitney was happy to let Bolivia know that the reason Hollywood had nearly dropped everything else to make the Bolivar biography was "so that all Americans will know the story of this immortal figure." While in Buenos Aires, it pleased him to observe that Argentinian audiences at the movie *Manhunt* had, just like North American audiences, sighed with disappointment when a sharpshooter with Adolf Hitler in his sights had failed to pull the trigger. In Rio, Whitney was less than enchanted when an actress he had brought along was smitten with their airplane pilot and decided to forgo a much-touted personal-appearance tour of the east coast of South America—even President Getulio Vargas of Brazil had promised to attend her first outing—in favor of a west-coast aerial liaison. Whitney stayed up most of one night convincing the lady that in times of crisis passion had to bow to patriotism, and the show went on.

The Brazilian Foreign Minister, Oswaldo Aranha, who had a small stable of brood mares, took Whitney to lunch one day at the Jockey Club in Rio. Just as one philatelist might, by way of saying thank you for another's hospitality, give him a stamp from his own collection, so did Whitney, upon his return to the United States, send a stallion to Aranha as a token of appreciation and Pan-American solidarity. "By virtue of Jock's wealth and social standing and general international acceptability," Rockefeller said afterward, "he was in a position to do things that perhaps nobody else could." In that instance, it was the chief co-ordinator's conclusion that the equine gesture of amity, coming as it did, late in 1941, at a moment when the precise extent of Brazil's concern for the Allied war cause was not yet certain, was a contributing factor in that country's decision to make available to the United States the air bases that proved so useful later on.

Whitney's shaky marriage finally fell apart early in 1940, concurrently with his giving up polo and basking in the success of *Gone With the Wind*. Liz went to Reno that May and after the customary six weeks departed with a divorce and, among other palliatives, the big estate in Virginia and three million dollars. Her ex-husband had plenty of other places to live. There was a suite kept ready for him at the Fifth Avenue town house, and another at Greentree; and several other residences, his or his family's, to which he had easy access.

Jock's personal life took a big turn the following year, when he met Betsey Cushing Roosevelt, a brown-haired, blue-eyed divorcée four years his junior. Her paternal grandmother had been a "Betsey," for reasons the successor to the odd spelling never did learn. Jock and Betsey were brought together at dinner one evening by his not yet alienated cousin C. V. Whitney and Sonny's wife of the moment, who was known as Gee. That was understandable: her given name was orthographically even more singular than Betsey's; it was Gwladys. Gee may have felt she owed Jock a favor; after all, he and Liz had introduced her to Sonny. Sonny had doubts about the evening his wife had planned. "You've got the completely wrong girl for Jock," he said. (When Jock remarried, his first wife sent his second one her leftover "Mrs. John Hay Whitney" calling cards; later, running into Betsey at Saratoga Springs, Liz said, sweetly, "I really want to give you my wedding ring," and began tugging vainly at a finger. "Don't bother," said Betsey, no less sweetly, "I've got one myself.")

Certainly, Jock and Betsey had their differences. He had been a high-living, hard-drinking, hell-for-leather horseman. She had her playful side, too, but they were both mature now, and after their marriage her primary concern was his happiness, health, and safety. Shipwreck Kelly liked to recall a World Series game at Ebbets Field, in Brooklyn. Jock had turned over the tickets in his season box there—he always seemed to have seats set aside for him at sporting arenas—to Betsey and her children and their friends; at the last minute he had decided to go to the game himself and had asked Kelly to accompany him. There were no seats left by then, but Whitney had influential friends everywhere, and one of his Ebbets Field acquaintances arranged to have a couple of folding chairs set up for him and Kelly on the roof of the stadium. They were near the edge, and there was no guard rail. After a while their cheers, fueled by bourbon, attracted the attention of some of the spectators below, including Betsey. She climbed to the roof, in Kelly's recollection, and insisted that Jock, who suffered slightly from vertigo, watch the rest of the game lying on his belly, while she clung vigilantly to his coattails.

Betsey's father was the renowned physician Harvey Cushing, third-generation doctor, pioneer in brain surgery, biographer of Sir William Osler, and still another Yale alumnus, having graduated in 1891. Dr. Cushing, who had died in 1939, was an unusual practitioner in many respects. For one thing, unlike most surgeons, he had no inhibitions about operating on his own family. He took out Betsey's appendix himself. His wife, Katherine Stone Crowell, had, like her husband and the John Hay family, grown up in Cleveland. When Helen Hay was seventeen, she would sometimes seek a reaction to her girlish poems by reading them aloud to her friend Kate. (It was a minor Cleveland saga that Helen had a crush on Kate's brother Ben, that he once gave Miss Hay a golden nugget, and that when he ditched her for another girl she flung the nugget angrily away.) The Cushings had five children, two boys and three girls. The older son, while an undergraduate at Yale in 1926, was killed in an automobile accident. His father, on being informed of the tragedy, took a deep breath and plunged into a delicate eight-hour brain operation.

The three Cushing daughters, when they matured, attained near-legendary status in American social circles. They were now and then—not altogether to their pleasure—likened to the three Soong sisters of China, who had married Sun Yat-sen, Chiang Kai-shek, and H. H. Kung. The Cushing sisters, too, would marry well, several times over. (It was easy for them, ultimately, to assemble more than a million dollars to endow a lectureship and a fellowship in their father's memory.) The oldest, Mary, more commonly known as Minnie, was married first to Vincent Astor and later to the painter James Fosburgh. (While Astor and Whitney were brothers-in-law, the former, who had a reputation for stinginess, would sometimes brag that because of his fiscal prudence he had more money than Jock had—"as if," Betsey once said acerbly, "it mattered.") The youngest, Barbara, known as Babe, was married first to Stanley Grafton Mortimer, a scion of an old Tuxedo Park family of entrenched worth and WASP social standing, and eventually, in 1947, to William Paley, who had emerged from a Philadelphia-Jewish-cigar-making background. "Babe was always the glamor girl and I was always the crumbum except when I was away from her," Betsey would say after the younger sister's death in 1979. "Babe was a perfectionist; compared to her, I always felt inadequate."

By chance Paley had bought a Long Island estate, in 1936, that abutted Greentree. There had been no road between the two demesnes, and to get from the one to the other by car took ten circuitous minutes. Once the Cushing sisters became country neighbors, their husbands leveled a hedge and had a road constructed between their properties. It was only one hundred and twenty-five feet long, but they gave it a fancy name, Baragwanath Boulevard—a tribute to the mining engineer John Baragwanath, who with his artist wife Neysa McMein had been a regular party guest at both houses.

Betsey Cushing was born in Baltimore while her father, who devoted much of his career to teaching, was on the faculty of Johns Hopkins University. As a girl, she would occasionally visit Thomasville, Georgia, but she never met any of the Whitney clan, although her parents knew not only the Hays but also Oliver Payne. When her father moved on to the Massachusetts General Hospital, she lived in Boston and made her debut in Massachusetts at the Brookline Country Club. She was twenty-two in 1930, the social calendar of which year was marked by two much-heralded weddings—that of Mary Elizabeth Altemus to John Hay Whitney, and that of Betsey Cushing to James Roosevelt, the eldest son of the governor of New York and Mrs. Franklin Delano Roosevelt.

Three years later, F.D.R. was in the White House, and his son James was serving as one of his father's administrative assistants. Eleanor Roosevelt was often traveling hither and yon, and Betsey would fill in for her mother-in-law as the President's hostess. Roosevelt had three other daughters-in-law, but Betsey seemed to be the one with whom he felt most at ease; indeed, after her divorce from Jimmy and her marriage to Jock, the President would still refer to her as "my favorite daughter-in-law." When he was relaxing at his Hyde Park home, having a drink and pasting stamps into his albums, Betsey was the one member of his large extended clan whom he particularly liked to keep him company.

She got on less well with the President's wife and his formidable mother, Sara Delano Roosevelt. One weekend at Hyde Park, the President picked up the phone extension in his study while Betsey and he were there. "Yes, Cordell?" he said. With Secretary of State Hull calling, conceivably upon some secret matter of international import, Betsey rose to leave. The President waved her back to her chair, and she sat there listening as he said, "Yes—yes, Cordell—yes—well—Ma, would you *please* get off the line—yes, Cordell, yes—yes—Ma, I can hear you breathing. . . ." Betsey burst out laughing, and the matriarchal Roosevelt heard that, too, and was not amused.

When King George VI and Queen Elizabeth came to Hyde Park in 1939 for the celebrated picnic during which they sampled American hot dogs, the President's mother almost upset all the precise arrangements by letting it be known that she hoped to have all her local friends in to meet the royal couple. Space was limited, and one of Her Majesty's ladies in waiting asked Betsey how to handle the ticklish situation. "Oh, pay no attention to Mrs. Roosevelt," Betsey replied. The President's mother was apprised of that, too, and exacted revenge; she contrived to have Betsey seated so far away from the guests of honor that the hot dogs had run out before her turn came to be served.

Betsey called Eleanor Roosevelt "Mama" (she called Sara Delano Roosevelt "Grandma"), but she never got along particularly well with her mother-in-law, either. Betsey and James had two daughters, named Sara (born in 1932) and Kate (1936) after their paternal great-grandmother and their maternal grandmother. But that marriage, too, began to go sour, and some of the interrelationships under various Roosevelt roofs —private roofs and, not least of all, the overwhelming White House one as well—became increasingly strained. Eleanor Roosevelt—who, of course, had a flock of other grandchildren—appeared to Betsey to be not especially attentive to Sara and Kate, possibly because the grandmother thought that the President was being too attentive to the little girls' mother. The Christmas stockings that Mrs. Roosevelt filled for Betsey's children disgorged such bleak objects as toothbrushes and cakes of soap. "A pair of socks would have been great," Sara reflected in later years. Once, to Sara's surprise and delight, she did find a five-dollar gold piece at the bottom of a Christmas stocking, the first decent present she could remember ever having received on such an occasion, but her father James snatched it away, saying, "This is for the bank."

All in all, Sara and Kate were much closer, as they were growing up, to their Cushing grandmother, whom they called Gogsie, than to Eleanor Roosevelt; and after Jimmy and Betsey split up, the girls seldom saw their paternal kin. In the mid-1950s, Betsey was sitting in an airport lounge at Heathrow, outside London, when Mrs. Roosevelt came in. Betsey rose, approached her, and said, "Mrs. Roosevelt, it's Betsey." "Who?" said Mrs. Roosevelt. "It's Betsey Whitney." "Who?" "It's Betsey Cushing." Betsey was never quite sure whether or not her ex-mother-in-law gathered who she was, but then Mrs. Roosevelt had encountered an awful lot of people over the years.

Betsey got on much better, after they became acquainted, with Jock's mother, though one of their early meetings had been unsettling. On an overnight visit to the Whitney mansion on Fifth Avenue, Helen escorted Betsey to a guest room and said, "This is the perfect room for you. It's the one in which Jock's grandmother died." Betsey might have felt even more abashed had not Jock's mother, even before he had got around to proposing, taken her aside one day and said, in her blunt fashion, "I'd like you to marry my son."

Jock and Betsey were married, on March 1, 1942, at the bride's mother's apartment in New York City.‡ There almost was a hitch. Apparently out of a sense of noblesse oblige, Jock informed Betsey that he thought it would be decent of him first to announce his engagement to Louise Macy, who'd been his fairly regular companion for a few years. Then the engagement could be broken, but the announcement of it, Whitney had reasoned, might help Louise in a dress business she was starting up. On hearing of this strange proposal, Betsey sent Jock a letter

‡ Later, Mrs. Cushing occupied a house at Greentree, where she lived until her death, in 1949. A day or two after she died, Whitney had a horse entered in a race. It was not an important stakes—the winner would get only twenty-six hundred dollars and the runner-up eight hundred—but he was anxious to test that particular horse in that particular contest. He did not want his colors paraded on a track while the family was in mourning, and he asked his friend Alfred Gwynne Vanderbilt to run the animal in his silks. Vanderbilt already had a horse in that race, so the Whitney one had to become part of an entry. Coming to the wire, the two horses were neck and neck. Then Whitney's horse flagrantly fouled Vanderbilt's and went on to win. Vanderbilt couldn't claim a foul, because if it had been sustained, both halves of the entry would have to be disqualified. So Whitney ended up with the first-place purse.

that was literally tear-stained, in which she said that if he went through with this outlandish scheme he would see no more of her. Jock abandoned his complicated notion and begged her to marry him at once, and she did.

He was thirty-seven, she thirty-four. There was a reception afterward at the Vincent Astors'. The Sonny Whitneys, appropriately, were among the guests. So were Edgar Woodhams, Whitney's valet-pilot, and Nelson Rockefeller. Tommy Hitchcock, who had been at Jock's first wedding, was present again, and Robert Benchley would have been, had not bad weather prevented him from flying in from the west coast with David Selznick and John McClain. With the country at war, the festivities were low key. Instead of a bachelor dinner the night before, Whitney had settled for a lunch at the Racquet & Tennis Club with a man who since Payne Whitney's death fifteen years before had come closer than anyone to being a surrogate father. (Whitney retrieved the chit he signed for the meal from the club's files and had it framed for display ever afterward with other prized memorabilia. For two gins, one pâté, one pepper pot soup, two shad roes, two broccolis Hollandaise, two Bries, and two coffees, his total outlay was seven dollars and seventy cents. The same meal in 1978 would have set him back thirty-four dollars and fifty-five cents.)

The lunch companion was Major Louie A. Beard, Jock's senior by sixteen years, a Texan who had graduated from West Point in 1910 and who at a time when the United States Army was prominent in polo circles had been a hero—a member of the army team that won the International Military Polo Championship in 1923, vanquishing a British foursome on Long Island; and the captain two years after that of the army team that sailed to Europe and beat the British, for the first time ever, on their home turf. Beard, who had an eight-goal handicap, had played in that historic match despite an injured ankle, and he returned home with a permanent limp. His martial career did not seem to be progressing fast, though, despite high praise for his horsemanship from General of the Armies John J. Pershing (Beard had had a temporary promotion to colonel during the First World War but, like many of his soldierly peers, had reverted to his permanent rank afterward); and he was accordingly willing to resign his commission that same heady year when Harry Payne Whitney asked him to oversee his stud farm at Lexington, Kentucky. After Payne Whitney's death, Helen lured Beard into her orbit, as manager of the Greentree Stud. The Major, as he was always known, became not only her adviser on horse business but also a sort of major-domo for many of her other enterprises, and eventually the supervisor of her estate in Georgia, where he died in 1954. When Helen Whitney had died ten years earlier, she willed him fifty thousand dollars.

The Major—who in 1934 helped found the American Thoroughbred Breeders Association and served for most of the rest of his life as its secretary-treasurer—had lofty standards in the horse world and could not abide sloppiness or ineptitude in any field of endeavor. He found it hard, despite the discipline the army had inculcated in him, to curb his rage when anybody accompanying him on a Thomasville bird shoot missed what in his knowledgeable view was a sitting duck. But he was so fond of, and quasi-paternally indulgent toward, Helen's son that any person Jock was fond of could in Louie Beard's eyes do no wrong. After Betsey materialized and took her daughters to Beard's Georgia fief (the Major called Betsey Ol' Miss, as if she were a regional football team), he did not even demur when one of the girls, sitting in a blind with him early one morning, confided that she loathed the very notion of shooting birds. "Fine," said the Major. "In that case, let's just sit back and enjoy them flying by."

The newlywed Whitney was still working for Nelson Rockefeller's Co-ordinator's Office. Betsey and Jock first kept house, as a result, in Washington, where they rented a mansion on Foxhall Road belonging to Admiral Cary Grayson. President Roosevelt stopped by not long after they moved in to call on his still favorite daughter-in-law and her new husband. Soon after that neighborly visit, the President invited the couple to dine at the White House. There would be just the two of them, he said, along with his secretary, Grace Tully, and they could have a nice cozy chat. Whitney was delighted. Naturally, he hoped to get to know the President better, even though Mr. Roosevelt, like a goodly number of stableboys, jockeys, and betting commissioners, was already calling him Jock.

Beyond that, however, Jock hoped to transact, or at any rate explore, some government business. There had been speculation around Washington that the Rockefeller operation was going to be merged, in the hope of getting rid of at least one bureaucratic apparatus, with the Office of Strategic Services run by General William (Wild Bill) Donovan. Rockefeller didn't relish that prospect (the merger never took place), and here, Whitney anticipated happily, would be a golden opportunity to present Nelson's arguments in privacy and at leisure. But Roosevelt had apparently foreseen that possibility and hadn't wanted to be put in a position of committing himself, one way or another: when the Whitneys arrived at the White House, the first person they bumped into was an added guest—General Donovan.

At the dinner table, the President, having achieved a position of neutrality, was in a jovial mood. His affability mounted when a servitor bore in a tray on which were arranged some wild ducks that a presumed admirer had sent him. Whitney knew that wild ducks were out of season.

He also knew from the odor emanating from the steaming salver that the presidential birds were long past their prime. Jock's first mouthful hideously confirmed that glum suspicion. But the host, smacking his lips, said, "Isn't this great!" and to Betsey's astonishment (she was trying to hide *her* duck under her napkin), her husband manfully swallowed a huge second mouthful of the tainted treat. Betsey decided then and there that Jock might someday make an ideal diplomat.

(Several months later, after Whitney had gone into uniform and had been sent to England, Betsey aspired to join him abroad, perhaps as an American Red Cross aide. She hoped the President would arrange this for her, and made an appointment to see him. Jock's beloved male dog Chillie was in her custody, and she took him along to the White House. When they entered the Oval Office, Mr. Roosevelt at once summoned his dog Fala. There ensued a confrontation so snarling that the Secret Service was momentarily alarmed. One upshot of the fracas was that a visitor to the White House, probably for the only time in its history, relieved himself on the Oval Office drapes. The other upshot was that the President said no.)

10

I Personally Prefer Russians to Germans

In the spring of 1942, the newlywed, thirty-seven-year-old Whitney, usefully and satisfyingly employed in war-related government work, was presumably draft-exempt. But being a civilian at such a time made him uncomfortable. It was in his view ungentlemanly, almost a show of bad manners. He had observed with admiration how his fellow polo player, Gerald Balding, had gone abroad to join the British army—the Royal Horse Guards, fittingly—in 1940, even though Balding was by then an American citizen and had a family in the United States. Balding had been impelled, Whitney knew, by a strong sense of duty. So now, in mid-1942, was Whitney similarly moved.

Whitney was commissioned a captain in the army on May 22 (he came out of his physical examination weighing two hundred and one pounds and measuring seventy-three inches tall); but his assignment to active duty was deferred at the request of Nelson Rockefeller. At a dinner for two, Rockefeller had vainly tried to persuade Whitney to forgo military service entirely and stay with the Co-ordinator's Office; now Jock did agree to wait until he'd gone to Mexico to help its government establish an indigenous motion picture industry. On June 18, Whitney's military service formally began. The occasion was marked by a farewell lunch at the Coffee House Club in New York, attended by fifteen members of the Co-ordinator's staff—among them, Kenneth Macgowan,

Jock's associate from Hollywood days; and John O'Hara, who performed some writing chores for the Rockefeller group. With Whitney about to go off to war, a natural subject of conversation was when the fighting would end. Before the celebrants disbanded, they chipped in, nicely combining patriotism with gambling, for a hundred-dollar war bond, which they agreed would go to the individual who came nearest to predicting the terminal date. The guesses ranged from August 1943 to October 1946. Whitney, with November 10, 1944, proved to be the closest, and in due course received the bond. He elected not to redeem it but to keep it as a souvenir. He never bothered to cash his initial army pay check, either, but that memento was worth a mere ninety-nine dollars and sixty cents.

By the end of June 1942, Whitney had reported in at his first station—an Army Air Corps intelligence school at Harrisburg, Pennsylvania, where he took a six-week training course. Betsey went there with him, and they rented what was for them an apartment of exceedingly modest proportions: only a handful of rooms and only one part-time servant to take care of them. Inevitably, there were intimations of their civilian mode d'être. At one cocktail party the Whitneys gave at Harrisburg, for instance, an Air Corps wife shyly introduced herself to an older man in mufti—a beautifully tailored dark blue suit—who to her eyes was unarguably the most distinguished-looking person present; he turned out to be a butler from Greentree, whom Helen Hay Whitney had dispatched to the hustings to see how the young master was faring in his strange and unfamiliar environment.

Once again, as at Plattsburg, Whitney found himself leading a schoolboy's life—long weekday stints of classes and homework, mitigated by Saturday night parties and Sunday picnics. The Harrisburg interlude was made the more tolerable for Betsey and Jock because among the students was a second lieutenant, C. Tracy Barnes, who was also a kind of second cousin. Barnes's mother was Payne Whitney's first cousin, and Jock's father, years earlier, had built a summer home for Tracy's parents on the Greentree estate. Lieutenant Barnes had, like Captain Whitney, gone to Yale, but Tracy was six years Jock's junior, and before they chanced to turn up at Harrisburg together, they were only casually acquainted. At the intelligence school, they began a friendship that lasted until Barnes's death in 1972. It would be especially pleasing to Whitney that Barnes, a lawyer by profession who for many years was an important cog in the Central Intelligence Agency, was head of the C.I.A. station in London during much of Jock's tenure as Ambassador there. Barnes's wife had accompanied him to Harrisburg, too; and they had an apartment in the same building that housed the Whitneys. Years later, Janet Barnes would recall vividly one night in the hot summer of 1942 when a bat flew into the Barneses' flat and began buzzing their bed. Lieutenant Barnes tried ineffectually to rout the intruder with a tennis racquet, and next appealed for reinforcement to Captain Whitney, who—putting bravely behind him his boyhood apprehensions about the winged creatures—marched onto the battlefield accoutered in shorts and a shower cap of Betsey's, and armed with a second racquet. Eventually the two fledgling intelligence specialists destroyed the bat, even though, Mrs. Barnes further recalled, they managed also to demolish a good deal of the furniture in the rented apartment.

At Harrisburg, on July 25, Whitney was routinely interviewed for the data required on an officer's qualification card. His interviewer noted, conceivably with awe, that Captain Whitney had a six-goal polo handicap; that his monthly prewar income was "private"; that his hobbies were fox hunting, horse breeding, and killing live birds with shotguns; and that he had spent at least two months a year in England since 1926.

On completing the intelligence course, Whitney was assigned to Eighth Fighter Command headquarters in England, at Watford, on the outskirts of London. He had long since begun to tidy up his civilian affairs, a process that for someone of his privileged status and complex affiliations was inevitably as different from that of most soldiers' as was his qualification card. The process, for instance, involved setting up three bank accounts in London—a sterling area account, a free sterling, and a registered sterling—and arranging for his New York office to deposit among these a thousand pounds a month, so he would not have to get by on his army pay. This sort of paperwork was smoothly handled for him, with little effort required on his part, by his financial staff in New York, which had been presided over, since 1937, by Richard Croft, an investment banker who would remain close to Whitney until his death in 1973, and to whom Whitney would write testimonially in 1966, when Croft retired, "You brought order into my chaotic affairs. You also brought a point of view which encouraged me in financial activity in terrific contrast to the stifling controls exercised by my mother's advisers."

Not long after Whitney was commissioned, Croft, too, became an army officer, and the burden of looking after Whitney's involved (if no longer chaotic) affairs was assumed by Samuel C. Park, Jr., another behind-the-scenes man whose role in Whitney's life was steadfast and significant. Born in Salt Lake City, Park had been in the class of 1925 at Yale, one year ahead of Whitney (they were unacquainted there), and had gone on to the Harvard Business School and J. P. Morgan & Company. Park was stricken with tuberculosis in 1934 and had to move to Lake Placid for treatment and recuperation. By 1941, his health was good enough for him to resume work, but not good enough for military service. With the war intensifying, Whitney and Croft were glad to be able to take on an associate who had both an impressive financial background and a 4-F draft status. Park would become, until *his* death in 1976, very nearly Whitney's fiscal alter ego (Croft meanwhile having taken on other responsibilities in the Whitney order of things), and one, it developed, with a gratifying intuitive capacity for sniffing out profitable investments. Any school or hospital or art museum seriously hoping to obtain a dime of Whitney money quickly learned that it would usually need first to obtain an approving nod from Sam Park.

In May 1942, Whitney had submitted his resignation as a member of the three-man State Racing Commission of New York, but its chairman, Herbert Bayard Swope, wouldn't accept it and wouldn't even grant him a wartime leave of absence, telling him, with typical Swope effusiveness, "You are always present in spirit; you are always represented by proxy; and when the need arises, you can be present *in propria persona.*" In June, Whitney resigned again, telling Governor Herbert H. Lehman, while he was at it, that "racing today in New York, at the peak of a period of unparalleled commercialism, has never been cleaner and has nowhere in the world been supervised more in the public interest." Whitney's offer to step aside was once more declined, and Whitney shrugged and gave his proxy to Swope. (After Thomas E. Dewey attained the governorship of New York in the fall of 1942, Whitney, by then in Europe, cabled him still another tender of resignation. Dewey was not especially fond of Swope, and, knowing that Swope held the Whitney proxy, he accepted the offer.) Whitney further debated resigning from some of the dozen or so social clubs he belonged to, but on reflecting that it would probably be difficult for such institutions to keep afloat during a war, with so many of their members away from home, he concluded that anyone who could afford his dues should refrain from letting the old places down. By then, Whitney's seventy-four-foot, forty-horsepower, sixty-five-thousand-dollar, custom-built yacht *Aphrodite*—a 1937 vessel named after his first yacht—had already been loaned, for the duration, to the Coast Guard, which would employ it principally as an escort for the trains that carried Franklin Roosevelt along the east shore of the Hudson River between New York and the presidential retreat at Hyde Park. The yacht's four-man crew was supposed to scrutinize the railroad tracks along the way for signs of sabotage, and the *Aphrodite* sometimes also ferried foreign personages spending the weekend with Roosevelt, giving them a leisurely offshore look at the river and its banks. (The Coast Guard returned the boat in 1945 with two new engines and a reinforced bottom. But Whitney abandoned it soon after that for a newer, faster *Aphrodite*—a yacht that Marshall Cassidy, the steward of the New York State Racing Commission, once had the temerity to try to overtake while cruising off Long Island. "Jock opened his thing up when I passed him," Cassidy said afterward, "and near washed me onto the shore.")

In England, Whitney was not compelled to live on an air base. Accordingly, he settled into a flat on Grosvenor Square, which he shared companionably with Tommy Hitchcock. Having furloughed polo for the war, Hitchcock was arranging for Rolls-Royce engines to be incorporated into American Mustang fighter planes. They proved to complement one another admirably in combat, a circumstance that made all the more ironic Hitchcock's death, in 1944, in a test flight aboard such an aircraft. Whitney's Grosvenor Square soirées, and later gatherings at other wartime digs of his in London, were social events happily attended by, as one titled Englishwoman would later put it, "all Jock's generals." Whitney did not attain even a major's leaves himself until December 1942, but he got along easily with bestarred officers, who as a group tended to enjoy the company of men with money or power or, best of all, both. Curiously, the one consequential American general in London whom Whitney never knew there—though they were to become fast postwar friends—was Dwight D. Eisenhower.

Whitney also found it congenial, some months after reaching London, to be reunited there with another intelligence officer, William H. Jackson. Whitney and Jackson, who was a couple of years Jock's senior, had first met on polo fields in the 1920s. In 1930, Jackson, a Tennessean by birth and Princetonian by education, had joined the New York law firm of Carter, Ledyard & Milburn, and there had handled some of the legal affairs of the Payne Whitney estate. Jackson had been counsel to the New York Stock Exchange and president of the Whitney-supported New York Hospital, and he had been best man at Jock's marriage to Betsey. Before the war was over, Jackson was a high-placed intelligence officer in General Omar Bradley's Twelfth Army Group. Among his principal postwar titles would be deputy director of the C.I.A. and managing partner of J. H. Whitney & Company.

One of Whitney's duties at Eighth Fighter Command headquarters was to give a daily intelligence briefing for its top officers before they launched their missions. Major Whitney had been there about six months when, unknown to him, trouble broke out at the next higher headquarters, that of the Eighth Air Force. Its commander, General Ira Eaker, was catching hell from Washington because he was losing aircraft that the Pentagon planners had intended to divert to, among other supplicants for added air power, General Douglas MacArthur. There was little Eaker could do, that general reasoned, to avoid having his planes shot down; perhaps the problem was that he needed a more convincing public relations spokesman, somebody who could explain his situation to Washington in terms that Washington would respect and accept. While

Eaker was thus brooding, another Air Corps officer who knew a good deal about public relations—John Reagan McCrary, Jr., until 1942 the chief of the editorial page of the New York *Daily Mirror*—had been asked by Robert A. Lovett, then Assistant Secretary of War for Air, to recruit somebody who could help convince skeptics both at home and abroad of the potential efficacy of precision daylight bombing, a primary concern of the Eighth Air Force. McCrary believed that the kind of person who could best carry out that task would be one who was accustomed to the limelight and was awed neither by the sight of a reporter nor by the sound of a British accent. On learning that Whitney was in England, McCrary recommended him to Eaker.

By then, Whitney's *curriculum vitae* disclosed that he had been influential in the movie industry as well as skillful at pursuing foxes and quail. Eaker, strangely, had never heard of Jock Whitney, but he knew about the impact of motion pictures. So, in February 1943, Whitney was summoned to Eighth Air Force headquarters. He had scarcely arrived when Eaker learned that General "Hap" Arnold, his superior, was sending a lieutenant colonel from Washington to London to inspect the revised public relations setup. Eaker wanted Arnold's envoy to be confronted by a resident spokesman of equal rank, so Whitney was promoted to lieutenant colonel.

Whitney found Eaker an agreeable and understanding boss. For a Regular Army officer, the general was unusually public-relations-minded. He made himself readily accessible to the press, and he was candid with it—too much so, Whitney came to perceive, for Eaker's own good. A journalist would stop by for a chatty briefing, and Eaker would tell him, like as not, that when the Allies were ready to invade the European continent his airmen would at once blast every single enemy plane clean out of the sky. When the interview was over, Whitney would have to run after the departing reporter and beseech him not to publicize the general's unequivocal assertion without qualification.

As a lieutenant colonel, Whitney was entitled to subordinates of his own, and he asked, not illogically, for McCrary, who would marry the onetime ranking tennis player Eugenia Falkenburg and with her would, until they parted, become the celebrated radio team of Tex and Jinx. (McCrary, after studying architecture at Yale, had gone into journalism and had progressed from copy boy to editor, thanks, in part, to having married a daughter of Arthur Brisbane, a high priest in William Randolph Hearst's pantheon. Whitney later introduced Tex to Jinx, whom Jock had met while she caddied for him in the thirties when he was playing golf with Bing Crosby in a charity tournament in California.) Whitney was delighted to have McCrary help him help Eaker. For one thing, Whitney was shyer than most press agents and McCrary was not; for another, as Jock once put it self-analytically to Tex, "nobody was ever commanded to do a job for which he was so ill equipped and which he hated so fearfully." (Whitney and McCrary had a falling out years afterward, but for a while Tex was one of Jock's principal postwar counselors. When, for instance, Jock's adopted daughter Sara married a concert pianist who happened to be the son of an Italian barber, a princess-and-pauper romance that the newspapers naturally made the most of, it was McCrary who advised the bride's father on how to reward the police who kept order at the ceremony: one bottle of scotch to each ordinary cop on the scene, and two bottles to each superior officer.)

It was just as well that Whitney had someone knowledgeable to assist him, because he was, according to McCrary, spending half his time conspiring to go on a combat mission—a role Jock had been strictly enjoined from trying to play, inasmuch as he was privy to many military secrets and could have been considered, if captured and identified, a lode of information to be painstakingly mined. Late one night, to McCrary's consternation, Whitney roused him by phone and announced triumphantly that he had arranged to hitch a ride on a daylight bombing raid. McCrary, who knew that such raids were accounting for most of the Eighth Air Force's losses—the attrition rate was then close to a dismal twenty-five per cent—tried to dissuade Whitney but got nowhere, and Tex finally agreed to drive Jock out to his take-off point. McCrary was pleased to find the airfield quiet: the mission had been scrubbed. Whitney was distressed and outraged. Eventually, he did wangle official authorization to participate—after due and proper training—in at least one operational mission, on the excuse that he would thereby "profit by the experience gained . . . so that the character and circumstances of our combat missions can be better expressed in our reporting responsibilities to the American public." That approval came through in August 1943, but it was not until the following May that he climbed aboard a combat-bound B-17 and embarked on an eight-hour aerial sortie. The mission turned out to be uneventful, with no serious consequences to friend or foe. The following month, less than a year and a half after going on active duty, Whitney was promoted to full colonel.

At the start of 1944, General Eaker was transferred to North Africa, as commander of the Mediterranean Allied Air Forces. General Carl Spaatz took Eaker's place in England, and Colonel Whitney was invited—nay, because of Eaker's reports of Jock's dubious prowess, all but commanded —to join his regular poker game. The other players were nearly all general officers, but they welcomed Whitney to their sportive jousts. He was the kind of colonel they enjoyed battling with: his credit was good, and he hardly ever ended up ahead. (General Eaker, who was always eager to cross cards with Whitney, once remarked at breakfast, after an evening poker game, "Gentlemen, we should propose a toast to Jock this morning. He almost won last night.") When cardplayers in Jock's circle referred to a "Whitney Straight" they did not have in mind his English cousin; they were thinking of Jock's inveterate habit of trying to fill an inside lower-case straight. As a civilian, Whitney somewhat protected himself against his own irrational behavior by playing poker for relatively small stakes; he could in later life recall no session he took part in that resulted in anybody's winning or losing more than seventy-five thousand dollars.

Possibly to the dismay of Spaatz and other gaming generals, Whitney soon followed Eaker south. McCrary tagged along, and on arrival he took over Whitney's public relations functions. Whitney became a political affairs officer. In that capacity, he maintained liaison and swapped intelligence with the R.A.F., the Office of Strategic Services, and friendly political factions in southern Europe. After the Allies landed there, Eaker set up his headquarters at Caserta, Italy. The Kings of Italy had had a summer palace at Caserta, complete with an English garden that boasted hundreds of trees and shrubs indigenous to the British Isles. Whitney and McCrary, surprised that no one had done so before, gleefully moved into the Queen's bedchamber, and they converted her bathroom into a bar. They soon discovered why the royal premises were vacant: they were infested with fleas. Regretfully, the newcomers evacuated the palace and occupied a tent. Whitney's personal coterie was further augmented, in Italy, by the arrival of an enlisted man, Sydney S. Spivack, whom Jock had got to know through the Cushings. Spivack had been more or less adopted by the physician's family. Whitney—who after the war attempted, not without difficulty, to find a suitable civilian niche for this particular friend, and once even bought a magazine for Spivack to try to edit—found it difficult to define their relationship precisely. "Spivy was my hair shirt," Jock once said, "in the sense of being a constant reminder to me that there was a great need for me to be helpful in the common weal."

Like Whitney, McCrary had wanted to get closer to combat than a staff officer's field desk, and Tex had got rather more than he might have wished. A plane he was aboard was shot down, and he landed by parachute. Whitney was relieved but envious. He asked Eaker to let him do something more exciting than confer. Wild Bill Donovan had turned up at Caserta, to consult his O.S.S. operatives in the area, and the two generals solemnly informed Whitney that they had found the ideal task for him: supervision of all O.S.S. activities on the outmost Bering Sea island short of Siberia. "Look," said Eaker, "if you want to be really uncomfortable, you can sling a hammock in my office and sleep in it." But the generals sympathized with his wishes, and ultimately Eaker agreed to let

Whitney embark on what appeared to be only a mildly risky errand for Donovan: the colonel was to investigate the field operations of the O.S.S. in southern France, where General Donovan's American agents had been working closely with French resistance forces in preparing for the Allied landings on the Mediterranean coast and sheltering air crews who'd had to bail out over the area.

This not terribly important mission—which would profoundly affect the rest of Whitney's life—began on August 21, when at an air base near St. Tropez he was introduced to the legendary "M. Henri," the French-raised, American lawyer Henry Hyde, who from his base at Algiers had organized and supervised O.S.S. operations in southern France. Hyde and Whitney traveled by jeep to one town, now abandoned by the Nazis, where the two men were joyfully welcomed by an elder who'd been caretaker for a French collaborationist's château and had hidden a radio vital for underground activities beneath some sacks in the collaborator's own kitchen. Nearby, the Americans met a farm family that had secretly harbored a B-17 crew for sixteen weeks. "One of the crew," Whitney wrote in a subsequent report, "was third-degree burned almost from head to foot, and required the most skillful medical treatment and special supplies. Without either," he went on, the farmer's wife and her two daughters "tended the shocking wounds while evading the searching enemy. When I told [the wife] that Gen. Eaker knew of their brave and generous work and had asked me to thank her on behalf of our Air Forces and America, the whole family crowed with pleasure, although denying that they had done anything more than their obvious duty. She said, 'Tell your General that this boy has courage beyond anything imaginable. Never once in all his agony did we hear him whimper or even complain.' That was the thing they remembered, not their own terrifying risk."

After spending the night of August 21 at Aix-en-Provence, Whitney bade adieu to M. Henri and headed north in a weapons carrier driven by an O.S.S. enlisted man named Moretti. Aboard, too, were two French civilians and their bicycles: the Americans were supposed to transport the Frenchmen close enough to enemy territory so they could slip through and communicate with Maquis behind the German lines. It was a tangled time. The Wehrmacht was retreating, and most military retreats are disorderly. Nobody quite knew what terrain was in whose hands. That afternoon, about four miles north of Aix, near the village of Cliousclat, Whitney's party ran into a small detachment of American ground troops, who, when asked if it was safe to proceed northward, told them the road was clear. The weapons carrier had not gone far when a German machine gunner materialized and opened fire. Moretti grabbed a tommy gun and fired back. Whitney leapt out, knelt for cover alongside the front wheel, and unleashed a carbine. The unbraked vehicle rolled backward, leaving all hands exposed.

The four men flung themselves into a ditch, still under fire but no longer visible targets, and crawled two hundred feet into the walled courtyard of a two-story farmhouse, which appeared to be abandoned and in which they took hard-breathing refuge. There was an earth bank at the rear of the house, and one of the French civilians started to climb it for a look around. He shakily withdrew: a German tank was astride the bank, practically on top of the building. Whitney in turn surveyed that area and through a hedge saw five pairs of legs walking by. Figuring that he and his companions were in armed combat, though manifestly outgunned, he fired at the leading pair of legs, and—although he had no gun dogs with him to fetch his prey—was reasonably satisfied that he had at least winged his target.

The battle, such as it was, raged for about half an hour. The Allies were convinced they had lost it when a grenade exploded in the only doorway that seemed to lead to egress, and a mortar round exploded on the roof. Whitney was the ranking person on the scene, and, as he put it in a report he later submitted to his superiors, "it appeared to me that our precarious position might require discretionary action." His action was to step outside and yell, "*Kamerad!*" He and his cohorts were prisoners. Their captors, without questioning them, marched them at gunpoint for half a mile or so to where another tank was parked. Its commander was busy; he was lying on the grass with his arm around a girl. A non-commissioned Nazi did pay enough attention to the captives to say, "Isn't war a wonderful thing?" Whitney was beginning to have his doubts about that, but he asked for some water. The non-com gave him a lemon to suck.

During this interlude, Whitney had a chance to concoct a story for Moretti and himself to tell their interrogators: the colonel was an Air Corps morale officer who'd been sent forward—unfortunately too far forward—to see how the ground forces' morale services measured up against those of his branch; the private was an infantryman whom Whitney had never laid eyes on till Moretti was assigned to drive him around; the two civilians were hitchhikers. But when their captors first questioned Whitney, they didn't ask for any information beyond his name, rank, serial number, and birthplace.

They searched him. They took his pocket knife and kept it. They took his money—about five hundred dollars' worth of French, Italian, English, and American currency—and returned it. They did not touch his wristwatch or his signet ring, which made him happy; the stone in the ring was his grandfather John Hay's garnet seal. They did not notice, fortunately, that in his hip pocket he had a folded piece of paper—his orders from General Eaker assigning him temporarily to General Donovan, which, if anybody recognized either name, would surely have aroused interest. That night, he managed to destroy the conceivably embarrassing document. In any event, the first Nazi officer who confronted Whitney evidently did not feel that the prisoner came under his jurisdiction; the German was infantry, and the American colonel was Air Force; he would be turned over in due course to the Luftwaffe.

That evening, the prisoners were separated. Whitney was bundled into a half-track and driven off under guard into the darkness. Around midnight, the vehicle came under machine-gun fire from, Whitney suspected, French resistance forces. During that skirmish, Whitney attempted to climb out, but his guard caught him by the seat of his pants and hauled him back. They kept traveling until early afternoon of the twenty-third, when Whitney was delivered to an interrogator in civilian clothes, who spoke English with an Oxford accent. "After I had given him my name, rank, and serial number," Whitney later wrote, "he asked me what my occupation had been in civilian life. For some reason, a word I would never have employed at home sprung to my lips. 'I am a capitalist,' I said on impulse. 'What was that?' he asked incredulously. 'Well, make it banker,' I said. He looked at me sharply. Apparently assuming that I was either insulting his intelligence or pulling his leg, he ended the interview abruptly and ordered me away."

After a three-mile walk through some woods to a château, Whitney was delivered to a Nazi colonel, elegantly outfitted and copiously bemedaled.

"Well, so you've had some bad luck," he began [Whitney recounted]. "But now, no more war for you."

Since I had a tricky story to tell, I decided to respond to his calculated chumminess, and let him lead me in conversation.

"What is that uniform you wear?" he inquired.

"Summer Air Force," I answered.

He regarded me critically. Hatless, tieless, coatless, and dusty, I presented an appearance sadly in contrast to his martial splendor.

"What indicates your rank? That does not seem a worthy uniform for a high-ranking officer in the American Air Force."

"We do not make a profession of war," I retorted, "so when it comes to uniforms, we simplify it as much as we can."

The colonel changed the subject. "When this unfortunate incident made you our prisoner, how did it happen you were so close to our lines?"

This was the critical question, and I watched him carefully as I gave him the answer Moretti and I had prepared. "I was on a mission," I said, "to study the morale services of the Army's ground forces, and to determine whether they were an improvement on those of the Air Force for which I am responsible."

For a moment the colonel stared at me in silence. Then he remarked scathingly, "So that's your job."

My heart sank, for I thought he disbelieved me. Then he added, "So your job is just to see to morale—and you a full colonel!"

It was apparent he had lost all interest in me.

Whitney was dismissed, taken to a farmhouse, and given some bread and cheese—the first food he'd had in over twenty-four hours. He found some paper and wrote two notes—one to his wife and one to Tex McCrary. "You son of a bitch," the second one said. "I'm finally having more fun than you had." (Long after the war, McCrary showed some films at Greentree of General Eaker's fighter planes strafing a line of re-treating German vehicles. "Good God!" said Whitney. "That's my con-voy!") That night, having been moved again, this time to a grain ware-house, he hid the notes under some straw and asked a Frenchman at the granary to give them to the first passing American soldier he encountered. There was another move, again punctuated by gunfire, on the morning of the twenty-fifth, and more questioning. One of the new lot of interro-gators was a German who said he'd been a floor waiter at the Waldorf-Astoria for fifteen years, and although he was decent enough to Whitney —he gave him two raw eggs—when four French civilians were brought in, "his behavior," Whitney recalled, "was not so friendly, indicating that he had learned other things at the Waldorf than when to knock on the door." Whitney ended up, that day, in a small, cramped room of a house with twenty-two other Americans, a few of them wounded. In the adjoin-ing room, "two young ladies of doubtful patriotism," he wrote, "did a great deal of loud laughing while the guards popped corks."

There was a different place of confinement nearly every night. During much of the daylight hours of the twenty-seventh, with his convoy stalled, Whitney sat at the side of a road, watching hundreds of German soldiers trudge by in forlorn retreat.

Their feet were often bound only in cloth and their uniforms ragged and filthy [he wrote]; their faces defying the most pessimistic efforts of car-toonist Mauldin.* There were vehicles of every kind except good; work

* After Whitney regained his freedom, an Air Force news release about his capture seemed to blame the infantry for his ordeal. This was too much for Bill Mauldin, the infantry's chief defender. He proceeded to draw one of his Willie and Joe cartoons for *Stars & Stripes,* bearing the caption "Colonel 'Jock' Whitney captured by Germans . . . official report states front line troops failed to inform the colonel and his party of their location." Willie and Joe were depicted standing at a barricade with signs on it saying "Stop! Nazis Ahead" and "Danger—Front 50 yds"; and one was grumbling to

horses thin and fat, lame and heaving, pulling wagons with no sides, loaded with every imaginable type of equipment. . . . For the first time these troops shook their fists at us, but in a desperate weariness. Once they had passed we learned there was but one escape, through a zone constantly under fire from our artillery. Finally we pushed through. The road was entirely unprotected for some three miles, and in the final daylight, through which we drove, it was a scene of burning vehicles half blocking the road and of literally hundreds of dead horses, some burning, all stinking with their poisonous stench. Our driver froze to the wheel and bent over it until his nose was flat against the horn, and with the accelerator down, somehow dodged both shells and shellholes, horses and fires, and reached the other side.

It was much the same on the twenty-eighth—more driving, more shelling, more dodging. Whitney ended up that day in the custody of yet another colonel, who like most of the earlier questioners was curious about the American's peacetime occupation. "I gave him the answer I had found most conducive to good will during previous interrogations," Whitney wrote. "I said, 'I'm a motion picture producer.' The colonel responded, as my other questioners had done, with a quick nod and a smile. 'Ach, Hollywood!' he grunted. Then his smile vanished and he resumed the brisk, military manner." That dialogue ended—after some side remarks on the Jewishness of Franklin D. Roosevelt—when the Nazi asked Whitney how it could be that the United States had joined forces with barbarian Communists, and Whitney replied, "I personally prefer Russians to Germans."

By August 29, Whitney had reached Valence and departed from there, in an old Renault bus, for Lyons. That vehicle was incapacitated when, during a strafing attack by American planes, its driver neglected to set its brakes before decamping, and the bus crashed into a stone wall. Whitney spent the next three nights in a windowless cellar teeming with bedbugs and made the acquaintance in the course of that stopover of a German soldier who had lived in the Yorkville district of New York and who, on learning that Whitney had also been domiciled in the East Eighties, assumed that he, too, was pro-Nazi.

More than a week had gone by. On the night of September 1, walking through Lyons on his way to his next unknown destination, Whitney was

the other, "We gotta lug that damn thing around from now on. . . ." Years later, Mauldin wanted to include that cartoon in a collection of his work, and he wrote Whitney, though he had no need to, soliciting his permission. Whitney said it was all right with him but added that he had thought the cartoon unfunny and unfair when it was first printed, inasmuch as he had been on a legitimate mission and had been told the road was clear. Whereupon Mauldin replied that now that he knew the truth he was eliminating the cartoon from the book.

heartened when some French civilians gave him and his fellow prisoners some bread, cheese, fruit, jam, and wine—and would have given them more had not their German escorts dispersed the succorers by firing over their heads. A few German engineers were demolishing bridges across the Rhône, and after one explosion quite close to the prisoners, Whitney wrote, "two German soldiers threw themselves on me for their protection so violently that they crushed flat two very juicy pears I had been nursing in my bosom. German officers had already complained that my cotton uniform was demeaning to my position; from now on I was to be obviously a bum and probably an impostor." (In peacetime, Whitney's immaculateness of dress was one of his unalterable characteristics. Gordon Simmons, the chief trainer of the bird dogs in Jock's Georgia kennels, told an acquaintance, after chasing doves and quail and wild turkeys with Whitney for nearly fifty years, "Mr. Whitney likes everything to look good. I never went hunting with him in my entire life without putting on a necktie.")

On September 4, Whitney was ushered into a boxcar that already housed twenty-eight American prisoners. They had been cooped up there for several days, and when the newcomers arrived one of the German guards exclaimed, "Ach! We have been like one happy family. Now strangers come and ruin it!" By September 6, Whitney had much more company—two hundred and fifty Americans locked up in a barracks at Dijon. He scouted around for some hole he could crawl out through but couldn't find any. Evidently two like-minded Americans had better luck, for at the next roll call they were missing.

> We were then marched to the railroad station by guards who had now become definitely hostile, as if surprised and disappointed at our treachery. We were put forty-five men in a boxcar, the floor of which was lined with about three bales of straw. A rather distinguished lady and gentleman of the French Red Cross then produced boxes of biscuits of the afternoon tea variety; a box for every four men and, in addition, some cheeses. This was to be our entire provision for a trip of undetermined duration, since the Germans had nothing for us. Of the cheeses I can say that mine had already evidenced its character by bursting through the side of its cardboard container. . . . It was delicious!

The train to which the boxcar was attached did not move much. At one point, it was a fat stationary target for some cruising Spitfires and Thunderbolts. On spotting the planes, one of the Americans let out a cheer; he had forgotten that he might be their prey. The guards locked the doors and dove under the train; the prisoners tried to bury themselves in straw. Fortunately, the fighters attacked a train parked behind their rolling jail.

The previous day [Whitney continued] we had acquired the crew of a B-17 of the Eighth Air Force, forced down in enemy territory when three of its engines failed in quick succession. The pilot of this aircraft, a 2nd Lt. Fulton, was one of the most singleminded men it has been my pleasure to know, and he led a determined crew. Their unanimous and guiding ambition was to get the hell out, back to their unit, so they could bust their crew chief on the nose.† I cannot report to what unit they belonged, since when I attempted that conversational approach I was firmly put in my place by four officers going quickly deadpan. These men had been well briefed. They didn't talk, they wanted to escape, and they found out how. Fulton reported to me that the lock outside our prison car could be hooked from the outside by putting someone through a small window, high in one corner, with a hooked stick as his tool. It was the first good risk; it had not required great ingenuity, chiefly an inquisitive will.

Of the forty-five people in our car, eleven wanted to go. They consisted of five from the bomber, an R.A.F. Flying Officer, a Lieutenant from the 36th Division, a B-47 pilot, a Chinese-American Medical 2nd Lieutenant, a 20-year-old private of the 36th who had left his native Munich for the U.S. so recently that he was not a citizen when he joined the army, and myself; eight officers and three enlisted men.‡

We decided to try it in the late night when our guards might most hopefully be asleep. The hazards were (1) That we didn't know where our guards were placed; (2) It was full moon and sinfully bright until dawn; (3) Immediately behind our cage was a flat car on which three tough and wide-eyed true Nazis were travelling with their tank. Already they had brutalized women who brought us fruit at the station, roughing them and firing low over their heads. They were forever shouting orders at our guards, jacking them up to sterner watchfulness. (4) We didn't know where we were. (5) Leaving a moving train is frowned upon, I understand, by the National Safety Association.

† Some weeks later, in London, Whitney ran into the pilot. He had a black eye. He said he had taken a swing at the crew chief but had missed. The crew chief hadn't.

‡ "Many people have been interested," Whitney said in a debriefing, "that so few of the group of prisoners with me were anxious or willing to attempt escape. There was a profound conviction among the great majority of these boys that once a ground soldier has been battle-tested he will not ever be replaced. Many of the men stated flatly that they preferred prison to going back with even a slight possibility that they might have to resume the battle. This might be called by some people an example of bad morale; I do not consider it as such. These boys with very few exceptions did not seek combat in the first place; without a single exception they hate every minute of the battle and yet, without exception, at least in the case of those with whom I was imprisoned, there was not one who would not go through with his duties with one hundred per cent of courage and efficiency. There was no fear in them, but neither was there any compulsion to do more than they had to. In all the arguments about 'why we are in this war' I did not once hear the thought expressed that we were forced to defend our human ideals or protect our free lives. It was always that we were dragged in; the only doubt, by whom. The fault lies in our training, which has put no vestige of sacred crusade in our cause."

Prompting us to try were (1) The train never had achieved a speed greater than twenty miles an hour; (2) If we were not seen we could obtain a valuable start on our jailers; and (3) Desperation.

We decided to get some sleep and to leave in two batches at about 0230 hours. From the moment the plan was fixed until the noise of a slat being pulled from the roof of the car woke me, I slept really deeply and without the nightmares which had hounded almost every minute of previous unconsciousness. The stick was made to order, the lock-picker of exactly the right size, and possibly training, and in a few minutes the pin was clear of the hasp. Then for a sickening time of tugging and hauling, my vanishing bulk [he lost twenty pounds in captivity] hit the right spot and it seemed for one moment that the whole side of the car had opened to the bright white world beyond. We lined up at the door, six in a line, while from various corners of the car came complaints that we were either endangering the lives of the others or disturbing their sleep! Lt. Fulton peered through the door, which I had left narrowly open looking for a good spot, and behind him I wished that the blanket wrapped around me was a parachute. For an hour there was not a hope of a safe fall. Before the great forests had reached out to the train, soft banks had run beside the track for miles. Now it was flat, bare, walled or wired. I was searching ahead for some cover and thought I heard someone say, "Go ahead— jump!" I looked down. That's what they said. Fulton was no longer with us! I hit the stones of the track side going too fast for my legs to keep up, but before the ground could smack me in the face, it ran out and I was rolling down the bank.* Where I stopped, I stayed, and after several brutal suggestions that it was going to stop, the train was gone, leaving a bright and beautiful countryside without a sound in it except for six somewhat lunatic kids (yes, I, too, the youngest of all!) blinking like moles at the moon, and shaking hands as if they'd won the Big Game. But we hadn't yet, as Fulton quickly reminded us, so we ran for cover about half a mile away—a thick wood. Here we split in threes, I taking the 20-year-old boy, and Lt. Stennett of the 36th Division; Fulton taking two of his crew—and the only compass.

We had gotten away at about 0345 on September 8th. We learned that we were near a small town in the Haute Saône named Soign, nearly midway between Gray and Vesoul. Although we crawled in the woods next day from tree to tree, we needn't have; the Germans regarded those for-

---

* Whitney had to jump from the left side of the boxcar, thus unavoidably disregarding a voice of experience—the voice of his cousin Whitney Straight. An heroic R.A.F. fighter pilot, Straight had been shot down over Europe and imprisoned for a year by the Nazis before he escaped. The R.A.F. wouldn't let him fly any more combat missions, because if he had been captured again he might have been forced to reveal how he'd escaped, and that might have hurt the chances of others. So he had been transferred to the R.A.F. Transport Command, based in Cairo. The cousins had been reunited in the Mediterranean theatre, and Straight had told Jock that, should he ever have to jump out of a train, he should do so from the right, because most people shoot right-handed and it was harder to swing a gun that way.

ests as a small boy does the dark, and with good reason. At about 1300
hours we were convinced that there were no Germans in the area, and I
led the way along a dirt road into what seemed to be a small and friendly
village. Luck holding, we were prevented by a small boy, a Parisian
évacué, from walking into some fifty Germans. I found that he was bright
and eager, so asked him to tell one trusted man, his *"patron,"* to send us
some clothes and food, and showed him where we hid. I trusted his dis-
cretion immediately and entirely. By now it was raining hard. For three
hours we crouched in the wood, shivering in soaked and ragged uniforms.
All of a sudden loud male voices sounded at the entrance to our hide-
away, and in a flash I knew the jig was up. They had caught my saviour,
tortured him, and he had told them all. We stood up to face our fate,
which then appeared in single file led by my bright boy in rain-cape and
hat. First, the butcher, with a basket full of his sausage and he the finest
genius of sausages in the Department. Then the baker with two great
loaves of bread still warm from the oven. Two for each of us. Then a lady
in a shawl, bringing eggs, both raw and hard-boiled. The owner of the
largest vineyard shepherding a demijohn of amber wine carried on the
back of a smiling peasant. There was the *Notaire,* and two of the leading
Fonctionnaires. Also, a very large red bull of a man who had in each of
his pockets a bottle of wine at the sight of which the faces of the initiated
glowed brighter with approval. He thought he spoke English and kept on
trying but without any consideration for the meaning of the words. But
most important of all, if we would wait just a moment, *M. le Maire, himself,* is coming. And he did, bringing two of his retinue. We all chatter
and laugh and embrace and gradually the food and the wine get the best
of our shivers, and we are warm and a little tight, especially the kid from
Munich, who is cockeyed. They keep saying, "Now, it's all over—no more
Boches—no more worries," and gradually we begin to realize that, by
golly, they're probably right. At the peak of the party, our burrow, our secret hole in the woods, must have held twenty-five celebrants, and nobody once said "Shush" or "Listen!" The Germans were less than half a
mile away, yet they wouldn't have approached this wood, if even Adolf
had ordered it.

At last the Mayor made his Franco-American-relations speech, with
extra bits in it about us. I attempted to reply for the U.S., Pres. Roosevelt,
our Army and Air Force and ourselves; and another bunch of refugees
had with pride and deep affection been gathered into safety in the only
way of fighting left to many brave Frenchmen.

As they roved off, we found that we were now with the FFI—the
Maquis, as we call them; "terrorists" to the enemy. We walked for two
hours through the dark wet forest, reaching a farm headquarters at about
seven in the evening. Here we had our first view of the wonders performed by these tough boys and girls and their equally fanatic elders.
Here is the determination of burning hatred and abiding love of honor.
Their weapons are few and poor, but a man who gets close enough can
do a lot with a Winchester .303, model 1894. The day of our arrival was

perhaps not typical, but I only know that without preparation these things happened: During the night 23 men had attacked 50 Germans at a bridge which would be important to our advancing troops. They had no machine gun. They lost one dead, one badly wounded, whom I saw. They took two prisoners and drove the Germans off the bridge, and it was there when the 7th Army came through. This was at a little town called Cubry. It wasn't much of a bridge. It probably wasn't worth killing that boy; the engineers would have had a temporary one up in three or four hours. But it aroused the whole countryside and must have shaken the hell out of the Krauts. The next morning their first machine gun arrived—German. Two women who had informed on Frenchmen were put to work at headquarters as prisoners, pending trial. One girl was crying in the yard while her mother tried to cover her shining bald head with a shawl. For a year it will be clear to all that she whored with the Boches. Always it will be remembered.

As we came in they were planning the ambush of a convoy for that night. We were fed and dried, then assigned to our billets. We walked another two hours to the village of Traves, our guide the leading spirit of that town. His neighbors said he could neither write nor read, that his wife did all his accounts, but that he had the genius-gift for making everything pay. He even dealt with the enemy, but he stuck them so hard no one in the town minded. There, in his big kitchen, we had a late supper, a snack consisting of melons, soup thick with beans, roast wild boar with potatoes and green leaves, and always the wine glass full. After this meal to end all remaining energy, we were taken to our hiding places, I alone in a little house belonging to a retired director of schools from Paris and his charming wife and daughter. They were waiting to see what the war had brought them. It was their first experience, their son having only recently vacated the extra bed to join the Maquis. When they led me upstairs, apologizing for the tiny room, and I saw that wide soft quilt-covered masterpiece with sheets on it, I blessed the spirit of France, which had sent that boy to the woods, and slept for twelve hours.

All the next day, September 9, Whitney rested up, and on the tenth he was presented—now clad in French peasant blue—to the regional commander of the Maquis, a man who called himself Commandant Vermont. Colonel Whitney and Commandant Vermont dined that night in a forest, partaking fraternally of a feast that began with a 1914 Perronnet and had for its *pièce de résistance* a stew of hare and pork, washed down with champagne. They bedded down under the moon and the stars and were aroused at four in the morning by the furious pealing of church bells. The local curate had been imprisoned for a year by the Germans, and this was his way of letting his world know his joy—he was slightly ahead of the fact—that the liberating Allied forces had arrived.

Commandant Vermont wanted to meet up with them whenever they did, and by dawn he set forth with Whitney, the Frenchman now in full military uniform, to make contact with the advancing troops. By noon, they had met up with forward elements of the 143d Regiment of the 36th Infantry Division, and soon they were at division headquarters, where Whitney found some officers of the O.S.S. "They kindly took charge of me and started immediately in the direction of the 7th Army," Whitney wrote. "They who sent me out brought me back. Amen."

In jumping from the train, he had chipped John Hay's signet ring. He would continue wearing it from then on, and, for all his fastidiousness, he would never have it repaired.

Unknown, of course, to Whitney, within a week of his being captured the news was out. An American war correspondent at Caserta had heard that he was going on a front-line mission. When he didn't return, the correspondent suspected that he'd been captured and sent home a "hold for release" story to that effect. There was a leak, and another journalist trying to confirm the rumor thought Major Louie Beard would be a good source. Thinking further that the Major could be found at the Belmont race track, that journalist asked a sportswriter out there to pursue the story. The upshot was that, by still further inadvertence, the Belmont Park public-address system was used, on the afternoon of August 28, to spread the melancholy tidings that an especially esteemed member of The Jockey Club had fallen into enemy hands.

Betsey, who was on Long Island with her daughters, received the news from a friend who'd gone to the races that day. Kate, aged eight, crawled under a bed. "I remember thinking," she said years later, "'Good Lord, we've just got ourselves a new father, and now it seems we've lost him again.'" Kate's Grandfather Roosevelt had already been informed that Jock was missing; now Harry Hopkins phoned Betsey from the White House and asked her not to mention the fact to anybody, lest the Germans discover, if they didn't know it already, that they had a high-ranking intelligence officer in custody. (It was presumably Washington's belief that Nazi agents did not frequent race tracks.†) But the news quickly spread. "Jock Whitney in Nazi Hands," proclaimed a headline in Tex McCrary's *Mirror* on the thirtieth—ten days before Whitney was free. (Nazis apparently did not scrutinize the *Mirror*, either.) Betsey was in New York City on September 10 and was called on by a couple of

† Not long afterward, Whitney was in Washington and called on Roosevelt. General Eaker had some ideas about postwar Europe that he wanted to convey to the presidential ear. The Commander-in-Chief seemed more interested in what news, if any, Jock had about his sons in service. That was awkward for the visitor, because the only hard intelligence Whitney had was that Brigadier General Elliott Roosevelt had passed through Caserta, had insisted on playing poker there for stakes higher than the conventional ones, had lost heavily, and hadn't paid off.

stern-faced officers on General Eaker's staff, who had been instructed to
ask her, as delicately as possible, what, should the necessity arise, she
wanted done with Jock's effects. The officers were with her when there
was another phone call from Washington. A general there said that the
Pentagon had just had preliminary word that Colonel Whitney had returned to duty and that confirmation could be expected within the hour.
When the good confirming word did indeed come through, Betsey
phoned Jock's mother, who was seriously ill, and his sister Joan. Then
she took the two officers to lunch at "21," and they all got drunk and
laughed hysterically and some of the other patrons who knew Betsey
and thought her husband was still a prisoner frowned at what they took
to be her unseemly behavior.

Whitney himself soon arrived back home, on a well-earned leave, but
too late to see his mother, who died on September 24. He was greeted
by, among other things, the news that Drew Pearson had suggested in
his syndicated column that Jock had bought his way out of captivity.
(Somebody once asked William H. Jackson what sort of a person he
thought Jock Whitney would have been if he hadn't had all that money.
"Money didn't get him off that train," Jackson replied.)

In 1951, although Whitney had never spent time in a formal Nazi
prisoner-of-war camp, he was happy to be accorded honorary membership in an organization of survivors called Stalag 7B. Two years after
that, while on a tour of the Continent, he took his wife and daughters
back to the remembered scene. They started off, as he had earlier, from
Aix-en-Provence, but this time in a chauffeured limousine. What had
triggered the expedition was Sara's spending a year abroad. She had sent
home, by chance, a postcard showing a bar in rural France, and Jock had
recognized the spot: the husband and wife running the café had rushed
out with a trayful of wine when the prisoners were marched by, and one
of the German guards had knocked the tray away. So Whitney had decided to go back. He found the ditch he had crawled through when first
ambushed (he did not essay to repeat the maneuver), and then he found
the house into the courtyard of which he and his three original companions had stumbled. It was occupied again by its prewar owners, and its
war-inflicted bullet holes were still visible. The French family pointed
these out, indeed, with some asperity; they intimated sourly that they
held Whitney accountable for the damage. When he and his entourage
beat a fairly hasty retreat, the *père de famille* waved them away with a
clenched fist. Whitney resolved then and there never again to visit that
village under any circumstances.

Whitney stayed on Eaker's staff for most of the rest of the war. The colonel was relieved from active duty in September 1945, having mean-

while been awarded a Bronze Star for "unusual tact and diplomacy in the establishment of close relationships with the personnel of other components of the military service and the Allied forces." Later there was a Legion of Merit, the non-combat medal often presented to staff officers who'd had few opportunities to win battlefield decorations.

On December 1, 1945, Whitney's terminal leave concluded, and he returned—at once permanently shucking, as noted earlier, his military title—to full-fledged civilian life. He had never received the promotion to brigadier general that Eaker had hoped to obtain for him; but Jock would become and remain a firm postwar friend of several of the Air Force eminences under whom he had served in Europe—Eaker, Spaatz, and, among other generals, Frederick L. Anderson, Everett R. Cook, and Edward P. Curtis (with whom, as an Eastman Kodak executive involved in Technicolor, Whitney had a prewar acquaintance). For more than twenty years, some or all of these senior officers would delightedly join Whitney for a winter week of bird shooting at Greenwood, his sumptuous Georgia plantation, often traveling there in a C-47 transport plane their host had bought while on terminal leave and had had converted into a comfortable air-borne yacht. General Spaatz, who had ridden aboard quite a few nicely outfitted aircraft in his time, once told Whitney that he ought to install a complaint box on his plane—because, Spaatz said, of the pleasure his crew would derive from never finding anything inside it. Pete Christensen, Whitney's postwar pilot for a quarter of a century, said that his friends in aviation could never quite get over the fact that he was in charge of a private plane that was not owned by a corporation but actually belonged to an individual.

Whitney called his high-ranking Thomasville guests "the Shooting Generals" and their repeated pilgrimages "my annual Air Force Week." (The generals sometimes referred to themselves as the "Spaatzwaffe-MAAFwaffe," but, having been instrumental in winning a major war, were probably entitled to such jocularity.) The lavish hospitality accorded them at Greenwood, on occasion even in Whitney's absence, was much fancied by the brass; it made them feel all the more at home that the plantation was supervised, until his death in 1954, by Major Louie Beard, a bona fide West Pointer. The Major's obituary in the United States Military Academy's alumni magazine was written by four-star general Spaatz, who said, for the moment downplaying the role of the bombing plane in the modern world, "We have lost one of the outstanding men of a passing era, wherein integrity, honor, and love for the horse were meeting the impact of a ruthless machine age."

Even the navy had had its share of the pleasure that Colonel Whitney could furnish fighting men. Admiral William F. Halsey and a few of his aides spent a relaxing week at Greenwood in the winter of 1945, girding up before embarking on their final campaign in the Pacific. Major Beard reported to Whitney afterward, "They drank up everything I had, plus what I could buy, plus a considerable amount that they had brought. The consumption per capita was four times the normal." The Major's notion of "normal" may, by conventional standards, have been abnormal. Delegated in 1947, for instance, to replenish the ebbing stocks of whiskey in one of Whitney's Long Island cellars, Beard bought forty-three hundred dollars' worth—five barrels of Golden Legend and forty cases of eight-year-old Bond Mill.

Whitney's Thomasville plantation—actually, he had three unconnected tracts there in three townships, covering in all eighteen thousand acres— often seemed to be his favorite retreat. The main house was not especially large, having only seven bedrooms, but there were plenty of accommodations for overflow guests in outlying buildings, and a ten-car garage. Roses, especially Banksia roses, grew everywhere. Thomasville called itself the City of Roses and had had an annual Rose Festival from 1922 on; a feature of a parade that was a highlight of the fiftieth such festival was a tractor driven by a native son of southwest Georgia, Governor Jimmy Carter. Betsey and Jock had their already decorative grounds further prettied up in the 1950s by the Italian landscape architect Umberto Innocenti, who gave them a palm garden and persuaded their indigenous gardeners to open up the areas around their lush camellia bushes; until Innocenti appeared on the scene, it had apparently not occurred to any Greenwood gardener that one should be able to gaze upon a camellia as upon a beautiful woman—to be able, as the Italian put it, to see and appreciate all the limbs. The driveway leading to the main residence was flanked by magnolias so stately that when one of them was felled by lightning it took three new trees to fill the breach.

Whitney's aunt Alice Hay said after one trip to Greenwood, "It is the kind of place where everything seems frightfully simple and is horribly elaborate." Another guest sought to convey its elegance by remarking that it was the only home she'd ever stayed at where the paper plates used at picnics didn't get soggy. There were stables for riding horses— most of these Greentree steeds that had been pronounced inadequate for running or breeding—and gun rooms and tack rooms and carriage houses and kennels that could house forty or fifty bird dogs at a clip but were occupied only for four months a year, from November on. It was considered inadvisible to school the dogs on the same terrain where they'd be hunting, so Whitney's spent eight months a year at the Myrtle, Mississippi, kennels of Gordon Simmons, who had become the chief Greenwood dog man in 1931 and, later assisted by his nephew Gene, remained so—except for a four-year stint during the Second World War training army dogs in Nebraska—ever afterward. (Whitney and his neighbors were extremely scrupulous about their dogs' comportment. The oil executive Walter C. Teagle, Jr., who had a place abutting Jock's, once wrote him that he had found the carcass of a large turkey just inside his property one day while quail hunting. Teagle learned that some of Whitney's dogs had tracked the bird to their mutual fence and stopped there. He wanted Jock and his people to know that thenceforth they should feel free to trespass in such circumstances; why, he added, he had already once had his dogs retrieve a crippled quail from Jock's preserve.)

A century after the Civil War, Greenwood retained something of the air of an ante bellum Southern plantation. Its tack room was in the charge of a black man, Fred Lundy, who'd been born on the place at the turn of the century, and whose own sixteen children had grown up there. (Seven or eight of his sons played on an all-black Greenwood semi-pro baseball team, which their father managed, and for which Whitney provided the uniforms.) Lundy was Whitney's number-one mule-wagon driver, commanding a fleet of ten hunting vehicles, each fitted out with gun boxes and game boxes and drink boxes and dog perches and picnic hampers with paper plates that did not sag.

Major Louie Beard had begun supervising Greenwood for Helen Hay Whitney in 1939, but mainly from his Greentree Stud headquarters in Kentucky. The Whitney principality in Georgia, thus governed *in absentia*, was in somewhat sorry shape when Jock's mother died in 1944. Beard moved there, but he was retiring, and he wanted a younger man to take over as general manager of the estate. In visits to Thomasville, he had got to know a settler in the area who had studied biology and ecology at the University of Chicago, Ed Komarek. He was the son of a Chicagoan engaged in wholesale produce, mostly potatoes sold to A & P stores; during the Depression, the Komarek family was noted for all the ingenious ways it could serve up potatoes.

Komarek, who with his younger brother Roy had developed a cattle ranch in Georgia, had interests that went far beyond mere estate management. Bird shooting was the major local sport, and in season it would usually preoccupy Whitney and his guests from dawn to dusk six days a week.‡ (Payne Whitney had decreed, in his day, that there would be no

‡ One of the most intrepid and indefatigable of all Jock's celebrated guests at Greenwood was General Sir Francis Festing, GCB, DBE, DSO, Chief of the Imperial General Staff of Great Britain. In 1959, while Jock was in London as Ambassador, he invited Sir Francis to spend a couple of days at Greenwood during a visit to the United States. The general started off one morning at 4 A.M. shooting ducks, then moved on to quail and doves, and at midnight, by which time his escorts were wilting, was still out in the woods on a coon hunt. He had in the meantime expressed an interest in some hogs the plantation was nurturing. (They were raised on corn rather than the conventional peanuts; that was supposed to make their bacon leaner.) The

shooting on Sunday. Jock and his generation didn't mind observing that tradition, but not necessarily out of deference to the Lord; there had to be room somewhere on the calendar for golf.) The proper habitation and feeding of quail, doves, and wild turkeys depended on how the land those birds frequented was treated. Pine woods and scattered open fields are conducive to the propagation of quail, and so, Ed Komarek had long since concluded, was controlled burning of both forests and fields. He was a knowledgeable and articulate advocate of the use of fire in agriculture and bird breeding, and was a loyal disciple of Herbert L. Stoddard, a onetime federal government biologist who'd been lured south in 1923 by a gentleman bird bander, S. Prentiss Baldwin, who had married one of the Hannas from Cleveland. For five years in the twenties, Stoddard conducted a Co-operative Quail Study Investigation in southwest Georgia, and he was the author of the 1931 classic, *The Bobwhite Quail.* Stoddard believed that game-bird production and conservation were inextricably bound up with scientific timber growth and curtailment of growth—the later by fire, among other means—and Komarek, who joined forces with him in 1934, came heartily to concur. He would become a consultant to the state Farm and Game Service and a prominent figure in just about every organization that had to do with quail.

When in 1945 Major Beard asked Komarek to go to work for Whitney, the fire buff at first declined. He had never met Jock, but he had had dealings with quite a few other rich Northerners with Georgia holdings and had been unimpressed. He finally capitulated, but only on condition that he be allowed time to pursue his own scientific research and that he be allowed to run Whitney's estates—there was a permanent staff of seventy, fourteen indoor people and fifty-six outdoor—without interference from Whitney or anybody else. Komarek did not expect to be hired on those stern terms. He has run Whitney's Georgia operations ever since. He would maintain after thirty-five years on the job that Whitney had only six times given him instructions, and those on personal, not managerial, matters.

"Roy and I realized from the outset," Ed Komerek said in 1980, "that social changes were coming to America. You couldn't any longer run a plantation the way you might run a yacht, purely for pleasure, although

following morning, accordingly, Festing set off early and eagerly to inspect some of Whitney's sows—thirty of them, each with a fenced-off quarter-acre estate of her own. A high-ranking American general had flown over from Fort Benning, splendidly accoutered and beribboned, to pay his respects to the Englishman, and somewhat glumly agreed to accompany Sir Francis on an inspection of the pigs, each of which had just produced a litter. The titled visitor climbed over fence after fence to look over the new crop, the natty American in his wake, and Whitney's pig handlers, several of whom had been enlisted men in the armed forces, had a hard time suppressing their mirth as the two bestarred officers wallowed around knee-deep in pig muck.

I suppose some people still do. That sort of thing was neither socially desirable nor economically sensible. We followed basically what was the Herbert Stoddard proposition—that game-bird production and conservation had to be tied in with timber and agriculture, and that that had to be tied in with fire ecology. Mr. Whitney once sent Sam Park down to Thomasville to look over what we were doing, and Park said Greenwood looked to him like the greatest example of negligence he had ever seen. But what he hadn't grasped straight off was that the ground was *supposed* to look neglected; that was what the quail liked. And our stands of timber, far from being neglected, were to become the most valuable in the South, and they may be more valuable—we cut a million board feet a year without its being conspicuous—than the land they're on itself."

Komarek contended that whenever Betsey and Jock were in residence he could expect to put on five or ten pounds a week, because of the two fancy chefs they brought along. "I once told General Ike," the manager said, "that running a place like this is like running an army; everything that happens depends on the mess." The manager would become increasingly interested, as the years of his stewardship added up, in fire ecology. "Back in the thirties," he said, "government agencies were all hipped on what they called 'fire control.' They were just simply opposed to all fires. Now they've come around to thinking, logically, about 'fire management.'" Komarek would in later, more enlightened days, be invited, with Whitney's blessing, to lecture on fire management in Japan and India, Germany and Sweden, South Africa and western Australia. "Before I talked to the Bureau of Land Management in Alaska," he said, "the so-called experts up there were doing more damage to the land by putting out fires than the fires were doing."

At Thomasville, Komarek would periodically conduct burn shows, with wide-eyed observers in attendance from, at one time or another, practically every state in the Union and forty foreign nations, including Argentina, Botswana, Chile, Finland, Iran, Israel, Malaysia, Uganda, and the Soviet Union. Jimmy Carter took in one such demonstration while he was governor, and told Komarek afterward that if wood smoke was harmful to human beings south Georgia boys like himself would long since have been dead. One Russian spectator, a man identified to Komarek as the chief forester of his country, was so enchanted when he watched Komarek studiedly set fire, with a drip torch, to a stretch of Greenwood, that he grabbed the torch and ran off through the woods unscientifically trying to light up trees right and left. Komarek had to run him down, before he could do any irreparable mischief, like a hound after a wild boar.

When Komarek took over at Greenwood, the state of Georgia had about four million acres in corn, with average yields of about eight bush-

els an acre. The going price was a dollar a bushel. Every extra bushel
that an acre could grow would mean an extra four million dollars for
Georgia farmers. Komarek had had a long but largely unrequited love
affair with corn. "Corn is truly a symbol of America's greatness," he once
wrote. "Throughout history it has been the one crop that in its success or
failure touched in some manner the welfare of everyone in all the
Americas." Fortunately for him, the laird of his manor liked corn, too,
though Whitney was more enamored of it by the ear than the bushel.
And how could Whitney not respond affirmatively to a project that entailed the improvement of a breed?

Jock thus readily assented when Komarek proposed, in 1948, converting some of Greenwood's cleared fields into corn patches on which he
could experiment with a newfangled hybrid seed called Dixie 18. It was
a promising variety. Its yields were twenty-five bushels or more an acre.
Georgia farmers, though, were slow to embrace change. At first, they
wouldn't buy Dixie 18, and Komarek had to give it away—to 4-H Clubs
and young members of the Future Farmers of America who were less set
in their ways than most of their elders. Komarek packaged Dixie 18 in
six-pound bags and donated these to county agricultural agents, to use
in productivity contests. (There was also a Miss Dixie 18 beauty contest.)

The new strain caught on. Whitney, somewhat to his surprise, soon
found himself the proprietor of a million-dollar-a-year corn-seed business. (Jock's accountants in New York were surprised, too, being largely
unaware of the extent to which the sideline had burgeoned until they received a bill one day for a hundred and fifty thousand dollars' worth of
fertilizer.) Whitney offered to turn over the corn business entirely to
Komarek, but his fire man begged off. Louie Beard took over the management of Jock's new offshoot. After the Major's death, in 1954, the
hybrid corn operation was incorporated under the name of the Greenwood Seed Company. The columned façade of Whitney's house was
emblazoned on its seed sacks, along with a picture of a white-haired
Southern colonel, complete with ruddy cheeks, twinkling eyes, and Van-
dyke beard, who was dubbed—Whitney, so finicky about naming his
horses, somewhat uncharacteristically approved the choice—"Kernel
Greenwood."

Komarek had by then become president of the Georgia Crop Improvement Association and had his own regional television show, which was
devoted largely to agricultural uplift. In deference to the pine trees that
were the glory of the area—some of Whitney's stood a hundred and
twenty-five feet high and produced ninety-foot poles—Komarek next established a small scientific institute called the Tall Timbers Research Station. Its base of operations was at the loftiest point between Thomas-

ville and Tallahassee, and for that reason the local television channel also emplanted its transmitting tower there. (Komarek at once embarked on a study of why migratory birds persist in bumping into guy wires, a distressful state of affairs that has long baffled TV transmission managers and ornithologists.) The Research Station attracted scholars from numerous disciplines more or less related to tall timber; by 1980, Komarek was fairly certain that Tall Timbers boasted, among other acquisitions, the greatest earthworm library in North America. The bobwhite quail seminars the Research Station sponsored were generally conceded to be incomparable in their class.

There was a certain archness to the generals' shooting parties at Greenwood, which Eaker called "the Whitney Political Conference," and which consisted largely of dove, quail, wild turkey, and duck shooting; eating and drinking; and poker playing. Sending out notices of the reunion one year, Whitney's telegraphed invitations went, PEACE TALKS HAVE DEFINITELY BEEN SPURNED BY FEATHERED POPULATION. BOMBING WILL BE RESUMED WEDNESDAY 3 JANUARY AT LEAST UNTIL WEDNESDAY 10 JANUARY. HOPE YOUR BOMBSIGHT WILL BE IN GOOD WORKING ORDER AND AVAILABLE THAT DATE; and another year he began with SOUND THE BUGLE and went on, ornithologically, UNDERSTAND ENEMY WILL BE PRESENT IN OMINOUS STRENGTH. And Eaker had phrased his acceptance that year: REFERENCE YOUR CALL TO ARMS I ENLIST FOR DURATION. SINCE YOU JOINED ME IN ONE WAR ONLY FAIR THAT I JOIN YOU IN THIS ONE. Similarly, a bread-and-butter letter from Spaatz had told Whitney that "your army of veterans behaved most gallantly and met all problems under your inspiring leadership. Although losses were heavy in some of the actions, appropriate gains equalized the losses."

One year, some of the generals misbehaved. Georgia has strict game laws. While Dwight D. Eisenhower, for example, once was turkey hunting at the nearby plantation of Robert W. Woodruff, the doyen of Coca-Cola, he downed four birds in ninety seconds. The limit was two in twenty-four hours. Woodruff had had a game warden first make a mock arrest of that distinguished guest and then release him, on the ground that such marksmanship was impossible. Whitney took Curtis, Eaker, Hunter, and Spaatz duck shooting one morning in 1969, to a hundred-acre Thomasville enclave reserved exclusively for that diversion. The limit was four ducks per person. Whitney filled his quota early and went home. His generals were not especially good shots (they were flyers by trade, not snipers), but they were persevering, and they kept firing away and not, as if on a bombing raid, keeping precise count of the casualties they inflicted. When they finally called it a day, they were confronted by a flinty warden—a federal one, at that—who, upon examining their bag and ascertaining that each had exceeded his legal catch by a brace of birds, announced, not in jest, that they were all under arrest.

Each general was ultimately fined twenty-five dollars, which was especially embarrassing to Spaatz, who didn't much like bird shooting anyway (he preferred bird watching, and was a particular devotee of the indigenous red-cockaded woodpecker) and had long prided himself on being so law-abiding that he had never even received a traffic ticket. And here was the former Chief of Staff of the United States Air Force picked up on a federal charge! Whitney, always the perfect host, arranged for a lawyer to go to the Thomas County courthouse and pay the culprits' fines, and he made them all feel better that evening by hospitably losing at poker.

II

Your Uncle Jock Didn't Start Off with a Pushcart

For a man of Whitney's age, experience, and upbringing, achieving a colonelcy in a world-wide war was not exceptional. Undergoing captivity was something else again. For once in his life, he had found himself in a situation where his privileged position was worthless. He had been forced, willy-nilly, to become a common man. His sobering ordeal had been another watershed moment.

By the end of the war, both his parents were dead (so, too, in November 1945, was Bob Benchley); and when Jock turned forty, just a few days before he fell into Nazi hands, he had come into those substantial segments of his father's estate that until then had been held for him in trust. Helen Whitney's own estate, which was mainly divided between her son and daughter, amounted only to an additional six-million-odd dollars. Joan Payson was bequeathed her mother's properties at Saratoga and at Lexington, Kentucky, along with a Houdon bust of Voltaire. Joan and Jock each received one of their mother's two Kentucky Derby trophies. Jock got the Greentree estate and the Fifth Avenue mansion. He had no use for the latter and soon began to sell off its furnishings. He sold the house itself in 1949, and eventually it was carved up into apartments.

Jock and Betsey slowly brightened up the main residence at Greentree, which had been rather gloomy in his mother's last days; Helen had spent most of her time, as a near recluse, with curtains drawn, listening to radio broadcasts of Brooklyn Dodgers' baseball games, a glass often at her hand. Betsey proceeded with caution in redecorating her mother-in-law's home. After all, Jock had spent his boyhood there; grown men do not lightly tolerate radical change in such a setting. Betsey asked Jock, for instance, if it would be all right with him if she removed some of the hundreds of photographs that were arrayed in his mother's mammoth parlor. He finally consented to the displacement solely of those persons whom he couldn't recognize; but to make sure that he would not inadvertently cast out someone whose face *should* have been familiar, he had his valet Edgar Woodhams—who had joined the household before Jock was ten—help assign names to some of the hoarier pictures. There were forty-five unidentifiable photographs on top of a single bookcase. When Edgar turned ninety, in the spring of 1980, he reminded Jock, in a "Dear Mr. J.H.W." letter from his retirement home in Florida, of an incident that had occurred back in 1914 at the Payne Whitneys' Fifth Avenue ménage. "Your father was in his bedroom and I was in the pantry when his bell rang (I forgot to say it had been a very hot summer day also very humid). When I arrived at the bedroom what do you think I saw. Your father was sitting in his chair and Martin Bray [a servant] had a large tin bowl with a huge piece of ice in it, also an electric fan directed at the ice and blowing towards your father. I must have looked amazed, because your father said, 'Well, Edgar, isn't this the nuts.'" Jock would sometimes contend that Payne Whitney had, that sultry day, invented air conditioning.

In the immediate postwar months, what concerned Whitney most, as he embarked on his fifth decade, was how to allocate his time and energy and money. His wild oats were tamed. He had savored the special delights, and suffered the special heartbreaks, that close association with the Broadway stage and the Hollywood screen could confer. He was almost unimaginably rich. He had an income of several million dollars a year; and he would in due course become eligible for a sop the government then threw to those few exceptionally well-heeled and generous individuals who for ten consecutive years parted with at least ninety per cent of their taxable income annually in the form either of federal income taxes or charitable contributions; such people, as long as they remained in that category, were allowed—until the law was changed at the end of 1957—to take unlimited deductions for their contributions, instead of being held to the fifteen per cent maximum that applied to lesser philanthropists. That meant, in effect, that the headmaster of St. Bernard's or the rector of Groton or the president of Yale could become the happy recipient of funds that Whitney would otherwise have had to consign to the Secretary of the Treasury.

The mere fact of his being in a financial bracket so markedly different from that of most mortals sometimes made it awkward for Whitney to communicate easily with others; and he welcomed any opportunity to demonstrate that he was—well, human, and could deal with money on a human scale. Thus when a desk clerk at the Mayflower Hotel in Washington, who knew that he had something to do with thoroughbred racing, asked him while he was on a postwar trip to Washington to place a two-dollar bet for her on some horse she fancied in a forthcoming event at Aqueduct, Whitney was delighted by the request. He said he'd advance the money for the bet, and if she lost she could reimburse him when he was next in town. He was pleased even more, when her choice came in first, to be able to send along his personal check representing her winnings of one dollar and sixty cents.

There were, as Whitney picked up and sorted out the pieces of his civilian life and sought to rearrange them in an orderly, satisfying pattern for his maturity, the inevitable and insatiable demands on a man of his position and purse. He did not want to rush into a host of commitments. On September 16, 1945, still on active duty, he had written to William Woodward, the patriarch of The Jockey Club, who wanted him to take a leading part in the activities of that august body:

> . . . I hope you will know how deeply I appreciate your thought that I could be useful in an important place in the councils of the Club. I have not given light consideration to my decision. I am conscious of the legacy which you spoke about [the Whitney family's three-generational interest in horse racing] and the responsibility which it imposes on me to do what I can for the best interests of the thoroughbred sport. However, that same legacy has imposed wider and more compelling responsibilities which, if accepted at all, must be undertaken with all my energy—at least for the present.
>
> I have seen quite a number of men of business and, for that matter, men of war, who can manage affairs of importance by an occasional fleeting visit in which problems are analyzed and policies established without a ruffled hair or a waste of time. I cannot do that. . . . We have talked before of plans, which were then tentative in my mind, but which now have reached the point where my entire future activity depends on their formulation. I intend to give a year to the analysis of the direction of my future efforts. . . .

Yet, within that year of proposed introspection, Whitney had consented to become a special assistant, dealing largely with motion picture matters, to the Secretary of State; to become a member of the United

States National Commission for UNESCO (on analyzing the make-up of that group, he was perturbed to find that among its one hundred members there was no representative of youth, and he managed to get a delegate from America's 4-H Clubs added to its roster); and had accepted both the chairmanship of the board of the Museum of Modern Art and the vice-presidency of the New York Hospital. The latter his family had richly endowed, his father alone having blessed it with forty million dollars. (Jock's perturbation there resulted in the hospital's putting on *its* board its very first Jewish trustee.) When the German Shepherd Club of Long Island was granted permission a few years later to hold its annual field trials on the Greentree grounds, and in gratitude offered to contribute to a charity of Whitney's selection, he suggested the hospital; the Shepherds' shepherds' subsequent gift of twenty-five dollars came to one four-hundred-thousandth of what Whitney himself would donate to that institution over the ensuing years.

But all these were detours off the main road of his contemplation. While a prisoner of war, Whitney had been impressed, and distressed, by the seeming indifference of most of his fellow captives toward the broader aspects of the war. "German interrogators would ask me why we were fighting," Whitney told a friend afterward, "and I'd reply, 'For freedom,' and the Germans would say, 'Oh, you know perfectly well you don't have any more of it than we have.' And then these American kids with me would corroborate the Germans. I never heard one of our soldiers say he was fighting because of anything Hitler had done or for any moral reason. I decided that there must be a fundamental block in our educational system, and that I'd try to do something to overcome it."

Whitney resolved after considerable reflection to channel his resources in three main streams, which corresponded roughly to an informal analysis his friend Jeremy Tree once made: "For Jock, money has three purposes: to be invested wisely, to do good with, and to live well off." The pattern Whitney conceived for himself to follow involved, first, investing part of his fortune successfully enough to have means to support him, and his family after him, in comfort and, yes, luxury; second, to sustain and strengthen the capitalistic system that had so splendidly nurtured his forebears and him by the imaginative financing of new, small businesses with growth and profit potential; and, third, to establish an innovative foundation that, during his lifetime, could, according to its charter, "promote the development of knowledge and the application thereof to the improvement of social welfare."

The John Hay Whitney Foundation—originally, after the Georgia plantation, called the Greenwood—was unveiled in the winter of 1946. Whitney allocated two hundred thousand dollars to get it under way and pledged an additional hundred thousand over each of the next five years. It evolved as an unusual foundation, in that it received no further infusions of capital. Each year, Whitney would give it enough money to cover the following year's anticipated budget. After twenty years of existence, he was allotting to it, and it was disbursing, about a million dollars annually.

The foundation's very first grant, when it was still in an inchoate stage, was, in 1947, to the National Planning Association, which wanted to conduct a study of labor-management relations—a solid, conventional sort of foundation-funded research project. But that was not the sort of adventure that Whitney had hoped his eleemosynary money would embark on, or the sort he could get especially enthusiastic about. He spent a good deal of his time then consulting with experts who he hoped could chart a livelier course for the foundation's endeavors. He wanted it to be experimental, to take risks, and to devote itself principally, at least at the start, not to activities in the areas of the natural or social sciences, but to the humanities. "The humanities have been suffering lately in relation to the social sciences, you know," Jock said to an acquaintance who hadn't seen him since a prewar yearling sale at Saratoga Springs. Whitney's companion, who had no idea that Jock's interest in education went beyond the schooling of thoroughbred horses, mumbled that sure, sure, he knew. Whitney shortly engaged a conference room at the Waldorf and filled it with a score of eminent educators—among them the presidents of Yale and Sarah Lawrence, the dean of Barnard, and the chairman of the New York City Board of Higher Education—and for several stimulating hours moderated a discussion among them on the subject of what a foundation like his could do for the humanities.

One of Whitney's first principal consultants for the foundation was Edwin R. Embree, a onetime alumni registrar at Yale, who administered the Julius Rosenwald Fund. Another, until she retired, at eighty, in 1979, was Esther M. Raushenbush, a progressive educator who spent much of her academic life at Sarah Lawrence; she was its president from 1965 to 1969. She regarded Sarah Lawrence as an offbeat, uninhibited institution of learning; she was happy to spend twenty years as senior consultant to the John Hay Whitney Foundation, because she regarded it as an offbeat, uninhibited institution of *its* genre. (Whitney's daughters both attended Sarah Lawrence while Mrs. Raushenbush was there, but she had never met Jock and had never—very offbeat, very inhibited for the president of a private college—pressed him for a contribution. When Whitney learned in 1978, not from her, of the existence of a building-fund campaign to name a new library at Sarah Lawrence after her, he sent along a check for a hundred thousand dollars; Mrs. Raushenbush heard about it at second hand.)

Whitney had resolved from the outset that, whatever his foundation might accomplish, it should try, within its resources and capabilities, to ameliorate the plight of the disadvantaged. One of his early advisers was Charles S. Johnson, the president of Fisk University, at Nashville, Tennessee, one of the nation's leading black academies of higher learning. Whitney had met Dr. Johnson when both were members of the United States Commission for UNESCO. It was Johnson who was in large measure responsible for the inception, in 1950, of the John Hay Whitney Foundation Opportunity Fellowships, which went to individuals from minority groups who had already shown some promise in their chosen field—most had already graduated from college—but who with outside support seemed likely to get wherever they were destined to go more quickly and less painfully.

Whitney told a friend, while the Opportunity Fellowship program was in formulation, that as his grandfather John Hay had established an open-door policy in the Far East, so did he hope to open doors at home. (A characteristic reaction, when the fellowships were announced, was that of the Wheeling, West Virginia, *Intelligencer*, which wrote about them under the headline "Millionaire Strikes Blow at Racial Bias.") Whitney and Johnson remained close. The educator became a trustee of the foundation. In 1953, at the Fisk commencement exercises over which Johnson presided, Whitney gave the principal address. (Befitting the occasion, Whitney was awarded an honorary degree. Over the years, he was similarly anointed by Colgate, Columbia, Kenyon, Yale, the University of Exeter—in England—and, in 1958, by Brown, in celebration of the hundredth anniversary of John Hay's graduation from that university.)

The first administrator of the Opportunity Fellowship program was another black who had demonstrably made much of his opportunities— Robert C. Weaver, professor of economics at the New York University School of Education, pioneer in federal interracial housing programs, and, later, Secretary of Housing and Urban Development in Lyndon Johnson's Cabinet. Nearly all the Opportunity Fellows, who received grants of from one to three thousand dollars per annum, were from underprivileged groups: blacks, Chicanos, American Indians, Chinese-Americans, Japanese-Americans, displaced persons, Micronesians, and natives of some of the less prosperous foothills of the Appalachians. Between 1950 and 1971, there were nine hundred and fifty-three Fellows. Every one, at the time he or she received a grant, was relatively obscure. "We've never given a penny to any established person," Esther Raushenbush once proudly declared. Quite a few Fellows ended up as very established persons indeed: the opera singers Grace Bumbry and Shirley Verrett (Leontyne Price was about to accept a fellowship when she was offered a Metropolitan Opera Company contract); the economist Andrew

F. Brimmer, who became a member of the Federal Reserve Board; the painter Seong Moy; the federal judge A. Leon Higginbotham; the lawyers Marian Wright Edelman and Julius LeVonne Chambers; the New York City Commissioner of Human Rights Eleanor Holmes Norton; the anthropologist Elliott Skinner, a United States Ambassador to Upper Volta;* and the Mexican-American Domingo Dominguez, who after earning his doctoral degree at the University of New Mexico wrote to a friend at the Whitney Foundation office, "I am the first Ph.D. in the entire history of my ancestors."

Not long after launching its Opportunity Fellowships, the foundation embarked on additional programs, all geared toward supporting individuals in the humanities. From 1951 to 1965 there were seventy-one Fulbright professors—academicians who were treated to one-year lectureships at liberal arts colleges and universities in countries other than their own. (The foundation also arranged orientation sessions for those coming to the United States, in the course of which they were warned, for instance, that it was not the habit of American students to rise from their chairs and snap to attention when a professor entered a classroom; and that failure to observe this nicety should not be interpreted as disrespect.) There was another program that gave professors at large American universities who had reached retirement age a chance to go on teaching, under Whitney sponsorship, at smaller institutions that couldn't afford men and women of their caliber and credentials; after one hundred and twenty-four retirees had availed themselves of this chance— Professor John Collier going from the City College of New York to Knox College, Professor Clarence Hamilton from Oberlin to Hamilton, Professor Helen Sandison from Vassar to Washington College—that program was abandoned, in large part because the teachers' original employers concluded that, if these savants were such coveted catches, it would make sense to find something for them to do, on *emeritus* status, back where they'd started from.

Then, beginning in 1952, there were the John Hay Fellowships. These grants were bestowed upon high school teachers; they got leaves of absence so they could pursue their studies at some university. Yale and Columbia each agreed, at the beginning, to accept ten John Hay Fellows. Harvard, Northwestern, and the University of Chicago joined in. Over a fourteen-year stretch, more than two thousand John Hay Fellows received altogether more than six million dollars. Most of the necessary funds were furnished by the Ford Foundation; it was one of the few in-

* After the 1952 elections, Whitney wanted Dwight Eisenhower to give an ambassadorial appointment to Dr. Johnson; but some members of the black community convinced the new President's staff that Whitney's candidate was too liberal for the Administration.

stances of a foundation's making a grant to another foundation. (McGeorge Bundy, the head of the Ford Foundation during the latter part of this program, would write Whitney some years afterward that "the work that your people do really is extraordinary in its combination of taste and venturousness, and they set an example that has a lot of influence in other foundations.") Whitney Griswold, the president of Yale in 1957, told Jock then that the John Hay Fellowship project was "the best single program of its kind in the United States, and, like the mustard seed in the Bible, is spreading its fruit in all directions."

The Whitney Foundation began to change its own direction in 1968. The shift in course was chiefly attributable to the foundation's coming under the stewardship of Archibald L. Gillies, a liberal Republican who had worked in various capacities, at home and abroad, for Nelson Rockefeller, and whom Whitney met that year while Jock was raising funds for Rockefeller's short-lived presidential campaign. (Whitney and Gillies would soon discover that they had another bond of sorts. It had been Gillies' father-in-law, Philip Boyer, Jr., who had been playing court tennis with Payne Whitney in 1927 when Whitney *père* was fatally stricken.) When Whitney offered Gillies the superintendency of his foundation, it was dispensing only about a hundred thousand dollars annually because Jock was then phasing out his fellowship program; Gillies made it a condition of his acceptance that the foundation would spend ten times as much. From 1974 on, the outlay hovered around the million-dollar mark.

Moreover, Gillies argued persuasively, the foundation should now consider switching its priorities from assisting individuals to improve their own lot—however admirable a concept that had been—to assisting them to improve their communities. (As one Mexican-American Opportunity Fellow rhetorically put it at a conference Gillies convened of alumni of that program, the Whitney Foundation had concerned itself for twenty-five years with the humanities; it was time now for it to concern itself with inhumanities.) If, say, the residents of a certain block in a certain ghetto wanted to enhance their sanitation services, the effort wouldn't require much in the way of financial support; but it was not the sort of proposal that most foundations would embrace. The Whitney Foundation, being relatively small and inherently flexible, could, Gillies convinced Jock, underwrite just that kind of thing.

On a broader scale, it was Gillies' contention, which Whitney came to share, that "foundations are not facing basic political and economic questions"; and some statistics that were compiled in 1972 and 1973 by a Commission on Private Philanthropy and Public Needs supported this view: of all foundation grants made in those two years, only seven tenths of one per cent related to political and governmental reform, and only three tenths of one per cent to economic matters. But to get into that kind of activity, Gillies issued an early warning, could cause difficulties, "usually because the project recommendations call for changes that mean some other part of the society has to give something up." There were social questions, too, that Gillies thought the foundation ought to help to face: for example, what were the attitudes of law-enforcement agencies and other authorities toward different kinds of emotionally handicapped children having trouble in school; was it true, as one researcher suspected and wanted funds to investigate, that if such children were white they were given special tutoring, but if they were black they were said to be maladjusted and often as not ended up in jail?

In working out the new order of things, Whitney and Gillies besought the counsel of, among other knowledgeable community leaders, two blacks—Vernon Jordan, of the Urban League; and, especially, Franklin A. Thomas, of the Bedford-Stuyvesant Restoration Corporation, which had been set up in 1967 to refurbish the squalid condition of one of Brooklyn's sorriest slums. A towering lawyer who had played basketball at Columbia, later a deputy police commissioner of New York City, Thomas had met Whitney while he was trying to raise funds for a cable television project that his Development Corporation hoped would brighten the quality of Bedford-Stuyvesant life. Thomas had needed a hundred thousand dollars for a feasibility study, and Whitney had unblinkingly proffered him that sum—not through the foundation but from his personal philanthropic funds.

Thomas, like Jordan, soon became a trustee of the Whitney Foundation—for a spell, while Gillies was unsuccessfully running for the New York City Council, he actually ran the operation—and also a close Whitney family friend. He once described himself to Whitney's daughter Kate as "someone who has been touched by Jock's special magic." Thomas' intimate connection with the Whitney Foundation was doubtless significant when in 1979 the trustees of the Ford Foundation selected him to succeed McGeorge Bundy as the president of that flowing cornucopia of philanthropy.

One of the projects that evolved from the foundation's revamped approach—ultimately, a two-hundred-thousand-dollar one—was a study conducted by two radical economists, Gar Alperowitz and Jeff Faux, a complex intellectual analysis of possible economic alternatives to the capitalistic system. "Are there ways to include those who are ordinarily excluded in economic decision making and in ownership of elements of the economy [in participating in the system]?" a Whitney Foundation report asked in introducing this project. "We see a need for both research and public discussion related to how people can participate in and change the economic system that is part of their daily lives." The implications of all that, of course, were enough to make some of Whitney's capitalistic cronies tremble, but he himself had no known qualms; his only stipulation was that whatever the researchers did they should do well. (A few of the foundation's trustees had qualms of their own about even offering this study for Whitney's consideration; and when he calmly gave it his blessing, they were momentarily overcome by giddiness and began making jokes, among these the invention of a newspaper headline that went "Jock Knocks Exxon.")

Among the less expensive grants that were approved under the new scheme were one for a group that wanted to strengthen enforcement of landownership reform laws in the San Joaquin Valley of California; and another, in the same state, for the organization of a laboratory to develop Spanish-language learning materials for the elementary grades in the school system of San José. An investigation of discrimination against women by mining companies in the Appalachians was conducted under the Whitney aegis. So, in due course, was the attempt by an ex-convict and reformed dope addict to rehabilitate a block in East Harlem. That one was budgeted at $31,000. The foundation gave $45,000 for the organization of tenants in a black section of New Orleans; $32,000 to an Italian woman in New York who wanted to advocate and protect the rights of welfare recipients in her neighborhood; $16,250 to further the efforts of a Quilters' Co-operative on the fringe of Los Angeles; and $37,500 to nurture a New Haven, Connecticut, food co-operative, one of the organizers of which was a fellow who had been a particularly prickly student activist at Yale in the early 1970s, when Whitney had been the Senior Fellow of Yale's governing corporation.

In all these bubbling foundation activities, Whitney did not much participate on a day-to-day basis. True, he did occasionally entertain recipients of his largess—he once gave a party for several hundred Opportunity Fellows—and he made a point of buying a painting once a year from some artist he had supported; but by and large he entrusted the routine operations of his foundation, as he did in others of his many spheres of interest, to the associates he had picked and in whose judgment he reposed confidence. Even so, the foundation that bore his name and was sustained solely by his beneficence was very much his own; and every now and then a beneficiary would thank him personally for the opportunities he had created. Thus, the American Indian writer and political activist Vine Deloria, Jr., who had first received a Whitney Foundation grant in 1972 for a study of Indian land claims, told Whitney in 1978:

> . . . I thought it might be a good idea to write you a letter summarizing some of what has taken place in the past six years and to express my per-

sonal thanks for everything you have done for me, for other Indians, and for people in general.

The past ten years were very traumatic for American Indians. We were really unprepared to deal with the sudden emergence in the communications media which the early seventies thrust upon us as the decade of activism drew to a close. Many of the problems that Indians have are longstanding problems generated primarily by the events of the past and not capable of easy or quick solutions. Yet the sixties seemed to have the temper of rapid movement and simple answers, and the fundamental intellectual and research work was not done in most instances. Thus it was very surprising and pleasing for me to meet the members of the Whitney Foundation. Universally they saw that problems were complicated, difficult to resolve, and generally required almost exact timing in the presentation of any possible solutions. I was then impressed, and I continue to be impressed, with the intelligence and forward-looking attitude of the foundation in this respect.

. . . I think the work you have consistently done over the past thirty years has been very important. Most important, as I see it, is that the foundation has not chosen to chase every sexy issue that surfaced but continued long lines of basic sound theory for many years and allowed many people to participate in the programs of the foundation. This kind of stability is very productive in the long run. I can think of dozens of foundations who approached me during the past decade and wanted to fund the "most important" Indian project. . . . Without naming any specific names, let me just say that the track record of some of the larger foundations is very poor in this respect, and their projects have not been fruitful. Human beings need the chance to grow and mature in their thoughts and actions, and the Whitney Foundation has encouraged this growth for many, many individuals and this has been very important. . . .

In the foundation's annual report covering the year from July 1, 1978, to June 30, 1979—a report that stated unequivocally, "Individuals submitting proposals should come from those groups that experience racial, gender, or economic discrimination"—Whitney independently signed a declaration about the recipients of his generosity: "Most of them have lived with adversity in the form of poverty or discrimination. They lean toward a practical vision of helping friends and neighbors work together on common and immediate problems rather than toward grand plans for social change." He noted that a number of foundation-backed projects had enjoyed governmental co-operation. "The point I want to make," he continued, "is that these two elements complement each other and are not, as some would have us believe, contradictory. Our American tradition of individual responsibility and our belief in using the public power and the public purse to help human beings whose interests have been neglected blend in interesting ways in the projects outlined in this report. I suspect that neither element can be truly effective without the other."

And in an introduction, written in November 1980, to the foundation's annual report for the previous year, Whitney firmly reiterated his views: "Central to the philosophy of the Foundation is its desire to help people achieve social and economic justice, with particular focus on the problems of minority persons and poor people and with a special concern [his wife and daughters were among the nine trustees] for equality of opportunity for women. This interest in those who experience discrimination in our country because of race or gender or economic condition guides the Trustees in choosing among many applicants for funds; unless this concern is reflected in a proposal to the Foundation, we are unlikely to respond favorably." It would have been hard to imagine Jock's father, or either of his grandfathers, or his great-uncle Oliver Payne, subscribing to such sentiments.

Whitney liked to have his life tidily organized. There were specific times of the year to be at Saratoga Springs, or at Thomasville, or in London; his friends could check a calendar and be fairly certain where to try to reach him. It was much the same, in the early postwar years, on a day-to-day basis: when he was in New York, more or less his home base, his mornings would be devoted to museums, hospitals, universities, and other philanthropic interests; his afternoons to the venture capital firm, J. H. Whitney & Company, that he founded concurrently with his foundation. He created the company in February 1946, writing a check for five million dollars to the order of J. H. Whitney & Company, and that May he reinforced its capital with a second five million dollars. The company, which was by design on the small side—it would never have more than forty employees—rented office space in Rockefeller Center, at 630 Fifth Avenue; the partners' dining room was paneled in butternut wood stripped from the Payne Whitneys' Fifth Avenue mansion and was decorated with some of Jock's paintings from his early American period.

Whitney soon surprised a few of his partners by urging them to hire some black secretaries. That was not easy to do in those days. The employment agencies that dealt with investment houses and banks did not customarily have any black applicants available. But J. H. Whitney & Company did find a few. One stayed with the firm for thirty-two years, until she retired; another, fired for incompetence, formally charged the firm with having violated the Fair Employment Practices Act, but she dropped her case after a black lawyer delegated to investigate it agreed that she *was* incompetent.

Initially, J. H. Whitney & Company had five partners, among them Jock's trusted money men, Dick Croft and Sam Park. None of the founding partners except Whitney put in any capital; the other four were to divide up one third of the firm's profits, if any; Whitney was to get two thirds. (In due course, several partners acquired an equity in the company, consisting of profits they could have taken out but elected instead to reinvest in it.) The partners, and no others, were eligible to play in an extremely exclusive annual golf tournament Whitney inaugurated; the trophy they competed for was a sterling silver replica of the front door to their premises. Whitney himself won the tournament twice, though his best score ever on a demanding course was a 78. On hearing of those two victories, Shipwreck Kelly observed that Napoleon had taken a chess champion along on some of his campaigns, and that the Emperor, curiously, had never been defeated by the master.

Another of the original partners was Benno C. Schmidt, Jr., who became managing partner in 1960. Twenty years after that, still running the firm, Schmidt would reflect, not without pride, that Whitney's ten-million-dollar stake in that enterprise had turned out to be the single most profitable investment Jock had ever made. It was a private company, not given to or required to make precise disclosures; but the probability was that Whitney's ten-million-dollar ante had increased tenfold.

A native of Texas, Schmidt had graduated from the University of Texas and its law school, had taught law there and at Harvard, and had worked, before Pearl Harbor, for the War Production Board. Later, in London, where he was a colonel serving as deputy purchasing agent for the army in the European theatre, he had gotten to know Whitney's close associate and personal lawyer Bill Jackson. Schmidt, though, had never met Whitney, and the Texan was therefore surprised just after the war, when he had returned to civilian life as general counsel of the Economics Division of the State Department, to receive a phone call in Washington that began, "I'm John Hay Whitney." Schmidt said yes, he had heard the name. Whitney said he was in Washington, and could they dine together that evening? Schmidt, wondering what this could be all about, said yes, he was free. They agreed to meet at the Mayflower. "You can recognize me because I'll have a ruptured duck in my lapel," Whitney said.

Several million other Americans were then wearing that emblem of military service, but Schmidt read the newspapers; he had seen plenty of photographs of a white-tied Whitney at a charity ball, of a tweedy Whitney leading a horse into the winner's circle, of a Whitney in khaki surrounded by Air Force generals; he said he would look for the ruptured duck.

At dinner, Whitney said he was about to launch a venture-capital company and wondered if Schmidt would care to come aboard. Schmidt was perplexed. He had never had any business experience at all. "Sure, I'm interested," he said, "but don't be surprised if somebody brings me a balance sheet and I say, 'What's that?'"

"Don't worry," Whitney replied. "We'll learn together."

It was not until years later that Schmidt got around to asking Whitney why he had phoned him in the first place. After all, in those immediate postwar days there were dozens of experienced men who were fresh out of the armed forces, seeking new opportunities, ripe for the plucking. Whitney then told Schmidt that within a short period Bill Jackson and two other men whose judgment he respected had separately spoken highly to him of the Texas lawyer. The three unsolicited and unconnected testimonials had sent Whitney to the telephone. Nearly thirty-five years after that exploratory dinner at the Mayflower, Schmidt, by then a pillar himself of finance and philanthropy—chairman of the board of trustees of the Memorial Hospital for Cancer and Allied Diseases, director of the Columbia Broadcasting System, trustee of the Whitney Museum and the Carnegie Fund for International Peace—would tell an acquaintance that over that three-decade stretch Whitney and he had had a relationship about as close to perfect as it was possible for two business associates and, by then, close friends ever to hope to enjoy.

Just as Whitney's foundation had as one of its paramount objectives backing people who were unlikely to obtain funds elsewhere, so was it a primary purpose of his venture capital company to invest in chancy enterprises of limited appeal to conventional sources of financing. Whitney felt strongly that a vigorous postwar influx of new businesses was vital to the dynamics of the capitalistic economy that had so handsomely enabled him to consider doing something along such lines. The prospective entrepreneurs who had conceived new businesses should, moreover, he believed, have access not merely to capital but to knowledgeable managerial advice. As matters stood, commercial banks were generally disinclined, in 1946, to give loans for dreams; investment banks were mainly interested in getting new businesses far enough off the ground to float issues for their stock; large industrial companies were usually interested in neophyte ones only if they could expect to buy them out or swallow them up. There really seemed to be nowhere for businessmen with fresh ideas to go except to wealthy individuals, and those individuals rarely had the facilities to examine and screen propositions or provide skilled managerial assistance.

So Whitney had started up his ten-million-dollar company. He and his partners were prepared to take risks and to take losses. They hoped they'd have enough successes to offset the failures they deemed inevitable. A number of financial experts whose views Jock besought had grave reservations about his perceptions of success; they argued that, however idealistic his notion of a venture capital business might be, surely—like most prosperous investment banking houses—he would need a brokerage department or a bond-trading department to provide his company with a bread-and-butter income base while it was embarking on its more fanciful, unpredictable flights. Whitney refused to share that pessimistic view, and he had the solid support of Benno Schmidt, who, ignorant at the start about business and having no money of his own to speak of, had no inhibitions to shuck and little to lose.

When a latter-day partner tried in 1963—long after J. H. Whitney & Company had been widely acknowledged to be a thumping success and had inspired the creation of many other such firms, among these Jock's sister's Payson & Trask—to spell out the credo that governed the firm's operations, he stated that "it is difficult to set down any very meaningful standards as to the types of business ventures which we will or will not go into. The range of our potential interest is wide. We will look at any business proposition which offers the possibility of using our capital *and organization* constructively. We do not work with other people's money and we have neither stockholders nor customers, so we are free to make any venture-capital investment which has a special appeal to us. To have a special appeal, it must offer the prospect of being satisfying, of being something with which we will be happy to be associated while it is going on, and proud to have been a part of when it is completed; and to meet this test it must offer the prospect of being profitable. We are not commercial bankers, investment bankers, underwriters, brokers, or investment counselors; we are venture capitalists—ready to use the combination of capital and entrepreneurial effort to create profitable and constructive new enterprises."

Replying to a friend who had congratulated him on the new company in March 1946, Whitney himself had put it more succinctly: "I think we can maintain a balance between the desperate temptation to point the finger of capitalistic rectitude at each proposition offered, as against the dizzy urgency of security."

Some of the original investments of J. H. Whitney & Company were ones it inherited from Jock himself. There was Sanoderm, for instance, a cultured-milk product that was supposed, when swallowed, to cure acne. A dentist had brought it to Whitney's attention back in 1937, and he had put $18,000 into it. But the magic potion got nowhere, not even after J. H. Whitney & Company took it over and tried to dehydrate it, as Minute Maid orange juice was so rewardingly dehydrated. The venture capital firm also took over Whitney's investment in Minute Maid. It was in connection with negotiations for one Florida orange grove that Schmidt displayed the sort of tanginess that Whitney had hoped he would bring to the fledgling firm. The grove was owned by a man who had started off his business career as a pushcart peddler, and a nephew was negotiating on his behalf. The Whitney company's principal negotiator was Alexander Standish, an early associate of the firm, whom Jock had met while both were wartime intelligence officers (Standish had ranked first in their training course at Harrisburg); and Standish kept being frustrated by the nephew's continually interrupting their haggling, on the ground that he had to telephone his uncle Joe for instructions. At an ensuing partners' meeting, Standish reported that a stalemate existed, that the uncle's asking price, as relayed by the nephew, was utterly unreasonable. Schmidt heard him out and then said, "You go back and tell him that your uncle Jock didn't start off with a pushcart, and he doesn't intend to end up with one, either."

The very first major investment that J. H. Whitney & Company made on its own—a $1,250,000 commitment—turned out to be a bonanza. As a result of that golden strike, the firm more than doubled its capital before it was a year old, and never again did it have to worry about earning, so to speak, its bread and butter. This venture was the Spencer Chemical Company. During the war, the government had built a synthetic nitrogen plant at Pittsburg, Kansas, to extract nitrates from natural gas for use in explosives. At the end of the war, the now surplus facility had been leased to the man in charge of it, Kenneth A. Spencer, a coal-mining executive. He wanted to convert it into a plant to make fertilizers, but he was short of funds. Spurred on by an invigorating infusion of Whitney capital, Spencer ultimately bought the plant and began profitably turning out ammonia, methyl alcohol, and other useful synthetics. In time, Spencer Chemical acquired a number of additional surplus installations, from the government, at bargain prices; and the company burgeoned marvelously. In the spring of 1950, J. H. Whitney & Company sold a substantial portion of its Spencer holdings for six and a half million dollars, but for some years it retained a stock interest that was still worth more than triple its original outlay.

During the firm's first decade of operations, it was approached by 5,750 individuals or groups desirous of its succor. It actually invested in sixty of these propositions, of which thirty-one—a healthy number, by its lights—proved to be profitable. It was a *sine qua non* of the firm's investment philosophy that it would keep a vigilant eye on the management of any enterprise it got involved with and would have appropriate representation on its board of directors. After another ten years, the partners could anticipate that they would receive about two hundred propositions annually that were worth thinking about at all, with perhaps fifty or sixty of these meriting serious study and reflection. About half of *those* would be *very* seriously scrutinized, and ultimately about ten, on an average, would be tapped for an investment of anywhere from two hundred and fifty thousand dollars to two and a half million. In that initial decade,

Whitney took an active role in the deliberations. "Jock was good enough at evaluating business prospects," Schmidt once said, "and he was all but infallible at spotting first-class people and also phonies. He had extraordinary insights about individuals, and, of course, his unusual financial situation provided him with more total objectivity than most of us are privileged to enjoy. He would sit in on a meeting with a bunch of applicants and come out and say he didn't want to have anything to do with them, because he regarded it as important whether or not an association with this or that person would be pleasant and would be fun. Otherwise, no dice. He would say, 'That bastard will probably make some money out of that scheme, but not with me.'"

Among the eventual rejectees who came around with high hopes were a man who had compounded a substance that, rubbed on the bottoms of shoes, was supposed to render them impervious to wear and do away with the necessity of ever resoling them; a man who had a drill that would go down a thousand feet and would, he insisted before being gently ushered out, awaken the dead; and a man who wanted to organize a nationwide chain of high-class bawdy houses. Some such propositions could be turned down, obviously, with trifling expenditures of time and money; others were discouraged only after lengthy and costly research. On one occasion, the firm spent a hundred thousand dollars, over a twelve-month period, looking into a revolutionary way of manufacturing bricks, before deciding not to subsidize it. In another instance, Whitney and his colleagues sank three hundred and forty thousand dollars in a film-making concern that they optimistically believed might become a flourishing rival of Eastman Kodak. Instead, they lost their entire stake. Before deciding to underwrite the inventor of a new kind of portable power saw, the company conducted eighty interviews and watched twenty demonstrations. Most such investigations were and would continue to be carried out by bright young associates—among them, at one stage, a fellow who'd been first in his class at M.I.T., another who was first at the Harvard Business School, and a third who squeezed in even though he was only second in his class at Harvard Law. The firm forthwith invested in a Harvard Business course for *him*.

There were more than enough hits, however, to carry the flops. The company's comparatively modest investment of forty-five thousand dollars in another chemical firm, for example, was liquidated after seven and a half years for three and a half million. There were notable successes in oil, in seaweed (from which chemicals useful for the food industry could be derived), in data processing, and in western Australian wasteland, of which, starting in 1960, J. H. Whitney & Company and some affiliates owned a million and a half acres. The land was so infertile when they got it that it couldn't produce enough forage even for kangaroos to graze on. But by the time the consortium had analyzed it and burned it off and fertilized and plowed and planted it, they had made that desert bloom, and their investment blossom, too. Looking back over the first thirty-odd years of the history of J. H. Whitney & Company, Schmidt—who ended up as a co-owner, with David Rockefeller, of a sixteen-thousand-acre showplace cattle ranch on that once dismal Australian tract—reflected, "It would be interesting if somebody could ever compute what Jock's original ten million dollars gave rise to—the dozens of new businesses created, the jobs generated in the tens of thousands, the millions made by managers, and the hundreds of millions spun off both in profits and corporate taxes. And all this, mind you, from what by almost any financial reckoning was a puny initial stake. It's remarkable what ten million dollars' worth of seed money, well administered for over thirty years, can do."

12

Being a Horse and Being Owned by a Whitney Is a Very Nice Thing

In a family where tradition and precedent counted for so much, it was practically a foregone conclusion that Whitney would race horses, and would do so on a formidable scale. His Whitney grandfather had been the leading American money winner and had built up Aiken, South Carolina, as an agreeable breeding ground for the American version of the sport of kings. Jock's uncle Harry was the pre-eminent stable owner of *his* generation. In the 1941 running of the Hopeful Stakes at Saratoga, five of the eight horses that went to the post belonged to Whitneys. Entries of Mrs. Payne Whitney finished first and second. Joan Whitney Payson took show money, and one of Jock's own horses came in fourth. A couple of outside nags somehow slipped through to beat out a horse carrying the silks of cousin Sonny. When the sportswriters called Jock's mother the First Lady of the American Turf, it was a title not lightly bestowed; it was roughly equivalent to her friend Babe Ruth's "the Sultan of Swat." Along with Helen's two triumphs in the Kentucky Derby—with Twenty Grand in 1931, with Shut Out in 1942—she won at least one running of every other big stake race in the United States. For many years, her contract jockey was Eddie Arcaro, an authentic sultan of the saddle. In

Shut Out's Derby year, Helen's Greentree Stable led all others in America in winnings, with $414,432. That year, she made Jock a thirty-per-cent partner in the operation and gave Joan a fifteen-per-cent share. On Helen's death in 1944, she willed the remainder of all her horse-racing and -breeding interests to her children. It was for both of them a legacy not to be trifled with.

Joan already had a stable of her own in the United States. She never cared about racing in England. Jock, of course, had already been highly visible on the racing scene of two continents—abroad, as one of a scarce handful of outsiders (the old Aga Khan was another) admitted to honorary membership in the Jockey Club of Great Britain; at home as the youngest member ever of the American Jockey Club, to which he was admitted at twenty-four; as an officer of the Westchester Racing Association and of the New York Racing Commission; and, from 1934 on, as an executive of the American Thoroughbred Breeders Association, of which for many years he was president and his cousin-by-marriage Alfred Gwynne Vanderbilt vice-president. (The association was even further a quasi-family affair: Major Louie Beard was its secretary-treasurer and chief operating functionary.) The association published the magazine *Blood Horse:* whatever profits the journal made went into research on horse diseases. Whitney and Vanderbilt were regarded in racing circles as men capable of effectively reconciling the often disparate concerns of stable owners and two-dollar bettors. At Belmont Park, which was operated by the Westchester Racing Association, it was Whitney, for instance, who neatly handled this liaison role by bringing about a fifty-cent reduction in the price of general-admission tickets to the track and, concurrently, an increase in the purses for some of the major stakes there.

Even in the 1930s, in the world of horse racing, commercialism was, so to speak, in the saddle, and few people could bring themselves to refer without snickering to the archaic, high-minded notion that the purpose of racing was, as Whitney and Vanderbilt genuinely believed it to be, the improvement of the breed of horses. Their attitude toward what had previously been primarily a gentlemanly pastime was still resolutely gentlemanly. Eddie Arcaro would say flatly in 1950 that they were the only two remaining sportsmen extant in horse racing in the United States. (The jockey would probably have included Joan Payson had he been thinking in terms of sportswomen.) A couple of years before that, Whitney and Vanderbilt, trying to democratize the regal sport, had actually signed contracts, as stable owners, with a trade union; some of the crustier members of The Jockey Club referred to the pair of them as the Young Turks.

Jock's own domestic stable, at the time of his mother's death, was a relatively modest one, based at Lexington, Kentucky, where in 1926 his father had bought some land adjoining the existing horse farm of his brother Harry—the same year in which Payne Whitney had given Jock, fresh out of Yale, two thoroughbred yearlings as a twenty-second-birthday present. Jock incorporated his stable, which he called Mare's Nest Farm, into the Greentree one, and Joan put in her own string, and after all these principalities were consolidated under one flag the brother emerged as a sixty-three-per-cent owner of Greentree, the sister with thirty-seven per cent. In effect, though, they were equal, trusting, sharing partners.

Jock and Joan soon employed, as their contract jockey, the gifted Ted Atkinson, who had gone to work for Helen as a stableboy in 1936, and who for eleven years would wear the Greentree silks. (Jock's personal ones, when he was racing on his own, had been a slight variation of his mother's—pink, black and white sleeve stripes, white cap.) The new owners of Greentree had further inherited their mother's trainer, John M. Gaver, who had begun working for the First Lady of the Turf in 1930. Gaver was an unusually cultured trainer. He had graduated from Princeton, in 1924, and before getting into the education of horses had been a prep school Spanish teacher. His relationship with Jock was solid and constant. It might be difficult in the ensuing years for an officer of the John Hay Whitney Foundation or a partner of J. H. Whitney & Company to reach Jock by telephone, but Gaver talked to him, wherever Whitney was, almost every day. It seemed only meet and proper to Jock, for whom racing was more of a family affair than a business, that when in 1978 Gaver retired (to a Greentree Stud residence at Aiken), he should be succeeded by his son John, Jr.

There were two operations, actually. There was the Greentree Stable, its summer headquarters on Long Island, near the Belmont track, and its winter quarters at Aiken and at Hialeah, in Florida, with fifty or sixty thoroughbreds in training at any given time; and there was from 1944 on the Greentree Stud, at Lexington—with, on average, seven stallions, fifty brood mares, and thirty-five weanlings. Major Beard was in charge of the stud at its inception, and when he retired and moved to the Georgia plantation to run that establishment, it was only logical, in the Whitney scheme of things, for him to be succeeded at first by *his* son Clarkson. Jock often attended sales of yearlings at Saratoga and Keeneland, but he did not enjoy racing horses he had bought as much as ones he had bred. The Greentree Stud—run from 1958 on by the aptly named Robert L. Green—occupied seven hundred and fifty grassy acres in Kentucky, and it also maintained a training area for young horses at Aiken, where there were traffic lights at the principal animal crossings. "We don't want no two-thousand-dollar cars crashing into no two-hundred-thousand-dollar horses," a stable hand at Aiken once told a visitor. (When Jock's sister died, in 1975, Joan's interest in the Greentree Stud was inherited by her husband, who had never shown much interest in horses. Five years later, Jock bought out Charles Shipman Payson's share of the ownership.)

Breeding was the main activity in Kentucky, but the stud farm also served as a retirement home for a few old horses, no longer useful either for racing or breeding, to whom Jock and Joan, like their mother before them, were sentimentally attached. Helen called these revered senior citizens the Gas House Gang, a baseball name borrowed from the St. Louis Cardinals, and her children carried on that tradition and that terminology. But sometimes there was no room at the inn. So they would often give horses away—horses that, while they were perfectly sound and would be perfectly acceptable for riding, couldn't because of one undesirable physical trait or another be raced and were deemed inferior for breeding. (These gift horses would arrive without a foal certificate from The Jockey Club, which meant they were no longer considered thoroughbreds; nor could any offspring they might have be thus described.) Or there might be a horse with what stable owners called "a case of the slows"—an otherwise fit animal that simply couldn't run very fast. Among the lucky recipients were friends, veterinarians, mounted policemen, blacksmiths (one of these, appropriately, getting a horse that had bad feet), and various institutions that conducted anatomical equine research. Two or three expendable Greentree horses would go each year to the University of Kentucky Experiment Station. On learning that a Greentree horse had arrived at the Veterinary Medicine School of the University of Georgia, an eleven-year-old girl in Hamilton, Georgia, once wrote Whitney that she would like one, too, maybe one worth a hundred dollars. He had to disappoint her: he had no other horses to distribute at that moment, and he had probably never had any that could still stand up and was worth so little.

Among the especially fortunate donees was a friend of John Gaver, Donald W. Griffin, the secretary of Princeton's National Alumni Association. Griffin once even got a horse named Donald. Princeton has long prided itself on its non-partisan attitude toward the Civil War. Inscribed in marble in the atrium of the university's main administration building, Nassau Hall, are the names of all seventy Princeton men who died in that conflict (thirty-five Yankees, thirty-five Rebs), but they are listed alphabetically, with no indication of which uniform they wore. In that vein, when the town of Princeton celebrated Memorial Day in 1961 with a parade, two latter-day cavalrymen fitted themselves out in blue and grey and clattered along Nassau Street, and, thanks to Whitney and Gaver, both riders were astride horses that had earlier borne the colors of the Greentree Stable.

Whitney understandably liked Greentree horses to win races. He relished competition—and why not, some people thought, in view of his having been born with so big a head start in the race of life? Except while a prisoner of war, it could certainly be argued, he had hardly ever had to initiate any competition of his own more or less from scratch. But much as he cared to win races, he cared equally about the quality and the welfare of the horses that he—and his sister with him—had entered in them. He felt strongly, and unshakably, that the commercialism of racing was harmful to the best interest of what he wished could be thought of not as a business but as a sport. In 1937, addressing the National Association of State Racing Commissioners, at Saratoga, he said, "We have allowed to have placed on racing in America the most blatant stamp of commercialism possible to conceive, and something should and must be done about it." There were, for one thing, too few good older horses in training, he believed; it may have been significant that over the years, despite the glamor attached to Derby-Preakness-Belmont three-year-olds, he achieved his greatest track successes with more mature color-bearers.

The following year, filling in for Helen Whitney, who at the last moment had been unable to honor a commitment to address the annual dinner of the Thoroughbred Club of America, he reminisced a bit about his Saratoga boyhood, when he had clocked dawn workouts for his mother, and went on, "During those early mornings I naturally came to love racing, but more than that, I began to understand and appreciate the courage and personality of thoroughbred horses; the generosity of winning owners; the uncomplaining sportsmanship of losers; the democratic comradeship of the turf, which plays no favorites; and behind all this, as its background, the varied color and excitement—all of which I now recognize as the spirit of racing."

Whitney was not hidebound about racing. He felt that it belonged just as much to the two-dollar bettors as to the multimillionaires, like himself, who could hold horses' halters inside a paddock while plebeians gaped across a fence; and he once referred sarcastically to "The Dear Old Guard, hankering for the Good Old Days before Joe Widener cluttered up the grounds with mutuel machines, saliva tests, and toilets for the poor." A quarter of a century after his stand-in remarks to the Thoroughbred Club, that body asked him to be its annual-dinner speaker on his own, and in 1963 he was once more dwelling on the same theme he had expounded in 1938:

> This is what my mother then asked me to say: "It is most urgent that you, who know what I mean by the spirit of racing, should see clearly this conflict of interest between commercialism and sport. We cannot allow the spirit of racing to be bought."

And this is what I think we still have to guard, more jealously than we have been doing: the spirit of racing.

What goes on eight or nine or, God forbid, ten times every afternoon at Aqueduct or Arlington or Santa Anita, or even here at your charming Keeneland, is horse *races*, and I enjoy these as much as anyone.* But the Thoroughbred Club represents the very fibre of horse *racing*. To preserve the spirit—and the sport—of racing, we have to remember that racing and races are not the same thing.

I don't say that we should try to go back to the racing of years ago. Even if we could, which we can't. Racing has become a mammoth industry. It takes money to support such an industry, and it takes a considerable degree of commercialization to provide that money. . . .

But money, if not exactly the root of all evil—and, having some, I have reason to think it's the root of quite a lot of good—is undeniably the source of a great deal of temptation. . . .

In the first eighteen two-year-old stakes of any consequence in America this year, there were fourteen different winners. One of these winners made more money—$75,000—for finishing second in one race than he had made for winning any of several other races.

Race tracks can and should do what they can to attract the best horses, and virtue should be rewarded. But I submit that $75,000 is a rather spectacular premium for failure.

I must admit at this point that perhaps the most spectacular reward for failure this season was received by Greentree. The prize wasn't gaudy, but the failure was.

Our trainer, John Gaver, received a package the other day. It contained a very attractive silver bowl. John naturally assumed it was a trophy for one of our horses that had won a stakes. He couldn't remember winning any stakes recently, so he put on his glasses and read the inscription.

It was for Malicious, our two-year-old colt that ran—if I may use the term loosely—for the opulent rewards in the Arlington-Washington Futurity. Of fifteen starters, Malicious finished fourteenth, seventeen lengths up the track. And the fifteenth horse hadn't finished. He'd jumped the rail and gone cavorting off into a parking lot. For this they gave us a silver bowl, and we shall treasure it. I don't know whether the fence-jumper got a trophy, too. . . .

The result of this kind of gold rush was races, some of them rather good races. But this was not racing, which is the name of our game. In racing, there is a greater purpose than a purse.†

---

* Whatever the length of a racing program, Whitney rarely sat through a whole card at any track. He was more likely to turn up shortly before an event in which one of his horses was entered, and to leave shortly afterward.

† The sentiments were Whitney's, but the words were put together for him by his first-cousin-once-removed Whitney Tower, then the chief racing writer for *Sports Illustrated*. Tower liked the speech so much that he asked Jock to let his magazine see

26. *Betsey and Jock Whitney on their wedding day, March 1, 1942.* (William T. Hoff photo)

27. *Joe E. Lewis trying out a new routine—apparently successfully—at a birthday party for Jock, at Saratoga.*

28. *Façade of the main house at Greenwood, in Thomasville, Georgia.*

29. *The main entrance to Greentree, Manhasset, Long Island. The court-tennis pavilion is at far left.* (John R. Wells photo)

30. *Aboard Jock's yacht* Aphrodite. *First row, left to right, Tony Mortimer, Tony di Bonaventura, Sara, Amanda Mortimer, Babe Paley; second row, left to right, Jock, Betsey, Kate.*

31. *War in the air: Jock at Plattsburgh, in 1940, for a citizens' military training course.*

32. *Colonel Jock Whitney (second from right) about to toast some new-made Free French friends after his escape from the Nazis.*

33. Kate Roosevelt squirms, in 1942, as her new father tries to share his new summer uniform with her during a family portrait session.

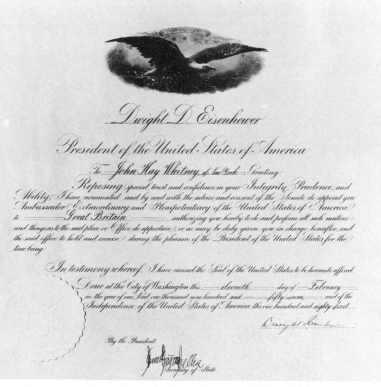

34. & 35. *Two ambassadorial appointments: John Hay's and John Hay Whitney's.*

36. *Ordinarily, Jock Whitney would have thought it gauche to wear white tie and tails in the morning, but protocol insists on such attire for the presentation of ambassadorial credentials to the Queen. Whitney's no less splendidly accoutred escort is Major General Sir Guy Salisbury-Jones.*

37. *Winston Churchill and Jock Whitney in London, 1958.*

38. *Secretary of State John Foster Dulles with the ambassador to Great Britain, at the State Department.* (Ollie Atkins photo, for The Saturday Evening Post)

39. *Jock and Betsey with her daughters Kate (l.) and Sara (r.) when the girls were teen-agers.*

Whitney knew horses. Once, after a considerable absence from his stud farm in Kentucky, he went down there for a visit. Bob Green paraded thirty-one horses for his inspection. Jock had never seen any of them before. The next day, he was able to identify two thirds of them on second sight. Preferring to breed his own racers, when he frequented yearling sales he would buy chiefly for stud purposes. He would stride up and down for hours, in deep contemplation, hands clasped behind his ramrod-straight back, trying to determine the quality of the horses on display. "There are many factors to consider, from the head to the set of the tail and the soundness of the legs," he once said. "Some people are fanatic about certain things. There was a time when the shape of a hock was a faddish thing with horse owners, who wanted a perfectly straight hind leg. Of course, by the time I look at a yearling, my trainer will probably already have examined it, and its heritage will be well known. And before I actually bid on a horse, I'll like as not have a veterinarian examine it. Vets bring portable X-ray equipment to sales, and with an X ray you might find a disturbing growth on a leg that the eye couldn't detect. When I was growing up, though, it was all quite different. It would have been sacrilege for a bidder to so much as lift a horse's foot. You and your vets had to do everything by eye and eye alone. The interest one has in a horse on sale is mainly a question of feel, or impression, plus, of course, its pedigree and the obvious examination for soundness. And there is also a lot of luck involved." (Once, after Jock married Betsey, he went along with her to a fashion show, and she was flabbergasted when he began scribbling notes about each new garment that was modeled—"as if," she said later, "he were taking notes on the hocks and withers of a horse at an auction.")

One of the first big winners Jock and Joan produced, after becoming joint proprietors of the Greentree Stable, was Capot, which as a three-year-old in 1949—a year in which Greentree's total earnings were eclipsed only by those of Calumet Farm—won the Preakness and the Belmont, came in second to Ponder in the Kentucky Derby, and was acclaimed as Horse of the Year by the *Morning Telegraph*. Whitney would have liked to win that Derby, but he had never had a particularly high opinion of that much-vaunted race, believing it came too early in a young horse's career. "It is thought by many of the horsemen I respect to take place at the wrong time and with the wrong emphasis," he once said, "to please the public rather than to test the best horse." Capot was a bay colt, by Menow out of Piquet, and Joan Payson named him. She was fond of all kinds of card games, including piquet, and in that game

it in advance, in order that *Sports Illustrated* could prepare an editorial agreeing with it. Whitney liked the speech so much that he sent Tower a case of scotch. It was one of Jock's few slip-ups; Tower didn't drink scotch.

the winning of all the tricks is called a capot. (Joan was more superstitious than Jock. Usually, the brother and sister sat in adjoining boxes at various race tracks. When Capot was at Pimlico, in Maryland, for that Preakness, she was urged by another horse owner, Walter J. Salmon, to move into *his* box; he had had three Preakness winners and Greentree nary a one. Capot might have won even if she hadn't switched seats, but she could never quite bring herself to believe it.) Capot was a dud at stud. He was too shy. So as a five-year-old he was castrated and assigned to the Gas House Gang, and he lived in contented sexless idleness until he had to be destroyed, at the age of twenty-seven, in 1974.

The 1949 triumphs of Capot attracted so much attention to the Greentree Stable that the following year its owners decided to have a documentary film called *Greentree Thoroughbred* made about their operations. Joe Palmer, the long-time racing specialist for the New York *Herald Tribune*, was commissioned to write the script; his commentary included the observation that "being a horse and being owned by a Whitney is a very nice thing." (Being commissioned to write for a Whitney could be a very nice thing, too. After Palmer had finished his stint, Whitney had five cases of eight-year-old bonded Jim Beam bourbon delivered to his home. This time Jock guessed right; Palmer did drink bourbon. Indeed, the mere sight of his *pourboire* had such a tonic effect that the sportswriter, who'd been down with the flu, at once got up and went out to the Jamaica track.) There were two versions of the film. One, in full blood-red color, depicted a foaling scene and was designed for adult viewing. Its first showing—Whitney liked when possible to blend his often disparate interests—was at the Museum of Modern Art. The other, for younger audiences, had a less explicit birth scene. When the unexpurgated version was shown the following year at the Illinois Thoroughbred Breeders Association, and Whitney's staff learned that the audience was to include a University of Illinois freshman who was the only female ever to have won a National Association of Thoroughbred Breeders' fellowship, they felt constrained to warn her father about the gory episode; but the young woman and her parents attended the screening nonetheless and stayed all the way through it with no apparent adverse effects. The foal in question was not so lucky. It fell ill as a two-year-old and died without ever entering a starting gate.

Of all of Greentree's thousands of thoroughbreds, Whitney's favorite was probably Tom Fool, which began to race in 1951. Sickly as a three-year-old, Tom Fool didn't even try for any part of the Triple Crown. In 1953, however, as a four-year-old, he won ten out of ten races and was acclaimed Horse of the Year. He scored one of those victories, in the Brooklyn Handicap, despite being burdened with a weight of one hundred and thirty-six pounds. On learning of that imposition, Whitney said,

"I'm honored to accept it." In 1980, the four-year-old Spectacular Bid was pulled by his owners from a similar race when he was assigned the same weight; his trainer called that outrageous. Commenting on the two incidents, twenty-seven years apart, Red Smith wrote in his syndicated column, "One man's outrage is another man's honor. . . . Tom Fool was a race horse, and when he was asked to prove it, his people did not flinch."

In 1960, the National Turf Writers' Association pronounced Tom Fool Horse of the Decade, rating him above such stalwart contenders as Nashua and Native Dancer. (When John Gaver was enshrined in the Racing Hall of Fame in 1966, he said Tom Fool had got him there.) That stallion was put to stud in 1954, and over the next eighteen years he sired thirty-five stakes winners. With heavy heart, Whitney finally ordered, in 1976, that Tom Fool, too, be destroyed; the beloved horse was already blind in one eye and was losing the sight of the other.

Meanwhile, though, Tom Fool had been immortalized in bronze by Herbert Haseltine, and in verse by Marianne Moore. The poet was not a habitual racegoer, but she had read a New York *Times* paean to the horse and had soon afterward betaken herself to Jamaica to watch him in action. She was inspired to write "Tom Fool at Jamaica," a poem that ran in *The New Yorker*. One of her lines called attention to the horse's distinctive marking—a white left hind foot—which she described as "a kind of cottontail to give him confidence." Whitney, who had commissioned the Haseltine sculpture but knew nothing in advance of Miss Moore's tribute, was enchanted—and he wanted to buy the original manuscript. But the poet wouldn't sell it. Instead, she gave it to him. "I thought it wouldn't be exactly fitting to be paid twice for the same poem," she said.

There were for Greentree, as there were for most stables, fat years and lean ones. Helen Whitney had had one hundred and sixteen stakes winners (Whitneys scarcely bothered to count ordinary races) in the thirty-four years she ran the stable. In the ensuing thirty-four years, Jock and Joan had only sixty-six. They had their quota of good horses after Tom Fool, but they did not have another great one until 1968, when their Stage Door Johnny won the Belmont—after Whitney, characteristically, had declined to enter that then three-year-old in either the Derby or the Preakness. Stage Door Johnny was, like Tom Fool, a memorable progenitor, and he sired, among other exceptional Greentree homebreds, the filly Late Bloomer (Tom Fool was her maternal grandfather), whose name was apt. She, too, did not bloom until she was a four-year-old. It was typical of the tender loving care that owners like Whitney lavished on their horses that by the time Late Bloomer was only a little over a year old she already had one hundred and twenty-six entries on her health record—more such data, undoubtedly, than many human beings accumulate in a lifetime.

Whitney regularly had made up for his convenience, and always kept close at hand, printed lists of all his horses in training or at stud. Each year, moreover, there would be separate rosters of newly purchased or bred yearlings, which had to be given names. Naming thoroughbred horses is no casual undertaking. To begin with, The Jockey Club, whose stud book is the unchallenged Bible of the sport, has its own annually printed roster of names that are in use or have already been reserved; no name inscribed therein may be conferred again upon a horse until fifteen years after the death of its previous holder—even longer if the name belonged to a dead stallion with daughters still at stud. No acceptable name may contain more than eighteen letters; spaces between words are included. Obscenity and innuendo are out. Race horses may not, except with the written permission of the concerned party, be named after living human beings. Dead ones are different. In 1969, the Greentree Stable had a horse in competition called Mr. Rollins. A newspaperman with that surname, who'd known Whitney, wrote him to inquire whether, as some of his friends had been suggesting, that horse was named after him. Jock replied that the horse had been named after Payne Whitney's secretary, a man "known to my sister and me to be the most careful guy with a buck ever to supervise allowances. So, when it came to naming this son of No Robbery, the old boy was recalled."

In the summer of 1964, John O'Hara, a sort of cousin of the Whitneys (his wife was Tracy Barnes's sister), was staying with Joan Payson during the Saratoga race meet. A run-of-the-mill Greentree horse named O'Hara happened to be entered in a race there, and people kept coming up to the writer and saying, "I see where Jock Whitney has named a horse after you." George F. T. Ryall, *The New Yorker*'s race-track columnist under the pseudonym "Audax Minor," alluded to that, too, in a dispatch from the scene. Not so, O'Hara insisted, not exactly so, anyway. He felt constrained, in a "Department of Amplification and Correction" he submitted to the magazine, to recount exactly what had happened: After dinner at Joan Payson's, she had given her guests pencils and paper and a roster of yearlings. There was one colt by Ballymoss out of Track Medal, and O'Hara had proposed naming it Tom O'Hara, in honor of a notable track star he admired. But then someone had pointed out that there was another Tom O'Hara known to the assemblage—John's very own brother Tom, a political writer on the *Herald Tribune;* and after the cries of "Nepotism!" had died down, plain "O'Hara" had been agreed on—its Irishness perhaps linking it to Ballymoss, but its relationship to Track Medal by now rather remote. (When O'Hara's *A Rage to Live* came out, Tex McCrary told Whitney the book's title reminded him of the kind of taxing routine Jock was wont to inflict on his house guests, whom he would round up practically at dawn, no matter how late he had kept them up the previous night, for four sets of tennis, eighteen holes of golf, and a softball game.)

Some plodding horse owners with unfertile imaginations, seeking names for anonymous yearlings, turn in desperation to agencies that charge one hundred dollars for each name that passes muster with The Jockey Club. Jock and Joan would have no truck with such services. Their poet mother, ever facile with words, had cared deeply about conferring apposite names upon her colts and fillies. In horse-naming circles, Helen Whitney was reverently remembered as having come up with Anchors Aweigh, by Man o' War out of Good-Bye, and Hash, by Questionnaire out of Delicacy. For offspring of the mare Fair Feint, she had conceived Uppercut, Spar, and Parry; for get of the mare Bonus, Twenty Grand, Easy Money, and Welcome Gift. She had named one of her Derby winners Shut Out because she was a baseball fan and his dam was Goose Egg. Following Shut Out's victory at Churchill Downs, Best & Company named a hat it was peddling Shut Out. There were no rules against naming a hat after a horse.

Jock and Joan felt no less strongly than their mother that good horses deserved good names. Joan was responsible for Coincidence (by Questionnaire out of Small World), Hall of Fame (Shut Out-Big Event), and Corydon (St. Germans-Sylvan Song). She picked Corydon because her grandfather Hay had once lived in a house with that name. Among the hundreds of horse names credited to her brother over the years were Repentance (Third Degree-Hasty Wedding), Singing Wood (Royal Minstrel-Glade), Blinker Light (War Admiral-Blinking Owl), Ball Hawk (Shut Out-Bird Hawk), Higher Learning (Arts and Letters-Royal Folly), Boomdeay (Amphitheatre-Miss Merriment), Writer's Block (Unconscious-Cold Type), and Sunday Evening (Eight Thirty-Drowsy).

Whitney had rules of his own. He thought it infra dig, by and large, to give horses names with outright connotations of victory or defeat (Well Done, say, or Left at the Gate), but he did accept Bright Finish (Nijinsky-Lacquer), and Capot got by because few two-dollar bettors could be expected to be familiar with the arcane terminology of piquet. Sometimes Jock and Joan offered prizes for exceptional names, and they recruited their friends to vie for these, distributing among them lists of the sires and dams of each new crop of Greentree yearlings. Irene Selznick, who had grown up naming horses for her father, Louis B. Mayer, was one Whitney horse namer. George Plimpton was another. In Plimpton's honor, Whitney named one horse Paris Review. Plimpton proposed in a subsequent issue of his *Paris Review* that future horses bear the names of titles of articles published in that journal, but the ones he picked out—

Looking Backward, Mister Horse, Ho Ho Ho Caribou, and The Flying Fix—all were struck down by Whitney's unoverridable veto. Still another quondam horse namer was Jacqueline Kennedy, who in 1963 contributed Graf Spee (Crafty Admiral-Gray Flank) and Igloo (Court Martial-Polar Princess), and who expressed the hope the next year that her daughter Caroline could help out, too. But Caroline had to be scratched; she was too busy naming canaries.

Two television luminaries in the Whitney coterie, Bill Paley of CBS and Richard Wald, of, in turn, both NBC and ABC, also joined the spirited competition from time to time. In 1976, they were protagonists in a mock donnybrook over the authorship of the name of a Tom Fool granddaughter, Trim the Sail (Graustark-Luffing). The to-do lasted for more than seven months and before it subsided involved reams of more or less humorous correspondence and nobody could calculate how many costly hours of executive and stenographic time. The root question was: Did or did not Whitney owe Wald five dollars for having named that horse? Paley was designated, all in good clean high-level fun, to arbitrate the dispute, and ultimately he decreed that Whitney did owe Wald that sum, and that if he wouldn't pay up the sheriff of Long Island's Nassau County should seize Jock's palatial home and sell it at auction, awarding five dollars from the proceeds to Wald and the remainder, if any—the estate probably then had a market value of ten or fifteen million—to a charitable fund for the benefit of the indigent living on Shelter Rock Road, a Manhasset, Long Island, thoroughfare, "such fund to be known as the 'J. H. Whitney Hot Soup for the Clean Poor Fund.'"

Before the sophomoric dust had settled, Wald had dragged his NBC commentator David Brinkley into the act, the broadcaster writing to Whitney on the printed letterhead of "Agnew, Fortas, Carswell, Ehrlichman, Mitchell & Colson, Attorneys at Law"; and Art Buchwald had written to Jock, "As you know, before I started the column I specialized in naming race horses. The other night out of the blue I came up with a name for a horse that blew my mind. Are you ready for this? The name is 'Trim the Sail.'" The recipient of that missive had Archibald Gillies detach himself from the worthy endeavors of the John Hay Whitney Foundation long enough to draft a response to Buchwald in which Whitney declared that "by now I believe Trim the Sail was my *own* idea." Jock at long last terminated the proceedings by sending Wald a sterling silver tray with the horse's name engraved on it and a five-dollar bill Scotch-taped to it; and by inviting all the principals involved—litigants, judges, witnesses, commentators—to a dinner at Windows on the World. But the only ones who turned up were Wald, Brinkley, and, for reasons nobody by then could ever quite fathom, Jimmy Breslin.

Late in 1948, when Jock and Betsey had been married six years, he proposed that he formally adopt her daughters. It was an unusual step to wish to take. James Roosevelt was still very much alive, and children with two living natural parents are infrequently adopted. By then, however, the Whitneys were convinced they would never have any children of their own; Betsey had had a couple of miscarriages and was past forty. Sara was sixteen, Kate twelve, and both were quite old enough to decide whether or not they wanted a new father. They had had little contact, during the war and the postwar years, with Jimmy Roosevelt. Adoption suited them fine.

Still, the girls were Franklin Delano Roosevelt's grandchildren, and until his death they had been under the constant protective watch of the Secret Service. While their father and their stepfather were both overseas in the armed services, these gun-toting federal agents became surrogate parents in the girls' eyes, and in the eyes, too, of their contemporaries. When it was Sara's turn, for instance, to provide transportation for her Brearley School classmates to a ballet or museum or whatever, a Secret Service man would be her driver; some of the other girls thought he was her father, and Sara did not bother to correct them.

A few of Whitney's friends asked him guardedly if he had thought through all the possible consequences of adopting children who already had a blood relationship with another, extant father. Whitney replied that he had indeed. "A relationship is something you must earn," he told one concerned acquaintance. He felt, and Betsey concurred, that he had earned the girls' fatherhood. Sara and Kate had been all but incommunicado with Roosevelt; at Christmastime, there had not even been a card from him. When Sara turned twenty, she would run into a Roosevelt half brother, who informed her that for a long time their mutual father had never let on to his second batch of children that a first batch even existed. The younger Roosevelt offspring had first learned about the girls, he said, when they found a book in their father's library inscribed "To Papa, from Sara and Kate"; and on asking Roosevelt who Sara and Kate were, had been told, "Oh, just two people I know."

After the girls agreed to be adopted, the only remaining snag was to obtain Roosevelt's consent. Without that, in writing, no court of law would have countenanced the move. Roosevelt furnished the requisite papers, and the adoption was formalized, by a Mineola, Long Island, judge, on March 30, 1949. The following day, the twelve-year-old Kate, after a chat with Jock, exclaimed to her mother cheerfully, "He's become my father already! He just asked me if I'd done my homework!" When Kate got married, the *Herald Tribune*, not quite knowing how to handle her parentage, had her the daughter of both Roosevelt and Whitney.

In 1950, Whitney received a plaintive, handwritten letter from James

Roosevelt, saying he would like to see the two girls sometime or other, if it didn't interfere with any of their plans. Jock and Betsey could let Eleanor Roosevelt know when such a reunion might be convenient. But that intermediary procedure was never observed, and from then on the girls' meetings with their first father were few and accidental. Roosevelt did not attend any of their weddings. Before the adoption, Sara and Kate had called him "Papa" or "Dad," and Whitney was "Boss." Afterward, Roosevelt was "Jimmy" and Jock was "Dad."

13

I Don't Care If the President Wants to See Me; I'm Going to Have Lunch with Jock

Jock's grandfather Hay had attained high status under Republicans, his grandfather Whitney under Democrats. Helen Hay Whitney, like her father, was a Republican. Payne Whitney, like *his* father, was a Democrat, but only when it came to state and city politics. In national affairs—like his doting uncle Oliver Payne—he had supported the Republican Party. Jock's political genes were a mixed bag.

Up to the end of the Second World War, politicians had on the whole been markedly more interested in Whitney than he was in them. They had courted him for obvious reasons. In the bleak Republican presidential year of 1936, for instance, he had enriched the G.O.P.'s coffers by fifty-six thousand dollars, though he was unacquainted with Alf Landon, owned not a single acre of the state of Kansas, and, while he had not yet met Betsey, felt socially more akin to Franklin Roosevelt than to any other star of the political firmament. Whitney then seemed to many of his friends to be politically ambivalent. One said of him that he would regularly go to bed a Democrat—indeed, after a few drinks and some debate, almost a socialist—but would always wake up a Republican.

As far as the Republican Party was concerned, Jock, at any time of

day, was certainly a middle-of-the-roader. He was not enchanted with either the polite, entrenched conservatism of a Robert Taft or the brash
new conservatism of a Richard Nixon. He hoped that the Republicans
would come up with some less close-minded spokesmen who could make
their party "fit to rule"—a phrase he was fond of because John Hay had
once used it as a title for a political speech. Hoping to accelerate the discovery of new blood, Whitney was an early, vigorous, and enduring supporter of the Ripon Society—a group of liberal young Republicans whose
aspiration was to have much the same ameliorating influence in Republican circles that the Americans for Democratic Action had among Democrats. From the time the Ripon Society was founded, in 1962, Whitney
alone furnished close to half of all its operating funds.

Jock was lukewarm even about Thomas E. Dewey, whom some entrenched right-wing Republicans regarded as dangerously radical. Whitney did routinely contribute to Dewey's gubernatorial campaigns in New
York—after all, it was Jock's home state—but with mixed feelings; two
and a half years before the 1948 national elections, Whitney gave Herbert Bayard Swope five-to-one odds—five thousand dollars to a thousand
—that Dewey would not be the next President of the United States. On
the eve of the 1948 voting, when practically everybody in the country except Harry Truman was sure Dewey would be, Swope telephoned Whitney and suggested that maybe Jock would like to make a settlement.
Whitney declined the offer, generous as it seemed to be, and he subsequently used Swope's thousand to help defray a pledge he had made to
Dewey's campaign fund.

The Republicans with whom Whitney felt most rapport, in the immediate postwar years, were of the iconoclastic stripe of Wayne Morse and
Harold Stassen. Stassen was Jock's presidential contender in 1948; the
Minnesotan didn't come close then or ever to being nominated, but
Whitney long felt that Stassen had done the G.O.P. an immense service
by demonstrating that it was a broad enough political umbrella to cover
a wide spectrum of beliefs. The grateful Stassen, who ended up that year
as president not of the United States but of the University of Pennsylvania, invited Jock to be his guest at the Penn-Army football game; but
Whitney, who felt, like some boosters of the Olympic Games, that sports
and politics should not be mixed, went to the Yale-Princeton game instead.

Another Republican to whom Whitney became partial in those days
was a newcomer to the national political scene—Jacob K. Javits. A young
lawyer fresh out of the army in 1946, Javits decided to run for the House
of Representatives from the New York City district encompassing Washington Heights, a middle-class neighborhood as remote as Kansas from
Whitney's habitual purlieu. Javits, like most unknown candidates for

office in need of financial backing from unfamiliar sources, heard that Whitney looked favorably on liberal Republicans and wangled an appointment with him. Javits turned up at Whitney's 630 Fifth Avenue office and, having heard further that Whitney did not suffer strangers lightly, expected to have a few minutes in which to make his pitch. To the candidate's surprise and delight, he stayed two hours. Javits left with a firm promise of support for that race—support from Whitney that would be forthcoming in all of Javits' subsequent Congressional and Senatorial campaigns—and with the onset of a friendship no less firm and constant. Nearly thirty-five years later, Javits, by then the senior Senator from New York and the senior Republican on the Foreign Relations Committee, happened to mention to an acquaintance that he was driving from Manhattan to Long Island to have lunch with Whitney. "I told my secretary, 'I don't care if the President wants to see me,'" Javits said. "'I'm going out to Greentree to have lunch with Jock.'"

By 1950, Whitney had several times been urged to run for the House himself. There would be no problem about footing campaign bills, obviously, and there was a family precedent: Cousin C. V. Whitney had won the Democratic nomination from the First Congressional District on Long Island, in 1932. (Cousin-by-marriage W. Stuart Symington became a Senator from Missouri.) True, Sonny had lost, but at least he had demonstrated that a Whitney of their generation could get on a ticket. Jock resisted all such overtures. He did not relish the possibility of having his life circumscribed by all the petty demands of constituents to which congressmen fall heir. He had not the patience for that sort of thing. For Nelson Rockefeller, who actually seemed to enjoy slapping backs, kissing babies, and eating Coney Island hot dogs, it was something else again. Rockefeller knew how different in that respect he and Whitney were. He once said of Jock, as if he had been a sportswriter describing a polo match, "His effectiveness in politics lies in moving in, concentrating, hitting hard, moving on." Moreover, Whitney believed that most amateurs had only about as much chance against professionals in politics as they did in sports. He changed his mind about that on the advent of one sensationally successful political amateur: Dwight D. Eisenhower.

Although Eisenhower's and Whitney's paths had never crossed in wartime London, Jock was one of the general's early presidential boosters. In May 1951, Whitney had to lunch, in his partners' dining room, General Mark Clark, Senator Howard Duff of Pennsylvania, and the editor Russell Davenport—all three of whom were already perched on the still frail Eisenhower bandwagon. Whitney climbed aboard. He was more optimistic about Eisenhower's chances than some of Ike's old army associates. When Jock convened his generals in Georgia early the next winter, the subject was much discussed; General Anderson bet Whitney ten dollars that Eisenhower would not get the Republican nomination.

It was with larger sums of money in mind, of course, that the Eisenhower adherents welcomed Whitney to their fold. By the spring of 1952, he was devoting much of his time to pre-campaign fund raising, and after the Republican convention in July he was working at it practically full time. By then, he was chairman of the finance committee of the Citizens for Eisenhower-Nixon, operating out of a room in the Marguery Hotel, in New York. Whitney's chief cohort was Sidney J. Weinberg, the senior partner of the investment banking firm of Goldman, Sachs & Company, whom *Business Week* once called "an ambassador between financiers and politicians."

Weinberg—a breezy ornament of capitalistic society who took pride in never having gone to college or even having finished high school, and whose ubiquitous presence in corporate boardrooms had won him the sobriquet of "directors' director"—was a political maverick. He had been one of the few prominent men in big-money circles whom Franklin Roosevelt could count on for support. During both the 1932 and 1936 presidential campaigns, Weinberg had been assistant treasurer of the Democratic National Committee. In 1940, opposed to a third Roosevelt term, he had popped up as a founder and diligent fund raiser of the Democrats for Willkie. Now, the diminutive Weinberg—standing five feet four inches, he was nearly a foot shorter than his Marguery roommate—joined Whitney in Eisenhower's peacetime ranks. Jock, who had been exposed to more than one skillful fund raiser in his day, came to admire Weinberg's expertise in that special field of enterprise. "Without any doubt, Sidney is the best money-getter I've ever seen," Whitney told an acquaintance. "He'll go to one of his innumerable board meetings—General Foods, or General Electric, or General Whatever—and make no bones about telling everybody there what he wants. Then he'll say, 'Come on, boys, where is it?'—and up it comes."

The Citizens group, a political midget compared to the monolithic Republican National Committee, had some trouble for a while establishing more or less cordial relations with the undeviating party organization. A rapprochement was finally reached when Whitney held a nightlong conference in Cleveland with the leaders of the G.O.P. Weinberg stayed in New York, and at two-thirty in the morning Whitney telephoned him to ask if it would be all right for the Citizens to make certain financial concessions—involving solicitation lists and allocations of revenues—that the National Committee was pressing for. Weinberg, who was given to blunt, earthy talk, at once replied, "The Republicans are not very bright," but after half an hour's conversation he capitulated, with a philosophical observation sharply at variance with his own immensely successful career: "Jock, if they cut us down, we got to go along. I learned long ago that if you're born a pygmy, you got to live a pygmy."

What made that trip to Cleveland especially eventful for Whitney, however, was that he finally got to meet Eisenhower. The general had come to Ohio to make a speech to all his financial henchmen, and Whitney wanted to make sure that Ike would mention, and mention favorably, the efforts being undertaken on his behalf by the Citizens committee. Jock pushed his way through a crowd of G.O.P. sycophants—as he later described them—who had Eisenhower besieged, and introduced himself. He told the general that it was crucial for the future of his group to obtain Ike's blessing. Somewhat to the consternation of the party regulars, Eisenhower spent as much time talking about the efforts of Whitney and Weinberg as about the national organization. "I was very touched by that," Jock said afterward.

He was slightly less impressed with Eisenhower's rhetorical style. Writing to General Anderson at the end of that month, Whitney said, "I personally believe Stevenson to be much overrated and certainly not a person who can clean out the rust of the party machinery which has been too long in motion. We must confess that Ike has not been the dynamic speaker which [sic] we had all expected, but I believe that his wonderful character and personality will come out as against the trained sarcasm of his opponent."

That same month, because of the Citizens committee, Whitney made another new friend who would ever thereafter be an important figure in his life. Jock had not long been holed up with Weinberg at the Marguery when his two principal deputies at J. H. Whitney & Company—Bill Jackson and Benno Schmidt—told him he ought to have a lawyer alongside him, someone who could knowledgeably answer whatever day-to-day questions might arise about the legal intricacies of political fund raising. They proposed Walter N. Thayer, an attorney originally from Ellenville, New York, in which Ulster County community he was still part owner, with his brother, of a weekly newspaper. A 1931 graduate from Colgate who had gone on to Yale Law School, Thayer had been general counsel of the Foreign Economic Administration early in the war and had traveled to London with W. Averell Harriman's lend-lease mission. Jackson and Schmidt had met Thayer over there, and he had the kind of postwar references that they suspected might appeal to Jock: he had also been an assistant United States attorney; and his law firm represented Rolls-Royce in America.

With Whitney's concurrence, Schmidt phoned Thayer, and he agreed to take a leave of absence from his practice and move into the Marguery with Whitney and Weinberg.* Thayer had never met either of them, and his introduction to Weinberg was a mite unsettling. The investment banker, who had been briefed about the lawyer, bustled into the room they were to share and said, in typical Weinberg fashion, "Who the hell are you and how are you going to keep me out of trouble? I don't know if I can trust you."

The triumvirate, with solid mutual trust, worked effectively together for more than two months, and the day after Eisenhower's victory, Whitney dashed off a handwritten note to Thayer saying, "I sometimes think what this would have been without you and I shudder, and utter cries in the night. . . . And besides, it's been good fun all the way, even at its toughest—and I suppose I value that the most of all." A few days before the polls opened, Whitney, Weinberg, and Thayer jointly calculated the outcome: they gave Eisenhower three hundred and twenty-nine electoral votes to Stevenson's two hundred and two. As it turned out, they had misjudged their own man's strength. Eisenhower won by four hundred and forty-two to eighty-nine.

In the flush of victory, the Citizens were easily able to mend fences with the orthodox Republicans. Whitney, Weinberg, and Thayer, indeed, had solicited so splendidly that they were able to give the United Republican Finance Committee eleven thousand dollars to help it meet some of its obligations. And even then, the Citizens had some cash left over. In February 1953, accordingly, they did something unprecedented in the annals of political fund raising. They notified the twenty thousand contributors to their coffers that they had spent only $1,432,345.40 of the $1,705,173.10 they had collected, and would therefore give everybody a sixteen-per-cent rebate on his or her gift. More than two thousand of the refund checks they subsequently distributed were never cashed. The recipients apparently either were saving them as victory souvenirs or just couldn't believe they were bona fide.

That same post-election month, Whitney became much better acquainted with the newly sworn-in Chief Executive. After spending half an hour with Eisenhower at the White House on February 12, 1953, Whitney wrote to Weinberg, "It is always something of a shock to find him frank to the point of some delicious indiscretions, but I guess, after all, that may be one of the few privileges of highest authority." Probably to Weinberg's disappointment, Whitney was too discreet to pass along any of the presidential indiscretions.

Whitney had since 1949 been a member of the exclusive Augusta Na-

* In 1955, at Whitney's urging, Thayer would abandon his practice altogether and join J. H. Whitney & Company as managing partner. He succeeded Jackson. Thayer was succeeded four years later by Schmidt.

tional Golf Club, in Georgia, which was triply famous: its links had been laid out by Bobby Jones, it was the scene of the Masters tournament, and it was one of Eisenhower's favorite retreats. (The course is often praised, too, for the beauty of its shrubbery. Jock became so enamored of one colorful variety of bush on the Augusta grounds that he sent the superintendent of his Thomasville estate over there to obtain some cuttings for planting around his own Georgia golf course.) Whitney was among a handful of princely benefactors who chipped in—his ante was twenty-five thousand dollars—to build a vacation house for the Eisenhowers, called Mamie's Cabin, on the country-club grounds. (On January 16, 1961, just before vacating the White House, the President wrote Jock that he had not known for his entire eight years in office to whom he was indebted for that agreeable retreat.) Whitney never quite made it into the innermost circle of the President's personal friends—the publishing executive William E. Robinson, the oil man W. Alton Jones, the Augusta National impresario Clifford Roberts; but he would become firmly encamped, along with the Coca-Cola chairman Robert W. Woodruff, the army general Alfred M. Gruenther, and Ike's Secretary of the Treasury George M. Humphrey, on the next highest tier of amity. Whitney sometimes felt that the top-level cronies tried to keep Eisenhower, at their frequent stag dinners, golf outings, and contract bridge sessions, from discussing anything of consequence; Jock would refer to them as "the gang of protectors." He himself would sometimes be referred to by outsiders, when it came to that, as "one of Ike's millionaires."

Whitney's admiration for Eisenhower was logical enough. Jock had developed real fondness for generals who'd served in the European theatre —service that in his own case had been so profoundly affecting—and anybody who was good enough to be the superior of all those other generals had to be a very good man indeed. Also, Eisenhower shared Whitney's enthusiasm for bird shooting. Whitney's Thomasville superintendent from 1945 on, Ed Komarek, said the President once told him that hunting was the best therapy for a soldier who'd been in battle.

Humphrey and Woodruff both had, like Whitney, luxurious birdshooting plantations in southwest Georgia; and Eisenhower was often to be found in that part of the country long before Jimmy Carter made it famous. When visiting Thomasville, the President usually stayed with Humphrey, but he usually hunted from Whitney mule wagons for Whitney birds and had picnic lunches in the field from Whitney hampers. (Eisenhower developed such a taste for the deep-dish hamburgers and black-eyed peas that were rustled up in the Whitney kitchen that from time to time Jock would have a batch of both concocted and frozen and shipped to the White House larder.) The fattest wild turkey ever brought down during a Whitney hunt—twenty-two pounds, two ounces—

was shot by the President on February 13, 1957; Whitney had it stuffed and displayed it ever afterward in one of his plantation guesthouses.

Whitney possessed, along with the kind of food and game that Eisenhower relished, three other attributes to which the President often seemed attracted beyond many others: Jock played golf, he played bridge, and he had his own airplane. Eisenhower was a demanding bridge player, and he found Whitney, however otherwise companionable, a barely tolerable partner. The first time they played together, in the locker room at Augusta National, Jock twice reneged in the course of a single rubber. Lapses that dreadful were of the sort that the short-tempered President could not easily bring himself to forgive.

Whitney's burgeoning friendship with Eisenhower resulted in, among other things, a change in Jock's political thinking. As he wrote the President in the summer of 1953, whenever before then he had thought of himself as a Republican, it had been as a qualified one—a "liberal" Republican or an "independent" Republican. "But now it is clear," Whitney said, "that you are reshaping the Party into what John Hay, my grandfather, often called it: 'the Party fit to rule;' and I am at last proud to be 'a Republican.'" It took a non-politician who had never had any known party affiliation until he ran for President to make Whitney a true believer. (By 1963, however, Whitney had backtracked and was again employing qualifiers, describing himself then in a letter as "a hopeful Republican.") Whitney did not receive any immediate reward, tangible or intangible, from the President for his assiduous activities during the campaign. Nor did Jock covet any. *Quid pro quo* had never been his style.

There was, that year, an exploratory invitation from the White House to run the country's foreign aid program, but that had no particular appeal to Whitney; his foundation aside, giving away money was for him a routine, unchallenging procedure. There was an appointment to a non-decision-making Washington group called the Business Advisory Council. There would, in 1954, be an appointment to a State Department advisory committee studying the reorganization of the Foreign Service. There would, the year after that, be a tentative offer from Secretary of State John Foster Dulles of an ambassadorship to Canada, but that was no more beguiling than the foreign aid job had been. Whitney said he would go to Ottawa only if the President "required" him to, and thought he could be of better service—should the President recover sufficiently from his September heart attack to run for re-election—as, once again, a campaign fund raiser. The President did not press the point.

(Whitney's only direct Canadian connection was a two-room cottage he had taken over from his father at an exclusive duck-shooting enclave at Simcoe, Ontario, called the Long Point Club, of which J. P. Morgan the Elder had been an early and enthusiastic member. "It was quite a stuffy place," Whitney told a friend. "You were supposed to line up your boat alongside the wharf at exactly ten in the morning to go off shooting, no matter how late you'd stayed up the night before, and you were supposed to take all your meals in a communal dining hall, as if you were a kid at camp." Whitney did not make frequent use of the Long Point Club, but when he went there—usually accompanied by a long-time bird-shooting accomplice, the stockbroker Roy F. Atwood—he wanted his surroundings to be as comfortable, even in that strict environment, as he could make them. Thus on his return from Ontario in the fall of 1949 he had given some rather precise instructions to his favorite interior decorator, Mimi Rand [Mrs. Charles P. Lineaweaver II], who by the time of her death in 1974 could list among her credits having refurbished two of Jock's offices and eight of his residences. Her Long Point Club assignment was one of the more austere of the lot: Whitney merely needed her to procure for him some lamps, towels, tables, and curtains. As to these last, he wrote, "There are four windows and I have measured them by standard equipment; namely five hands short one little finger knuckle by seven and one half hands." He had neglected, though, to give the decorator any vertical dimensions; and his secretary had to obtain these for her from the club's caretaker. Whitney never could remember accurately, from year to year, what he had left up there in the way of clothing or refreshments. On being informed in 1954, on the eve of a five-day, two-man trek northward with Atwood [on such rustic jaunts Whitney dispensed with his valet], that his on-hand supplies consisted only of six bottles of bourbon, three and a half of gin, three of scotch, and two of vermouth, he ordered that spartan stock augmented by six more bottles of gin and twenty-four of ale. This held them for a while; the following year, Jock's resupply demands comprised merely a dozen bottles of claret and a case of beer. That year, too, though he usually had plenty of staff people to run errands for him, on his way north he stopped off himself, at Abercrombie & Fitch, to buy a bottle opener.)

President Eisenhower was on one of his periodic visits to Georgia in April 1956—staying with Humphrey, shooting with Whitney—when he decided his health was good enough for him to run again for office. Whitney's private golf course there, though well watered and decoratively planted, was a modest layout with only three greens. The President usually preferred to play, with Jock and others, at the Glen Arven Country Club, whose own even better-watered fairways and velvety greens had been made fit for the presidential spikes to trod in large part through Whitney's generosity. The eighteenth hole at Glen Arven, a par 5, had a fairly steep uphill approach toward its green. A couple of hundred yards from the pin, Eisenhower disembarked from the motorized cart he'd been riding around in and took a brisk, testing walk up that incline. On reaching the green without difficulty, he pronounced himself fit to stand for re-election.

As the 1956 campaign progressed, Whitney once more served as a fund raiser. This time, however, he was no longer working outside the party structure. Sidney Weinberg, who treasured his independence, kept the Citizens committee going, but Whitney took over the chairmanship of the United Republican Finance Committee, a title that had been held four years earlier by the banker Winthrop Aldrich. Aldrich had hoped to be invited as a consequence to become Secretary of the Treasury in the first Eisenhower Cabinet. When instead, largely at the recommendation of Weinberg, that Cabinet post went to George Humphrey, Aldrich had told Secretary of State Dulles that the only other job he would consider would be Ambassador to the Court of St. James's.

Some of the President's staff had been boosting Whitney for that spot (the columnist Leonard Lyons had had him slated to occupy it more than a year previous, and when it came to prescience, David Selznick had mentioned Whitney as an ideal Ambassador to England while Harry Truman was still President), but when Jock had made it clear he expected no such acknowledgment of whatever services he might have rendered, Aldrich had gone to London. He did not expect to stay there more than four years, and as Election Day approached in 1956, it was increasingly rumored that, should Eisenhower win again, Whitney would be asked to replace Aldrich. The banker had heartily concurred. Indeed, he had so informed Whitney when Jock had called at the ambassadorial residence in 1955, and Aldrich had taken him on a tour of the establishment. "I got such a thorough showing-through," Whitney said later, "down to the last closet and the heating plant, that I began to wonder, What's he up to? Why the guided tour? Then, just as I was saying goodby, he took me aside and said, 'You know, I'm most anxious that you should succeed me in this place.'"

Whitney and Aldrich both went to San Francisco early in August for the Republican convention, and out there Aldrich was even blunter. "When would you like to take over?" he asked Jock at lunch one day. By this time, rumors of the succession were rife; Brendan Bracken had even written Whitney from London congratulating him on his appointment. On July 26, Whitney had informed his daughter Kate, who was visiting Moscow, that he was going to Washington the next week to learn "what happens to our little family *If* we win in November." On arriving in Washington, he'd been told by Sherman Adams, the White House majordomo, that there was some factual basis for all the talk that was going around; and then, between rubbers of a bridge game at the Executive

Mansion, the President himself had alluded to the likelihood of a formal offer of the job.

Whitney had misgivings. He had never done anything of that sort, and he himself, congratulating Aldrich when the banker's appointment had been made public, had described the task as "arduous." To be sure, being an ambassador, even to a major nation, was not quite what it had been in the days when Jock's grandfather Hay had represented the United States at the Court of St. James's. ("I get no comfort except in refusing invitations to dinner," Hay had written Henry James from London. "I am getting to be quite a dab at it." Hay's grandson could derive some comfort from the realization that, however arduous the social demands might be that were thrust upon him, he would never, like his forebear, be compelled in the exercise of his official duties to wear knee breeches.) Communications and transportation had become so rapid and sophisticated that governments could exchange messages in far less cumbersome ways than having an envoy hand-carry them around. Even so, an ambassador remained the overseas embodiment of his nation, the personal representative of its leader. But that meant, Whitney well knew, attending all sorts of ceremonial functions and making all sorts of speeches; and his marked shyness and mild stutter would be formidable obstacles to overcome. And how would the professionals at the embassy feel about his becoming their superior? Still, others outside the Foreign Service had filled high diplomatic posts without dissension and even with distinction—such friends of his as Averell Harriman and David Bruce. Aldrich, too, of course, against whose performance Jock's would surely be measured. And was not Aldrich a personage of such eminence that during the Eisenhower Administration he was reputed to be the only government official who addressed the President as "Ike"?

There was the further inhibiting consideration that Whitney would be tendered such a job only because circumstances had put him in a position to make robust political contributions—some sixty thousand dollars from Betsey and him to the 1956 presidential campaign alone. With all this in mind, Whitney wrote to the President on August 8, just after their bridge game, "But what could [going to London] accomplish for your administration and for the further development of modern Republicanism which we both consider to be so vital to our nation? It was my concern that the appointment in itself might only be taken as a further confirmation that the selection is designed to satisfy the amenities—high level, of course, but still amenities. On the other hand, the appointment of some person of such public stature as Chris Herter or Cabot Lodge could serve notice that we believe that the importance of our English-speaking alliance, to us and to the free world, is far greater than the reaffirmation of our good intentions. Such an ambassador would be on a mission and not on a visit."

The Anglo-American alliance was damagingly unraveled late in October, when the United States voted in the U.N. Security Council to condemn Great Britain for having joined France and Israel in an attack on Egypt over the Suez Canal. It was the general feeling in England that, considering the frayed state of the Anglo-American alliance that Winston Churchill had done so much to weave, the United States, however displeased with the Suez affair, could at least have merely abstained from the blame-casting U.N. vote. The gulf between the two English-speaking countries was wide, and Eisenhower and Dulles, hoping to bridge it, thought that Whitney, for all his lack of diplomatic expertise, stood as good a chance as any emissary of bringing that about. So they urged him to go.

Once the President had been returned to office, Whitney acquiesced. He wrote Eisenhower on November 21 that "the tragic state of our English alliance has brought the world close to war, and anything which can be done to realign our thinking must be of the highest importance. . . . I have never wanted to be the beneficiary of a reward for political work . . . but if that foreign post is considered crucial by you and if you think I can handle it, I would work at it with enthusiasm."

By then, Whitney had had his baptism in diplomacy. Just after the Republican convention, the octogenarian Syngman Rhee was to be inaugurated for the third time as President of South Korea. Eisenhower asked Whitney to be a member of the American delegation to the ceremony, with the rank of special ambassador. It was Whitney's first such official mission, and also his first—and only—trip to Asia. Betsey went along with him, and the others in the United States task force were Robert G. Sproul, the president of the University of California; Senator Bourke B. Hickenlooper, the Republican from Iowa; the Rev. Frederick Brown Harris, the chaplain of the Senate; and Congressman Walter H. Judd, of Minnesota, a long-time medical missionary in the Far East before he went into politics. The delegation further included two men who were already on the scene—United States Ambassador Walter C. Dowling, and General Lyman L. Lemnitzer, commanding the United Nations troops in Korea.

Dr. Judd was a staunch right-wing Republican, an undeviating supporter of Chiang Kai-shek; and at the outset he was somewhat cool toward Whitney, whose east-coast-establishment-liberal-Republican credentials were not altogether compatible with the Minnesotan's philosophy. Upon learning, however, that Betsey's father was Dr. Harvey Cushing, Judd's reserve melted, and he went out of his way to introduce her, and her husband, to a number of Korean physicians, who were equally impressed with the Cushing name. Whitney was in turn impressed by those doctors. "To witness the fantastic dedication of these professionals," he wrote to Eisenhower, "in the midst of such filth and poverty, stirred us deeply." He asked Ambassador Dowling what he could do to help them out, and the upshot was a fifteen-thousand-dollar Whitney pledge for tuberculosis research at the Severance Union Medical College. Whitney himself was entitled to a ten-dollar per diem while on the mission, but he waived that emolument, assuring the State Department that he could get by all right without it.

Whitney had scarcely returned to the United States from that junket when he had another new experience. He was summoned to Washington to testify, as Republican finance chairman, before the Subcommittee on Privileges and Elections of the Senate Committee on Rules and Administration. It was a routine hearing, but Whitney was wary; he requested, and was granted, permission to have Walter Thayer accompany him to the session, in the event that he needed any legal advice. There ensued a curious dialogue between Whitney and Senator Mike Mansfield:

MANSFIELD: I note in the list of individual contributions which you have furnished the Committee the name of Mr. A. S. Onassis. Who is this Mr. Onassis?

WHITNEY: I do not have the pleasure, Senator, of the acquaintance of all the people who contribute to our Committee, and I don't have the pleasure of his acquaintance.

MANSFIELD: Do you know if this man is an American citizen? I am just seeking information, because this seems to ring a bell having to do with oil tankers and things of that sort.

WHITNEY: I don't believe this is the same man who is as well known for that field of endeavor as you are mentioning. I am sure he is an American citizen.

Three days later, Whitney sent the Subcommittee a contrite letter of clarification: he had ascertained, he said apologetically, that this A. S. Onassis was not, indeed, an American citizen. But before that, when he left the hearing, its chairman, Senator Albert Gore of Tennessee, said he hoped the experience had not been unpleasant for him, and Jock had replied that it was "very pleasant indeed."†

† Being chairman of the United Republican Finance Committee had not deterred Whitney from sending a hundred dollars, that summer, to the sponsors of a testimonial dinner for the Democratic Senator Walter F. George, of Georgia. Georgia was for Whitney, after all, a home-state-away-from-home. In due course, Whitney received a form letter of thanks for that gift from another Democrat, Senator George Smathers, of Florida. "As you know," Smathers wrote, "the proceeds are going to the fine cause

In December, the victorious Eisenhower finally made it public: he wanted Whitney to be his man in London. Other non-professionals on the President's list of diplomatic appointees were Amory Houghton, for Paris; David Bruce, for Bonn; and James D. Zellerbach, for Rome. (Clare Luce, a non-career woman, diplomatically speaking, who'd been posted to Rome herself, wrote to Whitney, "Diplomacy is the labor of Sisyphus. . . . No ambassador was ever called upon to push a bigger diplomatic boulder up to its vital summit—good Anglo-American relations. Those who know you are confident that you have the courage, tact, and brains for this difficult and delicate labor.") The members of that quadrumvirate were all men of substantial means; one Communist columnist at home said that they "represent the narrow caste of the American super rich that wants to dominate the world," and called Whitney— presumably because of his affiliation with Freeport Sulphur—"a big exploiter of semi-colonial labor in Cuba."

Even Presidents have trouble in December getting their Christmas presents organized in time. On the twenty-fourth of that month, Ann Whitman, Eisenhower's personal secretary, wrote Whitney that her boss had just finished a painting entitled *Mountain Lake,* and that he wanted to send it to Betsey and Jock but didn't quite dare to. "I think he is secretly afraid (as am I)," Mrs. Whitman wrote, "of your reputation of being a connoisseur." (The President and his secretary had evidently forgotten that Eisenhower had already sent the Whitneys lithographs of two other works of his.) Whitney said it would be an honor and pleasure to add that work of art to his collection. *Mountain Lake*—snow-covered mountain, lake, trees, flowers—which the Whitneys suspected Eisenhower had copied from a postcard, duly arrived. Betsey and Jock, first having it preservatively varnished, took it to London along with some of their treasures. They did not know exactly where to display the Eisenhower ("It was quite hard to hang with our other pictures," Jock once mildly said), and they finally put it in an upstairs hall. But they were glad they had hung it *somewhere,* because when the President subsequently came to England he kept glancing around their residence until he finally espied it, whereupon he said, "I was looking for that." On his way inside, he must have been pleased, though, to notice that Jock and Betsey had placed in their vestibule, along with a Cézanne and a Picasso, a portrait of the President by his secretary, Thomas E. Stephens.

Whitney's name, as Ambassador to the Court of St. James's, was for-

---

of maintaining Democratic control of Congress, and the overwhelming response to the dinner had all the earmarks of a bandwagon festival, presaging a smashing victory in November." That was a bit much for the Republicans' chief fund raiser to take, and accordingly Whitney replied to Smathers, half in jest, "I feel like I've been panhandled only to see the bum (nothing personal intended) walk right into the saloon!"

mally presented to the Congress on January 29, 1957, and his nomination was confirmed by the Senate on February 12th. There was no opposition. This public approval was heartening to Jock; so were such private reactions as that of his liberal-minded aunt, Dorothy Elmhirst, who wrote him from her home in Devon, "Your attitude to the underlying problems of our civilization is one that I greatly admire. . . . I rejoice, too, when I think what this honour might have meant to your father." And at about the same time Jock would be writing to Lady Daphne Straight, Mrs. Elmhirst's daughter-in-law, "God knows what we can accomplish anyway, but it will certainly not be for lack of faith in us on the part of a great many people."

Because of the tensions that Suez had created, Dulles thought that Whitney should have "unusually complete and extensive briefings" before he set forth. Accordingly, Jock went himself to Washington, where over several crammed days he sat in on the Secretary's daily staff meetings and met with fifteen high-ranking State Department officials, with most of the members of the Cabinet, with the heads of the C.I.A., the Atomic Energy Commission, and the Joint Chiefs of Staff; and with several key Senators and Congressmen. It was not all work. The White House phoned late one morning and wondered if the Ambassador-designate would be available for golf with the President after lunch. Whitney, who had not anticipated having any time for recreation, rushed off to a store and bought himself a new set of golf clothes. "This is beginning to be expensive," he told a State Department official later. The State Department assumed he was joking.

Walworth Barbour, a career Foreign Service officer who was deputy chief of mission at the London embassy—the functionary, that was, actually in charge of the day-to-day operations, or what a British Ambassador to Washington would debonairly categorize as "the donkey business"—was summoned to Washington to help conduct Whitney's crash orientation course. One thing Jock asked Barbour right off was whether or not it would be a good idea for him to keep on racing horses in England. In the United States, Whitney said, racing was not always in good odor, and what would the British feeling be? Barbour replied tersely that—as Whitney of course knew—the phrase "sport of kings" had originated over there. (Barbour would say later that to him the significant thing about that exchange was that Whitney had been sensitive enough to bring up the subject.) Still, Whitney had his doubts. "As to racing," he wrote his English trainer Gerald Balding, "I will not be going for quite a while. I don't want to play it *down*, from the English point of view, but I must be careful about not playing it *up* on account of America's opinion. 'Sporting Ambassador' is not how I hope to appear too much." But then he received some reassuring counsel from none other than Prime Minister

Harold Macmillan. "The surest way for you to become a great ambassador," Macmillan wrote him, "would be for you to win the Derby."

There was time before departing for a sojourn at Thomasville. The President turned up there, too—he gunned down his record-breaking wild turkey on that visit—and on the Glen Arven links he gave his envoy succinct marching orders: to "stop the rot" in Anglo-American relations.

The Winthrop Aldriches, meanwhile, had been prodigal with advice of a more mundane but extremely helpful nature. Aldrich was the first American Ambassador to occupy a stately two-and-a-half-million-dollar mansion in Regent's Park, on the former site of St. Dunstan's Home for the Blind, that Barbara Hutton had built in the 1930s as a love nest for herself and the second of her seven husbands, Count Haugwitz-Reventlow. The residence was set on a twelve-and-a-half-acre lot; she called it Winfield House, after her five-and-ten-cent-store grandfather, Frank Winfield Woolworth. Its next-door neighbor was the London Zoo. During the mating season—at least when the wind was from the northeast—the air was full of sighs and cries. (Sea lions could be heard at any time of the year.) After that romance soured, Miss Hutton gave the place to the United States Government. Early in the war it had been used as a club by the Royal Air Force; later by the United States Air Force. Then it had been designated the American Ambassador's home.

The Aldriches, first colonists of this lavish settlement, wrote the Whitneys that they should bring along, or have shipped, breakfast sets (but not card tables), flower vases, clocks, reference books (especially an encyclopedia), throw rugs, cigars, pillows, mantel ornaments (there were plenty of those at Greentree), a coffee table, and a footman. They could buy heaters in London. Their official limousine, a Cadillac, was in good shape, but for their personal use they could buy a Bentley, easily enough, from Jock's cousin Whitney Straight, who was a Rolls-Royce executive. They would have access, of course, to the diplomatic pouch, but they should be forewarned that ordinary air mail was twice as quick. They were welcome to take over some wine left in the ambassadorial cellar and to keep on the Aldriches' butler, but he had an ulcer. (Jock replied that he hoped the butler would stay on anyway, because Betsey also had an ulcer—a singular upstairs-downstairs bond if ever there was one.) They might find handy an enclosed list of names—dentist, osteopath, packers and shippers, children's conjurer, theatre-ticket agent, dressmaker who comes to the house, and proprietor of small craft on the Thames. Whitney was enormously grateful for all that inside information, and he bought $1,078.99 worth of leftover Aldrich wine.

As had been the case when Whitney went off to war, there were many arrangements to be made. Cartier was called upon to pack and ship Betsey's jewelry. Cards were left with the florists Wadley & Smythe, to be enclosed with flowers that might, alas, have to be sent to New York funerals. Jock's last at-home social event of consequence was a farewell stag dinner at "21." Among the guests, testifying to the catholicity of his close personal relationships, were Secretary of the Treasury Humphrey, Shipwreck Kelly, Robert Woodruff, John McClain, Sidney Weinberg, Tex McCrary (who sent a foghorn to London as a housewarming gift), William Paley, Alfred Vanderbilt, Walter Thayer, Henry Cabot Lodge, and Generals Eaker, Spaatz, and Lucius D. Clay. Spaatz, alluding to another senior officer of his era, wore a big lapel button that read "I Shall Return."

Whitney had already prepared for his homecoming. He had bought a forty-foot-wide New York town house on East Sixty-third Street, had had it stripped down to its structural steel, and was having a brand-new residence put up on the site. It was only eight minutes away by car (he had clocked it) from his Fifth Avenue office. It would have a ground-floor picture window that slid into the basement, so one could walk out into a garden; and eight fireplaces. Assured by his architects that all would be in place when he returned, the novice Ambassador Extraordinary and Plenipotentiary flew off to Europe. He arrived at Winfield House on a Sunday and surprised the household staff by taking a quick look-around and then asking to be driven to his office, so he could get right down to work.

14

You Can't Expect Every Place to Be Like Greentree

Whitney was the eighteenth American Ambassador to Great Britain. Among his predecessors, men of means predominated. The roster included Whitelaw Reid, Walter Hines Page, Andrew Mellon, Joseph P. Kennedy, W. Averell Harriman, Walter S. Gifford, and Aldrich. But being wealthy was not a *sine qua non;* during the Second World War, the United States had been represented at the Court of St. James's by John G. Winant, who had not much more economic clout than what belonged to an ex-governor of New Hampshire.

The precursor who mattered most to Whitney, naturally enough, was John Hay, who had assumed the post in 1897. Hay was only the second Ambassador. Up to 1893, when President Cleveland sent Thomas Bayard to London, the chief American envoy had held the rank of minister. (A plaque at the embassy lists all ministers and ambassadors, in two columns, in chronological order. By chance, "John Hay Whitney" ended up directly alongside "John Hay." Whitney liked that juxtaposition.) Hay had come to London, Jock well knew, under circumstances not dissimilar to his own, at a moment in history when relations between the two countries were strained—in the grandfather's day, because the United States had favored Venezuela in a border dispute that nation was engaged in with the imperial colony of British Guiana.

At his embassy office, on Grosvenor Square, Whitney installed a portrait of Hay in a place of honor, directly above two stuffed quail. Betsey's older daughter, her pianist husband, and their two small children moved to London, too, into a flat of their own; Sara Roosevelt di Bonaventura could look out of Jock's office and see her presidential grandfather's statue occupying a place of honor in the square itself. (A man of rare family loyalty, even to rather remote kin, Ambassador Whitney paid a thousand pounds to Christie's for a silver beaker that had once belonged to the wife of a first cousin of one of Franklin Roosevelt's grandparents.)

The London press knew who Whitney was and was generally welcoming. The *News-Chronicle* heralded his presence with the headline "60-Million Dollar Envoy." The *Times,* more in keeping with its habitual reserve, said "Mr. J. H. Whitney Arrives." Whitney was fairly well known to the upper reaches of London society and to the race-track set, but in between his name was less than a household word. (He was not universally known at home, either. On Groucho Marx's television show, "You Bet Your Life," more than a year after Whitney had established himself in London, a woman who had already won a thousand dollars could have moved along to five thousand by identifying the United States Ambassador to Great Britain. She said, "Rockefeller.") The Lord Mayor of Manchester, on the brink of escorting the Ambassador into a banquet there, began some chitchat with "Well, Mr. Winant . . ." Whitney didn't hear the gaffe, but it was caught by his aide-de-camp, James W. Symington, a young lawyer and singer who was the son of Senator Symington of Missouri and, on his mother's side (she was the sweet-voiced café singer Eve Symington), a John Hay great-grandson.

Symington's duties, like those of any personal aide, were varied. Whitney expected him to, among other things, "save me from . . . the numerous requests I get to help on everything from building colleges to putting Japanese through them." In Manchester, Symington construed it to be his duty to save the Lord Mayor from an embarrassing public misidentification. The aide rushed over to that worthy and said, loudly, "I just want to let you know how much Ambassador *Whitney* and Mrs. *Whitney* enjoy being here." In a subsequent toast, the grateful Lord Mayor saluted Symington as a young man who would undoubtedly go far in diplomacy. He did. He became chief of protocol of the United States.

At noon, on February 28, 1957, Whitney handed over his ambassadorial credentials to Queen Elizabeth at Buckingham Palace. In white tie, tails, and decorations, he rode in the first of a procession of three gold-and-black horse-drawn landaus sent to fetch him from the royal stables, each vehicle in the charge of a coachman and footman in scarlet livery. (Whitney had a Legion of Merit and a Bronze Star to wear from his wartime service, and was also a Commander of the Order of the British

Empire. The most splendid title he would ever attain was not conferred on him until after he'd finished his term as Ambassador—Associate Knight of the Grand Priory in the British Realm of the Most Venerable Order of the Hospital of St. John of Jerusalem.) Betsey followed in an automobile. "You wouldn't believe how carefully orchestrated a ritual it is," Jock said afterward. "You have to have your picture taken—in tails, at that hour—at your departure point, standing with one foot on the carriage step, your credentials in one hand. And then at the palace there is a precise moment to take off your top hat, and another moment, inside, after a precise number of steps, for you to bow, and then the Queen says, 'Did you have a good journey?' and you say something like 'Yes, ma'am, but very uneventful,' and then she says, 'But of course you know the house, don't you?' and then I forgot just what *I* was supposed to respond and instead I found myself staring vacantly up at the ceiling."

Back at Winfield House, Whitney and his aides toasted the occasion with champagne, and he had a glass sent out to each of the escorting redcoats. Then he dispatched formal word that the ritual deed was done to the State Department at home and to his own dominions in the United Kingdom—the American consulates at Belfast, Birmingham, Cardiff, Edinburgh, Glasgow, Liverpool, Manchester, and Southampton.

Whitney may not have known Buckingham Palace very well at the start, but he had long felt at home in England. He had relatives there galore: Dorothy Elmhirst, the Straights, and various Paget kin of his grandfather Whitney—among these Olive Lady Baillie, the proprietress of Leeds Castle, at Maidstone, Kent, a stately home so venerable that King Edward had thought it in need of sprucing up in the year 1278. (Later, Henry VIII had ensconced Anne Boleyn in it.) Jock had many close friends, too—among others, Lady Alexandra Metcalfe, whose husband, the Duke of Windsor's equerry and crony, died that year; the Alexander Freres, he the publisher, she the daughter of Edgar Wallace; Sir Solly (later Lord) Zuckerman, the South African-born scientist who was honorary secretary of the London Zoo; and Jeremy Tree, one of the few horse trainers who regularly supped with royalty. Moreover, Whitney was at the start of his stint already acquainted with most of the ranking politicians he would be working with—Harold Macmillan, for instance, who had taken over the Prime Ministry from Anthony Eden after the Suez adventure; and Foreign Secretary Selwyn Lloyd. And then there were Jock's old-school-tie associations, dating back to Oxford, with Alan Lennox-Boyd, the Colonial Secretary, and Hugh Gaitskell, the Leader of the Opposition.

As for the royal family, Whitney was as close to it, probably, as any American Ambassador could ever hope to be. The Queen called both Jock and Betsey by their first names (they called her "ma'am"), and from time to time they would spend weekends with Her Majesty at one of her palaces or castles. (There were stiff rules of protocol to be observed; it was *de rigueur*, for instance, for Her Majesty's guests not to keep her waiting. At Windsor Castle one Ascot weekend, Betsey was dressing for the evening and told the page stationed outside her bedroom door—there seemed to be a lackey posted at every chamber—that she would be a bit late for dinner. "Quite all right, madam," the page replied. "You have thirty seconds.") There was a movie one Saturday night at Sandringham, and according to tradition the front-row seats in the viewing chamber—the only really comfortable seats—were reserved for royalty. Perched awkwardly one row back, his long legs constricted and cramped, Jock conveyed his distress to Betsey, who shushed him by whispering, "You can't expect every place to be like Greentree." Betsey did think, though, that the Queen's food was quite as good as what they had at home. (The teen-age son of one of Whitney's embassy assistants, after being invited to stay at Jock's Long Island and Thomasville homes during a holiday in the United States, attempted in a bread-and-butter note to Betsey to put those spacious establishments in some sort of proper perspective. "First Windsor Castle, then Greentree and Greenwood," he wrote. "Now we've seen everything.")

One time, when the Whitneys were having lunch *à quatre* with the Queen and Prince Philip, they got onto the subject of the lost art of enameling. As an example of what Whitney was talking about, he tugged loose an enamel tie clasp that had not long before been fashioned for him by an Italian duke in the jewelry business, Fulco de Verdura. The Duke of Edinburgh admired the gewgaw so profusely that Jock therewith gave it to him. "Dear Jock," the Prince wrote afterward, "Thank you so much for the pin! I enclose mine in exchange." He enclosed a safety pin. (Royal levity is not much different from that of ordinary folk. A couple of years later, at a gala London première of an American motion picture, Prince Philip rushed up to Whitney in the foyer, clasped his hand, and said, "How do you do and what part do you play in the film?")

Of all the royal family, the Whitneys knew the Queen Mother best. Betsey had first met her when, as Queen, she had munched hot dogs at Hyde Park. Elizabeth *mère* was a frequent dinner guest at Winfield House, and once, hearing that rabbits were becoming a nuisance on its lawns, she offered amiably to stop by someday and help shoot them. After one evening, when the other guests included the Macmillans, Sir Harold Nicolson, Jeremy Tree, Baba Metcalfe, and the not yet disgraced John Profumo, Sir Harold grumbled that, "while surrounded by all those distinguished and charming people," he had had to pretend to be interested while the Queen Mother talked all but uninterruptibly to Tree about their respective race horses. And then, of course, there was Princess Margaret, who once brought a pet Pekinese to dinner. Whitney's ambassadorial tact had been put to a test that night. Britain had relations with the People's Republic of China. The United States did not. The only China it recognized was Taiwan. When Whitney asked Margaret, "Ma'am, did you get that little dog from Nationalist China?" and she replied mischievously, "No, *proper* China," he came back with "Well, in any event China proper."

"How very diplomatic," Princess Margaret said.

Whitney had not been installed for a month before there was more serious business to attend to. In the aftermath of the Suez Canal dust-up, Macmillan had let it be known that to try to bolster sagging Anglo-American relations he would welcome an invitation to get together and talk man to man with Eisenhower. The President proposed a late March meeting on more or less neutral territory—the Mid-Ocean Club at Bermuda. Eisenhower brought along his golf clubs, but there was so much to discuss—the uncertain status of the Gaza Strip, China (Britain wanted the People's Republic admitted to the U.N.), NATO (Britain wanted to reduce the size of its committed forces), guided missiles (the United States agreed to provide some to its old ally), and Hungary (the two heads of government jointly deplored the Soviet incursion there)—that there wasn't time enough to work in a full round.

Whitney flew over with Macmillan and Lloyd, and while he had little to do with the substantive discussions—the two Englishmen, and Eisenhower and Dulles for the United States, were the chief protagonists in all of that—he had a chance to observe foreign policy in the making. And he sensed a helpful thawing of Anglo-American relations. "From the point of view of my problem," he wrote Dulles immediately upon returning to London, "[the Bermuda conference] will be worth at least a year of work in its effect on British opinion towards the United States. It gives their Government a chance to speak on our behalf—which the Prime Minister told me he would push." (Whitney added gossipingly that Randolph Churchill had said before Bermuda "while in his evening cups" that he was going to take Dulles apart at a press conference, but that after Bermuda had declared that the Secretary of State was worth "five of our so-called statesmen."*)

* While Whitney was dining at the Mid-Ocean Club one evening, an American journalist in *his* cups marched over to his table and began loudly singing, to the tune of "I've Got a Pocketful of Love," some lyrics that went, in part, "We're Ike's millionaires/We're Wall Street bulls and bears/We've got a pocketful of dough." Whitney stoically endured the serenade, while various State Department functionaries tried in their embarrassment to crawl under the table, and when the reporter was finished

Nearly three months later, though, Whitney felt that there were still ruffled waters to be calmed. "Feeling about us is difficult to analyze," he would then write his long-time business associate Langbourne Williams, who had got him into Freeport Sulphur. "On the surface things are better, but the wounds of injured pride are deep and don't quite ever clot and heal. Any little irritation and the blood flows again. We're at it every day, and make a little progress here and there."

One of the many traditions to which United States Ambassadors to the Court of St. James's were supposed to adhere was an appearance as guest of honor at a dinner of the Pilgrims of Great Britain. The event took place on April 4, 1957, at the Savoy Hotel. Lord Halifax, the then president of the Pilgrims, drew a laugh by asserting that if Whitney "ever had a horse that is going to win the Derby and is able to tell the British public about it three or four days before, his reputation as an Ambassador will be made."† Selwyn Lloyd, who knew that Whitney was an important shareholder in the Great Northern Paper Company, got *his* laughs by saying of the honoree, "I have only really read of one doubtful activity. I understand he has much to do with the production of newsprint. What greater catholicity of taste or occupation could any man display? It only remains for him to become a politician."

After more such badinage, Whitney finally got a chance to deliver the remarks that were expected of him. He concluded them by, he thought appositely, quoting what Ambassador Hay had said at a similar introductory banquet fifty-nine years earlier: "All of us who think cannot but see that there is a sanction like that of religion which binds us to a sort of partnership in the beneficent work of the world. Whether we will it or not, we are associated in that work by the very nature of things, and no man and no group of men can prevent it." On other occasions, Whitney was fond of quoting some remarks the very first American Minister to St. James's, John Adams, had addressed while presenting his credentials to

Jock said, for want of any better riposte, "Perhaps you have an inferiority complex." Whereupon the besotted bard said, "Oh, perhaps you want to hear the second verse," and launched into it.

† Whitney's English trainer, Gerald Balding, would die a few months later. Jeremy Tree, who had been in the Royal Horse Guards with Balding, and who as a teen-age conscript had briefly met Whitney during the war, took over Whitney's English racing operations. Whitney's breeding operations, which Cecil Boyd-Rochfort had been in charge of for nearly thirty years, had been taken over by Boyd-Rochfort's nephew, David McCall, an Etonian who became manager of the London Bloodstock Agency. In 1960, while Whitney was still Ambassador, the precious-metals mogul, Charles W. Engelhard, turned up on the racing scene there, and soon asked McCall to work for him full time. With some trepidation, McCall agreed, and conveyed that news to the Ambassador. Later, at the Buck's Club bar, another member said to McCall, "Congratulations. You must be the first person who ever sacked a Whitney."

King George III in 1785: ". . . I shall esteem myself the happiest of men if I can be instrumental in . . . restoring an entire esteem, confidence and affection, or, in better words, the old good nature and the old good humor between people who, though separated by an ocean and under different governments, have the same language, a similar religion, and kindred blood." On his own, Whitney would say that "the business of ambassador is still the very basic business of mankind—helping to find ways to get along with one another."

Whitney conceived his mission to be threefold: to obtain information he could pass along to Washington, to act as the representative of the United States where he was stationed, and to negotiate treaties. (John Hay, his grandson was acutely aware, was probably far better remembered in history as a treaty maker than as a historian or a composer of light verse.) At Grosvenor Square, he found himself, with seven hundred employees, responsible for a larger force than he ever had before. It was a particularly complicated embassy. There were a couple of dozen quasi-independent American federal agencies with emissaries on the premises —people from the Department of Agriculture or the Federal Aviation Agency or whatever—and they tended to act in free-wheeling ways; one such operative might go off to Czechoslovakia to deliver a speech on a conceivably sensitive subject, and the embassy might have no idea what he was going to say until, too late, he had said it.

To try to maintain some semblance of order, Whitney presided over semi-weekly conferences of a dozen or so of his top assistants—economics minister, political officer, military, naval and air attachés, public affairs officer, consul general, and so forth—and once a week there would be a larger gathering of forty or fifty persons. Walworth Barbour stayed on as deputy chief of mission, and Whitney let him handle most of the operating details. The Ambassador more or less had to; his prescribed social calendar was awesomely time-consuming. At the start, there were seventy-five other ambassadors to be formally called upon, and in turn to be received. They all gave parties, too, and while it would have been possible for Whitney to send a subordinate to some of these, he couldn't. The Soviet Ambassador, Jacob Malik, made it a point to attend every one, and the state of Russian-American relations was such at the time that Washington felt that whatever Malik did Whitney should do, too.

And then there were the endless lists of other functions at which an American ambassador was supposed to put in a jovial appearance—the George Washington birthday ball, say, of the English-Speaking Union Educational Trust; or the annual livery dinner of the Worshipful Company of Coachmakers and Coach Harness Makers of London; or the Memorial Day service at St. Margaret's Church, in Westminster, for members of the United States armed forces who were buried in the Brit-

ish Isles. "I remember the faces and Betsey remembers the names," Jock
said after a few months on the ever moving social treadmill.

But when they first reached London, Betsey was still suffering from
her ulcer, and she had to follow a restricted schedule. As in earlier days
she had sometimes substituted as a hostess for her erstwhile mother-in-
law at the White House, so now did her daughter Kate sometimes stand
in for Betsey at Winfield House soirées. (At one formal dinner, sitting
alongside a gentleman whose place card provided no clues to his line of
work, the then twenty-one-year-old Kate asked him pleasantly what he
did for a living. "I am Chancellor of the Exchequer," he replied.) To
give the family some chance to relax, Whitney bought a country place at
Wentworth, near the Ascot race track, where they managed to spend
several relatively tranquil weekends.

Even so, their schedule was demanding and exhausting; and the only
person who seldom seemed fazed by it was Jock himself. When Betsey
had recovered and her husband came by Winfield House one evening to
escort her to one of three or four receptions he felt duty-bound to take in
that day, she was not surprised to find their chauffeur, groggy from his
rounds, dozing on the back seat of their limousine, and the Ambassador
at its wheel. "The other Monday morning," Whitney wrote back to Bill
Jackson, "I woke up muttering 'Dear God, make it Sunday again.' Just
like school." He had so little time for himself, he lamented, that he'd
been able to squeeze in only a single round of golf a week.

From the beginning, Whitney kept in close touch with the President
whose alter ego he was supposed to be. "Once when I was faced with
what seemed at the moment like a particularly grave crisis," Jock would
say in later years, "the President told me, 'Well, Jock, now you're learning the loneliness of command.' It was very comforting to have him say
that. There were certain moments when you felt utterly abandoned."

The President knew Whitney better than he knew most of his many
dozens of ambassadors around the globe, and he corresponded with him
far in excess of the White House norm. On April 5, 1957, for instance,
seemingly unaware that the English newspapers sent sportswriters to
Georgia to cover the Masters, Eisenhower took pains to transmit to Whitney the first-round scores at Augusta. Eight days later, Whitney would
be writing back, "My life is a brand new one for someone who has
avoided strangers with almost fanaticism. . . . But when it's part of a job
it's easy enough, isn't it?"

There was much byplay about golf. "I can do better practicing at
home than you, Sir, by the way," Whitney wrote the President just after
the Bermuda conference. "I can hit a spoon on *my* lawn." The following
month, reporting gloomily to Eisenhower that his time had already been
booked solid at fifteen-minute intervals for the next two months ("For-

give my mentioning being busy to you!" Jock added in a postscript), he recounted an adventure on the links with Foreign Secretary Lloyd, on a long hilly course without caddies, and how he had had to tote his huge, bulging leather bag around while everybody else was sensibly making do with a little cloth bag containing only a couple of rusty clubs. "From the vigor with which you were cracking those tee shots," Whitney wrote the President on another occasion, "I feel I can look forward to good news on your important legislative programs."

One time Whitney traveled north to stay at a Scottish castle of which the British people had given Eisenhower life tenancy in gratitude for his wartime services on their behalf. ("I motored up to Culzean from Black-pool," the Ambassador wrote, "where I did everything to satisfy the lo-cals that I loved Blackpool, except jump off their famous Tower, on a wet and windy day.") He had a chance afterward to get in a round of golf, and shot, for him, a glorious 79—his handicap was then 12; he could not resist sending the President his card. He would not usurp the Chief Executive's precious time, he added, by asking him to glance at his *next* day's card, when he had shot a 90.

President Eisenhower was not a race-track habitué, but he felt con-strained to report that same May that he had won a hundred and fifty-eight dollars on a Whitney-bred horse named Banned, which belonged to their mutual friend George V. Allen; and to report further in June that Banned had finished sixth in his next race and that Allen had phoned Ann Whitman and told Eisenhower's secretary, "I recommend the Presi-dent recall that fellow Whitney." That jest was incorporated into a com-munication of more serious content; the President was distressed because Macmillan was angry because Harold Stassen, Whitney's old choice for Chief Executive and now an Eisenhower negotiator on disarmament, had shown a draft of a memorandum to Moscow without clearing it in ad-vance with Paris, Bonn, or London.

Pleased as he was to be getting so many private communications from the President, Whitney was unhappy, not long after taking up his post, to learn that he was not being made privy to all communications be-tween the two nations that were his concern. The State Department, it seemed, had been disturbed because some of the messages it routinely sent to American embassies abroad, especially in Europe, were being leaked. Accordingly, it imposed new restrictions on the dissemination of copies of various documents. The upshot was that several ambassadors, Whitney among them, were finding out about matters within their pur-view later than numerous officials of the capitals they were assigned to. Whitney first became aware of this state of affairs when he called on Sel-wyn Lloyd one day and the Foreign Secretary told him, apropos some

Anglo-American situation, "Of course, you know that the President talked about this yesterday with the Prime Minister."

Whitney didn't know anything at all about it, was indignant (on checking with Ambassador Amory Houghton, he discovered that the Paris embassy was being treated in the same fashion), and complained to the State Department. He received the usual through-channels demurrers and the usual Foggy Bottom replies—that there were certain delicate communications that were better, in the circumstances, left undistributed. But Jock believed that if he was going to be kept in the dark he would lose whatever influence he had attained with the Foreign Office. When he next saw Eisenhower, he complained about not being considered a trustworthy representative of the Administration—he personally hadn't been accused of any leaks—and said that perhaps he should resign. Nonsense, the President replied; and he instructed the State Department to keep Whitney completely informed.

In his first year as Ambassador, Whitney traveled fifty-six hundred miles within the United Kingdom. He visited twenty-two cities and delivered fifty-one speeches, not counting offhand responses to toasts and the like. He gave eighty-two lunches and went to sixty-five. He gave three formal dinners, for a total of three hundred and eighty-five guests, and went to seventy-six dinners; he gave thirty receptions, for fifty-two hundred guests, and went to fifty-seven receptions; and he put in an appearance at fifty-two miscellaneous public functions. He was invited to switch on the lights for the Autumn Illuminations at Blackpool (that involved having his picture taken on a roller coaster)—an honor which delighted the State Department, inasmuch as the Soviet Ambassador Malik had turned on the current two years earlier.

Whitney had hoped at the outset to be able to visit, before his expected four-year tour was finished, every single one of the forty-five counties in Britain, but he never quite realized that goal; he did tell one London acquaintance that, if he had had time to follow all his English horses around to all the tracks where they were racing, he would certainly have ended up calling at more spots than most ambassadors got to in the line of their duty. Before he was through, he did achieve the distinction, as the *Telegraph and Argus and Yorkshire Observer*, in Bradford, proudly noted, of being the first American Ambassador ever to set foot in a textile factory in the West Riding. Whitney himself, on the first of several trips he made to Wales, asked, trying to strengthen bonds of amity, if any of a group of miners he was chatting with had ever before seen an American Ambassador. One collier raised his hand and said, "Yes, sir; I had the honor of escorting the body of Whitelaw Reid to the boat train."

Almost wherever Whitney went, there was a speech to be made. He had never much liked public rostrums, in part because of his lifelong slight speech impediment; once he wrote to President Eisenhower, who in his second term sometimes slurred a word or two, "I know I mix up far more words than you do, and nobody thinks that my health has anything to do with it." Before leaving for any engagement, Whitney would inquire of somebody on his staff what oratory would be expected of him. "As often as not, I'd receive solemn assurances," he said later, "that *this* time nothing of the sort would be required. After a few such assurances, I learned that, whenever a glass would be struck, someone would have to say a few appropriate words, and more likely than not that someone would turn out to be me." So he would usually discuss in advance, with Jim Symington or with W. Bradley Connors, his public affairs aide, what he should say if called upon. He would rely on them, too, to keep him supplied with appropriate jokes and stories with which he could pepper his remarks. When they ran out, he appealed for help to, among others, his fellow member of Augusta National, Freeman Gosden—the Amos of Amos and Andy.

Whitney had a natural, dry wit, and it stood him in good stead when, as often happened, he could not rely on prepared texts and had to engage in off-the-cuff colloquy. During a question and answer period after his formal address to a dinner of the United and Cecil Club, for instance, he was asked, "What is the United States' view of the Commonwealth's role in the future? In asking this, I am encouraged to know that His Excellency studied at Oxford." His Excellency replied, "I could answer that one better if I had completed my education at Oxford. . . . We feel about the Commonwealth as we do about love and mother—great." And when another member of the group—the last part of whose remarks elicited cries of "Shame!"—said, "I am a guest here myself, and don't know if it's protocol, but would like to ask this: Would the United States go to war over Berlin? In my view the United Kingdom wouldn't," the Ambassador responded, "Well, I've only been here about two years and haven't learned everything about protocol either, but I know enough not to answer *that* one." That elicited laughter.

Whitney was on the whole well received in his public appearances, but it was not always smooth sailing. Whatever the United States did, or was believed to have done or to contemplate doing, he was by some Britons held accountable. The Royal Society for the Prevention of Cruelty to Animals growled at him, for instance, on hearing that Americans were going to shoot chimpanzees into space; and when it was later made known that a rhesus monkey had perished in the nose cone of a Jupiter missile, he was taken to task for that by both the National Society for the Abolition of Cruel Sports and the Conference on Animal Welfare Societies, the latter advising him, as one nation might advise another on the brink of severing relations, that it viewed that incident "with the gravest concern." It was hard to please everybody. When on another occasion Whitney consented to unveil a statue of Sir Walter Raleigh opposite the Air Force Ministry, in London, he was chided by the National Society of Non-Smokers.

Whitney's ambassadorial salary was $27,500 a year—roughly, what his life style at home cost him a week. His annual allotment for entertainment as an ambassador was an additional $10,000, which would probably have sufficed in Upper Volta. It was traditional the world over that on the Fourth of July every American envoy everywhere would open up his residence to any fellow citizens who happened to be in the vicinity and elected to stop by. There were apt to be more Americans in London at that time of year than in Ouagadougou. Jock's first Independence Day gathering attracted a crowd of three thousand, and by the time he had greeted nearly all of them—including one tourist who, inspecting Jock's celebrated Van Gogh self-portrait, allowed as how he, too, was a fan of Kirk Douglas—he had to soak his right hand in Epsom salts. Soon afterward, Whitney commissioned some research, the findings of which were that the average man and wife could, at reasonable speed, shake no more than twenty-seven hundred hands an hour. Whitney didn't like to make anyone feel neglected, so he recommended to Washington that the open-house custom for the Fourth of July be abandoned in Britain; a few years later it was, all over the world.

There was a constant parade to London of junketing congressmen, moreover, and it was expected—by most of them, at any rate—that the Ambassador would accord them due reverence and hospitality. "The more one learns of Congressional delegations," Whitney would confide to a diary that he sometimes kept, "the more one knows that with rare exceptions they don't really expect to learn anything, and would resent it if they did."

The prodigious amount of entertaining the Whitneys had to do, and enjoyed doing, did not in the long run involve a net loss. President Eisenhower was happy to be able to instruct Jock to notify his accountants that any such expenses his envoys incurred above their allowances would be considered tax-deductible by the Internal Revenue Service.‡ When two members of the House of Representatives turned up that fall, Whit-

‡ Whitney got another unexpected fiscal break just before that first Independence Day shindig. Back in New York, Sidney Weinberg let Walter Thayer know that he could procure for Jock five barrels of eight-year-old Chapin & Gore bourbon, a Whitney staple—enough to make seventy-five cases of the stuff—at $26.50 a case, which was almost forty dollars a case less than what the Ambassador had been paying, though Weinberg added a warning that there would be a dollar-per-case delivery charge for shipment to England.

ney would write to Eisenhower, without naming them, "One had his aide (how do they get aides, I wonder?) telephone from the *Queen Mary:* He wants to be met by the Military Attaché, he wants such-and-such and so on, and, by the way, he wants a car with an *English-speaking driver.*" The other Congressman, Whitney went on, had been at Winfield House with Sir Patrick Dean, the British Deputy Under Secretary of State, indulging in small talk in a room that held the Whitneys' Impressionist paintings, and Sir Patrick had said, "It's always such a pleasure to come to this house and be able to see these pictures," and the Congressman had said, "Yes, and I didn't even know the Ambassador painted."

Eisenhower's reaction to that is unknown. Whitney's was to give his consent when Sir Solly Zuckerman proposed bringing some chimpanzees' paintings over to the residence from the zoo next door and having them touted as the latest acquisitions in the ambassadorial collection.

On July 15, 1957, the same day on which he was privileged to attend the opening of an Anglo-American Exhibition on Brain Function, Whitney wrote the President proposing that Eisenhower visit Britain—it would be his first return to his wartime headquarters since he moved into the White House—to demonstrate that the Allies were once again marching in step and to "put an end to the Suez frustration." But Eisenhower and his advisers were not yet ready for him to make that dramatic personal appearance. That was presidential business.

When it came to presidential pleasure, Jock was happy two weeks later to be able to inform his boss that a horse of his named Gettysburg, in honor of the Eisenhower farm in Pennsylvania, had won the Cotswold Maiden Stakes in Yorkshire, at four-to-one odds. In September, an English journal called *The Manager* nominated Whitney, whom it described as "on barbecue and bridge terms" with the President, as its Man of the Month. Its further appraisal of him struck a no less accurate note. "He has used his money to do good," it said, "and to have fun."

Whitney would periodically return to the United States, for consultations, philanthropies, and fun. When Queen Elizabeth made a five-day state visit to America in October 1957—the excuse was the three-hundred-and-fiftieth anniversary of the Jamestown settlement—Whitney was a member of the official party; subsequently, at his own expense, he had ten thousand copies of a pictorial souvenir album of Her Majesty's trip distributed to British schools and other institutions. In London, he had Winston Churchill, then eighty-two, over for lunch, and diplomatically made that elder feel sprightlier by inviting as another guest Senator Theodore F. Green, of Rhode Island, who was ninety.

By the end of 1957, the London *Sunday Times* would be saying of the Ambassador, commendingly, "He has thrown long shadows, and will continue to do so"; and, more important to Jock, Eisenhower would be writing him, "Of one thing I am certain: We have the best possible person in London to advance the idea of US-UK interdependence."

The pace did not slacken appreciably in 1958. Queen Elizabeth and Prince Philip came to a small dinner at Winfield House in February—it was Her Majesty's first meal under that ambassadorial roof—and the Whitneys assembled to break bread with her the Henry Cabot Lodges (Lodge was Eisenhower's spokesman at the U.N. and had cast the anti-British vote on the Suez Canal resolution, but the Queen, of course, was supposed to be above politics), their daughter Sara di Bonaventura, the David Ormsby-Gores (he later Lord Harlech), the James Symingtons, Selwyn Lloyd (he in politics but post-Suez), Lady Elizabeth Cavendish, the Earl and Countess of Euston, and Jeremy Tree, who, should the conversation flag, could be counted on to talk to the Queen about horses.

It was not easy, as a rule, for the Whitneys to reciprocate Her Majesty's own hospitality; they were forever being invited to state banquets at Buckingham Palace—for the presidents of France, Italy, and West Germany, for the King of Nepal, for the Shah of Iran—or to join her at Windsor Castle to witness the annual Procession of the Most Noble Order of the Garter. Still, there were fewer surprises for Whitney at such gatherings than at some others he felt obliged to attend. At a June 1958 dinner of the Worshipful Company of Glaziers and Painters of Glass, for instance, he had to be initiated into one ancient tradition of the group: when after dinner one passed the loving cup to one's table companion, one was immediately supposed to turn one's back on him, to protect him, as in the good old days, from possible assault while he was busy drinking.

Throughout it all, Whitney was keeping in his usual close touch with the White House. Hearing in June, for instance, that the President was having trouble with crows at his Gettysburg farm, Whitney was glad to be able to refer him to a crow-shooting expert. (In Whitney's circle, specialists abounded. Had he thought the President needed one, he could undoubtedly have come up with a crow-breeding expert, a crow-stuffing expert, or a crow-cooking expert.) Eisenhower cared no less about his friend's similar problems. The following month, he would be writing Jock that he'd been disturbed to hear from George Humphrey that invading tropical red ants were killing off quail in Georgia. The President had no solution for that, but, he said, "At least he brought me something to think about besides Khrushchev, Lebanon, and deficits!"

By the time of the Ambassador's 1958 Fourth of July party, he had the gout, and no wonder. At some of the luncheons he had to go to—one, for example, following the unveiling by the Queen Mother, at Cheapside, of a statue of Captain John Smith—he would have to work his way gamely through five wines, brandy, and liqueurs. He had recovered his agility by the end of the month, when Secretary Dulles arrived in London for a conference of foreign ministers of the then significantly regarded Baghdad Pact Organization. In August, Whitney furnished the trophy for a larksome cricket match, held on the Royal Artillery officers' pitch at Woolwich, between an American and an English team. The Americans won (largely because of the prowess of a British schoolmaster on their side who happened to have been born in California), and the local press took the fray in good spirits. The Manchester *Daily Telegraph*, for example, said, "There was one short period when the ground actually looked like a real English cricket pitch and that was when the players were off the field."

The Chicago *Tribune*, though, which suffered from chronic Anglophobia, was not amused. In an editorial entitled "A Sticky Wicket," it noted that the match had been ill-timedly held on the one hundred and forty-fourth anniversary of the British burning of the White House; and that the contents of the Ambassador's Cup, which Whitney had been persuaded to fill with tea leaves, had been provided by the same merchants whose tea had been dumped into the harbor of Boston in 1773. "These gestures, we suppose, are thought to convey the impression that bygones are bygones," the *Tribune* groused. "We trust that this byplay is not carried to the extreme that the War of Independence is laughed off as simply a good joke."

An ambassador could never be sure how his words and actions might be construed. Addressing the Royal Empire Society in October, Whitney had touched on the China situation and had said that the United States would continue to oppose a U.N. seat for the People's Republic. For thus speaking up, he was chastised in a letter to the *Times* by the soldier-writer Lord Elibank; and was in turn defended by both Lord Halifax and Sir Harold Nicolson, who said it seemed perfectly reasonable to them for an ambassador to be enunciating the foreign policy of his own country. No one took exception that same month when Whitney went to Northern Ireland to do the sort of thing that conscientious ambassadors are expected to do: at Newtownards, in Ulster, he visited a factory that made nylon hose, and according to the following issue of *Knitwear and Stockings*, "Mr. Whitney was shown each stage in the process of manufacture of fine gauge stockings, from the delivery of yarn to the final boxing and packaging." The article was illustrated by a photograph of the Ambassador gazing with seeming rapture at a process called seam-free linkage.

Whitney had much else on his mind. At the end of August, he had assumed control of the New York *Herald Tribune*, for the ownership of which he had been negotiating, off and on, for more than a year; and after he came home from London the publication processes of this newspaper would preoccupy him more intensely than any other undertaking of his life.

The President had not yet decided that the time was right for him to go to England, but late in 1958 he authorized a visit by the Richard Nixons. The Vice-President was to represent Eisenhower at the dedication of a United States memorial chapel at St. Paul's Cathedral. Whitney had met Nixon several times but did not know him well and had not much admiration for his past political performances. Still, Nixon was the highest-ranking American government official yet to come to London during his ambassadorship, and the occasion was one to be accorded suitable pomp and circumstance. The Nixon visit was scheduled for the end of November, and it seemed appropriate to have a Thanksgiving dinner, with all the trimmings, at Winfield House. Nixon was the nominal host. The Queen headed the guest list of fifty-six. (Prince Philip couldn't make it; he was off boar hunting in Germany.) Among the other indigenes were the Macmillans, the Mountbattens, the Duchess of Devonshire, the Dowager Marchioness of Reading, the Lord Chief Justice, the Dean of St. Paul's, and two Marshals of the R.A.F.

The menu, it was announced in advance, would include roast turkey and cranberries, sweet potatoes, pumpkin and mince pies, and, along with a selection of wines, what the *Daily Express* called "vintage cider." The first course was to be oyster stew, and that provoked a minor flurry. The Master of the Queen's Household felt constrained to send Whitney a long handwritten letter in which, "hoping that you will not consider my letter unwarrantable cheek and ill-mannered interference," he said that Her Majesty was not fond of oysters. "I believe a somewhat similar case occurred a year or two ago and it was solved by the host serving grapefruit or melon or some such fruit as an alternative dish," the Master of the Household went on. "I might add," he added, "that the Queen has no idea that I have written to you and will probably undermine my good intentions by eating the oysters after all!" The Winfield House kitchen was forthwith instructed to serve Her Majesty chicken soup.

There was another Nixon-connected crisis when it developed that the Vice-President's valet had neglected to pack a dinner jacket. Whitney's clothes were far too big for Nixon to get into without looking like a clown; so the Vice-President borrowed a jacket from an embassy officer about his size, and the embassy man borrowed a dark jacket from a security man, and the security man borrowed a black coat from a bobby, who spent the evening trying to look as dignified as he could in his shirt sleeves. Once that had been settled, the evening was on the whole a success, though the Vice-President, who had consumed more wine than cider, surprised the assemblage by insisting, right in the middle of dinner, that he dictate a cablegram to President Eisenhower telling what a good time was being had by all.

In a thank-you note to the Whitneys, Her Majesty mentioned "so many interesting people," but alluded neither to the Vice-President nor to the chicken soup.

Among the members of the Nixon entourage was his military aide, the Marine general Robert Cushman. Cushman took Whitney's aide James Symington aside, shortly before the Nixons' departure, and said there were so many people to whom the Vice-President wanted to send thank-you notes of his own that he wondered if Symington could lend a hand drafting them. So Symington dashed off letters to, among others, the Queen and the Ambassador; and when Whitney in turn asked Symington to compose an acknowledgment of Nixon's letter, Symington had the pleasure of corresponding with himself.

A couple days later, writing to his parents on his own, Symington told them, "It was interesting to see the Nixons in action . . . he moves about easily; chats with people, and handles the press as the *Observer* notes like a 'player' (professional) 'versus the gentlemen.' As a speaker, he is both glib and sincere-seeming—but not powerful. He had some fine things to say—but while his voice is pleasant—low and modulated—it does not convey passion—the compelling urgency of leadership. He seems to me like a nice young man who would deserve and manage competently a cabinet post. But in watching his boyish, dark face, the furrowed brow, the quick smile, I begin to wonder if I do not understand why he appears 'tricky.' I feel he lacks the deep springs of imagination that would give strength and substance to his analysis. It's hard to tell if the analysis is his, or if he has memorized the notes of advisers, and rephrased them through a technique of translation that is purely superficial—as if he studied a lesson, and wants everyone to think he wrote it. Consistency is not likely to be the mark of such a man. . . ."

The President may have been both pleased and surprised when he received Whitney's own assessment of the Nixon visit. "He and Pat were a smashing success," Jock wrote. "His candour and great range of knowledge over the widest possible variety of subjects has been really impressive. A great many people here were prepared to find slick toughness, but instead discovered an informed sympathy for their past and future and a true appreciation of our joint problems in the modern world. . . . All my efforts, and those of my staff and the hundreds of programs we have throughout the country, are a weak ray of light compared with the expanse of brightness which the interest in this individual caused to shine. Dick was marvelous. . . ."

Eisenhower also received a firsthand report on the dinner for the Queen from another guest, Senator John Sherman Cooper of Kentucky, who had been in Europe for a NATO conference and whom Whitney had asked to join the Thanksgiving feast. After the Senator had told the President at a White House breakfast how much he had enjoyed the dinner, Eisenhower suddenly blurted out, "Do you know the person I like best in my Administration?" Senator Cooper waited. "I like Jock Whitney the best," the President declared.

The following month, in a Christmas message to his staff, the Ambassador described the relationship between the United States and the United Kingdom as "a unique institution upon which rests the best hope for peace across the world." Then the Whitneys were off to Sandringham for a couple of days of shooting with the Queen; on the first day, the royal hunting party bagged one hundred and nine pheasants, twenty-six hares, two rabbits, two woodcocks, seven wood pigeons, and, according to the official score card, "one various."

As 1959 got under way, the State Department was in some turmoil; Secretary Dulles had cancer (he would die in May and be succeeded by Christian Herter), and Nikita Khrushchev was acting up with, by American lights, uncommon abrasiveness. By now, however, Whitney was comfortably wearing his ambassadorial mantle and was being more and more commended for his diplomatic skills. When at a Birmingham dinner in February, for instance, of the English-Speaking Union, he was asked to comment publicly on the prickly matter of Berlin, over which the United States and the Soviet Union were thrusting and parrying, he responded by quoting Mark Twain, who, asked what he thought about heaven and hell, had answered, "I am silent of necessity. I have such good friends in both places."*

Whitney was on free and easy terms with Prime Minister Macmillan, who told Jock, during one of their tête-à-têtes, that in fifty years the United Kingdom and the United States would both be socialist nations and the Soviet Union would be a bourgeoisie. Jock replied cheerfully that the prospect didn't alarm him; he didn't expect to be around when and if Harold's prediction came to pass. James Reston was in London that spring, and saw Whitney, and afterward wrote in his New York *Times* column that Macmillan had described Jock to the Shah of Iran as "the best American ambassador here in many years." Whitney feared

---

* Every now and then, Whitney seemed to carry circumspection to excess. During a conference of the leaders of Western powers at Geneva in the spring of 1959, he dined in a hotel restaurant with two journalists with whom he was chatting off the record about President Eisenhower. Although there was no reason to believe that the room was bugged, Whitney insisted on switching tables three times.

that he would be criticized for having been the source of that flattering statement and wrote Macmillan to apologize. "Please do not worry about the remark," the Prime Minister wrote back. "I make it to everyone I meet and I expect that it has got about."

(Not all the world's press, at home, in England, or elsewhere, treated Whitney quite so kindly. Lord Beaverbrook, whose papers often nipped at Whitney's heels, said of him to Robert F. Kennedy one evening, as Arthur Schlesinger, Jr., recounted, "There are rumors of his demise, but as of this time I understand he has refused to lie down." And after Whitney had told the Press Association, in London, at its annual lunch in June 1959 that "no single agency has a greater responsibility than the press in a democratic society," *Izvestia*'s riposte was that the West didn't know what freedom of the press smelled like, and that any Western journalists who dared to print the truth were not invited to lunch with J. H. Whitney but, rather, were grilled by the F.B.I.)

To others Macmillan would say at that time that, while he was fond enough of Eisenhower, he didn't really know him terribly well; and that Whitney was a first-rate conduit for letting Washington know how London felt about things in general, and for keeping London similarly informed about the Washington point of view. "Jock vitiated the argument that all ambassadors should be drawn from the career Foreign Service," James Symington would say later, after he had been elected to Congress. "Some ambassadors don't meet too many people—outside of those connected with their official duties and those they bump into at diplomatic receptions—in the countries to which they're assigned. In London, everybody wanted to meet Jock, and he wanted to know everything that was going on. He could really tell the British what the U.S. position was about almost anything. He had the skills to operate effectively and also the political sanctions conferred by the President's trust and friendship; and the British sensed this. They knew they had got a champ, and they loved it."

Symington, of course, was a cousin, but the Ambassador was no less fondly regarded by most of his unrelated subordinates at the embassy. Indeed, without his knowledge, sixty-odd members of the staff at Grosvenor Square had banded together in an informal group called the Back the Ambassador's Horses Friendly Society. They would each chip in a shilling or two every time Jock had an entry in a race, and place a bet on it. They were loyal but not quite patient enough. The first nine Whitney horses they bet on failed to win. The tenth one to go to the post had the promising name of No Fear, and when its pre-race odds were discouragingly astronomical, the club laid off. No Fear won, at seventy to one. (Jack Forrest, the onetime St. Bernard's waiter who in later years became steward of Whitney's New York office mess, was a native of Liverpool, and after he went to work for Jock he sent five pounds to a friend in the old country with instructions to bet fifty pence on every Whitney horse that ran. In five years, he had a seventeen-pound profit. "Just think," Forrest told a Whitney lunch guest, "all those horses have cost Mr. Whitney a fortune, and I've never lost a cent.")

One of the few commercial establishments on Grosvenor Square was a United States navy commissary catty-corner from the embassy. Whitney did not have much occasion to use the little store, but one Saturday, informally dressed and on his way to a golf date, he realized he didn't have any golf balls and stopped off to buy some. There was a sign on the door: "Ties must be worn." The petty officer on duty wouldn't let Whitney in. On Monday, Jock got hold of the admiral in charge of American naval forces in Europe and complained about the restriction. The sign was removed. Whitney had not been aware that there was a resourceful Englishman who eked out a livelihood by stationing himself outside the commissary from Monday through Friday and renting ties to prospective customers who were too scantily clad to obtain admittance. The tie man stormed into the Ambassador's office and complained that Whitney was undermining the free enterprise system. The Ambassador heard him out and forthwith did what seemed to him the only fair thing: he bought the fellow's entire stock of neckties.

Whitney had plenty of ties of his own, of course. He knew how important the wearing of club ties, the right one at the right time, was to many of the Englishmen in whose circles he moved; and after he had been in London for a while, wishing to be prepared for any eventuality, he asked his staff to draw up a list for him of all the clubs he belonged to over there. There were fifty-five of them, ranging from the Royal and Ancient Golf Club of St. Andrew's, which had its tie, to the Pan American Clipper Club, which didn't. The roster, which included some organizations of which he hadn't even realized he was a member in good standing, embraced, along with such conventional clubs as Buck's, White's, and the Athenaeum, the Ends of the Earth Club, the Cavalry Club, the Bushey Park Officers Open Mess, the Household Brigade Polo Club, the Jesters Club, the Royal Thames Yacht Club, and Helen Cordet's Cercle de la Maison de France.

For more than two years after Whitney's appointment as Ambassador, he had been urging the President to come to England, but Eisenhower had always demurred; he did not want any lingering resentment over the Suez Canal contretemps to cloud what would presumably otherwise be a triumphal return. By mid-1959, such doubts had been largely dispelled. Time had passed, and Whitney's persevering courtship of all strata of British society, all the lunches and dinners and toasts and visits to coal mines and schools and parish houses, had paid off. The Allies were allied again. "We are on the edge of our shooting-sticks for the arrival of Our Imperial Ike," Whitney wrote Walter Thayer on August 26. "Everybody loves him—as before." The President arrived the next day. His meticulously planned automobile ride from Heathrow Airport to Winfield House had been clocked in advance at fifty minutes. The welcoming crowds that gathered along the way to hail the much-loved hero were so dense that the trip took ninety.

A highlight of the presidential visit was to be a stag dinner at Winfield House (black tie, no medals), with Eisenhower as the host, for thirty men, among them Winston Churchill, Prime Minister Macmillan, and most of Ike's high-ranking British Second World War colleagues—Field Marshals Viscount Alanbrooke, Earl Alexander, and Viscount Montgomery; Marshals of the Royal Air Force Sir Arthur Harris, Viscount Portal, and Lord Tedder; General Lord Ismay; and Major General Sir Francis de Guingand.

There was a last-minute hitch. The British might have got over their hurts about Suez, but Eisenhower had not yet fully let go of a grudge he had held since the 1940s. He did not want Montgomery invited. Whitney and his staff were appalled. There was nothing the English press would find juicier, they knew, than an opportunity to dwell at length on Monty's conspicuous absence from that glittering throng. The embassy begged the State Department to persuade the President to relent. The President was adamant. Eventually, Walworth Barbour told Whitney he would have to do something about this personally, and to do it through his special access to the presidential ear. Whitney got hold of Eisenhower's son and aide John, and beseeched him to instruct his father about some of the facts of life. Montgomery came to dinner.

After that hurdle had been cleared, all went smoothly, and on September 2, just before moving on to the Continent, Eisenhower wrote to Betsey, after he and Jock had whacked a few golf balls across the spacious lawns of the ambassadorial domicile, "My secret dream would be not to go to Paris at all, but to spend the next two days in your lovely home." That same day, Whitney wrote to Macmillan, with reference to the improvement in Anglo-American relations in the time that had passed since the 1957 conference at Bermuda, "I, the happiest and most fortunate of bystanders, watched a miracle born and grow, and can ever bear witness to what you together have created. It is the fashion of today's cynicism to sneer at decent striving; at fairness, and patience and dedication. The people know otherwise, and are grateful."

And to Eisenhower Whitney would write within a fortnight, "The aftermath of your trip is to leave us in the warm sunshine of Anglo-American well being. It seems incredible that two years ago politicians were running for office in by-elections with anti-American speeches. Today such a one would be lynched!"

Early in 1960, the Whitneys were much preoccupied with the royal family. The Queen gave birth, in February, to Prince Andrew. Jock and Betsey sent a Charles II silver porringer as a baby present. That was too much, Her Majesty replied in thanking them; the child was already spoiled. There was a dinner in March for the Queen Mother. Then in May came the wedding of Princess Margaret to Anthony Armstrong-Jones. The Whitneys gave a party at Winfield House for all the American journalists who'd flown over to cover the epic event. They also gave the bridal couple, at the Princess' request, a Winfield House butler. The newlyweds had figured that anyone who was good enough to serve the likes of Churchill, Eisenhower, and Montgomery, not to mention the bride's mother and sister, would be admirably suited to their Kensington Palace digs.

They did not ask for references, which was just as well. The butler had sort of come with the house, and Jock and Betsey had long been wondering how they could gracefully get rid of him. He had once half scared to death their grandson Christopher di Bonaventura by pulling out his false teeth and snapping them in the child's face. Also, he would sometimes have overnight guests at the residence—ladies whom Betsey had never met, let alone invited. The newlyweds soon regretted having asked for him, and sacked him within three weeks. The butler claimed to have his own grievances; why, he told the enthralled English press, the master of his new household wanted to be addressed as "Sir" rather than "Mr. Jones" and would summon him by snapping his fingers. P. G. Wodehouse, who couldn't have known of the servant's own snapping predilections, told the New York *Journal-American* that "Jeeves wouldn't stand for it for a moment." (In later years, when Princess Margaret and the by then Lord Snowdon visited the United States, they put up at the Whitneys' a couple of times. Betsey and Jock were glad to have them but not always appreciative of what such hospitality might entail—police barricades around their New York town house, for instance, with angry crowds of I.R.A. supporters pressed behind them ready to shout, as soon as anyone stuck his head out of the front door, "Down with England!" During one such visit, when the headmaster of a New England school wrote Whitney asking for an introduction to Her Royal Highness and citing as his reason that his wife was a Plantagenet descendant, Jock's secretary Isabel Hill told him that the request reminded her of the letters he used to get in London from American tourists who thought they deserved to be introduced by him to the Queen because they could trace their ancestry back to William the Conqueror.)

Then came the ill-fated Paris summit conference of May 1960, when Khrushchev exploded over Francis Gary Powers and his U-2 airplane. Whitney was there, staying at the Crillon, and worriedly scrawled some notes on hotel stationery: "Dear beautiful summit our fault—Eisenhower tarnished—State Department tarnished—Defense stupid, only CIA emerges as brilliant but unlucky. And on top of this we continue to blame the British for being soft. . . . Please let us not forget our best friends, difficult as they may sometimes be. Let's not, for instance, ignore their problem to the extent that we berate them for not agreeing that the C.M. [Common Market] is an unmitigated wonder, designed to unite a Europe which is perhaps not all Europe."

What was worse, in covering the summit the *Herald Tribune*, of which Whitney was by then the owner but a notably absent one, had said that following the Paris meeting Prime Minister Macmillan's esteem had markedly dwindled with the Administration in Washington. The Beaverbrook papers in England, never very friendly toward Whitney, were quick to pounce on him again. "Mr. Whitney should lose no time in explaining to the public what motive his newspaper has for these successive attempts to belittle this country," said the *Daily Express*. The *Evening Standard* chimed in with "What has Mr. Whitney to say? No one, in this country at least, is slow to impute responsibility for a newspaper's views to its proprietor. And President Eisenhower's prompt personal intervention should indicate to his ambassador the action demanded if Anglo-American relations are not to suffer."

Anglo-American relations survived, in part perhaps because the Paris edition of the *Herald Tribune* was able to report on Jock's next speaking engagement, before the Commonwealth Correspondents Association in London, under the headline "Macmillan Praised by Whitney." The Ambassador then gratefully retreated from the limelight until, a few weeks later, a thirty-five-foot-wide American bronze eagle arrived to be installed on the façade of his building on Grosvenor Square. There were some Englishmen, especially those partial to understatement, who thought that wingspread was a bit much. (It was actually only one sixth as wide as the embassy itself.) But Whitney staunchly defended its dimensions, and the big bird was soon taken in local stride.

Whitney's fifty-sixth birthday, on August 17, 1960, was a particularly agreeable one for him: three of his English horses won races that day. He had not won an English Derby—over the next twenty years he never would win one—but he had become the fourth-ranking money winner among all horsemen in Britain. His stable there was doing better than Greentree was at home. The Back the Ambassador's Horses Friendly Society was having a field day. A presidential campaign was under way in the United States, and Whitney was concerned about the lack of support his *Herald Tribune* was giving the candidacy of Richard Nixon. (One of its regular columnists, Walter Lippmann, had called Nixon "an indecisive man who lacks . . . inner conviction and self-confidence"; and another, Joseph Alsop, said he "has been simple, folksy, elaborately humble, constantly platitudinous, and full of marshmallow-type optimism.") Jock himself was not wildly enthusiastic about the Republican candidate (neither, for that matter, he was told by Walter Thayer, chairman of the Finance Committee of the National Volunteers for Nixon-Lodge, was Eisenhower); but he felt that he, and his paper, had to exhibit loyalty to their chosen party.

Regardless of whether Nixon or Kennedy prevailed, Whitney knew that his London days were numbered. It was time to start making long-range future plans. There were all sorts of options. For instance, John J. McCloy, the chairman of the Chase Bank, had invited Jock to join its board of directors on his return. Whitney invited Thayer's reaction to that. In the week before Election Day, Thayer recommended that Whitney decline: David Rockefeller was slated soon to succeed McCloy at the Chase, and it might not look good for Jock to seem to be cozying up too close to the Rockefellers. Being a bank director would be all right, Thayer thought—he himself was already on the board of the Bankers Trust, with which J. H. Whitney & Company did most of its banking—but perhaps the First National City would be better for Whitney. In that connection, Thayer went on, Jock might consider going on the boards of several other large corporations that would presumably be glad to have him—General Electric, for one, any big automobile, steel, or food company.

Whitney replied in a joint letter to Thayer and Sam Park with what was, for Jock, unusual asperity. If that was the way they thought he proposed to spend his time, he said, they didn't understand him. "I've been giving a lot of thought to what Whitney does after his return," Jock wrote. He was not going to get any more enmeshed than he already was in hospitals or museums or Freeport Sulphur or Great Northern. And he did not want to go on *any* boards except the Yale Corporation, which he was already on. "I must make it clear that the *Herald Tribune* is *paramount* in importance. I feel I must identify myself with it (and, frankly, how much time I must put in to learn its problems). . . . I intend to be—must be—the *Herald Tribune*. . . . I have learned, Sam and Walter, the importance of having a job. I've got another job coming up, which needs me again. How nice that is: to be needed and to know that you—and only you, have what it takes to do the job."

Whitney had hoped when he arrived in England more than three years earlier that, like John Hay, he would have a chance to negotiate some kind of treaty. That opportunity finally cropped up as his time abroad was running out. As part of the 1941 lend-lease program, the United States had received from Britain, in exchange for some destroyers, a ninety-nine-year lease on a considerable expanse of acreage on the West Indian island of Trinidad, where four American military bases had ultimately been set up and, after the war, a missile-tracking station. As the winds of independence began to blow over that part of the world, the West Indians wanted their land back, lease or no lease; and on November 3, 1960, at Lancaster House, Whitney began trying to work out an arrangement with a new (and short-lived) political entity, the West Indian Federation, which wanted to establish its capital on one of the American-occupied sites. Some of the West Indian conferees came to London in a fighting mood. They anticipated stout American resistance to their proposals and were prepared to denounce this as another instance of big-nation imperialism. They were taken aback, at the first meeting, when Whitney declared that, even though the United States had a legal right to use their territory until the year 2040, he and his country believed that the West Indians needed more of their land and should get it back to do with whatever they wished.

Even so, the negotiations dragged on for more than a month, until, on December 8, the United States, through Whitney, agreed to yield up all but one of its four bases. The treaty—the West Indian American Defence Agreement—was formally ratified, in the Governor-General's house at Port-of-Spain, on February 10, 1961. Kennedy had, of course, been inaugurated by then, and could have rewarded some deserving campaign contributor by appointing him or her to head up the delegation for the ceremonies, but he graciously asked Whitney to go and thus be able to sign the final documents he had helped to draft.

On November 24, 1960, President Eisenhower sent another of his many letters to Whitney and, along with some reflections on the *Herald Tribune* and on Georgia quail shooting, said, "I am quite sure that your four years' service in your vital post has done much to strengthen the basic friendship between the governments of Great Britain and the United States and, indeed, our two peoples. Your presence in London has always given me a feeling of great confidence that our affairs there would prosper."

By then, Whitney had embarked on one last gesture of amity. Sir John Rothenstein, the director of the Tate Gallery, had seen and admired Jock's works of art while dining at Winfield House; and now, on the eve of the Ambassador's departure, he wanted to mount at the Tate a public exhibition of the John Hay Whitney collection. Jock and Betsey had brought eighty-one of their paintings over with them, but only fifty-six that they considered major ones. That would not be quite enough for a full-fledged show. So Whitney had the art historian John Rewald, back in

New York, select and crate and ship a dozen more—among these a Derain of Charing Cross, which seemed fitting—and also prepare the notes for the catalogue, in the introduction to which Rothenstein acclaimed the exhibit as "beyond comparison the most splendid collection of impressionist and post-impressionist painting in these islands in private hands." (The catalogue afforded Rewald an opportunity that rarely comes to an art historian—to correct himself. In discussing Whitney's famous Renoir, *Le Bal au Moulin de la Galette,* one of three such paintings, Rewald wrote, "The similarity of the Louvre and Whitney versions has led to frequent errors, some of them committed by the Louvre authorities themselves. In 1929, J. Meier-Graefe published the Whitney painting in his book on Renoir, p. 90, but credited it to the Louvre and gave the dimensions of the latter's canvas. In 1933, when the Louvre organized a Renoir retrospective at the Musée de l'Orangerie, Paris, its own version was catalogued with the dimensions of the Whitney canvas as well as with its pedigree, that is as having belonged to Chocquet. In subsequent publications, such as M. Florisoone, *Renoir,* Paris, 1937, and M. Drucker, *Renoir,* Paris, 1944, the Louvre painting is reproduced but the dimensions given are those of the Whitney version. This in turn has prompted J. Rewald, in an article in *The Connoisseur,* to state that the two versions were of identical size, which of course is not the case.")

Whitney imposed only one restriction on the Tate. There was to be no discussion, if possible, of the monetary value of any of his works. When, accordingly, the art critic of one English newspaper asked Rewald to put a price tag on the collection, he replied, following Whitney's instructions, "If you were invited to dinner at Buckingham Palace, would you ask Her Majesty how much her china was worth?"

The Tate show—which contained paintings by, among others, Braque, Cézanne, Chardin, Courbet, Degas, Gauguin, Van Gogh, Manet, Matisse, Monet, Picasso, Pissarro, Rousseau, Seurat, Toulouse-Lautrec, Utrillo, Vuillard, and Whitney's brother-in-law James Fosburgh—opened on December 16, 1960, and ran for six weeks. The critics thought it a civilized collection. Anthony Tucker wrote in the *Guardian* that "Mr. Whitney seems hardly to have a footfall out of place; the only thing one might regret is that they could have fallen more adventurously. But such regret is overwhelmed in the face of so much that is magnificent." The *New Statesman* said, "The Rousseau jungle scene floats above everything else like a message from another planet." Another critic thought the collection both earthbound and contemporary. "Enlightened conservatism in painting," he wrote, "like Eisenhower Republicanism in politics, is the keynote here." Whitney had never assembled so many of his paintings under one roof before, preferring to keep them scattered around his various homes and offices; and he was especially pleased, accordingly, by what John Russell had to say in the *Sunday Times:* "It remains, in the true sense, a family collection."

There were numerous farewells, formal and informal. At a good-by dinner given by the English-Speaking Union, Lord Birkhead said he'd heard the President-elect of the United States did not like to be addressed as "Jack." "That is odd," the English speaker continued. "'Jock' is good enough for us." The Queen, one day after taking in the Tate show herself, had the Whitneys to lunch at Buckingham Palace. (She did not have to worry that they might ask her to appraise her tableware.) There was a farewell dinner—white tie, decorations—given by the Pilgrims. The Right Honorable Lord Birkett was in the chair, and he called Whitney "the friendliest American ever to come to our shores." The Earl of Home, by then the Foreign Secretary, was the highest-ranking British official to speak (among the four hundred others present were the Archbishop of Canterbury and the Lord Mayor of London); and Lord Home said, "We come here with mixed feelings—feelings of satisfaction and of fulfillment in the distinction with which you have borne your arduous official duties and the honour with which you have represented your country. We are losing a staunch and true friend of Britain."

Nine days before the Pilgrims' dinner, Whitney had been called to the Foreign Office to listen to a formal expression of British concern about the escalation of American activities in Southeast Asia; and had, unhappily, seen his picture alongside one black London headline that went "U.S. Envoy's Paper Launches a Violent Attack on Britain and British Policy Over Laos." In his remarks to the Pilgrims, he took occasion to say that the "rumor that the United States wanted to use force in Laos," which was rife in Britain, was "totally false." As to his role as a publisher, "It has sometimes seemed to me—being a newspaper owner and Ambassador—rather like trying to balance a teacup on each knee while dodging custard pies." In conclusion, dabbing at his eyes, Whitney said, "I am sure that no Ambassador and his wife were ever made to feel more at home and that no Yank in Britain was ever more kindly treated."

Lord Salisbury, who had been extremely critical of the United States and all its spokesmen and emissaries at the time of the Suez Canal dispute, then led the guests in singing "For He's a Jolly Good Fellow."

Prime Minister Macmillan hadn't been able to make it to the Pilgrims' party (he had sent a message saying that during "four difficult and testing years" Whitney had "done so much to strengthen the friendship between our two countries"), but on January 12 he and Lady Macmillan gave a farewell dinner of their own, at Admiralty House (10 Downing Street was under repair), with most of the Whitneys' close London friends in attendance—the Mountbattens, Lady Alexandra Metcalfe, the Solly Zuckermans, the Whitney Straights, the Dowager Duchess of Devonshire, Ava Viscountess Waverley, the Earl of Home, the Alexander Freres, and a dozen or so others. The Prime Minister ad-libbed a gracious toast, following which Whitney, who did not like to go anywhere unprepared, pulled out a carefully composed and convoluted response. "Heavens," Macmillan whispered to one of his guests, "if I'd known he was going to make so long and eloquent a reply, I'd have done better myself."

Tributes to Whitney's ambassadorship came in from all sides. General Lauris Norstad, the Supreme Allied Commander in Europe, who by now had a firm perch in Whitney's coterie of generals, said his departure would be "an evil day." Lord Salisbury told Betsey that she and Jock had demonstrated genuineness and kindness—"the qualities," he said, "that the British esteem more than anything else." Harold Nicolson told her that "Mr. Whitney was a wonderful channel and one who was liked and trusted by both sides," and he added, "Please tell your husband from me that although I regard success as rather beastly, it is pleasant, on the conclusion of a Mission, to realize what a success one has been." Viscount Lambton told her that Jock had been "the living embodiment of Modesty, Honour and Simplicity, and I do not believe an American Ambassador has ever before or will ever again do such good and make so many friends." And the Queen Mother wrote, "My dear Betsey, Thanks for all you & Jock have done during the last four years to bring our two dear countries even closer together. Goodness, how we shall miss you!"

When Jock and Betsey were moving into Winfield House in 1957, they had had five hundred and ninety-nine pounds' worth of copper cooking utensils shipped over from Paris to supplement the ambassadorial kitchenware. These they donated to their successors' chefs. As a further household gift, they bequeathed a couple of dozen handsome dinner-table ashtrays that they had a London silversmith fabricate. They were first laid out at a farewell dinner for a couple of dozen of the Whitneys' best London friends. The next morning, it developed—perhaps because some of the friends wanted solid reminders of their hosts' stay in residence—that six of the ashtrays were missing. (Earlier that year, Betsey had received a small parcel with a typed note enclosed: "Lady Violet Bonham Carter returns with many apologies this lovely napkin belonging to Mrs. Whitney, which she stuffed into her bag with her pocket handkerchief yesterday at tea. She sends all her apologies for this accidental 'shop-lifting' and hopes that the missing napkin has not caused trouble to the staff.")

On January 13, there was a farewell gathering of the embassy staff at Grosvenor Square. The retiring Ambassador was presented with an engraved sterling-silver loving cup from the Back the Ambassador's Horses Friendly Society; the overall success of his horses had more than made its purchase possible. It was Jock's first inkling of that fraternal group's existence. ("Before leaving," the *Observer* reported laconically of this occasion, "Mr. Whitney tipped his horse Belgrano for the 2:30 P.M. race at Birmingham. At the seventh fence, Belgrano refused and unseated his rider.") Whitney had some gifts of his own to bestow in exchange— among them a bronze replica of the Daniel Chester French statue in the Lincoln Memorial, to which he had a plaque affixed saying it was in memory of John Hay, and a bronze head of President Eisenhower by Nison Tregor.

Back at the residence, the Whitneys found a letter written to them jointly that day by a veteran Foreign Service officer on the embassy staff: "Your performance here will so long as I am interested in the profession be the model of accomplishment and of leadership. In my opinion you were the perfect Ambassadorial couple and the finest representatives our country could have had here." There was another letter waiting, a handwritten note to Jock from Betsey. "Thank you," it said in toto, "for the best four years of my life."

Asked later what he considered his chief accomplishment as Ambassador, Whitney thought for quite a while and then replied, in carefully chosen words, "I like to think that we did set an aura of good feeling."

Sixteen years afterward, Jimmy Carter designated Kingman Brewster, Jr., as his Ambassador to the Court of St. James's. As president of Yale while Whitney was the Senior Fellow of its governing corporation, Brewster had been extremely close to Jock, and on agreeing to take the London job had naturally consulted his friend on how to prepare for it. Whitney's advice had been succinct. "Always carry a card in your left-hand pocket with some appropriate sentiments written on it," Whitney had replied, "because as soon as you get out on the street somebody is sure as hell going to ask you to say a few words."

15

I Did It Because I Had To

Shortly before Whitney left London, his ambassadorial chores had taken him to a banquet of the Printers' Pension Corporation, where he dutifully professed his confidence in the printed word. "We are word creatures," he told that gathering, "as sure as we are two-legged. We need words to grow as we need vitamins." The printed word, and especially the printed journalistic word, had long attracted him. It was, in a sense, in his blood. Not only had his grandfather Hay written for and briefly edited the New York *Tribune*, but Grandfather Whitney had written occasional editorials for the *World,* had invested with clattering success in Ottmar Mergenthaler's newfangled linotype machine, and for a while had owned the *Morning Telegraph.* Uncle Harry Payne Whitney had edited the *Yale Daily News,* and Aunt Dorothy Elmhirst had run the *New Republic.* Jock himself had dabbled in the writing side of journalism at college, and later on the business side as an investor in the *Outlook, Newsweek, PM, Polo.* There would subsequently also be *Interior Design* and the *Scientific American.* But his connection with all those magazines had been passive. He had always hankered to become an active word creature. The *Herald Tribune* made that wish come true, and publishing that stellar, ill-starred journal proved to be in turn the most exhilarating and most exasperating experience of his adult life.

Established by Horace Greeley in 1841, the *Tribune* antedated the New York *Times* by a decade. The Scotsman James Gordon Bennett had begun putting out the *Herald* in 1835, and his son and namesake took over in 1867. The junior Bennett—it was he who sent the reporter Henry

Stanley to Africa in search of Dr. Livingstone—almost became a peripheral member of the Whitney clan. He was on the point of marrying a sister of Edith Randolph, the second Mrs. William C. Whitney, when on New Year's Day in 1877 he confounded New York society by urinating into his fiancée's parents' drawing-room piano. After being horsewhipped by the young lady's brother, Bennett, Jr., removed himself to permanent exile abroad. He edited the paper by cable for ten years. In 1887, he launched a Paris edition of the *Herald*. Soon after his death, in 1918, his papers were sold to Frank A. Munsey. Meanwhile, Whitelaw Reid had succeeded Greeley at the helm of the *Tribune*. The two old papers were merged in 1924, with the Reid family—Whitelaw's son Ogden Mills and Ogden's wife Helen—in command.

After the demise of the *World* in 1930, the *Herald Tribune* was the only non-tabloid morning newspaper in New York City in competition with the by then pre-eminent *Times*. A generation later, the *Herald Tribune* was widely thought to be the livelier of the two. It had comic strips. It also had Red Smith on sports, Walter Kerr on theatre, John Hutchens on books. It had Walter Lippmann and the Alsop brothers—Joseph and Stewart. (President Eisenhower didn't much like that. He regarded Joe Alsop as a nettlesome scourge to the placidity of his Administration.) It had a batch of bright young reporters—one of whom, not long after officiating as best man at Kate Roosevelt's wedding, defected, to the bride's adopted father's dismay, to the *Times*. If the *Trib*, as it was commonly known, was sprightlier than its rival, it was also markedly punier; neither in circulation nor in advertising linage had it ever come close to its competitor.

During a six-month stretch early in 1957, the *Trib* had lost one tenth of its daily readership, falling to an average circulation of 326,478; the *Times*, meanwhile, had increased its daily readership by twenty-three thousand, to 570,717. The Sunday figures were even worse. The *Trib's* circulation had dropped over a decade from more than seven hundred thousand to just over half a million—only fifty per cent of the *Times's*. Politically the *Times* had always tended to endorse Democrats; the *Tribune* was staunchly Republican. That had never much seemed to influence businessmen who directed the placement of ads. They were more concerned about profit than partisanship.

By the 1950s, New York City was changing. The middle class was moving to the suburbs, and most of it was reading the *Times*. Still, the *Trib* had its loyal following, urban and suburban. A 1957 Roper survey disclosed that thirty-seven per cent of its readers had been faithful to it for at least twenty years, fifty-one per cent for at least ten. They were "disproportionately male, old, upper class, college educated, Protestant, Republican, and suburban"—a fairly accurate thumbnail sketch of, among others, John Hay Whitney.* There were not enough of them, however, to encourage the Reids to believe there might be any appreciable diminution of an operating deficit projected for that year of more than a million dollars.

The *Tribune*'s plant on West Forty-first Street, just off Seventh Avenue, had by the 1950s become woefully old-fashioned. In 1954, the widowed Helen Reid and her sons Whitelaw and Ogden—the latter usually known by his nickname Brown—were hard pressed for the additional capital they felt they needed to revitalize their paper. The year before, when Whitney had received a medal from a civic group called the Hundred Year Association of New York, the *Tribune* had favored him with an editorial that said, in part, "merely to recite his activities would be to compile a guidebook to much of what is best in New York." Whether or not that flattery was calculated to make him receptive to the paper's subsequent importunities was moot.† In any event, Whitelaw Reid paid him a more than social call the following July, dropping in on him at Fishers Island, off New London, where Betsey and Jock had spent a few weeks every summer since 1947, and where they had built a house in 1949.

Fishers Island was only twenty-five minutes by Whitney's plane from Roosevelt Field, on Long Island; and three or four hours from Manhasset by his yacht. (When people asked Whitney why he had got himself involved with the *Trib*, he would sometimes jokingly reply that some rich men had yachts, some had mistresses, and some had newspapers. He was rich enough, of course, to have all three. When a fellow publisher was

* Soon after Whitney took over the *Tribune,* he sent a research team out early one weekday morning to the Hartsdale railroad station, in Westchester County, to check commuters' reading habits. Lester Zwick, the paper's knowledgeable circulation director, went along. A black woman got off a train coming from New York City, presumably on her way to work as a housecleaner, and as she approached the platform newsstand Zwick predicted that she'd buy the *Daily Mirror*. She did. A man in overalls with a lunch pail turned up next. Zwick said he'd buy the *Daily News*. He did. He said a tall, serious-looking woman in tweeds would buy the *Times*. She did. A conservatively dressed man with Anglo-Saxon features, a scuffed briefcase, and a dirty, sweat-stained felt hat that had an English look to it came along. Zwick said he would buy the *Tribune*. He did. When this intelligence was eventually passed along to Whitney, he said he had better have Betsey check the state of his hats.

† Earlier, in 1953, *The New Yorker* had run an anecdote, written by Geoffrey T. Hellman, about two Yale men, one rich, one poor, both of whom had been out of college for twenty-five years. They were lunching together at a hotel. "I'd like to buy the *Herald Tribune*," the rich one said. "Well, I think there's a newsstand in the lobby," said the poor one. "That's not what I mean," said his companion. "I mean buy the *paper*." We can surmise that Hellman, who had graduated from Yale in 1928—two years after Whitney—was one of them (though it is hard to picture him having lunch at a hotel rather than a club); the identity of the other will probably forever remain unknown.

apprised of Jock's remark, he reflected for a moment and then said, "I'd trade in my paper for a yacht or a mistress any day.") That first summer at Fishers, Whitney had innocently had his skipper berth the boat in a vacant slip at the Fishers Island Yacht Club. Jock did not know that the space had been rented by an absentee owner. In October he received a stern letter of reprimand from Pierre S. du Pont, Jr., the club's secretary-treasurer, with a bill enclosed for two hundred and forty dollars. "You were docking your boat on someone else's money," Du Pont admonished him. Jock had never liked to be considered a sponger. It was not his way of life to cadge or welsh, and Du Pont had lectured him further, "Morally I think this procedure could be considered unfair." Along with his instant remittance, Whitney wrote, "I am sorry you felt it necessary to make so lengthy a statement of the situation." Whitney's private airplane pilot was more familiar than his yacht captain with the lay of the Fishers Island land. During the war, the airman had been the personal pilot for an Air Force general stationed in New York, and had often flown over to Fishers to procure fresh lobster for the general's dinner parties. When the Whitneys began sojourning at Fishers, they would occasionally have fresh corn flown over for their dinner parties from their Greentree garden, but it was peacetime, and hardly a cause for raised eyebrows. After one such mercy flight, Jock, whose reputation as a trencherman was legendary among his friends, looked up from his plate and said to his guests with schoolboyish enthusiasm, "This is the best ear of corn I ever put into my whole mouth!"

It was at Fishers Island that, in many years of playing golf on several continents, Whitney scored his only hole in one. The achievement was less than totally satisfactory; a fog hung over the course that day, and nobody in his foursome saw the ball land in the cup. Among the many guests whom Jock and Betsey entertained at Fishers over the years were Cyrus L. Sulzberger, the *Times* columnist, and his wife Marina. Mrs. Sulzberger wrote to her daughter, after five days there, "It really was marvelous. We had two cars to pick us up, one for us one for the luggage. The private plane is all polished wood and chintz and soft cushions. The house is a dream of bright colours and pretty things and white wicker beds and arm chairs and flowers in baskets at every corner and such comfort and it is all covered with pale pink fat old fashioned roses. . . . But one can't have everything in life, that was apparent. Their sea is beige. Shallow and sea weedy and to add insult to injury it is melted ice." Mrs. Sulzberger left Fishers Island, she also reported to her daughter, "with two delicious dresses and the softest pullover in the world. What hospitality. And a huge bunch of roses to take back to the hotel."

Whitelaw Reid, in 1954, did not fare as well. Whitney waited for several months before responding to his plea for help for the *Trib*, and finally wrote to him, early in December, that in view of Reid's request for secrecy in any financial arrangements that might be made between them, he would have to turn him down; it would be impossible for Whitney to initiate the kind of research into the paper's fortunes that his partners would demand of him, he explained to the supplicant, without the news leaking out. "I want you all to know, also," Jock went on, "that I understand the emotional involvement which you have with the paper, and I realize fully that this is not just any business venture to be analyzed. Generations have woven these roots deep into your hearts in an almost passionate attachment. I can share that feeling, but, after all, it is not my business or my child, and I must put my own affairs first. I know you understand this, but I wanted you surely to know that I am profoundly sympathetic to your problem."

Only three years later, the *Herald Tribune* would be his affair and his problem.‡

Still, the Reids kept after him. When Whitney's appointment as Ambassador to the Court of St. James's was announced, Brown Reid, who'd assumed the *Tribune*'s editorship in 1955, instructed his chief editorial writer, Harry Baehr, to compose a suitable encomium, stressing the point that, whatever the average American citizen might think of John Hay Whitney, the paper knew him to be no longer a playboy but a serious-minded mature man—a transition that in the view of most people who knew Whitney had already occurred more than a decade earlier. (Baehr, Dartmouth '29, wanted to teach history. He did his doctoral thesis at Columbia on the post-Civil War history of the *Herald* and the *Tribune*, and in the course of his research got acquainted with the Reids. Academic jobs were hard to come by in the thirties, so Baehr went to work for the paper as an editorial writer and never turned back.) It was only later, when he learned that the Reids were after Whitney's money, that Baehr began to wonder if there might have been an ulterior motive behind the laudatory editorial he'd been asked to write. The Reids had further enlisted the aid of Jock's long-time friend and, now, Greentree estate tenant, Tex McCrary, who'd written a column for the paper in the early 1950s. McCrary had set up a public relations firm—Barbara Walters and William Safire both worked for him for a while—and the *Herald Tribune* was one of his clients. He advised its owners to keep after Whitney, and there were a few desultory meetings among the principals and various

‡ Earlier in 1954, David Selznick had wondered if Whitney might be interested in the Los Angeles *Daily News*, which was also looking for an infusion of capital. In begging off, Jock told his old friend that he did not like putting money into any enterprise, all things considered, unless he could acquire control of it.

deputies in 1956, but nothing definite had evolved by the time Jock took off for his post in London.

Whitney left a New York City that had four morning dailies—the *Times,* the *Herald Tribune,* the *News,* and the *Mirror.* They all cost a nickel. There were three afternoon papers—the *World-Telegram & Sun,* the *Journal-American,* and the *Post*—each a dime. A half century previous, the city had had fifteen dailies. Then they had cost a penny apiece. Whitney delegated to Walter Thayer the burden of handling any further approaches the Reids might make. Anticipating some, Thayer turned for counsel to a number of experts in the field, among these Samuel I. Newhouse, who in an era when many harried publishers would gladly have swapped a newspaper for a mistress or a yacht had accumulated a fortune by gobbling up rickety journals and making them prosper. The diminutive Newhouse came around to J. H. Whitney & Company and, perched on a chair in Thayer's office with his feet not quite touching the floor, said he thought it might be too late for Whitney or anyone else to save the *Tribune.* "But let Jock try it; he can afford it," Newhouse went on. "It probably can't be done—the *Times* has too big a lead—but Jock ought to give it a shot. There might be a miracle, and he will never regret the effort."

It was Thayer's own best guess from the advice he'd received that if Whitney should buy the paper he might be able to turn its fortunes around after three years—and after an incurred loss of three million dollars for each of those years. Thayer consulted others whose opinions Whitney and he esteemed—notable among them William S. Paley, who on Whitney's departure for London had leased the new Ambassador's private plane for the use of the Columbia Broadcasting System.* Indeed, at that stage of the proceedings, Paley was visualized as a large-scale participant—about a four-hundred-thousand-dollar one—should Whitney assume the proprietorship of the *Tribune.* Paley's enthusiasm cooled when his associates at CBS said that in view of Whitney's owning a couple of television stations any joint venture of theirs into publishing might attract the interest and even incur the displeasure of the Federal Communications Commission.

All this was going on at home while Whitney was still mainly preoccupied abroad with learning how to keep afloat in diplomatic channels. There were, however, innumerable letters and phone calls about his involvement in the paper, and frequent transatlantic flights of envoys to

---

* In 1959, Whitney sold the plane to CBS. It broke down three years later, and Paley joshingly suggested that Jock owed him a rebate. Whitney's rejoinder to that was typical of the way in which men of extraordinary wealth discuss the tawdry subject of money. He retorted that there would be no refund because he had just come upon an old gambling chit indicating that Paley owed him nine dollars.

Whitney from concerned parties in the States. And the concern was deepening. The *Tribune* lost half a million dollars in the first six months of 1957; the Reids were pressed for cash. One of the problems that had to be solved had nothing to do with money: should Whitney come to the rescue of—maybe even take over eventually—the *Herald Tribune,* who would edit it?

By the end of September 1957, Whitney had agreed to lend the *Tribune* $1,200,000, in twelve monthly installments, beginning in October. On October 1 another eulogistic editorial about Whitney appeared in the paper. This one, headed "Renewing a Valued Association," was accompanied by a portrait of Abraham Lincoln and John Hay. The editorial declared, "We welcome Mr. Whitney as a friend and associate," and in an adjoining statement Whitney said:

I am happy to make this investment in the future of the New York *Herald Tribune* and in this manner to participate not only in its ambitious program for increased service to its readers but also in the future of the newspaper medium as a vital instrument of public information. I have always had a personal interest in the New York *Herald Tribune,* partly because my grandfather (John Hay) was an editorial writer and reporter on the New York *Tribune* from 1870 to 1875 under Whitelaw Reid, and later, in 1881, acted as editor-in-chief while Mr. Reid was in Europe. They were close friends throughout my grandfather's life.

Almost at once, Whitney came to realize that being an ambassador with journalistic associations could lead to ticklish situations. On that October 1, the *Tribune* hired away from *Life* a new editorial writer, William J. Miller. Three days later, the Soviet Union launched its first Sputnik. Eisenhower's Secretary of Defense, Charles E. Wilson, who had come to Washington from General Motors and was known as "Engine Charlie," dismissed the satellite as a "basketball." Miller had come to the *Trib* determined, as he put it, to restore outrage and indignation to the American scene. He wrote not one but three editorials chiding Wilson for his brush-off of the epochal event. The first editorial began, "The nation has been asleep."

The quick-tempered President was outraged and indignant. For a time, he refused to look at the *Tribune,* which, in October 1951, had been the first consequential American paper to propose him for the White House, and to which on becoming Chief Executive he had paid as close attention as he did to any journal. He would fume now and then, to be sure, about a column by Joe Alsop, but by and large Eisenhower regarded the *Trib* as the most stalwart advocate of the kind of liberal Republicanism that he espoused. Indeed, Whitney would sometimes tell acquaintances that pressure from the President had been the determining factor in his deciding to get involved with the paper. When Miller first met Whitney, in December 1957, Jock was still upset about those White-House-shaking editorials. The editing of the *Tribune* was not yet, of course, Whitney's sole responsibility. Even so, when he had accompanied Queen Elizabeth to the United States in October, he felt constrained to apologize to the President for the paper's editorial thrusts. Not long after that, Miller's superiors began blunting the edge of some of his jabs at the Administration.

The *Herald Tribune*'s net loss for 1957 came to $1,277,738.92. The $1,200,000 Whitney was committed to invest in it would be simply bail-out money. Just before Christmas, Thayer, Paley, and McCrary had had lunch with Sam Park, Jock's chief fiscal agent, and the four of them concurred that there would be little point in Whitney's becoming only an investor in the newspaper.† If he was going to be held accountable, as he surely would be, for its fortunes or misfortunes, he might as well own all of it. The quadrumvirate also agreed that Whitney needed a new corporate entity to embrace his various publishing ventures. Soon after that lunch his advisers began talking about a "hen house." The idea was that, if Whitney were to take over all or most of the troubled *Trib*, it could be shored up, until its tide turned, were he to acquire other publishing properties—other chickens—that could be counted on to show a profit. When the time came, in 1958, for his associates to give their hen house a formal name, they thought at first of "H. H. Publications." That was rejected, though, on the ground that people might believe the initials stood for Jock's mother Helen Hay. So they chose, as an interim name, Valley Road Publications (Valley Road was Jock's Long Island street address), later switching back to the chicken concept they'd begun with— Plymouth Rock Publications.

In January 1958, while Whitney was on one of his frequent trips to the United States, Lee Hills, the executive editor of the Detroit *Free Press*, came east and had lunch with Jock and Paley in the CBS man's suite at the St. Regis Hotel. Hills said that the *Herald Tribune* seemed to him a risky investment, a tough prospect, but that if Jock went ahead and bought the paper "it could be the most exciting, challenging, personally satisfying thing he ever did." Paley concurred. Whitney was left with the feeling—the hope, at any rate—that, if he accepted the challenge, Hills would be the editorial captain of his ship. Always one to move prudently—except perhaps back in his polo-playing days—Whitney dispatched Senator Javits to sound out Arthur Hays Sulzberger, the pub-

† McCrary shortly departed from the scene. At a time when the *Tribune* was supporting Sherman Adams, the White House major-domo who had accepted a vicuña coat and other favors from the manufacturer Bernard Goldfine, McCrary's public relations firm had set up an exculpatory press conference for Goldfine.

lisher of the *Times*, as to how that paper would react if John Hay Whitney were to become its principal rival. Sulzberger was non-committal, but he did say he'd be glad to talk to Whitney whenever their paths might next cross. (They did meet for drinks and polite chitchat when Sulzberger was in London the following October, and Whitney inferred that the *Times* would look upon him not exactly as a fraternity brother but at least as a friendly enemy. One subject they did not discuss was that Jock was considering as his editor-in-chief, should he take over the *Tribune,* Sulzberger's nephew Cyrus, the *Times*'s chief foreign correspondent. The younger Sulzberger was interested in the job but felt he could not make so monumental a switch of allegiances while his uncle was alive.)

By now, Walter Thayer was searching for purchasable chickens—newspapers, magazines, radio and television stations—to support the *Tribune* until it got turned around. In April 1958, Whitney asked Secretary of State John Foster Dulles for permission to return to the United States for "consultations." The Ambassador didn't have to consult his government but, rather, his own people at home, because the *Herald Tribune* situation was, as he told Dulles, "a good deal sicker than when we began." The doses of dollars that by this time were being mentioned as the means of restoring the ailing paper to health were disconcerting even to a man in Whitney's enviable position—fifteen, maybe twenty million dollars—and there seemed to be nobody else around who had either the resources or the resolve to lend a hand. "The only ray of hope," Whitney wrote Dulles, was that the situation had become "so desperate that Brown now agrees to step down in favor of a really top newspaperman who was willing to do it a few months ago, but for whom I couldn't get chief control. The decision, based on all the factors now available, must be taken in the next ten days. I have concluded that, even if I decide against any further investment (and this time it will require just about my *whole* neck!) I must be there and make the decision myself." Lee Hills was the editor Whitney referred to, and on April 21, just after Jock returned to London with matters still unsettled, he was cheered by a cablegram from Thayer: MET LEE AND HIS LAWYER TODAY STOP HE LOOKS LIKE HENHOUSE ROOSTER IF WE CAN NAIL CHICKENS.

His hopes high, Whitney made another quick trip to New York at the end of May. He had what seemed to be a crucial meeting scheduled for June 7 with Hills and Brown Reid. But the day before that he received a puzzling letter from Reid's mother. That matriarch said that she believed there might be better alternatives for the future of the *Tribune*—she did not mention any specific ones—than for him to take it over. "Even though Brown will represent us at any future discussions," she wrote, "in the final analysis my decision may be the determining factor."

That was enough for Lee Hills. He washed his hands of the affair and went back to Detroit. Whitney wrote Brown that the *Tribune* had seen the last of any money of his that it would get. (HAVING SUDDEN AND UNEXPECTED TROUBLE WITH TRIBUNE DEAL, Whitney cabled Betsey in Majorca, where she was on a holiday with the Whitney Straights, DUE TO DESPERATE DIVERSIONS BY BROWN.) Mrs. Reid took what she hoped would be quick ameliorative action. On June 13, she called on President Eisenhower. She told him Whitney had misunderstood her, that the Reids wanted to co-operate with him, and wouldn't the President intercede? Jock had returned to London by then and was almost at once the recipient of a letter from the President saying he had told Mrs. Reid that Whitney's taking over the *Tribune* would be "a civic service of the highest order." Negotiations were resumed. They might have been in any event, for, as Walter Thayer told a friend at the time, "I don't think there is a chance in the world that Jock is out, because he will not let this thing fold if he can keep it alive."

Now the President introduced a diversion of his own. One of Eisenhower's top-tier bridge and golf cronies was William E. Robinson, a sometime publicity man but for most of his business career involved in journalism. Robinson had worked for the *Herald Tribune* from 1936 to 1954, with a number of titles, among them business manager and executive vice-president. He had met Ike in France in 1944, when Robinson had gone there to supervise the resurrection of the *Herald* after the liberation of Paris. In the fifties, certainly in part because of the friendship between Eisenhower and Robert Woodruff, Robinson had become president of the Coca-Cola Company. But that hadn't lasted long; the story went around Georgia that Robinson had interrupted a speech Woodruff was making in Atlanta, a lapse that was roughly comparable to interrupting the Pope in Rome. So the President suggested to Whitney that, if and when he took over the *Tribune*, perhaps he could find a spot there for good old Bill Robinson—business manager or something of the sort. Jock had by then been an ambassador for nearly eighteen months and had become a polished diplomat. "I have the greatest respect for Bill's judgment and will always turn to him for advice," he replied, tactfully, to Eisenhower. But he said nothing about a job.

By the end of July, Thayer had caged for Whitney his first plump chicken—the Sunday newspaper supplement *Parade*. It was bought from Field Enterprises, Inc., for $6,600,500. Jock had partly owned it once before. *Parade* had been instituted by Marshall Field in 1941 as a weekend appendage of *PM*—to make use of stories and pictures for which there wasn't enough space in that slim daily. Whitney had lost most of his investment in *PM* when Field bought him out for twenty cents on the dollar. But after *PM* folded, Field had syndicated *Parade*. By 1958, it was lucratively tucked inside fifty-nine Sunday papers with a total circulation of eight and a half million, and was making a profit of two million dollars a year. It was a fat chicken indeed. There was a further irony. *Parade* could not be distributed with the *Herald Tribune,* because two of its best-paying customers, the Newark *Star-Ledger* and the *Long Island Press,* were in the same broad geographical area. The *Tribune* used *This Week* instead. (Whitney sold *Parade* to the Booth Newspapers, early in 1973, for sixteen million dollars. Even allowing for inflation, that hen laid more than its share of golden eggs.)

The first step leading toward Jock's acquisition of the *Herald Tribune* had been the agreement made with the Reids in the fall of 1957. This provided that after his initial loan of $1,200,000, he could, by lending an additional $1,300,000, obtain a fifty-one per cent interest in it. His rights and obligations were transferred to Valley Road Publications and in due course to Plymouth Rock. The paper's financial condition and prospects, though, did not seem to warrant the Whitney interests' putting up the additional $1,300,000, all the more so since there was a substantial amount of preferred stock that outranked the common. Next, a plan for the reorganization of the *Herald Tribune* was endorsed by all the concerned parties, and that intent was set forth in a complex option agreement—a lawyers' delight—dated July 18, 1958. That agreement provided that Plymouth Rock could acquire fifty-one per cent of the equity *and* eighty per cent of the voting power for stock purchases totaling $1,250,000 ($500,000 of this for common and $750,000 for preferred) and a commitment for a further loan of $900,000. It all added up to $3,350,-000. That option was implemented through a reorganization agreement signed on August 28, 1958.

Whitney had now assumed full responsibility for the *Herald Tribune,* but its appetite for continued financial aid seemed insatiable. By the time the paper had run its course, he had put nearly forty million dollars into it, and the Reids' share of ownership had shrunk, as debts ballooned, to six thousandths of one per cent. But from Jock's point of view, the money involved was only a part of the picture. There was a sense of noblesse oblige, too. Somebody had to save the good old *Herald Tribune,* and who had better reason to than John Hay's grandson and Ike's friend? "I did it because I had to," Whitney told an acquaintance afterward. In a more formal statement, he would say:

> I took over the *Herald Tribune* because I believed in its importance to
> our community, and because I could bring in resources to strengthen
> it. . . . I won't belabor the well-worn theme of "the role of a newspaper
> in a modern world." Let me only say that it must be a force in the com-

munity, a force for good, a force for reason and a force for understanding. . . .

In saying that the *Tribune* should be a force for good, I recognize that
I am in an ill-defined area to which each person has his own chart. I think
there is good in a spirit of moderation, one which doesn't wear the brands
of extremism or intolerance, but rather welcomes diversity and proceeds
with patience. I think there is good in a concern for human welfare and
human dignity, recognizing that neither by itself is enough but both are
necessary. There is good, too, in the spirited political life this nation
enjoys.

I took over a newspaper that called itself "Independent Republican," a
term I had been in the habit of applying to myself. But I found that the
Tribune had come to be widely thought of as being just plain Republican,
in the "my party right or wrong" sense. I believe in what the Republican
Party has traditionally stood for, not because it is Republican but because
I think it is right—or at least, because I think that on balance it is more
nearly right more of the time.

A newspaper doesn't have to compromise; freedom is the essence of a
responsible press. And responsibility—by which I mean a devotion to
truth and conscience, wherever this scatters the chips—is, I deeply feel, an
inescapable obligation of a free press. In short, I have tried and I think
with some success, to restore the "Independent" part of our "Independent
Republican" label.

I think there is a lot of good, too, that can be done in a practical, hard-
headed way right here in New York. Our town loses the individual all too
easily in its noisy maze. But with the right combination of enterprise and
inspiration, a newspaper can give voice to his needs and wants. I think
the city can be brought to respond to the kind of public appeal only a
newspaper—yes, still only a newspaper—can make.

We are not proclaiming omniscience or the discovery of a new and
magic formula. But I do hope, through the combined and concerted
talents gathered at the *Herald Tribune,* to provide a voice that will be
heard.

On August 28, Helen Reid told the *Tribune* staff, "We are having a
man who cares about newspapers come into the field." A few days later,
her son Brown, who had agreed to stay on as editor until Whitney could
find one of his own, wrote to Jock, "The ship is yours. The very best of
luck." Walter Lippmann cabled Jock that he had told Mrs. Reid, "It has
been wisely done and all will be well with the paper." John O'Hara sent
Jock a letter in which he noted that he still used the *Herald Tribune* library as a research source for his novels, and he said, "I think that your
coming to the rescue now is an act of public service in the public good
that is of much more significance than you realize, and as an old pro I
honor you for it." O'Hara called to Whitney's attention that he was writ-

ing on a letterhead he had salvaged from the wreck of *Collier's* magazine. "When a journalistic institution is allowed to die," the author
wrote, "every man and woman who has ever read a single word in that
publication—in agreement or disagreement—is the loser. The loss to non-
readers is incalculable, and the loss to freedom is absolute."

(A year afterward, Stanley Walker, the then retired legendary city editor of the *Tribune,* wrote in the *Saturday Review* that, while the ship
undoubtedly had barnacles, its new skipper should be careful in the
course of scraping them off not to damage the superstructure. "The coming of Mr. Whitney was an effective specific in itself," Walker said. "His
name and personality alone brought a certain confidence. The people at
the paper felt better, the readers were reassured somewhat, and even the
advertisers felt a new, healthy glow, a sort of pride to have a part in a
Whitney venture. . . . He's solvent, civilized, not easily scared, in excel-
lent health, and he means to do right. . . . The old-timers, who never
quite give up hope, are in his corner." Whitney himself was aware—
sometimes disturbingly—that his solvency was to many of his associates
more significant than his character. In a 1964 speech at Colby College,
on the occasion of his being dubbed the Thirteenth Elijah Paris Lovejoy
Fellow, he said, "I think it is clear that though I have worked at journalism, I am here today primarily because I am a millionaire. It is not polite
to go into this sort of thing. Heaven knows it is not comfortable." He also
said—could he have been thinking of his poet mother?—that newspapers
had "the capability to write the real poetry of everyday life."

Never in his life had Whitney had to worry about money. When he
took over the *Tribune,* there were moments when little else seemed to be
on the mind of anyone he dealt with. On October 22, for instance,
Thayer, a meticulous man, told him the paper was going into the red at
the daily rate, three hundred and sixty-five days a year, of $5,479.45. "It
scares the hell out of me," Thayer wrote to London. "I think it's the
toughest assignment you have ever taken on." And within a year Sam
Park was warning Whitney—who had philanthropic pledges outstanding
for 1959 of nearly two million dollars—that he should hold back on other
major contributions and even on large personal expenses. "The *Tribune*
is causing a revolution in your accustomed style of operation," Park said.

The first few months of Whitney's stewardship of the newspaper were
unexpectedly unrewarding. For eighteen days in December 1958, a time
of year when advertising was usually heavier than at any other period,
the paper had to suspend publication entirely because of a deliverers'
strike. During that bleak hiatus, Brown Reid agreed to a suggestion
made by Whitney the previous month that he resign. As president of the
Herald Tribune, Whitney installed Howard Brundage, a partner in J. H.

Whitney & Company. Brundage was a businessman, not a journalist. Whitney needed an editor-in-chief.

For a while, he thought he had his man in Bernard E. Kilgore, who in less than twenty years had boosted the circulation of the *Wall Street Journal* from 32,000 to 625,000. Kilgore did consent to join the board of directors of Plymouth Rock Publications, but advice was all he would provide; he did not, understandably, wish to leave a proven commodity for one with a shaky past and a cloudy future. Kilgore proposed Eugene S. Duffield, an eminent *Wall Street Journal* alumnus who by then was a vice-president of Federated Department Stores; Duffield begged off when he was offered the presidency of the Popular Science Publishing Company.

It was a difficult period for Whitney. In his ambassadorship, he was engaged in perhaps the most strenuous assignment thus far in his life. The *Herald Tribune* was his most provocative undertaking. It was hard to handle the ongoing and the forthcoming all at once, and across an ocean at that. But for all the intensity of his commitment to the Court of St. James's, by the spring of 1959 Whitney was referring to the *Tribune*, in his voluminous correspondence to his surrogates back home, as "Topic A." He had had Thayer engage McKinsey & Company to study the paper and its prospects, and that research organization's findings had not been particularly heartening. McKinsey predicted that most of the *Trib*'s readers thought the paper was too stodgy. (It was that analysis that inspired a subsequent *Tribune* advertising slogan: "Who says that a good newspaper has to be dull?") The results of another survey, made by Elmo Roper, jibed nicely with Whitney's long pursuit of both excellence and gratification. The *Herald Tribune*, that study concluded, should be aimed at "those who want a *first class* paper but who want to *enjoy* it, too."

Whitney had not too much time for introspection, but when he had, his reflections were not always heartening, either. On May 23, 1959, spending a rare weekend alone with Betsey at their English country retreat, after a round of golf he wrote a longhand fireside letter to Thayer:

I had thought that my life's experience, rather highlighted by the fabulous opportunity that this current wrastle affords, gave an extra reason for me to be the owner of this newspaper, gave me a reason and a challenge for personal activity on the paper, which would be exciting, useful, and proper. This may have been a half-baked, really an unbaked, reason for what *otherwise* would have been an idiotic, Quixotic contribution to the survival of a tradition. A bit, perhaps, because Ike believes in its importance—as everyone does who doesn't have to pay more than a nickel for it!

But now I am suddenly faced with a challenge to my romantic notion that I can perform a working function in this revival—this Phoenix shaking its ashes away. The challenge is put, quite kindly, by more than a few experts in journalism in searching questions as to my intentions. I have answered these questions frankly and they have all fled away!

In other words I have kept to my innocent hope that I, and Betsey, have something to give, something effective, something of a personal, actually unique kind . . . if this isn't so, then one of the real reasons for this huge lifesaver having been chucked overboard seems a bit silly. . . . I still believe that, unless the new *Tribune* is associated with the Whitneys, as it once was with the Reids, that there's no sense, no sense at all in my giving it a reputation and a fortune, in both of which I have a proud stake, and which they can exploit.

I can cut it now, and I do think you should know I am prepared to. . . .

Thayer replied six days later:

The issue is the form this participation of yours may take, not the substance of it. You have a tremendous talent to bring to the venture. As I have become acquainted with and have dealt with the moguls of the newspaper industry my faith in what you can bring to it has increased rather than decreased. I am sure there is no endeavor you could pursue which could *tap* or *use* to such full extent the great assets you have to offer. I don't know anyone who can match you in this respect. Therefore, not for a single minute have I contemplated a management solution that would bar active participation for you. If we cannot get management which will not only accept but encourage such participation by you, I would rather see you out of the picture entirely, for it makes no sense to me for you to put up your wealth and reputation at risk in a business from which you are excluded, whether voluntarily, or involuntarily.‡

Topic A remained the recruiting of an editor. In mid-1959, Bernard Kilgore came up with a new candidate. It was a long shot. Kilgore recommended Robert M. White II, the forty-four-year-old editor of a family-owned daily, the *Evening Ledger*, in Mexico, Missouri. Mexico had a population of fourteen thousand, the *Ledger* a circulation of

‡Not long before, Thayer had happened to be on an airplane and spotted one mogul, Arthur Hays Sulzberger of the *Times*, seated up ahead of him. Thayer was pleased to see that Sulzberger evidently took the *Tribune* seriously. The *Times* publisher was scrutinizing both his own paper and the opposition one, apparently comparing their treatment of that day's news developments. The *Tribune*'s role in daily journalism vis-à-vis the *Times* was of considerable interest in other circles, too. After Christian Herter succeeded Dulles as Eisenhower's Secretary of State, Herter wrote Whitney that he hoped the *Tribune* would succeed if for no other reason than to disabuse some foreign governments of their notion that the *Times* was the official newspaper of the American government—a misapprehension, the Secretary said, that sometimes prompted its holders to leak stories to the *Times*.

8,500. It covered the regional news, it boasted, "like dew covers Little Dixie." Not only was White from a small Midwestern town (if a notable one: Mexico called itself the fire-clay and saddle-horse capital of the world), but he was a Democrat. But he was no country bumpkin. He was a director of the American Newspaper Publishers Association and a consultant to the Chicago *Sun-Times*. Still, one of the few things White seemed to have in common with Jock Whitney was that the Missourian liked to shoot quail.

Walter Thayer met White at an A.N.P.A. convention in New York and was sufficiently impressed with him to pack him off to London so Jock could look him over, too. Thayer described White to Whitney, in advance, as "young Lochinvar." Whitney, after meeting him, was put in mind of another non-New-York-born editor he had known, the founder of *The New Yorker*, and Jock described White as "a civilized Harold Ross. He puts his feet on the table but doesn't entirely mean it." Notwithstanding, Jock was impressed, too, and he offered White the editorship of the *Tribune*, which White accepted as of August 3. (Whitney made haste to assure the President that under White, whatever his political antecedents might be, the paper would remain "Eisenhower Republican.") White was no less impressed himself. "I found that Whitney is the kind of guy who puts a newspaper ahead of the ownership," he later told *The New Yorker*'s Talk of the Town department, "which is the only way a newspaper can be great."

Soon after White moved in as editor—also president, chief executive officer, and a director of Plymouth Rock, with a hundred thousand dollars a year in assured income and stock options to boot—Whitney wrote to Stanley Walker, "where are the present-day counterparts of you and your heroes? Will newcomers one day write in whispered words of Bob White and the men he brought to the paper? Or are they even now with us, haloes invisible? I may never find out, but at least I can give them room and air—and time."

There would be less time than Jock had anticipated. White was certainly an innovation in the upper reaches of the New York journalistic scene, and he was also, to a degree, innovative. When Nikita Khrushchev came to the United States, for instance, White ran a front-page editorial explaining the United States and the capitalistic system to the Soviet premier, and he had the text printed in both English and Russian. But White also had traits that came to trouble Whitney, not least among them a seeming devotion to astrology. The editor wrote his boss late in October 1959 that he had just had a reunion with a female astrologer of his acquaintance who had predicted two years previous that he was destined to move from a small town to the editorship of a big metropolitan paper; this time she was predicting that 1961 would be a great year for

40. *After a wild-turkey shoot at Thomasville: left to right, President Eisenhower, a plantation hand, Major General Howard McC. Snyder (the White House physician), Secretary of the Treasury George M. Humphrey, Jock Whitney.*

41. *Ike as chef, and a trencherman at Greenwood. The chef's doctor hovers nearby, just in case.*

42. *Jock—he is easily identifiable by his prominent ears—and guests watching a court-tennis match at Greentree.* (Frank Ross photo, for The Saturday Evening Post)

43. *Friends and relatives: left to right, William S. Paley, Jinx Falkenburg, Mary Cushing Astor Fosburgh, John McClain, Betsey, Jock, Babe Paley, Tex McCrary.*

44. *After the strike: Publisher Jock Whitney happily holding up his* Herald Tribune *when the presses begin rolling again.*

45. *A tea at the Whitney town house in New York, in 1963, for delegates to the annual Youth Forum of the* Herald Tribune. *The painting is Toulouse-Lautrec's "Marcelle Lender dansant le Boléro dans 'Chilperic.'"*

46. In his office at J. H. Whitney & Co., at his grandfather Hay's desk, with, behind him, Seurat's "L'Île de La Grande-Jatte." (Frank Ross photo, for The Saturday Evening Post)

47. *At a Museum of Modern Art reception for the United Nations General Assembly: left to right, Mrs. Tom Connally, Senator Connally, Jock, Nelson Rockefeller.* (William Leftwhon photo)

48. *Jock's first important painting: Pierre Auguste Renoir's "Le Moulin de la Galette," painted in 1876 and acquired by Jock in 1929.* (John D. Schiff photo)

49. *Photographic portrait, of Betsey Cushing Whitney.* (Cecil Beaton photograph; courtesy Sotheby's Belgravia)

50. Jock Whitney.

51. *Joan Whitney Payson, Jock's sister, at the racetrack, watching a Green-tree horse while keeping up by radio with the Mets.* (Associated Press Wirephoto)

52. *Capot wins the Belmont Stakes in 1949: In presentation picture, left to right, Jock, George Widener, Joan Payson, Greentree jockey Ted Atkinson, and Greentree trainer John M. Gaver, Sr.* (Mike Sirico photo)

53. *The President of Yale and his Senior Fellow at New Haven in 1973. Behind Jock and Kingman Brewster, Jr. is a portrait of Brewster's predecessor, A. Whitney Griswold.*

54. *Ambassador Whitney in his embassy office, with Whistler's "Wapping" and Bellows' "Introducing John L. Sullivan" on the wall, and a photograph of his grandfather Hay on the table.* (Douglas Glass photo. Copyright by Glass, 43 Black Lion Lane, London W6)

the *Herald Tribune*, that any newspaper owned by a lion (Whitney was a Leo) and run by a ram (White was Aries) couldn't miss; and, finally, that Castro would soon be shot. (White's personal secretary was Kathryn A. Ritchie, who later became Whitney's secretary. White had not long been on the job when he confessed to Miss Ritchie that he was worried about a phrase she kept transferring from one day to the next on her desk calendar. The words were "Period of Adjustment." Why did that bother him? she wondered. "When is my period supposed to end?" he wanted to know. He was much relieved to be told she was jotting down the name of a play she had it in mind to go to when she could find a free evening.)

That same October, Thayer concluded a reorganization, for Whitney, of the corporate structure that was underwriting the *Tribune*. Plymouth Rock became the Whitney Communications Corporation, and into this new entity were transferred a few radio stations, *Parade*, the monthly *Interior Design*, and five television stations under the aegis of the Corinthian Broadcasting Corporation, until then itself wholly owned by J. H. Whitney & Company. The idea still was that profits generated by all the other elements of Whitney Communications would be used to shore up the *Tribune* until it could get by on its own; meanwhile, the venture capital firm could go about its regular business without having to fret about the paper's woes. Four partners in J. H. Whitney & Company— Thayer, Sam Park, Robert F. Bryan, and C. Wrede Petersmeyer—left that concern to become, with Jook, partners in Whitney Communications. On the occasion of its establishment, Whitney issued a statement: "It is my conviction that the whole communication field is basic to our modern life, and that it has a profound political, social, cultural, and economic importance not only in the United States, but throughout the world."

As 1960 got under way, Thayer predicted to Whitney, not with horoscopic advice but on the basis of a detailed study of the paper by McKinsey and Company that the *Herald Tribune* could, if all went well, be expected to break even in five more years; and that Jock could expect to put another fifteen million dollars into it before things got turned around. That seemed manageable. The annual gross profits from the other Whitney Communications properties figured to be about eight million dollars—the largest share from Corinthian's television operations. In view of that, it did not amuse Whitney, who received his paper daily in London by air and who sometimes had to take a deep breath before reading portions of it, that under White some of the *Tribune*'s columnists and, worse yet, its editorial writers, kept attacking the medium of television. "If you want to know what's wrong with television," said an editorial on November 3, 1959, "turn it on. Its few worthwhile evening programs struggle for life in a sea of mediocrity. Its daytime programs are a uniform mess of triviality. Its children's programs are of a sort that a conscientious parent puts on only after great hesitation." The usually mild-mannered Whitney informed his editor that such broadsides were "fatuous piety."

That year, of course, was a presidential election year. Eisenhower was a lame duck. Whitney had breakfast at the White House in January, and to Jock's surprise and delight his host said that when his term was over he might go into publishing himself. Whitney and Thayer at once began to talk about a "Mr. X Project," and Jock wrote Eisenhower wondering whether, at the appropriate time, he would like to be associated in some capacity or other with either Whitney Communications or the *Herald Tribune*. It was not the President's way of doing things to give flat "nos," especially to overtures from friends with a lot of money. He replied evasively that "there would be a great personal pleasure in some kind of association with you." But all that ever evolved from this exchange was a vague understanding that the *Tribune* might someday get first serialization rights to Eisenhower's as yet unwritten White House memoirs.

By the spring of that year, with the presidential primaries under way, it was fairly obvious that Whitney would play some role in the campaign, as he had before—if nothing more than contributing substantially to candidates of his choice. But this bothered some of his editors, who felt uncomfortable, for instance, about running an editorial one day endorsing a Republican Senator's re-election and then, a couple of days later, running an Associated Press dispatch mentioning that Whitney had contributed a thousand dollars to that Senator's campaign fund. It did not especially bother Jock that he seemed to others to be wearing two hats. He could hardly help it if he had a closetful of hats. If one of his horses won a big stakes race, surely his sports department should have no qualms about chronicling that legitimate news—or, when it came to that, about reporting the triumphs and tragedies of his sister's New York Mets. Only rarely did Whitney exercise his rights of ownership to influence his paper's handling of the news. On the death in 1965 of Joseph Grosso, who had joined the Whitney household staff in 1917 and had stayed on for forty-eight years, thirty-three as a butler and fifteen as Jock's valet, the sole obituary notice the deceased received in any New York City newspaper was a handsome one in the *Herald Tribune*.

Most of the *Tribune* staff found Bob White a congenial, likable boss; and Whitney, though largely removed from the editorial scene, was still on reasonably good terms with his protégé, whom he had forgiven for his sniping at television.

One final word on the editorial page and television [Jock wrote White from London on March 18, 1960]. I am glad that you know that I will allow no sacred cows to bear my brand in any part of our building. I do feel that you and Dwight [Sargent, by then running the editorial page] missed my point about being "holier than thou," which I must have expressed very badly because the last thing that I had in mind to suggest was that we should not judge. So it seems to me that a good deal of language and thought was devoted to swatting a straw man. I still think we should not be "holier than thou" because to me this description cannot be used in connection with honest judgment but only when the judge is stuffy or deals in unsupported generalities.

Yet Whitney was beginning to have reservations about White's overall judgment. Jock had not demurred when he'd been told that his editor was negotiating with Al Capp to have that cartoonist-turned-polemicist appear in the *Tribune*. The publisher had assumed it was Capp's "Li'l Abner" comic strip that was under consideration. When, however, Whitney learned instead that White had had a contract drawn up for Capp, whose political views by then were often considerably to the right of Eisenhower Republicans, to write a thrice-weekly column for the paper, he balked. Capp got even. The following year he came up in "Li'l Abner" with a character called Jock Wetknee, Hambassador from Lower Slobbovia.

Thayer, too, was beginning to have doubts about White. Thayer was supposed to be the chief conduit of communication between Whitney in London and the *Tribune* staff in New York, and here was White communicating directly with the distant owner. For another thing, the paper simply wasn't making the headway all hands had hoped for. For still another, it irked Thayer that White was living in the suburbs and commuting to his Manhattan office from Westchester County not by train, where he might at least have rubbed elbows with some of his readers, but by private limousine. What would have been perfectly acceptable for a Whitney, Thayer felt, was wrong for a White.

Whitney, who had seen many a horse come from behind in many a race, was naturally concerned about all this, but he remained sanguine about his paper's long-range prospects. When a real estate man in New York proposed that election-year spring that Jock's name be high on the Republican national ticket, he replied, "ill-equipped as I would be for the Vice-Presidency, I may—just may—be able to bring to the revival of the New York *Herald Tribune* qualities (including money!) to restore it as a vital voice in this country's affairs."

Vice-President Nixon was, of course, the leading candidate for the top spot on that ticket. He was not one of Whitney's favorite persons, although they had got on well enough during Nixon's Thanksgiving visit to London in 1958. (When Nixon's daughter Tricia happened to mention to Jock once she had always wanted to be a jockey, he sent her a set of

Greentree silks.) At the Republican convention in August, 1960, when Nixon was nominated to run against John F. Kennedy, Congressman Walter Judd of Minnesota, with whom Jock had traveled to South Korea for the Syngman Rhee reinauguration, was the keynote speaker. The *Tribune* ran an editorial—it was written by Dwight Sargent; William Miller had long since returned to *Life*—chiding Judd for, among other things, excessive party partisanship. Whitney was running a Republican paper, Eisenhower was still President, Whitney was still Eisenhower's Ambassador, and he was not pleased. He was even less happy when White seemed to him dilatory about formally endorsing Nixon's candidacy. "Good grief," Jock wrote to White (sending a copy of his lament to Eisenhower), "for the life of me I cannot see why. . . . We are not *independent* in postponement, we are silly. . . . You are running a Republican newspaper. Do you feel a personal concern that you are in an anomalous position in so doing? If there is any doubt in your mind about where the paper should stand—and when it should take its stand during the campaign, then we must resolve that immediately—I want our paper to be free but free Republican."*

Privately, Whitney had misgivings about the candidate his newspaper was backing. (His journalist son-in-law at the time, William Haddad, was writing campaign speeches for John F. Kennedy.) "I now think Nixon may win," Whitney wrote Thayer on October 26. "I hope that's good!" After Kennedy won, one of Jock's assistants drafted a telegram for him to send to the loser, which went, in part, "It is incredible that we must do without you in public life for a while longer. Nobody could point up with greater force the tremendous job still to be done by the party if we are to restore the kind of leadership we must have to perpetuate the principles which are so uniquely American." Whitney kept the message on his desk for a few hours, then tossed it aside. His staff filed the unsent message notwithstanding. There is no evidence extant that the *winning* candidate actually transmitted a telegram that a rear admiral addressing the 1960 Thanksgiving Dinner in London of the American Society, at the Dorchester, contended in his remarks that Kennedy had sent to the Ambassador: JOCK PACK JACK.

It had not bolstered Whitney's ebbing confidence in the judgment of White that on election night, when Nixon was narrowly defeated, the

---

* Whitney had another grievance for which White could hardly be faulted. The *Tribune* was running well behind the *Times* in all categories of advertising linage. One area in which it might logically have expected to rank at least even was paid political advertising from Republican sources. But the Republican Party kept putting most of its ads in the *Times*—and this despite the fact that (or conceivably because) Walter Thayer was serving as the finance chairman of an ad hoc group separate from the party called National Volunteers for Nixon-Lodge.

Tribune went to press proclaiming that Kennedy had scored a victory of "Rooseveltian proportions." On November 18, White resigned, effective as of the start of the new year. ("It was a great idea," Thayer said later, "but it didn't work.") On being apprised of that development, Whitney wrote to White, "I know that I am taking on an immense job, but I have come to the conclusion that only the owner can *be* the paper and to do that he must clearly be around." By the end of 1960, the *Tribune* that Whitney would soon be commanding in person had already consumed seven million dollars of his money.

16

The Only Millionaire I Ever Rooted For

On January 4, 1961, just before leaving London to take over the *Herald Tribune,* Whitney wrote to a friend, "The problem of the *Trib* is appalling to one who hoped for ease, but we'll have to give it a whirl." On arriving thus purposefully in New York, Whitney was welcomed by a *Times* editorial that said, "This newspaper warmly wishes him well." The editorial also commended him on his diplomatic mission. "Mr. Whitney would have been popular and useful," it said, "even if he hadn't been amply supplied with money of his own; but if he hadn't been so supplied he couldn't have afforded the London post at all. He did not complain. He is not a complaining man. He merely observed that it is 'intolerable to have to have money to have the job.'"

Whitney arrived at the *Tribune* just ahead of a new editor Thayer had recruited for him. This was John I. Denson, a peripatetic Louisianan who had been the managing editor of *Newsweek* and who before that had bounced around the editorial staffs of nine daily papers and three other magazines. Denson was a fussy man. So determined was he to have his first edition of the *Tribune* as nearly letter-perfect as he could make it that it rarely got to press on schedule. He was a quixotic editor, too, hard-driving and temperamental, not always easy for his subordinates to get along with. Some of them called him the Lone Ranger, others the Mad Genius. He loved flashy, attention-getting headlines. On March 2,

1962, for example, the day after the astronaut John Glenn had had an
acclamatory parade in New York City and an airplane had crashed at the
city's Idlewild Airport, killing ninety-five people, Denson had had
splashed all the way across the paper's front page two banner heads:

TRIUMPH—THE NEW YORK WAY

and

TRAGEDY—END OF FLIGHT 1.

Denson was wholeheartedly committed to converting the *Tribune* into a
full-fledged rival to the supremacy of the *Times*. "If this paper survives,"
Whitney said, "there should be a plaque to John Denson in the lobby."

Denson presided over a publication that by now Whitney had resolved
would be a "newspaper of analysis and interpretation rather than the
newspaper of record." The *Tribune* could hardly have hoped to challenge the *Times* for the latter distinction; it didn't carry enough advertising to give it room to cover all the news in depth or even superficially.
The *Trib*'s circulation had gone up since mid-1959 by about 40,000 a day,
but it was still steadily losing money; and Whitney had to fret not only
about that but also about the impact of the paper's improvidence on the
fortunes of its sustaining Whitney Communications Corporation.

> It must be recognized [Jock was told by Thayer in a memorandum dated
> April 18, 1961] "that the drain of the *Tribune* is causing a feeling of frus-
> tration, if not despair, among some of our associates. The *Tribune* losses
> consume all present W.C.C. combined earnings after debt service. . . . It
> is imperative, in my judgment, that all concerned be given the assurance
> that we will not subsidize the *Tribune* to an extent and in a manner that
> will permanently stunt the growth of these companies. We have a very
> unique and a brilliant group of people associated with us. They must be
> made to feel their personal futures will not be impaired because of the
> sacrifices in time and money being made in the *Tribune*.

Concluding that Thayer should play a more direct role in guiding the
paper's shaky course, Whitney soon installed him as president of the
Herald Tribune. (Whitney's own titles were Editor-in-Chief and Publisher.) Thayer tackled the job with verve. Walking along Fifth Avenue
one day, he noticed that a mannequin in a Saks show-window display
was holding a copy of the *Times*. He phoned an executive of the department store, demanded equal space, and got it. But he never got much
more Saks advertising, or, when it came to that, ads from many of the
other New York stores whose patronage was so crucial to a daily's
well-being. The *Tribune* would have been happy to obtain a forty-per-
cent slice of their morning-newspaper advertising allocations, and it did
get that from Lord & Taylor. But the R. H. Macy & Company *Times-*

Tribune ratio was closer to eighty-twenty; a Macy executive to whom Thayer protested that this was a disproportionate state of affairs rejoined that he could hardly be expected to tell his handbag people that they had to promote their wares in the *Tribune* when they were rewarded for their sales, and when those sales seemed to be clearly more affected by advertising in the *Times* than in any other medium.

Thayer's advent did not sit entirely well with Denson. The editor did not take kindly to the new president's hiring of a couple of efficiency experts who were supposed to monitor and speed up press-time procedures in the composing room—where Denson's perfectionist dilatoriness, some expert efficiently calculated, was costing the paper eighty-five thousand dollars a year in overtime charges. (It was ironic that Denson's vice was Whitney's virtue: both craved excellence.) Denson thought the presence of Thayer's watchdogs was humiliating. One night one of them, while the editor was fiddling with the wording of a headline as the presses were ready to roll, stamped his foot and pointed an accusing finger at him. Denson, a chain smoker, snarled, "If you don't get your finger out of my face, I'll burn it off!"

Thayer and his efficiency experts, moreover, had in their analyses of the paper been impressed by the realization that fifty per cent of the *Tribune*'s revenues, such as they were, derived from the Sunday paper alone. They believed, accordingly, that Denson should concentrate on improving that end-of-week issue. Denson, on the other hand, was more interested in the future of the Monday-through-Saturday *Tribune*. It may have been significantly indicative of his attitude toward Sunday papers that he decided to print the comic strips they carried not in color but in black and white.

Whitney, who did not like controversies, found himself in the uncomfortable position of having to serve as moderator between his two principal surrogates, one of whom seemed to believe in the first half and the other in the second of a dictum once laid down by *The New Yorker*'s A. J. Liebling in "The Wayward Press"—"The function of the press in society is to inform, but its role is to make money." In one of innumerable memoranda that Whitney and Thayer kept exchanging, Jock, by now beginning to wonder if a plaque on a wall was such a good idea after all, said, of Denson, "This is a really horrifying bear we have by the tail. I feel so much tonight like shaking him till his poor old teeth fall out that I can barely resist going out to the bullpen and shouting at him. But then I sit here in my office knowing that if I really let fly he'd have to go and then so would we. That disastrous indispensability—how long will we have it?"

Whitney decorated his office, on the fifth floor of the *Tribune* building, with fittings he thought appropriate: John Hay's desk, to begin with, a number of Hay memorabilia, and a Currier and Ives print of Horace Greeley. Jock's sister Joan added a Toby jug that *she* thought appropriate; it portrayed an old man in a dressing gown, reading the *Times*. After a few months on the premises, Whitney evolved a routine that he fancied. He had a working-press card (he never actually used it to get close to an accident or a fire), and he worked. At his East Sixty-third Street town house, he would attend to his many other interests for an hour or two each morning and be driven to the *Tribune* in time for a daily 11 A.M. editorial-page meeting. There was often a lunch for some dignitary, in the paper's fourteenth-floor dining room. At 4 P.M., there was a meeting to determine, aside from late-breaking stories, what the make-up would be of the next day's front page. Scattered throughout the week there were other sessions he usually sat in on—editorial planning, promotion, circulation. He didn't talk much at any of these, beyond asking an occasional question. Denson once referred to his "unquenchable curiosity." Volubility had never been Jock's forte. "You hardly ever know what he's thinking," Betsey said one time. "Of course, that's one of the reasons he's so fascinating."

Barring a crisis, Whitney would stay around until six-thirty or seven— the first edition was supposed to go to press, if Denson could be persuaded to let it go, at nine—and he would often phone in (somewhat to the distress of Betsey) later in the evening, to be kept abreast of what was going on. Wherever he happened to be after dinner, a copy of the first edition would be rushed over to him as soon as it was printed, in case he had any changes to propose before the last edition was locked up. Now and then he would have lunch or a late afternoon drink with some of his staff at Jack Bleeck's convivial saloon one block south, an establishment formally designated the "Artist and Writers Restaurant (Formerly Club)" and memorable for, among other things, the nurturing of the strenuous indoor sport called the match game. Whitney did not go there often enough to become one of the boys. Indeed, a *Tribune* reporter recalled one time when a number of Jock's employees, seeing him materialize in the doorway, took him for a plainclothes detective, possibly from the Vice Squad, and instantly stopped gambling. Whitney reserved most Tuesday evenings, when he was in town, for a fourteenth-floor buffet supper with his senior editors, who could recognize him anywhere.

It was a continually demanding routine, quite different from anything he'd been accustomed to. London had been a strain in its own way, but an ambassador didn't have to be responsible for the publication of a major newspaper every day of the year. There were also social events that Whitney felt he was more or less obligated to attend, much like some of the receptions and dinners he'd felt constrained to show up at in England—testimonial banquets in New York, for example, for leaders of the men's-wear trade, few of whom had ever sold any kind of suit that Whitney wore, but all of whom might someday choose to advertise their merchandise in the *Tribune*. By October, the daily grind had taken its toll. Whitney went to the New York Hospital for four weeks, suffering from a severe case of influenza and a mild cardiac disorder. While he was there, Dwight Sargent wrote an editorial about health care, and in view of his boss's circumstances thought it prudent to carry the text to Jock's bedside and let him scrutinize it before publication. Whitney was bemused. "If you had to come to me every time an editorial touched something I'm interested in," he told Sargent, "there'd be no time to write any editorials."

On being discharged, Whitney went himself to his Georgia estate to recuperate. He was on a strict diet. Writing to Joseph Alsop just after Christmas, he said, "We are off to Thomasville tomorrow—no spare ribs, no sausage, no bacon—God!" In the hospital, Jock had had much time to mull over the path his paper was taking, and on December 20 he had dictated a memorandum establishing an eight-man editorial board, which was to meet—starting in February after his return from the South—for not more than an hour and a half every Friday morning. "The broad purpose of the board," he wrote, "will be to discuss and to agree, where appropriate, on the general editorial policy and direction of the paper. . . . It is important, however, at the outset to establish one principle to which I shall rigidly adhere. The editorial board shall not, at any time, concern itself with the problems which arise in the daily preparation of the paper. These will be handled in the daily editorial conference or, where circumstances require, by discussion between Mr. Denson and me or, in my absence, Mr. Thayer."

Whitney's hospitalization prevented him from attending one editorial lunch at the *Tribune* at which the honored guest was Attorney General Robert F. Kennedy. Jock's relations with the new Administration in Washington had got off to a pleasant enough start—he had represented the United States at the Trinidad treaty signing soon after President Kennedy's inauguration—but he was still at heart an Eisenhower man. Whitney told the ex-President that summer that he had declined three invitations from Jacqueline Kennedy to serve on a committee to round up American paintings for the White House walls; and Ike's response had been to return Jock's letter with "Fine!!" and "Hooray!!" scribbled on it. Soon after returning to the United States, Whitney, at the personal request of President Kennedy's press secretary, Pierre Salinger, had deferred publication in the *Tribune* of an exclusive story about the imminent release by the Soviet Union of two captured B-47 pilots—the White House feared that if the news broke the captors might change their minds—and the grateful President had had Salinger send him a wire of thanks. "As a beginner in this trade," Jock had said afterward, "I've learned already that every good newspaperman has to have at least one scoop to give for his country." In December 1961, President Kennedy himself had told Robert J. Donovan, the *Tribune*'s White House correspondent, that he considered the paper's editorials "very responsible."

Then, in the spring of 1962, the *Herald Tribune* editorially scolded the Administration, and especially its Attorney General, for not pushing hard enough to get to the bottom of the tangled affairs of Billy Sol Estes, a Texas Democrat who subsequently ended up in prison for transporting fraudulent mortgages across state lines. Robert Kennedy was angry, and his irritation rubbed off on his brother. The White House had twenty-three subscriptions to the daily *Tribune* and thirteen to the Sunday; it also received ten free copies of each. (There, too, the *Tribune* lagged behind. The White House's daily and Sunday subscriptions to the *Times* were forty-five and twenty, and to the Washington *Post* forty-one and fifteen.) At the President's order, Salinger canceled all the subscriptions to the *Tribune*, and when a truck rolled around on the morning of May 29 to drop off its regular free copies, a gatekeeper tore the wrapper off the bundle and said, "You can junk them or sell them. We don't want them around here." (There was a precedent. Eisenhower had once canceled the *Times*. His anger at it had been so far-reaching that the Augusta National Country Club, way off in Georgia, for a while hadn't dared let a copy be visible on its premises.) "You have always been a bit too much of a gentleman," Tex McCrary wrote Whitney on hearing of the banishment; "ride this one a little rough because you are in a dark alley with a dead-end kid. You have always been something of a legend to the working press; they adore you, but they never thought the day would come when they could find you on the firing line with them. But now, Colonel, as Bill Mauldin would have drawn it, you have joined the dogfaces!"

The storm soon abated. While in Washington for a meeting of National Gallery trustees in January, Whitney had a gentlemanly meeting with both President Kennedy and Salinger. The *Tribune*, they told him, would be taken off their blacklist. Its restitution was not instant. Whitney was back at the White House again in April, this time invited by the President to attend his signing of a Congressional resolution conferring honorary American citizenship on Winston Churchill. "Saw no *Tribs*," Jock said in a note to Thayer. By summertime, though, the paper was back in the Administration's good graces, and by October, five weeks before the President's assassination, Salinger—whom Whitney then characterized as "our more or less constant reader"—was a guest at the unveiling in the *Herald Tribune* building of a plaque given by the journalistic fraternity Sigma Delta Chi in memory of James Gordon Bennett and

Horace Greeley. (Salinger characterized himself at a lunch following the dedication as a "long-time though sometimes interrupted subscriber.") Art Buchwald, who the year before had transferred the source of his *Tribune* column from France to the United States, could not let this comic opera conclude without getting in a word of his own. He was in Beverly Hills that day, and sent Jock a telegram that went, in part, UNDERSTAND . . . PLAYING HOST TO PIERRE SALINGER THE FATHER OF NEWS MANAGEMENT ALSO HAVE HEARD YOU SHARING SAME PLATFORM WITH HIM AS WELL AS LUNCH. IF THIS IS TRUE PLEASE CANCEL MY SUBSCRIPTION TO THE HERALD TRIBUNE.

The previous October, the *Tribune,* under Denson's editorship—one of the feathers in his cap was a vigorous campaign against New York City potholes that caught the public fancy—had increased its daily circulation to 400,000. The climb to that encouraging plateau had been slightly helped by the administrators of the North Shore Hospital, a one-hundred-and-ninety-six-bed institution that abutted the Whitney estate at Manhasset and to which he was a lavish contributor; they decided to make a copy of the *Trib* available every day to every one of their patients who had the strength to hold it. By that month, too, one of Thayer's efficiency experts had calculated worrisomely that since Whitney had taken over the paper it had been administered *seriatim* by three presidents, four vice-presidents, two secretary-treasurers, two assistant general managers, six advertising managers, and a dozen senior editors. The total rose when Denson left that month and moved over to the *Journal-American,* one of the few papers around where he had never previously been employed. He said he quit because he didn't have enough independence. Others said it was because he couldn't come to grips with the eighty-five-thousand-dollar difference between putting the paper to bed at 9 P.M., when the press run was supposed to begin, and nine-fifteen, when he was usually satisfied with the look of its front-page headlines. What some people around the premises had called the Denson Revolution had come to an end, and nobody put up a plaque in the lobby to mark its demise.

Whitney was leery about hiring any more editors from outside, no matter how promising they might seem. He told Thayer he wanted all replacements, including Denson's, to come from within the ranks. Accordingly, James G. Bellows, an alumnus of the Miami *News* who had had the fancy title of Executive Editor (News Operations), succeeded Denson. Bellows wanted as his second in editorial command Richard C. Wald, then the paper's correspondent in Bonn, who happened to be in New York on home leave. Wald had a long-standing *Trib* affiliation; he had been a campus stringer for the paper while a student at Columbia, and on graduating had been promoted to office boy. Wald was planning to return to Europe and stopped by Bellows' office to wish him good luck and say good-by, whereupon the new editor told him he should stay in New York. All Wald's luggage was already aboard the S.S. *France*. (It was part of the charm of the *Herald Tribune*—perhaps also one of its failings—that it let its correspondents travel around the world at a leisurely pace, while *Times* men grappled with jet lag.) Wald agreed to become an editor, but only on condition that he could first accompany his wardrobe across the Atlantic. He took the boat over—Whitney sent champagne to the dock in celebration of Wald's new promotion—and when he got to London flew straight back (one boat trip was considered enough to get him properly relaxed) to join the home team. Whitney, his editorial headaches momentarily alleviated, took a deep breath and wrote a memorandum to Bellows:

> Our first problem is to define what kind of a paper *we* want, whether there is a market for it, and then to determine if we are capable of publishing this kind of paper.
>
> What does it take to be different from the *Times*, department by department, and at the same time be a quality paper that the discriminating, adult, responsive reader will come to believe he must have? I shouldn't really try to answer my own question in detail, for I haven't the training and background to do so. I can only, then, give an impression of where I think we are, from *untrained* observation. . . .
>
> I feel that under John Denson quality too frequently was sacrificed to form. The "new era" was to be one in which the reader was to be lifted out of the slough of meaningless words and become educated—in the best sense. John knew, and we believe, that a modern newspaper has a new job to do, and illustrated this avowed new purpose in a number of extraordinary papers. But not a great number and certainly not consistently. Instead the face—the new face—sometimes became a mask which covered lack of quality, failure of our agreed purpose. . . .
>
> Clearly, however, the effort was of the utmost importance in attracting attention to the fact that the *Trib* was no longer an imitation—it was worth attention. And often enough and *whenever* the news warranted, the treatment became brilliant and compelling.
>
> But what was happening to the other boast—that this would be, for the first time, an *edited* newspaper? I submit that very little effort was devoted to improvement of the quality of writing and layout through the paper. Correspondents were given encouragement and latitude to speak their minds, but I doubt much guidance to mind their words. I really believe that the kind of heads used, especially on the front page, would be a discouragement rather than an appeal to quality.
>
> In summary, a great change was brought about, under the direction of Denson, in the selection and handling of the news and in the appearance and style of the HT. Excitement ran through the building for many

months and out of it to a somewhat startled group of old readers—and, fortunately, found many new ones who liked what they saw. But, in my view, it was essentially not what they were told they would see.

But the questions do gradually emerge—

1. What is our basic editorial goal? Quality? Best in town? Difference? Understanding? Excitement? Entertainment? Ease of reading?

2. Would there be an adequate responsive audience for it to make it economically feasible?

3. Are we capable of accomplishing this goal within acceptable time limits and costs?

Bellows had scarcely taken over when disaster struck, in the form of a sixteen-week strike called by Bertram A. Powers, the formidable head of Union No. 6—Big Six, it was informally called—of the International Typographical Union. At first, only the *Times*, the *News*, the *Journal-American*, and the *World-Telegram & Sun* were struck. But if the other papers in town—the *Mirror*, the *Post*, and the *Herald Tribune*—continued to publish, that would undermine the bargaining position of the shutdown newspapers; and in any event, they all belonged to the New York Publishers' Association and knew they would be bound by whatever the terms were of an ultimate settlement. So all the papers stopped publishing. (The *Post* resumed before the strike ended.) Whitney, like other frustrated New Yorkers for whom radio and television could never supplant newsprint as a guide to contemporary history, made do with whatever papers he could lay his hands on—principally the Philadelphia press, the Boston-based *Christian Science Monitor*, and the Paris *Herald*, which was part of his own domain. (During a speaking engagement in Philadelphia a few months afterward, he said, "I find that arriving here now is a little bit like greeting a pen pal for the first time.") When the strike was finally settled, the *Times* and the *Tribune* felt impelled to raise their newsstand price from a nickel to a dime, and the *Mirror* soon disappeared. The *Tribune*'s daily circulation, when it resumed publication, was down by 92,000, and its Sunday circulation down by 57,000. Its payroll had gone up by $1,262,000. It did collect $350,000 in strike insurance, but even so its loss for the fiscal year ending April 30, 1963, was a discomfiting $4,238,000.

Whitney wrote another one of his introspective memoranda on July 18, 1963. This time he said that, whenever he asked an acquaintance what it was about the *Tribune* that made that person feel he had to read it, he would get some such answer as "It is that the *Trib* is the only really *interesting* paper I know." As for himself, Jock went on, "Actually, I often think of it as fascinating, but I guess that's for my private lexicon." He thought he detected a special enthusiasm for the *Trib* that other papers did not attract. "This is what we must bottle because it is our unique appeal," Whitney concluded, with a jab at the *Times*. "Imagine anyone really liking the NYT."

Whitney's editors began bottling some of what they hoped he was talking about. There was a new Sunday literary supplement, *Book Week*, on the launching of which Jock stated, "This newspaper has had a long and honorable association with the world of books. Ideas and language are important to us, and we have tried to discuss them with the intelligence and liveliness that is their due." There was another Sunday supplement, livelier than it was intelligent, which was entitled *New York* and evolved into the magazine of that name. Two of the *Tribune*'s younger feature writers, Jimmy Breslin and Tom Wolfe, were among its notable early contributors. (John O'Hara, who had worked for the paper in 1928, wanted to be, but a piece he submitted for the first issue was rejected on the arcane ground that it wasn't New Yorkish enough.) Breslin, who prided himself on his raffish approach to journalism and life in general, would later declare that Whitney "ran the paper with great class and grace. . . . Jock Whitney is the only millionaire I ever rooted for."*

Tom Wolfe gave *New York* a certain instant notoriety by contributing to it a two-part piece about *The New Yorker*, the first section of which was liberally laced with falsehoods and vicious personal remarks about that weekly's editor, William Shawn. After the publication of that installment, Shawn, hoping somehow to get the second one killed, asked to meet Whitney to discuss that possibility. Whitney hadn't much liked Wolfe's remarks himself, but Bellows had approved the article *in toto* and the owner was reluctant to intercede with his editor. (One of the few instances in which Jock spoke up at a meeting of his top editors was soon after *New York* got under way. The minutes of a meeting recorded, "Mr. Whitney would like to see unnecessary slang and jargon give way to proper English.") Whitney did not like confrontations of the sort Shawn proposed, but he reluctantly agreed to receive the *New Yorker* editor at his home. Shawn, who didn't much like confrontations either and who by then had had second thoughts about a get-together, begged off at the last minute, and Wolfe's concluding part went to press without further ado.

* In the spring of 1970, long after the *Herald Tribune* had ceased to exist, Whitney Communications finally settled a libel suit brought against the paper because of an article Breslin had written nearly seven years before. It was a piece about a bartender who had gone into hiding after inadvertently being a witness to a gangland slaying. The bartender had sued, apparently on the ground that Breslin had impugned his manhood by describing in graphic detail how he had hit the floor when the shooting began. Before the case was finally disposed of out of court (but not before Whitney Communications had run up forty thousand dollars in legal fees), Jock was obliged to file a notarized affidavit saying that he was unacquainted with the gentleman who'd felt so aggrieved and that he bore him no animosity.

On November 22, President Kennedy was killed. Whitney, who was pressed into emergency service that tumultuous night as a copy reader, had a speaking engagement four days later, in Massachusetts, at the annual dinner of the Nieman Foundation, Harvard's sometime home for professional journalists. "In this period of national involvement," Whitney said, "the nation has turned to its news media—and especially to its press." He went on:

> Throughout the country, millions watched the funeral, the burial—even the moment a man was killed—on television; and then they turned to their newspapers. For together, the papers have served to crystallize the moment. Men will not remember these days as a long period of continuing event. Few will recall for long the exact timing of every sequence. Their personal history will be a succession of images—a President shot in an open car; a careening drive to the hospital with a wife holding her husband's head; a hurried swearing-in; a face of grief behind a dark veil; the roll of muffled drums; a flag-draped caisson; a eulogy perhaps; a little boy saluting; white-gloved hands slowly, precisely folding the last flag.
>
> In these images is the poetry of memory, and these the press captured and held freshly, recording the event as it became history. Most of the country's editors were conscious that they were preparing a record for the future. When the television pictures had gone, the people in my city went out to buy the papers they would put away and save as recollection for some future time. . . .
>
> Writing in the *Herald Tribune* just a year ago, your honored guest tonight, Louis Lyons [the Nieman curator], commented: "It is the key communications problem of our times that the news grows more complex. It is the challenge of the press to deal with it."
>
> At the *Tribune*, we're trying to do just that. We still are experimenting, we still are learning, we still are attempting to find new ways of producing a better newspaper than now exists. . . .
>
> I'd like to see this same process going on all across the country. I think the country needs it. And, as public life grows more complex—and this is happening, inexorably—we're going to need it even more. It may be we will not get it. It's hard to edit and publish a good newspaper. Increasingly, the task is one of selection, of organization, of distillation—of putting more into each possible reading minute. . . .
>
> The main thing is to be unafraid of ourselves, unafraid of the truth, and to trust our capacity for action. That has been our strength; that is still the glory of our present ability to continue, even through dark days like those past, not faltering before the unexpected and the unknown. And that will be the strength of enterprises like the *Herald Tribune*—that we can argue freely because we seek the truth; that we trust our fellow man to choose well, if only the truth is set before him.

Meanwhile, the *Tribune* was limping along, still trying to recover from the trauma of the strike. Thayer was working practically full time at the paper, and he told Whitney, on January 20, 1964, that "immediate steps, maybe drastic ones," were needed to produce "a fresh, new approach to the daily paper." He urged Jock to engage in yet more soul searching. The *Tribune* needed a firmer hand at the tiller, Thayer suggested—perhaps his own, but *somebody's*. Whitney had a lot of demands on his time—his family, his houses and horses; his hospitals, museums, and other philanthropic interests; his businesses, his personal investments; Yale—but his newspaper had become almost all-absorbing. "I agree with you that strong leadership is needed," he responded to Thayer on February 4, "but I think I'm going to have to be the one to provide it." He continued:

Organizationally, as I suggested above, I've decided that I've got to assume a much greater role as editor-in-chief, at least until we've got the daily paper going the way we want it to. I've discussed with Jim Bellows the idea of his largely detaching himself from routine day-to-day operations, and concentrating instead on long-range product improvement. He feels strongly that he has to keep his hand closely in the daily production of the paper, both for purposes of staff morale and because our top editorial staff is already spread paper-thin. He is, however, going to give a greater portion of his time to basic improvements, detaching himself from the daily routine to whatever extent is necessary and possible in order to do so. I intend to work out with him a schedule to ensure that the long-range planning doesn't get short-changed.

At the same time, I'm going to work much more closely and more constantly with him on improvements. . . . The editors and I are agreed on a need for change—or improvement—and on a need for a stepped-up effort. And, in my own activated role as editor-in-chief, I plan to do everything I know how to see that the effort is made and to make it succeed. I think we can make this arrangement work; I certainly think we've got to try. . . .

As I see it, the kind of changes you have talked about have been largely aimed at producing the kind of paper we've been saying right along we were producing. I think we were on the right track when, with John Denson, we launched that "new way to edit"—and the 1962 circulation figures would certainly seem to bear this out. It was a bumpy track, admittedly. Jim has smoothed out most of the bumps; now, not to get too metaphorical, we need to build up a new head of steam, but still to go in the same general direction that we started on three years ago. . . .

As far as the kind of improvements we'll be seeking is concerned . . . We'll be reconsidering all the techniques of newspapering; and, as a starting list of goals, I'd set down the following (many of which will seem not unfamiliar to you):

1) To overcome the "total news problem"—to give readers the impression that the *Trib* does give them, in Gallup's words, "complete coverage

of the *important* news;" to provide an answer for the man who says, "I like your paper, but I've got to read the *Times*."

2) To ensure that we do live up to our billing as a paper that's "organized for understanding."

3) At the same time, to keep our franchise as a paper that's easy to read.

4) To find better, more clearly evident ways of giving not only the facts but their meaning—to convince the reader that he's getting an extra measure of understanding by reading the *Trib*.

5) To give the business and financial pages the authority and substance they still lack.

6) To build into our women's pages a more universal appeal.

7) To get the paper more intimately and more broadly involved with the life of the city; to identify its interests with those of New York, and to win for it recognition as a paper that not only cares about the city, but does something about it.

8) To get more force and more consistency into the editorial page; to make it urbane, witty, and thoughtful, with an occasional roundhouse punch up its sleeve; with a worldly view of imperfect man, but with a conscience and a temper.

9) To invest the paper with a clear aura of leadership, not only in newspaper techniques, but in news development and in active citizenship.

10) But, in both news and editorial columns, to be fair—not only to competing candidates in the months ahead, but also, and always, to competing, even unorthodox points of view.

The kind of improvement we're talking about can't be done in a day, and it's going to have to be made by a staff acutely sensitive to our own enthusiasms—or lack thereof. It's going to require their enthusiastic cooperation. On our part, it's going to demand a careful blending of tact, patience and insistence. I know I've carved out a difficult job for myself, but I think it's one that can be done, and that, in our present circumstances, I've got to be the one to do it.

Another national election was coming up that fall. In August 1963, Whitney had said in one of the speeches his publishing role imposed on him, "It would be a calamity if the *Trib* should ever have to support a Democratic presidential candidate, without there having first been a complete, unthinkable change in the Democratic Party's attitude toward government, and toward the process and ethics of governing." He had qualified that slightly: "A newspaper does have the freedom of its own conscience. And a desire for the unrestricted exercise of that freedom is at the heart of my purpose in owning a newspaper."

At about that time, the *Tribune*, always searching for a Republican whom it could in good conscience support, was leaning toward William Scranton; later, it would tilt toward Nelson Rockefeller. Whitney dined

at the White House with Lyndon Johnson in December, three weeks
after that President's being unexpectedly sworn in, but Jock did not
know him well and had not the slightest intention of endorsing him until
Barry Goldwater won the Republican nomination. Whitney began to
think another unthinkable. He had persuaded Clare Boothe Luce to write
a political column for the *Tribune* early in 1964 but dropped her when
she became a Goldwater advocate. Now Whitney felt, he told Thayer in
another of their exchanges of memos, that the *Tribune*'s editorial page
"should have definite personality"—it had always been a Republican personality—"without being too predictable." Thayer demurred. He told
Whitney that unpredictability was a character defect and that "most
definite personalities are predictable."

"Not mine," Jock retorted. He added, "I have strong personal convic-
tions which I'm prepared to defend and support. And it is largely to have
an opportunity to do this that I bought the *Herald Tribune*."

On Sunday, October 4, 1964, the leading *Tribune* editorial, under the
headline "We Choose Johnson," started off, "For the Presidency: Lyndon B. Johnson. Travail and torment go into these simple words, breach-
ing as they do the political traditions of a long newspaper lifetime. But
we find ourselves, as Americans, even as Republicans, with no other acceptable course." The apostasy continued:

> For many Republicans, this has been a season of soul-searching—
> whether, out of loyalty to the party and the two-party system, to embrace
> Goldwater; whether to defect to Johnson; or whether, caught between
> two unpalatable alternatives, to abstain from choice.
>
> For us, as we suspect may be true for others, these considerations were
> decisive:
>
> Abstention is impossible. Office-holders and candidates for office, be-
> holden to the party, are limited by their obligations in what they can say.
> A newspaper cannot take refuge in this; and no agony of indecision can
> make the choice go away, unless we maintain that the White House
> should be vacant for the next four years. One or the other has to be
> elected; the choice is only which, not whether. . . .
>
> We believe strongly in Republican principles; we feel that the Republi-
> can party is best fitted to govern a free nation. And we urgently want to
> see the Republican party, already dangerously diminished, grow stronger.
>
> But this, in our judgment, does not justify making Barry Goldwater
> President of the United States.
>
> In supporting Lyndon Johnson, we do so with our eyes open and our
> fingers crossed. . . .
>
> Senator Goldwater says he is offering the nation a choice. So far as
> these two candidates are concerned, our inescapable choice—as a news-
> paper that was Republican before there was a Republican party, has been
> Republican ever since and will remain Republican—is Lyndon B. Johnson.

The editorial was written by Raymond K. Price, Jr., who had been on the *Tribune* staff for nine years and in charge of the editorial page for the last two. He had helped Whitney write speeches—the Nieman Dinner address among them—and earlier in 1964 had collaborated with ex-President Eisenhower on an anti-Goldwater article for newspaper syndication; in later years, Price would be recruited by Walter Thayer to become President Richard Nixon's principal amanuensis. There was some confusion, at first, about the authorship of "We Choose Johnson." Whitney's friend Sidney Weinberg, who liked to be privy to and pass along inside information of all sorts, confided to his friend Henry Ford II that Jock himself had written it—an attribution that earned Whitney about an equal amount of accolades and accusations. President Johnson didn't much care who had strung the words together, but he was so pleased by them that the day they appeared he both phoned Jock and sent him an appreciative telegram. Jimmy Breslin offered to buy Whitney an appreciative drink. Jock replied that he'd buy *him* one if only Breslin would for once get his copy in on time; the publisher added, about the controversial editorial, "The only difficult part of the decision was to say it so that our readers would understand the reason why." (Breslin had been hired by the *Tribune* in part on the strength of a book he'd written, a not very flattering tale about Joan Whitney Payson's New York Mets. Running into Jock at Bleeck's one day, Breslin said, "Hey, I got to hand it to your sister. She's one hell of a broad." She had become that, according to Breslin's peculiar standard of values, by having had him thrown off her private railroad car—after he had boarded it uninvited—for drunkenness.)

Among those who felt differently about the pro-Johnson editorial were quite a few men and women who said they'd been faithful subscribers to the *Herald Tribune* for fifty years, and who now let Whitney know in stern, aggrieved terms that they wanted their subscriptions canceled immediately. As late as 1980, some especially hard-shelled Republican acquaintances of his could not bring themselves to forgive him for what they regarded as outright perfidy. What mattered more to Jock at the moment was that Dwight Eisenhower, in retirement at Gettysburg, saw nothing amiss with the tack he had taken.

That year, the *Tribune* lost another $4,223,400. By April 1965, one of the bookkeepers who had the unenviable job of trying to keep Whitney's accounts in order calculated that thus far he had poured $26,455,000 into the paper with nothing much more to show for it than his unused working-press pass, a set of working-press license plates for one of his automobiles, and eligibility to attend the annual Gridiron Club dinner in Washington, D.C. The *Tribune*'s contract with the typographers' union, costly as it had been to achieve, expired at the end of March 1965, and when that year began there was little expectation that the terms of the next contract would be any better. Anticipating another year of torment, and of an argument about automation, a technological advance that the union had been stoutly resisting because it understandably feared that the innovation would result in smaller work forces, Thayer had written on January 22, 1965, to Gardner Ackley, the chairman of the President's Council of Economic Advisers, "The solution to the so-called automation issue is the key to the survival of one or more papers in New York. We have been unable because of union restrictions in New York to take advantage of technology now available to newspapers in every other city of the United States and, by the use of this technology, to reduce substantially our publishing costs. . . . The papers in New York, collectively, lose several million dollars a year. If we are to survive, we must become more efficient. . . . For this reason several of us are strongly of the opinion that these negotiations will be the most decisive so far as the future of papers in New York is concerned that we have ever experienced."

In mid-February, Thayer circulated among the *Tribune*'s employees a memorandum citing many bleak statistics: Since 1950, the circulation of all New York newspapers had decreased by 34 per cent. The total lines of advertising had increased by 11.7 per cent; the hourly rate in composing rooms, meanwhile, had increased by 55 per cent. "What we need in these negotiations," the memorandum concluded, "is freedom from the restrictions which thus far have prevented the introduction of these methods and equipment in New York or which have made their introduction so costly that we cannot afford to employ them." A further memorandum the following month said that the publishers had decided not to try to ask for automation for the time being. "There's a limit beyond which we cannot go," the employees were now advised. "The *Herald Tribune* has been losing money for years. We now are engaged in a massive determined effort to put the paper on a sound basis financially, and, by doing so, to insure both its survival and its success. We simply cannot do this if, on the one hand, we yield to pressures for higher wages and costly new benefits; and if, on the other hand, we accept a technological freeze which will deny us, perhaps forever, the savings from which these wages and benefits can be paid. In these negotiations, we, and, in our opinion, some of the other newspapers quite literally are negotiating for survival."

Discussions—with other papers, with unions, with *Tribune* employees—went on all spring and summer, but to no avail. On September 16, there was another strike, this one called at the *Times* by the Newspaper Guild. The other New York papers that belonged to the Publishers' Association (the *Wall Street Journal* didn't) silenced their presses as a gesture of solidarity. It was the third shutdown since Whitney had come on the journalistic scene. True, the strikes had not cost him any cash—the paper was losing money every day it was published—but they had disrupted the flow of continuity he was trying to establish. It was like halting a horse race in the backstretch and then telling the jockeys to start up all over again.

In the previous strike, the *Post* had flouted the Publishers' Association and resumed publication ahead of the other papers, but to no particular lasting advantage; it had settled afterward on the same terms as all the others. Now, Whitney and Thayer decided to withdraw from the Association, allegiance to which hadn't seemed to get anybody anywhere in any event. The *Tribune* resumed publication on September 27, and for fourteen heady days had practically a monopoly. Its daily circulation skyrocketed to a giddy 1,000,000. The strike ended on October 11. By November, the daily paper's circulation had dwindled to 309,000.

As early as 1963 there had been talk in the higher echelons of the *Tribune* hierarchy of avoiding its daily confrontation with the *Times* by becoming an afternoon paper. One deterrent to that was the awkward location of the plant. Delivery trucks could move in and out of there readily enough at night, when traffic was slight; but during business hours, when the adjoining garment district was in full swing, there would be formidable traffic jams to cope with. A possible solution was to have the paper printed at the *Times*, which although only a couple of blocks to the north was in a somewhat less congested area. Thayer had had several not unpromising talks about such an eventuality with Orvil E. Dryfoos, the *Times*'s publisher, but Dryfoos had a heart attack and died in May 1963. After that, there seemed to be nobody of authority at the *Times* who really cared whether the *Trib* continued to exist as a morning or afternoon paper or at all. "The Sulzbergers would say nice things to Jock when they ran into him at social functions," Thayer said years afterward, "but most of the *Times* people, especially their advertising people, were pretty rough. They acted the way we'd probably have acted had we been in their shoes. They weren't interested in the health of the *Herald Tribune*."

Meanwhile, starting as early as the summer of 1964, exploratory talks had been carried on among the *Tribune*, the *World-Telegram*, and the *Journal-American*. The three papers had a total daily circulation of 1,250,000. They were losing altogether ten million dollars a year. As a last resort to solve the financial problems that were plaguing them, they were contemplating a merger. Independently, they had 4,598 employees. In unison, they figured they could get by with 2,834. The payroll savings could be expected to be enormous. (So could be the anguished screams of the unions representing the employees who would have to be let go.) The merger conversations were shrouded in secrecy. They were held not in offices but in homes or hotel rooms; and inasmuch as the *Telegram* and the *Journal* were not independent entities but links in chains—respectively, Scripps-Howard and Hearst—there were all sorts of complications involved. Thayer was the chief *Tribune* emissary to these secluded gatherings. The basic idea was that, if a merger ever materialized, there would come out of it a morning *Herald Tribune*, an afternoon *World-Journal*, and a Sunday *World-Journal and Tribune*. (The last would be known from its initials, inevitably, as the "Widget.") Whitney sat in on some of the early meetings, with more concern than enthusiasm, but by April 1965 he was telling Thayer, "I really am becoming violently excited about the 'big deal.' I suppose I did turn with a little difficulty. But the direction this is now taking seems to be so *right* for us that it can't be true—(probably isn't!)."

There were too many people involved in the tricky negotiations for the proposed merger to remain secret. By the winter of 1966, rumors had spread all around the publishing industry. Employees who feared layoffs were getting edgy, and newspaper unions were threatening to strike again. On March 21, the three principals issued a statement confirming that they were in negotiation, and on April 1 they signed an agreement. Under its terms, the *Herald Tribune* would abandon its midtown plant and move down to the *World-Telegram*'s premises on Barclay Street. Business at Jack Bleeck's friendly neighborhood pub might suffer dreadfully, but this was no time for sentimentality.

The new arrangement would go into effect on April 25. On the seventh, the Newspaper Guild, calculating too moderately, told its members, in a city-wide bulletin, that nine hundred of them could expect to lose their jobs under the proposed setup. Whitney and Thayer told the *Tribune*'s employees on the thirteenth, "Delay in beginning the operation of our new company will be extremely prejudicial to all concerned, management and employees alike." Whitney alone signed a statement on the twenty-second:

> I bought the *Herald Tribune* eight years ago because I believe deeply in the value of articulate, intelligent discussion of our world. I wanted it to continue to be what in fact I always thought it was: a lively companion to a wide circle of friends. I did not buy it to make myself wealthy or famous or powerful. You cannot buy the traditions and principles of this newspaper, you can only lend them a hand toward survival.
>
> That effort has not been completely successful.
>
> Newspapers are a business and businesses need a profit to survive. The problems are easy to say and hard to solve. The competition was fierce, the turn-around was hard to make, the strikes were each an enormous setback, the settlements were hard to live with, the cost of each part of doing business rose while the price of the newspaper could not and circu-

lation always lagged a little behind expectation. And always, the fruits of automation and modern practices were kept beyond reach.

My own clearest aim was to keep this voice alive in our community; to make it survive. The last thing I wanted to do was sell it or merge it.

But the *Herald Tribune* is not a child. It's not a toy or a whim of one man. It is an institution that has something to say to our times and it is an institution on which many people depend. It must have a stable future independent of my pocketbook.

He had decided, Whitney went on, that merger alone could keep the *Tribune* alive, but the demands of the unions were now thwarting that possibility. He concluded:

Tomorrow, there will be the final daily edition of an independently owned *Herald Tribune*. On Sunday, we will give you for the last time the newspaper we have tried to create for New York that others are beginning to imitate around the country.

Although these are my last papers and this is my last statement as owner of the New York *Herald Tribune*, we look forward to a long and secure future in partnership with a bright, strong afternoon newspaper and a fine new Sunday paper.

If we are crippled by a long strike, the future will be even more bleak than the recent past.

We are now at a crucial moment in the history of this newspaper. It is 125 years old and many men and women have given their best to it. I write this because here and now I want to put on the record how I feel and how I share their pride.

The unions did strike, on Sunday, April 24, concurrent with the appearance of the last *Herald Tribune*. While the management of the paper was waiting around to resume publication as part of a jerry-built troika that might or might not be able to stay ahead of the wolves, the staff began to look for more secure jobs. One hundred and sixty of the *Trib's* three hundred and fifty editorial employees departed, and among them, Wald estimated in a survey made on Whitney's behalf, were sixty per cent of the paper's "quality" people. "To put it bluntly," James Bellows said in an August 11 message to Matt Meyer, the publisher of the *World-Telegram*, "the *Tribune* staff has been devastated. I think it almost impossible—with the present staff—to publish a *Herald Tribune* I would be proud to be the editor of, or be able to compete with successfully in the morning field."

On August 15, the one hundred and thirteenth day of that particular strike, Whitney gave up. "I have never been involved in a more difficult or painful decision," he said in a formal statement that the *Times*, as the now unassailable paper of record, was happy to print in full. "The toll of a long strike—the loss of readers, advertisers, the cost of starting up again —all these things entered into the decision. But though a newspaper must meet the exacting test of profit and loss, it is something more than a business. The *Herald Tribune* had a voice, a presence, a liveliness of thought and a distinction of style that many have appreciated. It was an attempt I am glad to have made—one that did succeed in bringing together men and women of great talent and sensibility. They made it a newspaper to be proud of."

Jock held a press conference that day, too, in the *Tribune's* ninth-floor auditorium, where in more halcyon times those four hundred or so high school seniors who had been lucky enough to be chosen as delegates to the paper's annual World Youth Forum had met in spirited conclave. "I know we gave something good to our city while we published," he said, "and I know it will be a loss to journalism in this country as we cease publication. . . . I am glad that we never tried to cheapen it in any way, that we served as a conscience and a valuable opposition. I am sorry that it had to end."

Two days later, Whitney observed his sixty-second birthday, and Wald sent him an anniversary note on a *Tribune* letterhead—one of the terminal uses of such stationery—"We greyed your hair a little more, but you held up pretty well." On August 22, Jock wrote to General Eisenhower, whose own seventy-fifth birthday he and Thayer and one hundred and fifteen other old friends had celebrated at Augusta National the preceding October, "It is a very bitter blow to have finally had to abandon the *Herald Tribune*. All of a sudden we looked around and found the ship nearly devoid of crew. . . . Labor is directly to blame, of course, but the leadership in labor relations exercised by the New York *Times* and the *Daily News* over the past fifteen years has been so weak that the blame is there, too. It seems almost to have been designed to accomplish what has just happened. Quien sabe?" Whitney also wrote personal letters of thanks and regrets to some two hundred *Tribune* employees who had stayed aboard the sinking ship until it capsized.

The *Tribune* had vanished. A *World-Journal-Tribune* incorporating some of its features—*New York*, the Sunday book section, sundry others— did start publishing on September 12, 1966. Its first issue sold 875,000 copies. Its first month of operations showed a net loss of $839,770—about a dollar a reader. On May 5, 1967, after two hundred and thirty-three lackluster appearances, it threw in the towel. (Its last issue carried an obituary of John McClain, one of Jock's longest-standing friends, who died in London; Whitney had got him installed as the Widget's travel editor.) Thus ended all at once the battered remnants of seven once thriving New York newspaper names: the *World*, the *Telegram*, the *Sun* (which had earlier been swallowed up by the *World-Telegram*), the

Journal, the *American,* the *Herald,* and the *Tribune.* Whitney later told
Harry Baehr, "I still wake up at night and wonder whether there was
anything more I could have done to keep the *Tribune* functioning."

He could hardly have been faulted for stinginess. Whitney Communications' total investment in the paper had amounted to $39,475,929.
(Whitney Communications was, of course, able to write off much of this,
and it did also get $6,575 from the successor proprietors of *New York.*)

The Widget had led too short a life to be much mourned. It was something else in the case of the *Herald Tribune.* "The saddest thing about
the *Trib,*" Jock wrote Daphne Straight in England, "is the avalanche of
letters I get from people who can't believe their old friend has gone. The
loss is unbearable to them, and one wonders how it has been that this
passion for the paper has not transmitted itself to more readers and to
more advertising in these past three years."

Among the senders of condolences whom Whitney actually knew were
such old friends as Tallulah Bankhead, Gene Tunney, John O'Hara,
Nelson Rockefeller, and Robert Benchley's son Nathaniel. Rockefeller
said, "You did a superb job against heavy odds." O'Hara said, "You can't
buck these unions. They have a horrible power to screw things up."
Tallulah called him "Darling." Nathaniel Benchley said that if his father
were alive he'd have given the editorial staff a farewell party at "21" and
would then have reserved seats for all of them in preferred lifeboats on
the next sailing of the *Ile de France.* The drinks at Bleeck's were laced
with tears. Red Smith—whose sports column would soon move to the
Times—wrote an obituary entitled "My Best Girl" for the Paris *Herald.*
"When you know she has been kicked to death," he said, "there is blind
anger along with grief." In that same paper, Art Buchwald wrote a letter
to a little girl named Virginia, who had ostensibly written him to say she
didn't believe what someone had told her—that the paper was dead. "It's
True, Virginia," was his title, harking back to the famous editorial about
Santa Claus. "No, Virginia," his text went, "there is no *Herald Tribune.*
You are too young to understand why it is no more and so am I." The
headlines over a few of the many obits that appeared in other newspapers were "The *Herald Tribune* Murder" (Washington *Evening
Star*), "The Latest Tragedy in New York" (Burlington, Vermont, *Free
Press*), "Death at 131 is Untimely" (Spokane *Daily Chronicle*), "A Death
in the Family (Wilmington, Delaware, *Evening Journal*), "Death in the
Morning" (*Arizona Republic*), "Death of a Great Lady" (Yakima, Washington, *Herald*), "Death of a Giant" (St. Louis *Globe Democrat*), and
"Botched Surgery" (Dunkirk, New York, *Observer*). There were also numerous editorial cartoons, quite a few of which the artists passed along to
Whitney. Typical was a Bruce Shanks drawing entitled "Obituary Page"
in the Buffalo *Evening News*—it appeared on Jock's birthday—in for-

warding which Shanks appended a note saying, "I'm very unhappy to be able to send you the original."

Whitney had devoted the better part of eight of his prime adult years to the *Tribune*, and now there was the tedious task of disposing of the corpse and its few remaining assets. After he had had the paper's sixteen Pulitzer Prize plaques unscrewed from its lobby walls, he sold the building, for $3,900,000 (less $474,269.64 that was still owed on a thirteen-year-old mortgage the Reids had taken out), to the Group Health Insurance Company. Some of the furnishings and equipment, when auctioned off, yielded a further return, but a modest one; one batch of machinery that had cost $2,000,000 fetched a mere $21,469.32. (The *Times* took over the stewardship of the *Herald Tribune* Fresh Air Fund—which underwrote rural summer holidays for deprived urban children—and while it dropped the *Herald Tribune* from the fund's name, it courteously did not substitute its own.) The *Tribune* had a lot of photographs of Harry Truman in its library. Whitney had these sent to the Truman Library at Independence, Missouri. He sent a comparable collection of Eisenhower memorabilia to the presidential library at Abilene, Kansas. He sent a batch of baseball photographs to the National Baseball Hall of Fame at Cooperstown, New York. The disposal of the meat of the library —a morgue dating back to 1927, made up of three hundred filing cabinets containing 200,000 photographs and 500,000 envelopes with 30,000,000 clippings inside them—posed a problem. The Columbia School of Journalism couldn't cope with anything that monumental. The main branch of the New York Public Library didn't have room for it. Finally, New York University, which was building a new library in Greenwich Village, agreed to accept the morgue. The clippings were moved there in 1967, but after five years N.Y.U. had a change of heart. It was costing the university, its librarians declared, twenty thousand dollars a year to look after the collection, and only five per cent of the visitors using it for research were N.Y.U. students. The university was glad to turn over the *Tribune* files to the City of New York, and along with the Pulitzer Prize plaques they ended up, largely unsought and unseen, in a Queens branch of the Public Library.

All Whitney himself had left in the United States to show for his time, effort, and money was *New York Herald Tribune Crossword Puzzles*, a monthly with a circulation of 80,000.

17

In Jock We Trust

On the death of the *Herald Tribune,* Kingman Brewster had written Jock that he felt sorry for the Republic, for himself, and for Whitney, and had added that the immediate question was: "How do we mobilize JHW for —the Republic—for me—for JHW?"

The university president might well have said "also—for Yale?" Whitney's loyalty and generosity to his alma mater had by then already far transcended those of most old Elis, rich or poor or in between. He was not a banner-waving, tailgate-picnicking alumnus who whooped it up at the Bowl when the Harvard football team came to town. Yet who with a long Yale football memory could forget what he had done way back in 1939 in his motion picture prime—arranging with United Artists to have Hal Roach's *Housekeeper's Daughter* privately screened for a Yale varsity sequestered outside Detroit on the eve of a challenging confrontation with the University of Michigan? On pushing off in 1957 for the Court of St. James's, Whitney had tendered his resignation from the Yale Corporation, the university's supreme governing body, which he had joined two years previous; but President Griswold had refused to accept it; a Jock Whitney *in absentia,* he had insisted, was better than no Jock at all.

In the spring of 1963, after Griswold's death, Whitney, though mainly preoccupied with the ongoing tribulations of his newspaper, had served on a five-man Yale Committee on the Nature of the Presidency, which was supervising the search for a successor. During one of the group's deliberations, he scribbled to himself, about Brewster, "In essence—very

strong character—could move Yale—could be said to be obstinate."
Brewster had been a professor of law at Harvard and had come to Yale
in 1960 as its provost, or second in command; but Whitney was then
based in London, and the two men were barely acquainted. "Whit Griswold learned he had cancer in the fall of 1960, the weekend of the Princeton game," Brewster would say years later. "Dean Acheson was the
Senior Fellow of the Corporation, and it was up to him and me to keep
everybody cool while we waited to see what happened. Jock came back
soon after that, and I met him at a Corporation meeting. But he was shy
and taciturn, and made little impact on me at the start. Then in the fall
of 1962, Whit was stricken again, and around Christmas we learned it
was terminal. It was a difficult time for all of us, and especially for me; I
had to keep Whit's spirits up and keep the university going; also, I had
to keep the trustees sufficiently informed of the situation so that they
wouldn't later feel they'd been left in the dark—but not too intimately informed, lest they depress Griswold. Jock's sensitivity to all this made a
big impression on me. Then Whit died, and while the Fellows were looking for a new president, I was the acting one. I got into hot water at one
point by discouraging a student group that had invited George Wallace
to speak on campus not long after the bombing in Birmingham that
killed the black schoolchildren. I didn't forbid the students to have
Wallace. I simply persuaded them to disinvite him. But there was one
of those flaps over the matter. The education editor of the *Herald Tribune* phoned me and said Mr. Whitney had told her to ask me certain
questions about the incident, and I told her to tell Mr. Whitney that if he
had any questions to ask he should ask them himself. Apparently, he had
felt initially that if he had approached me directly he might seem to be
scolding me. He called himself, and I told him that I hoped he and I
would never have to discuss anything through an intermediary. And
from that moment on, Jock and I were well on the road to rapport."

Kingman Brewster was inaugurated as Yale's seventeenth president on
April 11, 1964. The Yale Corporation—ten self-perpetuating successor
trustees (successor to the ten ministers, mostly Harvard men, who had
founded the New Haven institution), six elected alumni trustees, and, ex
officio, the president of the university and the governor and lieutenant
governor of Connecticut—regularly met once a month, during the academic year, from Friday morning through Saturday noon. Now and then,
the trustees, or Fellows, would convene in New York, but for the most
part they held their weighty deliberations in New Haven, where, on fall
home-game Saturdays, they always tried to finish up their business before the opening kickoff at the Bowl. During the decade starting in 1963,
Whitney, for all his other obligations and inclinations, hardly ever missed
a meeting. (He would usually spend Friday night at Brewster's home.)

Among the other Fellows, during Jock's span of service, were Cyrus Vance, William Scranton of Pennsylvania, John Lindsay of New York, J. Irwin Miller of Indiana, William McChcsncy Martin of the Federal Reserve Board, and Paul Mellon. (In Mellon and Whitney, Yale boasted a one-two philanthropic punch the like of which few other academic institutions have ever matched, although Princeton did have two Rockefeller brothers.)

The trustees' meetings took place at Woodbridge Hall, a building put up in 1900 to provide working room for the president and his staff and for the Corporation. The Fellows' chamber, on the second floor across a hallway from the president's private office, was dominated by a huge oval mahogany table, with twin chandeliers above it and the walls around it hung with portraits of Yale eminences—the largest, appropriately, a painting of Elihu Yale himself. Like members of Cabinets of Presidents of the United States, Yale Fellows would normally take their leather-upholstered chairs away with them as souvenirs when their terms expired. There has been one exception. The trustees' room still contains, off in a corner and unused, a wooden chair with an outlandishly wide seat. It was custom-built to accommodate, during his service between 1913 and 1924, the extraordinary bottom of William Howard Taft. (Just before one meeting broke up, Jock's classmate Carlos Stoddard, who had stayed on at Yale after graduation as a fund raiser, stopped outside Woodbridge Hall to gaze in awe at an extraordinarily long chauffeur-driven limousine waiting at the curb next to a No Parking sign. Stoddard knew it was one of Whitney's cars. While Stoddard was looking it over, he heard Whitney approaching, turned around, and said, "I don't want it." "Why?" asked Whitney. "It has no swimming pool," Stoddard said. "True," said Whitney, in one of his infrequent jokes about his affluence, "but it does have a nine-hole golf course."

Brewster was, as Whitney had sensed in the note he wrote himself in 1963, a strong-willed man. Whatever success he enjoyed during his fourteen years as president of Yale was attributed by people close to him in part to his own toughness and pragmatism, and in part to Whitney's common sense and good judgment. Whitney, admirers of both men liked to say, tempered Brewster's steel. "Jock was the voice of reason," Brewster himself would reflect after he had left Yale. "He never panicked. He was always thinking things out—worrying about their implications. One of his favorite words was 'why.' He would ask that whenever anybody suggested anything. In the later 1960s, there were many tensions among Yale's trustees about the university's policies, and Jock was very good at finding common ground on which they could all comfortably stand. He showed them, as he had in London, that he had diplomatic skills."

It was during Brewster's regime that women undergraduates were admitted to Yale. Throughout the controversy that then radical move generated, Whitney stood solidly behind his president. Yale had planned originally to merge with Vassar, but Vassar backed off. Then Brewster recommended simply admitting women, and a lot of alumni—also, a couple of trustees—were vociferously opposed. Whitney went on record as favoring the new policy, and his stand is believed to have muted the criticism of (and curtailed the diminution of gifts from) some of his more hidebound contemporaries. "Among Yale's trustees at the time," Brewster would say later, "Jock and Irwin Miller did the most to change the university from being excessively homogeneous and dominated by an inherited elite to achieving greater diversity. Co-education, of course, was a major aspect of that. On the eve of a trustees' meeting at which that momentous change was going to be voted on, I asked Jock and Irwin to get together with me. You know, someone said that the faculty of the Yale Law School was made up of Old Turks and Young Fogies. I used to think of Jock and Irwin as sort of the Old Turks of the Corporation. That night, I had a question to put to them. It was, 'Will Yale get more financial support by first going co-educational and then asking for approval, or by asking first and then doing it?' They both said, 'Do it, then ask.' That was gutsy. They knew I was talking about *them*. That made me bite the bullet and put the issue up to the Corporation."

Whitney backed up Brewster, similarly, during some of Yale's troubles engendered by the war in Vietnam. Jock hadn't been especially outspoken all along on that issue, although he made up his mind sooner than some—calling the war in a letter to a friend, just after Nixon's re-election in 1972, "a rocky disaster." In the late 1960s, one of the country's most articulate opponents of the war was Yale's chaplain, the Rev. William Sloane Coffin, Jr., whose attendance record at major anti-war protests was practically flawless, and whose views and actions even got him indicted for conspiring to counsel draft evasion. The Yale chaplaincy was not a tenured job. It was a five-year appointment, and Coffin, who had held the post for a decade, was due to be considered for a new term in 1968. Women—radical clergymen—what, some crusty old grads wondered, would Yale embrace next? They began to slam their fists down on their checkbooks.

Whitney had spent time with Coffin during holidays on Fishers Island, where only gulls and golfers ordinarily raised their voices, and had got along well enough with him, but Jock had ambivalent feelings about the continuation of the chaplaincy. "I agree that he is hard to take—really impossible," Whitney had written to his cousin Eve Symington the previous November. But to fire him, or not rehire him, would have caused more trouble, Whitney had concluded, than to keep him on. Brewster wanted to retain Coffin. He knew there would be problems whatever the university did, and he felt that a matter as ticklish as this one would have to go before the Corporation. It was traditional for that body to refer all its decisions, for preliminary consideration, to committees from within its ranks, but there seemed to be no standing committee—Budget, Finance, Educational Policy, whatever—that could logically handle that order of business. So a new one, an Institutional Policy Committee, was formed, and before Whitney knew exactly what had happened the other trustees had unanimously, and with relief, chosen him to be its chairman. It fell upon him, thus, to be the advocate of Brewster's wish to have Coffin reappointed, as he duly was. The president did suggest one change in the chaplain's status. Brewster said that to spare Coffin, and any future holder of the office, the awkwardness of having to seem to be running for re-election every five years, thenceforth perhaps the chaplain should serve for an unspecified number of years "at the pleasure of the Corporation." Whitney had faithfully sided with the president, but he still harbored faint misgivings. "Don't you think," he asked after the appropriate resolutions had been voted on and passed, "that we could find some phrase other than 'serving at the *pleasure* of the Corporation?'"

In 1970, Whitney became Yale's Senior Fellow. A Secretary of State (Dean Acheson), an Episcopal bishop (the Right Rev. Henry Knox Sherrill), and a distinguished scholar (the Horace Walpole expert Wilmarth Lewis) had been among his predecessors. Now Whitney was unarguably a Yale B.M.O.C.—Biggest Man Off Campus.

There was an enormous difference between Whitney the investor-philanthropist and Whitney the Senior Fellow. As the former, he was always surrounded by associates who would make either semi-decisions for him or strong recommendations. But as Senior Fellow, he was on his own. Yale's Senior Fellow has no statutory authority. He is merely senior in point of service. Still, by tradition, he is the one to whom the president of Yale turns when he needs a quick decision from his trustees and hasn't the time to consult more than one of them. And it is he to whom the president turns when drawing up agendas, he who admonishes his fellow trustees to work harder and attend meetings more conscientiously, and, yes, he, too, who urges them to make larger contributions. "I would go to Jock for advice on all sorts of problems—personal as well as institutional," Brewster said. "Jock generated trust."

Brewster had to steer Yale through murky waters. Columbia had exploded in 1968, Harvard in the spring of 1969. After Harvard had called in the police to break up a student uprising that April, the Cambridge institution had tried to calm things down by inviting its entire constituency to a meeting in its football stadium. Brewster decided to hold a similar conclave at Yale's hockey rink. Among the university's Fellows were both

William P. Bundy, who had been President Johnson's Assistant Secretary of State for East Asian and Pacific Affairs, and Cyrus Vance, who had been his Deputy Secretary of Defense; even without their provocative presence, a student response to Vietnam was bound to be clamorously voiced. As soon as the meeting was announced, some students had denounced it, maintaining that the proceedings would be rigged by the administration, and that honest dissent would surely be stifled. "At dinner the night before the meeting," Brewster said, "Jock and a couple of other fellows suggested mildly that if the students were that suspicious of how proceedings were going to be conducted, why not let the students preside? It had never occurred to me. Over and over again, the trustees were ahead of me. In theory, as most people viewed Yale, the faculty always had to be prodding the president to get the trustees to do something. But in actuality, just as I was often ahead of the faculty, so were the trustees often ahead of me."

The meeting was ultimately chaired by a radical professor of political science, Robert Dahl, who was respected by all shades of student opinion. Eventually, a resolution on some such cataclysmic issue as whether or not R.O.T.C. should be abolished was proposed from the floor and was put to a vote. It was agreed, in the interests of pure democracy, that every one of the more than five thousand persons present would be entitled to vote—students, professors, trustees, wives, campus cops, voyeurs. Tellers were appointed and went around scrupulously counting hands. "The trustees had been sitting there for a couple of hours listening to some pretty nasty abuse directed at them personally," Brewster said. "Then the votes were added up. The outcome was an exact tie—something like 2,885 to 2,885. When the senior professor who was chief teller disclosed that, everybody burst out laughing and went home."

Whitney was not especially fazed by student agitation. Had not his Yale class of 1926, after all, been revolutionary, too, in its way and in its day—forcing a startled university administration to do away with compulsory chapel? Still, some of the latter-day demonstrators stretched one's tolerance. The Fellows could not enter Woodbridge Hall for their monthly meetings, for a while, without having to squirm through picket lines of jeering students. (The trustees' sessions could, of course, have been moved elsewhere, but Brewster and Whitney both refused to take that easy way out.) To try to establish some sort of bridge between his students and his trustees, the president proposed an amendment to the Corporation's monthly timetable: each Saturday morning, every trustee would go to an undergraduate residence and have breakfast with some students.

Whitney did not much fancy that kind of face-to-face confrontation, and before retiring to his bedroom in Brewster's home, on the Friday evening preceding the first such scheduled breakfast, he asked to be excused. Brewster refused to do *that*. When Jock came down the following morning and his host asked routinely how he had slept, Whitney replied, "Not at all." Why not? "I was too nervous about breakfast." Why? "If I go, I'll have to answer all their questions." Brewster finally got him under way—it was, the president would recall, comparable to sending a small child off for his first day at a new school—and Whitney arrived, with little appetite, at Ezra Stiles College, where he had barely taken his designated seat when a militant black student challenged him to state what Yale was then doing for what was called at the time "the black experience." Jock invited him and the others at the table to say what they thought Yale should do about that and other matters of special concern to them. Soon he was listening intently, also eating with his usual gusto. At nine-thirty he strode into Woodbridge Hall, his shoulders thrown characteristically back ("Jock always walked as if there were a strong wind behind him, about to bowl him over," a friend once remarked); and when Brewster asked him, less routinely, how the breakfast had gone, he said, "Super! Super!"

Perhaps Yale's most worrisome day, in that era, was May 1, 1970. On May Day, Bobby Seale, the Black Panther out on bail after being indicted for kidnapping and murder, was due in New Haven to speak at a much-heralded rally convened by his supporters. At a faculty meeting just before the Black Panther rally, the question arose as to what extent, if any, Yale should institutionally participate in the demonstration, which was inevitably going to arouse strong feelings, and probably violence. Brewster said that he did not construe it to be the function of any university officially to support blacks or anyone else on trial for alleged crimes. He added, almost as an afterthought, that in any event he wasn't certain that in the atmosphere of the times any black could get a fair trial anywhere in America. Someone leaked that last offhand remark to the press, and the news spread across the nation that the president of Yale had said no black in America could get a fair trial. Vice-President Spiro Agnew demanded that Brewster resign. Many Yale alumni had been upset and irate when they heard what Brewster had said, and some of *them* were demanding his resignation, though there were heartening exceptions. SPIRO AGNEW? WHAT CLASS WAS HE? one old grad telegraphed.

"At the next trustees' meeting," Brewster said when the dust had settled, "it was suggested that what I'd said to the faculty, in or out of context, was perhaps unwise and unnecessary. 'I'm not sure it was wise,' I responded, 'but it sure was necessary.' It did have the effect, too, of making me a hero for the moment among some blacks, and that wasn't harmful at all when May Day arrived." When the day came, Yale students, black and white, helped keep the Panthers' demonstration from turning into a large-scale melee; one undergraduate even approached a Fellow who was observing the scene and said, politely, "I don't think you should go any farther, sir. Otherwise you'll get into the tear gas." "Yale was lucky that day," Brewster said afterward, "and in my view the students were heroic."

Inevitably, there remained alumni who wanted Brewster's hide. One of Whitney's classmates, a man of lofty dudgeon, even urged Jock to head up a campaign to rid the university of its president. "You ask the wrong man," Jock replied. "I have seen him during these terribly difficult times and in my opinion no man could have shown more courage and more dedication to the safety and survival of Yale. . . . It seems to me that those of us who believe in Yale must do so with a sense of history—with a look into the future when the madness of these days will have passed. I truly believe that Kingman Brewster is fitted to bring Yale through these embattled days, if anyone can, into a time when reason and respect will be restored. . . . I think it takes a great deal more exposure to the kids now at Yale than most alumni can have to realize how very far from being 'bums' they are. They are bright and dedicated to a better Yale as they see it." Brewster's breakfasts had borne fruit.

Even so, Brewster was sufficiently concerned about what effect his words and actions might have on alumni support to ask the Corporation to review and re-evaluate his presidency. Another ad hoc committee was formed—William McChesney Martin chaired this one—and it sought out the feelings of students, faculty, and alumni. Based on its findings, the Corporation decided unanimously that Brewster should stay. In July 1970, Whitney personally reaffirmed his faith in Yale and its leader by pledging fifteen million dollars for the construction of two new undergraduate colleges on a high school parking lot alongside the Payne Whitney gymnasium. The additional residences would have enabled Yale to accommodate two hundred and fifty more students, who would, it was predicted, generate half a million dollars a year in increased local spending. But there was a long wrangle with city officials of New Haven about the tax-exempt status of the proposed colleges and the land they were to stand on, and ultimately the project was abandoned. Whitney thereupon footed the bill to have five old campus buildings overhauled and refurbished. In the course of the work (it was the sort of thing that some old grads heard of with relief—all hope for Yale was not lost) one soundly sleeping student was prankishly sealed into his room with bricks and mortar.

Whitney retired from the Yale Corporation in the comparatively tranquil spring of 1973, when he was nearing his sixty-ninth birthday. He had been a Fellow for eighteen years. The last trustees' dinner he attended, before his big leather chair was packed up and trundled to his New York office (he did not sit on it there; he put it across from his desk, for visitors), was on May 11, 1973. There were the usual laudatory remarks, principal among them Brewster's description of Jock as "my mentor and senior partner." Whitney himself confessed that as a Yale undergraduate a half century earlier he had barely been aware of the existence of a president of the university and had never heard of anything called a corporation. He added, on a less jocular note, that "the big issues are what count in our lives and will matter to those who come after us, and while none of us is given the time to know all the alternatives, we in this room have the obligation to make an unreasonable effort to find solutions that satisfy both competing ends."

Brewster had long been mulling over what Yale might present to Whitney that evening as a symbol of its gratitude for what he had done for, and meant to, the university; and now he unveiled a gift that he deemed suitable. It was something that Yale had never bestowed on any of its sons or daughters: a silver yale, the yale of heraldry, a fabled beast that according to Pliny had a flexible horn. The yale that Yale gave Whitney—its design was based on a picture of the creature that Brewster's wife Mary Louise had come across in England—had three tusks, chin whiskers, and a three-tufted tail. A plaque affixed to its marble pedestal read, simply, "In Jock We Trust."

When the Yale class of 1926 celebrated its fiftieth reunion, Jock's classmates commissioned a portrait of him for the university. (The plaque affixed to that inadvertently assigned him to the class of 1923.) The original idea was that the painting would be hung in one of the colleges Whitney's largess had renovated. That testimonial notion was discarded when someone pointed out that, however much student comportment might have changed since 1970, there was still no assurance that a larksome undergraduate might not, in the throes of cramming for an exam, relax by using the portrait as a dartboard. Whitney's likeness was thereupon consigned, for safekeeping, to an office in Woodbridge Hall.

The closest Yale ever came to naming a building after John Hay Whitney was when in 1980 it designated a new faculty facility—one acquired with funds supplied by both Jock and the National Endowment for the Humanities—the Whitney Humanities Center. Brewster's successor, A. Bartlett Giamatti, wrote to Whitney, "It is a dream many of my colleagues and I have had for many years, and you have made it happen." Giamatti hoped that Jock could attend the formal dedication of the center—he couldn't—because "It is also an opportunity for grateful faculty and others to salute one of Yale's greatest men and to carry on in the spirit he has taught us."

In 1977, Yale embarked on the first fund-raising drive in half a century to which Whitney was not asked—was not allowed—to contribute. His undergraduate club, Scroll and Key, was observing its centennial, and after its officers consulted with Brewster how best to memorialize the anniversary, they decided to raise some three quarters of a million dollars to endow a new academic chair, and to call it the John Hay Whitney Professorship in the Humanities. Brewster particularly relished the idea because it gave Yale a chance to solicit contributions from non-Yale sources. He called on Bill Paley, and in due course they compiled a list of a hundred and seventy-eight of Jock's friends, who were invited, without Whitney's knowledge, to chip in. In no time at all, seventy-five of them had made pledges of six hundred and fifty thousand dollars. Among the donors were three Rockefeller brothers, Joseph Alsop, Mrs. Vincent Astor, Harry Baehr, Walworth Barbour, David Bruce, William A. M. Burden, C. Douglas Dillon, Jacob Javits, Vernon Jordan, Benno Schmidt, Irene Selznick, Walter Thayer, Franklin Thomas, Jeremy Tree, and Lord Zuckerman. Brewster had left for *his* stint at the Court of St. James's by November 1977, when the establishment of the chair was revealed both to Whitney and to the general public by Yale's acting president, Hanna H. Gray—later the president of the University of Chicago—who to Whitney's delight had become the first woman member of Yale's thitherto doggedly patriarchal Corporation. Mrs. Gray installed Bart Giamatti, a Scroll and Key man, as the first John Hay Whitney Professor. Whitney had not yet met Giamatti, who had been on the Yale faculty since 1966 and specialized in Italian and English Renaissance literature, but on learning of his selection Jock said, "If they thought they were picking somebody according to my predilections, they were certainly right." Soon afterward, Giamatti became president of Yale himself, and on ascending to that summit wrote Jock, "The hardest thing to give up last Tuesday was the John Hay Whitney Professorship. It represented everything fine Yale stands for, as do you, and I was profoundly proud to have that chair. Someone else will have it now but if I may I shall always think of myself as the John Hay Whitney Professor. It meant everything."

Back in 1965, Whitney had received a Yale trophy called the Mory's Cup, named after the New Haven restaurant much patronized by Yale blades and given annually to an alumnus for service to the university. The sponsors of the dinner at which the presentation was made had a fake first page of the *Herald Tribune* printed for the occasion; the level of its humor was epitomized by one "news item" to the effect that, at Joan Payson's initiative, the New York Mets had just traded Yogi Berra for Mory's treasurer. A year later, there would no longer be a *Herald*

Tribune in New York to spoof; but Whitney was by no means out of publishing. He was still the patron of the *Trib's* offshoot abroad, the Paris *Herald,* and because of that proprietorship he had, when the paper celebrated its seventy-fifth birthday in 1962, been invested with the Légion d'Honneur and the Grand Médaille de Vermeil de la Ville de Paris. (Before he could legally preside over the *Herald,* he had been obliged to submit an affidavit to the authorities over there to the effect that he had never declared bankruptcy; he was surely one of the few newspaper publishers extant who could have poured forty million dollars into a lost journalistic cause without having so to declare.)

The Paris edition of the younger Bennett's *Herald Tribune* had drifted along amiably for much of that three quarters of a century. It was put together in some comfortably musty old offices on the Rue de Berri, earlier the site of the first American church built in that tolerant city. Its circulation when Whitney acquired it was a modest thirty-five thousand. Because it contained both comic strips and stock market quotations from home, it had a loyal following among Americans in France—not least of all the doughboys of the American Expeditionary Force of the First World War—and those across the English Channel, too. Its editor for many years had been Eric Hawkins, an émigré Englishman who during the hard times of the thirties had succored many down-and-out writers— including Ernest Hemingway and Ezra Pound—by buying articles from them. The *Herald* had published uninterruptedly, six times a week, aside from a four-year shutdown during the Nazi occupation of Paris. In 1966, when its parent paper folded in New York, it was not in very good shape itself; it was losing two hundred and eighty thousand dollars a year. (During the 1965 strike in New York, Whitney and his associates had ten thousand copies of their Paris paper flown over daily to that newspaper-starved city.)

By then, the *Herald* had a competitor in the form of an international edition of the New York *Times,* which had been inaugurated in 1960. (Earlier, there had been brief sorties into Paris by both the London *Daily Mail* and the Chicago *Tribune.*) The overseas fight for advertising and circulation between the *Herald* and the *Times* was financially draining. Whitney was persuaded that an infusion of additional news sources for Paris was desirable, and in August 1966 he sold a minority interest in the *Herald* to the Washington *Post.* Then, early in 1967, the *Times* abandoned its international edition, and there was a further shuffle of ownership. The end result was that the *Post* had thirty per cent of what became known as the *International Herald Tribune,* the *Times* thirty-three and a third per cent, and Whitney Communications—which it was agreed among the three would manage the joint enterprise—thirty-six and two thirds, minus a six-thousandths-of-one-per-cent sliver of a Whitney Communications subsidiary that belonged to the Reid family.

Under the new setup, the *International Herald Tribune* had unlimited access to news, editorials, and features from both the *Post* and the *Times*. Whitney was the chairman of its board of directors, responsible for naming its publisher; its stateside editorial writer, Harry Baehr, had an office at Whitney Communications. As editor of the paper, the owners picked Murray Weiss, the terminal managing editor of the New York paper. As a publisher, for one stretch, Jock picked Philip S. Weld, the owner of a chain of newspapers in Massachusetts. In 1980, at the age of sixty-five, Weld would break the world's record for a one-man crossing of the Atlantic Ocean, in his sailboat aptly called the *Moxie*. When he did, Whitney cabled him, "The *International Herald Tribune* has been called a Mid-Atlantic newspaper and it has crossed that ocean many many times but unlike the *Moxie* it has required many crew members and pilots to make the crossing and we were never at the mercy of winds and seas, so our very special congratulations to you, Phil, and our thanks for being the American who set so remarkable a record for this gallant form of ocean passage."

The *International Herald Tribune* began to blossom. Between 1966 and 1979—in 1968, the Soviet Union let it be sold in Moscow for the first time in forty years—its circulation rose from 60,000 to 130,000, and its annual gross revenue from $3,270,000 to $30,000,000. It was on sale in one hundred and forty countries.* But its publishing costs were formidable. Of eleven dailies then coming out in Paris, only *Le Monde* and the *International Herald Tribune* (which long-time readers persisted in calling the "Paris *Herald*" no matter what its masthead proclaimed) were in the black, and the *Trib* barely so. Murray Weiss was getting out the paper with linotype machines that dated back to the 1920s, and the presses were even older. The *Trib* printed only sixteen pages every day, yet there were one hundred and sixty-five employees in its production department, seventy-seven of them in the composing room alone. They worked a twenty-five-hour week—five hours a day, five days a week—and had six weeks' paid vacation. With modern technology—computer terminals, cold type, all of that—five competent people in the composing room would have sufficed. There was little hope that more advertising income

---

* Late in 1978, the paper came under fire from Jewish groups in both the United States and England for deleting Israeli advertisements from the three thousand copies that were normally distributed in Arab territory. The *Tribune* argued that without such deletions the paper would be barred from such areas, and that it was better to have its editorial voice heard there under wraps than not to be heard at all. Two years after that, the paper announced that it would no longer accept "escort service" advertising that contained racy implications, and there were no protests except from a few traveling businessmen and some fringe feminists.

could remedy the situation. The *Trib* was already charging its advertisers more for a full page than was the New York *Times*, which had a circulation six times as large. The only solution seemed to be—as it had in New York—automation. The seven trade unions representing the employees wanted no part of that.

Then the proprietors had a radical idea: why should the paper have to be published in Paris at all? It was an *international* journal now; why couldn't it just as easily be printed in Frankfurt, say, or Geneva? True, it would undoubtedly be easier to attract a top-notch editorial staff to Paris than any other city on the Continent. True, Whitney wanted to stay in Paris. True, the French government, which could probably bring the unions around, if it chose to, wanted it to remain there. Or did the government really care? It would have to be tested.

Early in 1978, the *Tribune* leased a new building at Neuilly, on the outskirts of the capital, and there it installed up-to-date composing equipment. It set up an exact duplicate installation in Zurich. The unions knew this was going on, but they seemed unimpressed, nor did they respond affirmatively to a pledge from the management to give exceedingly generous severance pay to those employees who would have to be let go. Meanwhile, the *Tribune* was sending its editorial employees, three at a time, to Zurich, to learn how to master the newfangled machinery there. The trips were "secret"; the management made sure that the secret got out. Finally, the *Tribune* went to the French government and said that, unless an accommodation could be reached with the unions, it was ready to pack up and leave for Switzerland, and that it could do so, indeed, in twenty-four hours. The government persuaded the unions to accept the new order of things.

Soon the paper was being printed in three places—at Neuilly (with thirty production employees), at Zurich (for distribution to southern Europe), and outside London (for the British Isles). The paper prospered mightily, and by September, 1980, it was challenging the *Wall Street Journal* in Asia, transmitting photographs of its pages by satellite to Hong Kong and printing there. By the end of that year, those of Whitney's associates who had been worried about his involvement with bigtime print journalism were glad to have a *Herald Tribune* under their wing after all. Harry Baehr concluded an unpublished history of the newspaper under Jock Whitney and Walter Thayer by saying that "both served American journalism—and the people it serves—to the best of their extensive ability, and for both the name 'Herald Tribune' on a newsstand in, say, Istanbul, is at once a Distinguished Service Cross—and a Purple Heart."

When the *Herald Tribune* gave up in New York, in 1966, Whitney could have made his business headquarters the offices of J. H. Whitney & Company, a very much thriving concern still at 630 Fifth Avenue, in Rockefeller Center, where he had hung his business hat before he went to London as Ambassador. He elected instead to address himself mainly to the problems of his Whitney Communications Corporation, which in 1961 had set up shop, also in Rockefeller Center, on the forty-sixth floor of the Time-Life Building. There he emplaced his broad John Hay desk, his ambassadorial flag from London, his Haseltine bronzes of Easter Hero and Royal Minstrel; an ashtray built upon the shoe worn by his mother's 1942 Kentucky Derby winner Shut Out; and, of course, the sculptured likeness of his own beloved Jones terrier Chillie. Yale's fabulous yale would join the real animals in due course. (So, after yet another New York newspaper strike, in 1978, would the original of a *New Yorker* cartoon by Robert Weber referring to a short-lived daily that emerged in those troubled days; the caption read, "This doesn't look like the 'Trib' to me!") Whitney brought a few of his works of art to Room 4600, too, among them his mother's cherished Sargent portrait of Robert Louis Stevenson and various paintings by Hopper, Derain, Géricault, Signac, and William Harnett—the last represented by *The New York Herald, 1880.*

He had plenty to keep him occupied. In 1971, for instance, the New York Hospital, which had been practically a Whitney fiefdom throughout the twentieth century, was about to celebrate its bicentennial. (Whitney and his family had been so generous to the hospital, tens of millions of dollars' worth of largess over the years, that when a doctor on its staff performed a minor operation on Jock's foot one time he declined to submit a bill. Whitney insisted this was unprofessional and sent the surgeon fifteen hundred dollars.) Having opened its doors while America was still a British colony, the hospital thought it might be nice if a member of the royal family came over to grace the ceremonies. Jock was asked to put on his ex-Ambassador's hat and provide a suitable personage. He couldn't, whereupon he put on his Yale hat and provided Kingman Brewster.

Room 4600—it was actually a whole floor—sheltered among other entities the John Hay Whitney Foundation, the Whitney Communications Corporation, and the Whitcom Investment Company, this last a partnership—Jock as the senior partner—that he established (initially as WCC Associates) in 1967 and that would own, among other assets, all of Whitney Communications. The foundation, several of whose employees were gentle ladies in their middle years, did not have a softball team, but Whitney Communications and its magazine subdivision did, and they would now and then march out into Central Park to meet in lively fraternal competition—the Whitney Communications side sporting T-shirts inscribed "The Jocks," the magazine side labeled "The Profit Center."

Whitney himself did not play, although he owned all the bats and balls; he had by then become strictly a spectator sportsman.

In the first few years after the collapse of the *Herald Tribune*, Whitney Communications functioned pretty much like a run-of-the-mill investment firm, trafficking in fairly large blocks of stocks of organizations like Dun & Bradstreet and Booth Newspapers, but exercising little managerial control over such of its assets. The only communications properties in which it had a majority interest were the *International Herald Tribune* and the monthly *Interior Design*. Jock had recruited Richard Wald from the ranks of the New York *Herald Tribune* unemployed to work for Whitney Communications. Wald was supposed to look for new print properties, but the only publication in the acquisition of which he figured was another monthly, *Art in America*. For a while, Wald thought that he had *Gourmet* also added to the Whitney magazine stable. He had Jock convinced he should buy it, and its owner was tempted to sell it, but the latter wanted first to make sure that whoever took over from him would have a proper appreciation of good food. Wald, who knew at first hand the splendor of the meals that routinely emerged from Whitney kitchens, proposed that Jock give a small lunch at his East Sixty-third Street town house for the *Gourmet* man. It was an unexceptionable repast, enhanced by some of Whitney's finest wines and choicest brandies, and built around a magnificent game pie made from quail flown up from the host's larder at Thomasville. After the guest of honor had taken his leave, Wald asked the host when he wanted to close the deal for *Gourmet*. "I don't want the magazine," Whitney snapped. Wald wondered why. "He never mentioned the game pie," Jock said.

Wald soon moved on to become, at one time or another, the head of the news divisions of both the National and American Broadcasting Companies. Not long afterward, Whitney Communications did actually begin buying other magazines. (Some—*Basketball News, Gridiron*—went almost as quickly as they came.) It ended up with eight of them, all special-interest publications, which would produce in 1980 an annual operating revenue of twenty-two million dollars, and involved so many people that Room 4600 couldn't hold them all. They were duly ensconced in still another Whitney office, over on Third Avenue. Among them were *Hockey News,* a seasonal weekly for ice-hockey buffs; *Waterway Guide* and *Boating Industry,* two monthlies for sailing and cruising aficionados; and a monthly for senior citizens that, when Whitney had first bought a minority interest in it in 1962, was called *Harvest Years*. In 1970, when Jock was sixty-six, his aides suggested that the name of that one be changed to *Leisure Years*. He dissented. "The concept of leisure is to most people very negative," he said. He agreed to *Retirement Living*, but after a spell he and his publishing partners concluded that that title had too narrow an appeal, and the magazine ended up, in 1978, as *50 Plus*. Rosalynn Carter, who was fifty-one, appeared on its first cover. That honor was originally to have been conferred on Jacqueline Onassis, but she was passed over on the ground that she had already appeared on a slew of magazine covers and, besides, she was only forty-nine.

By 1980, Whitney Communications had also acquired twenty-nine small newspapers in Florida, Delaware, and Maryland, including the *Kent County News*, at Chestertown, Maryland, which had begun in 1793 as *Apollo; or, Chestertown Spy*. Most of these were weeklies. Two exceptions were the daily Easton, Maryland, *Star-Democrat* and *Oil Daily*, a very special publication with a circulation of 6,500 and a subscription price of $227 a year; it was coveted by its small band of readers because it furnished them such vital intelligence as the price of a particular shipment of crude oil en route from Bahrein to London. There was also a comparably esoteric semi-monthly, the *Coal Industry News*.

In 1978, Whitney Communications cast a covetous eye to the north, and it bought and briefly held a controlling interest in a one-hundred-and-ten-year-old weekly paper in Maine, the Camden *Herald*. Thus began a business relationship with Walter Cronkite. The doyen of television already owned ten per cent of the *Herald*, which he had become fond of while plying Maine waters during summer holidays. Whitney's Thayer was, like Cronkite, an avid boatsman; the two Walters had been friends since 1963. Cronkite had traveled to Normandy then to film a CBS special on Dwight Eisenhower and the twentieth anniversary of the D-Day landings, and Bill Paley had invited Thayer to go along and watch the proceedings. Cronkite's path had not often crossed Whitney's, though the commentator did sometimes go to football games at New Haven; his agent was a Yale man.

When, largely at Thayer's instigation, Whitney Communications bought *Waterway Guide*, Cronkite was elated. That was *his* kind of magazine. When he was offered a ten-per-cent slice of that investment, his joy was boundless. He had started off his career in print journalism, and now he was getting back into it. During the 1979 motorboat show at the New York Coliseum, he wandered around the arena with a copy of *Waterway Guide* under his arm, and at one point stood behind a counter set up by that publication and sold subscriptions. He is not known ever to have peddled a TV set. Eventually, Whitney and Thayer decided to put all their newspaper holdings under a new corporate umbrella—it was called WCC Newspapers—and they invited Cronkite to buy a five-per-cent share of that organization and join its board. He did, once the matter, which had Paley's blessing, had been probed and approved by a CBS conflict-of-interest committee. But somebody at the network thought for once Cronkite had gone too far. A CBS executive chided him—to the extent that anyone there would ever chide Uncle Walter—for having delivered the evening news while sporting a Whitney Communications Corporation club tie. Not long after Cronkite joined the Whitney publishing family, *50 Plus* put him on *its* cover. "Why He's the Most Trusted Man in America," read a picture caption. The text inside said that, whenever Cronkite retired from CBS, "He'd like to serve on the board of a major newspaper group." He was already a director of a newspaper group, of course, though still, by most criteria, a comparatively minor one.

Whitney had been involved in television long before Thayer drew Cronkite into Jock's widespread orbit. Whitney had tentatively explored the commercial possibilities of television way back in 1937, when David Selznick had asked him to try to find out, while on a jaunt abroad, how the then infant medium was faring in Europe. In 1940, when television was first unveiled in the United States, Whitney had invested in Dumont Television. J. H. Whitney & Company had bought a TV station in Tulsa, Oklahoma, in 1954; and in the very early days of cable television, also in the fifties, it had helped build the first cable stations in the country—in Pennsylvania, West Virginia, and the state of Washington. Whitney Communications would become heavily involved in cable television, and for a while it also had a subsidiary called the Corinthian Broadcasting Company, which owned five conventional television stations across the country. Corinthian was merged into Dun & Bradstreet in 1971. Four years earlier, Jock's interest in Corinthian had had a value of $18,000,000. At the time of the sale, he had transferred some of his shares to Whitcom, his investment firm, of which he was the major partner. His personal proceeds from the Dun & Bradstreet transaction came to $67,949,655; he was also the principal beneficiary of Whitcom's proceeds of $32,952,750. His great-uncle Oliver and his father would have been proud of him.

Whitney had a further link to television. Bill Paley was his brother-in-law, confidant, and fierce bottle-pool opponent. (Their wives once tried, to no avail, to distract them from dueling with cues by piling a Greentree billiard table high with books; the next thing Betsey and Babe knew, the floor was strewn in all directions with precious first editions in hideous disarray.) When it came to *looking* at television, Whitney was, in Paley's judgment, an exceptionally discriminating viewer. (Jock was especially critical of TV sports coverage; he said once that he had never heard a television commentator give a proper account of a horse race.) Whitney was forever nagging at Paley to be sure to catch this or that show on somebody else's network. "Jock's sort of my TV monitor," Paley once admiringly said.

In the late 1960s, Whitney had got much involved—partly at Paley's urging—in non-commercial, public broadcasting. He became a director, and solid supporter, of the Educational Broadcasting Corporation, which ran New York City's Channel 13. It was mainly through Whitney's beneficence that Channel 13—to which he gave $413,900 between 1967 and 1975—was able to carry live telecasts in 1970 of the Knapp Commission hearings on corruption in the criminal justice system of New York. The following year, at the instigation of Senator Javits, Whitney was nominated as a director of the Corporation for Public Broadcasting, which Congress had established in 1967 to oversee non-commercial programs on a national level. "I have never approached any job or assignment with more enthusiasm than I do for this work," Whitney told the Senate Committee on Commerce, which had to approve him, and which did. Soon there were snags. President Nixon thought that commentators on non-commercial stations were unappreciative of and unfriendly to his Administration; the way to get rid of that annoyance, the President and his communications advisers resolved, was to have a law passed forbidding broadcasters to use public funds for discussion of public affairs.

The *raison d'être* for the establishment of the Corporation for Public Broadcasting was to have an agency free of government interference. Late in 1971, the Administration started to interfere, and by January a director of the Corporation, Thomas W. Moore, a former ABC television executive who by then was running a subsidiary of General Electric called Tomorrow Entertainment, sent Whitney a draft of a resolution that Moore hoped the Corporation itself would adopt: "The Corporation will not fund the production of, nor will it fund any organization which provides any interconnection for news, or news analysis and news commentary by professional broadcasters. In addition, it will not fund the production of, nor will it fund any organization which provides any interconnection for panel discussions and interviews on national political affairs or on public affairs subject to national political debate. . . ."

What that gobbledegook seemed to mean was that if the Corporation didn't behave the way the Nixon White House wanted it to, the Administration would, with Moore's concurrence, try to strip it of its funds. Whitney was dismayed. "I have given a great deal of thought to this question since we last met," he wrote to Moore. "Taking into account the urgent requirement for permanent financing, it is not an easy question to resolve. It is clear to me, however, that the course we pursue in seeking permanent financing must be one which will not in any way restrict CPB in its support of programs dealing with public affairs, including news coverage and, where appropriate, analysis and commentary. There is simply no way, in my judgment, to generalize on this subject. I believe if we attempt to do so, either on our own initiative or in response to pressure from whatever source, we will do a great disservice to public broadcasting and the role it should fill as part of the broadcast media. I

cannot, therefore, subscribe to the proposal you have drafted. . . ."
Thanks in part to Whitney's adamant position, the proposal was scuttled,
and while the Nixon people did not give up trying, they were never able
to stifle the public broadcasters. Eventually, it didn't much matter; the
Watergate hearings were carried on all television channels, commercial
and non-commercial alike.

Whitney had reached the watershed age of sixty-five in August 1969. As
a birthday present, Richard Wald, one of the few individuals who knew
him well enough—and was well enough liked by him—to josh him with
impunity about his money, sent him a senior citizens' reduced-fare card
for use on the New York City public transit system. Wald had trouble
obtaining it, because it hadn't been easy for him to extract Jock's Social
Security number, which was a prerequisite, from the recipient's vigilantly protective staff.

In the post-*Herald Tribune* years, Whitney hadn't busied himself over-
much with the day-to-day activities of any of his enterprises. He had
Benno Schmidt to handle the venture capital firm that bore his name. He
had Walter Thayer to run Whitney Communications. He had Frank
Streeter, who had joined his staff in 1952 as an assistant to Richard Croft
and Sam Park, to look after his personal financial affairs and his philanthropies. He had Archibald Gillies, a Young Republican Turk, to supervise his foundation and his political activities. The art historian John Rewald had come along to look after his paintings, the value of which was
becoming astronomical. He had secretaries and valets and butlers and
chauffeurs and gardeners and airplane and yacht captains and horse
trainers and jockeys and dozens of other retainers to cope with all the
ramifications of his existence. He had so many people doing so many
things on his behalf that just keeping track of them all might have been a
full-time job for anybody else. On the other hand, his associates were as
a rule so carefully selected and so proficient that they didn't need much
guidance. He believed strongly in letting people to whom he had delegated authority exercise it. When somebody asked him once, for instance, to intercede personally in a matter that involved a substantial
sum of his own money but that he had turned over to a trusted surrogate, he refused. "That would be meddling," he said.

One of the rare occasions on which Whitney differed from any subordinates was when his cousin Whitney Tower was planning, late in 1975,
to start up a horse-racing journal called *Classic*. Tower felt confident that
Cousin Jock would like to sponsor anything of that sort, even without a
family connection, and he made a conventional overture for backing
through Whitney's staff. He was turned down flat. Rightly suspecting
that the proposition had never even been called to Jock's attention,

Tower wrote him a personal note about it and sent it to his home. The reply was affirmative. Jock apologized for having been overprotected. It turned out, though, that his staff had exercised shrewd investment judgment. *Classic* was short-lived.

Now there was, with so many people to look after so many things for him, more time for Jock to devote to his horses and his golf and his strictly non-business cronies, such as the social and sociable stockbroker Joseph E. Sheffield, a childhood friend and contemporary at Yale (his grandfather had founded the Sheffield Scientific School there). One of Sheffield's chief claims to postgraduate fame was having named a female dog Harry Luce. Betsey was glad that Jock had more time for himself. The fewer things he had to do, the more attention he could pay to their children and grandchildren. Both Sara and Kate were by then divorced and, in Sara's case, remarried. Sara had five children, Kate three. It was after Kate's divorce, in 1974, from William Haddad, that she decided to change her surname. She went to her adopted father one day and said she had resolved to give up "Haddad," and how would he feel if instead of calling herself "Kate Roosevelt" she used "Kate Roosevelt Whitney"? It was characteristic of Jock that he said that before coming to a conclusion he'd like to think it over. When they next saw each other, he reached out to her and said, "You've made me very proud." That was that.

Whitney was an indulgent grandfather but a prudent one. Whenever one of his grandchildren finished high school, he gave the young graduate a new car, but he took pains to see it was not a flashy one. He was eager to have his oldest grandson, Christopher di Bonaventura, become a crack shot, but Whitney—his father would have approved of that—would not let the boy take aim at a dove or a quail until he had had several years of training in Georgia with BB guns and air rifles and on a skeet range. That paid off. At Yale, in the class of 1977, Di Bonaventura, thanks to his arduous apprenticeship, was a member of an undergraduate skeet-shooting team that won a national championship.

Early in the 1968 presidential campaign, Whitney was staunchly behind the candidacy of his old friend Nelson Rockefeller. As the Republican nominating convention drew near, Rockefeller asked Whitney to assume the chairmanship of his finance committee. Whitney agreed, but two days later Rockefeller withdrew from contention. A decade earlier, President Eisenhower had proposed that Whitney come home from London and run for the governorship of New York. Jock had no taste for elective office. Campaigning would have been anathema to him. He would as soon have kissed a pet crocodile that for some years dwelt snugly in a

Greentree greenhouse as a stranger's baby. He turned Eisenhower down. Then Rockefeller decided to run for the gubernatorial job. The endorsement of Senator Javits of New York, Rockefeller believed, was indispensable. On one of Jock's trips home, he had the two of them to breakfast at the Mayflower Hotel in Washington.

Javits was on a spot, of sorts. Rockefeller's chief rival for the Republican nomination for governor was Leonard Hall, a former chairman of the Republican National Committee who had been instrumental in getting Javits elected to the Senate in 1956. In large measure because of his fondness for Whitney, Javits agreed after the breakfast to support Rockefeller; and when Rockefeller held his first big political rally in New York City, in the heart of the garment center, it was Javits who presented him enthusiastically to that crucial segment of the state's electorate. Rockefeller won the nomination and the election, becoming as he did New York's principal Republican challenger for even higher office. The moment Rockefeller ascended to the state capital in Albany, according to Javits' later view of American political history, the Senator lost his own last chance to become the first Jewish President of the United States. (Eisenhower didn't give up. In 1961, he wanted Whitney to run for mayor of New York. The ex-President said he would support Javits for that office, but only if Jock first begged off. Whitney had no intention of seeking that job, either. Nor, at the time, did Javits. "I think that, in essence, he just couldn't face it," Whitney wrote to Eisenhower about Javits. "Well, neither could I!" Nearly twenty years later, Javits, then seventy-six and on the brink of losing his bid to be re-elected for a sixth Senatorial term, expressed regret that he hadn't pursued the mayoralty after all. "New York is my town," he said, "and in a sense I should have been mayor of it even if I didn't want to be.")

Before the 1968 election year was over, Whitney had contributed thirty-one thousand dollars to the Republican presidential campaign chest, but with little enthusiasm. After Nixon was elected, Whitney's relations with the new President were amicable enough—Jock and Betsey were invited to four White House dinners early in the first Nixon Administration—but not markedly warm. By the time Nixon ran for a second term, Whitney had switched from his long-standing role as a concerned Republican to that of a thoroughly disgruntled Republican. He was not at all pleased early in 1972 when Maurice Stans, Nixon's Secretary of Commerce and sometime bagman, came around to his office one day soliciting a cash contribution of two hundred and fifty thousand dollars, or, failing that, a check before April 7, the cutoff date for the public disclosure of contributions. Whitney was not interested. Stans said he'd take a hundred and fifty, a hundred thousand, whatever Whitney might have on hand. "You want to go to the White House for dinner

again, or be out?" Stans asked. Whitney said he'd wait until April 8 and
then make up his mind. By then, he didn't feel like giving anything at
all, over or under the table. That September, he was chivied by a Republican fund raiser he respected into taking a ten-thousand-dollar table at a
New York State Republican Party fund-raising function, and some of
that money probably trickled into Washington; but he never made a direct contribution to the Nixon coffers.

He was never again asked to dinner at the Nixon White House. By the
following July, the John Hay Whitney who over four decades had probably been as handsome a benefactor of the Republican Party as any other
living individual would be writing to a friend in Australia, "We are all so
fascinated by the unholy developing monstrosity of Watergate that nothing else seems important. The Administration seems to have been almost
totally infected by the disease of distrust and unbridled cheating. . . . I
spend hours at the telly, almost totally stunned."

Whitney turned seventy in the summer of 1974, but he didn't celebrate
that milestone until October, when some friends—Thayer, Paley,
Brewster, Javits, et al.—tendered him a stag dinner at "21." Art Buchwald was imported from Washington to provide a bit of levity, and he
brought along some typed "Offhand Remarks":

> When I was invited tonight to Jock Whitney's forty-third birthday
> party, I stopped off at the FBI in Washington, D.C., to find out what they
> had in files on him.
> This is what they gave me:
> "Jock Whitney was born in a small condominium on the lower East
> Side of New York.
> "His father used to be in the piece-goods business.
> "He owned a piece of Park Avenue—a piece of Grand Central Station—
> a piece of Fifty-ninth Street—and a piece of Long Island.
> "While many people claim to have bought the Brooklyn Bridge, Jock's
> father was the only one who *really* owned it.
> "As a boy, Jock and his father used to play with trains—the Northern
> Pacific, the Southern Pacific, the Atlantic Coast Line and the Atchison,
> Topeka and Santa Fe. . . .
> "Jock lived the simple life of any New York boy—playing in the city
> streets. Only in his case it was more dangerous because he was playing
> polo. . . .
> "After Yale, Jock got a job as a runner on Wall Street. Two days later
> they made him a full partner when Jock promised to bring his brokerage
> account to the firm.
> "Then Jock got bored with the finance business and went to Hollywood
> where he discovered that if he invested his own money in movies, he
> could get laid. . . .

"Fortunately for Jock's health, the war started and he enlisted in the U.S. Air Force where he shot down twenty-three planes—three of them theirs. . . .

"After the war, Jock took his G.I. pay and invested in a little shop called the J. H. Whitney Company. Since anything you did after the war made money, Jock couldn't help but become rich.

"But once again he became bored. Eisenhower suggested Jock become the Ambassador to the Court of St. James's and make it up to the English for all the havoc he did to their women during the war.

"Jock agreed and the rest is history. As soon as he was sworn in as Ambassador, Great Britain lost India. . . .

"While Ambassador, the Reid family came to him and offered to sell him what they described as New York's most thriving newspaper—the New York *Herald Tribune*. . . .

"Jock built up the paper to a point where he was able to merge it with the *World-Telegram* and the *Journal-American*. This merger was considered one of the greatest ever made in history and was only topped by the merger of the New York Central and the Pennsylvania Railroads. . . ."

We love you, Jock, and we're all glad to be here tonight.

18

What Is the Outlook?

A much-traveled friend once asked Whitney how it was that Jock, who liked hunting and had the means to go anywhere (and a yacht and a plane to take him there) had never been to the game lands of Africa. Whitney shrugged. "I guess I'm just a European man," he said. He had never been territorially ambitious. Through J. H. Whitney & Company and other outlets, he sometimes let his capital venture on heady expeditions, but not himself. John Hay, the grandfather in whose footsteps he often aspired to tread, had no yacht and had never heard of a plane, but Hay was forever exploring the globe. Jock did not try to emulate that side of him. He took, rather, after his other grandfather: Will Whitney, for all his far-flung business enterprises and for all the real estate he owned in half a dozen American states, never in his life set foot west of St. Louis. Jock's only sortie into South America was on behalf of Nelson Rockefeller's Co-ordinator's Office; his only trip to Asia for Syngman Rhee's reinauguration; he owned some acreage in Australia but owned it sight unseen.

A typical European Whitney expedition, when he was in his prime, would last a couple of weeks—perhaps a week in and around London while the Derby or the Ascot Gold Cup was being run (he bought a flat on St. James's Place toward the end of his ambassadorial stint and installed his ambassadorial chauffeur as resident caretaker), and then a few days' grouse shooting in Scotland (he generally took along his own custom-made 16-gauge Purdy shotguns); perhaps also a brief stopover in Paris to visit friends or editors. His junkets were always meticulously laid on, with innumerable communications in advance between his secretaries and the managers of the Crillon or—before he had his own flat— Claridge's (there should be two limousines to meet the Whitney party at Orly or Heathrow, one for Mr. and Mrs. Whitney and daughter Kate, the other for Mr. Whitney's valet and their luggage); between the secretaries and Whitney (remember to go to Peal & Co. on Oxford Street for grouse-shooting shoes, to Davies & Son for a new shooting outfit, oh, also to Peal for your blue velvet monogrammed slippers); and between Whitney and himself for a suitable allocation of travelers' checks (fifteen hundred dollars for wife, five hundred dollars for daughter, seven hundred and fifty for valet). Returning from one such trip, Jock asked a secretary to count the leftover French francs he had tossed into a desk drawer. He believed he had about fifty dollars' worth. The secretary came up with a hundred and seven. The rich are often richer than they think.

In his later years, Whitney seldom strayed from a pattern of movement he had evolved and thoroughly enjoyed: Georgia in early winter, next New York City and Long Island, with perhaps a brief look at his horse-breeding establishment in Kentucky; England in May; Fishers Island in early summer; Saratoga for two weeks in August; then back to New York. "I don't know quite why I got so committed to such a routine," Whitney said, almost ruefully, when he was in his mid-seventies. "There were all those places to stay at, and it seemed like the thing to do. I'm afraid it was rather establishmentarian."

Whitney was basking in Greenwood early in 1976—the centennial year, as it happened, of his mother's birth—when he suffered a severe heart attack. He had had minor cardiac troubles before, and rheumatic fever while in college, but this was a massive coronary. He spent three months in the John D. Archbold Memorial Hospital at Thomasville (it was named after one of Colonel Oliver Payne's Standard Oil associates) and then another three months recuperating, until he was pronounced fit to travel north. For a while, early in his illness, he couldn't speak, and he was convinced, wrongly, that he had suffered a stroke—like his sister Joan, who had died just the year before.

The Archbold Hospital was, for a town with a population of less than twenty thousand, an exemplary institution, in no small part because of the beneficence of the neighborhood plantation owners. Whitney, for instance, had endowed the Louie A. Beard Memorial Scholarships that it conferred each year on apprentice nurses. In 1951, further, he had bought a field that served Thomasville as a landing place for light aircraft, and had stipulated that, when and if it was no longer used for that purpose, it would go to the hospital. The last plane touched down there in 1960; the hospital sold the land for fifty thousand dollars. After his recovery, "as a token of appreciation," Jock gave the hospital another seventy-five thousand dollars, for the establishment of a new coronary unit. It was to be named after Dr. Oscar M. Mims, a local physician who'd taken care of Whitney during his prolonged sickness. When Jock sent the doctor himself, as a token of appreciation, a check for seventy-five hundred dollars, Mims wrote him, "My usual gifts from grateful patients are in the form of tomatoes, corn, fruit cake, or jelly, or an occasional bottle of Bourbon or Scotch."

(Jock's daughter Sara's second husband was Ronald A. Wilford, the president of Columbia Artists. Sara arranged for Mstislav Rostropovich to play a benefit in Thomasville for the hospital. The cellist stayed at Greenwood, and while strolling around the grounds came upon some blossoms, on an unidentified tree, from which, he wrote his bedridden host, he was going to try to concoct a new strain of vodka. "I think this will be a very successful experiment," Rostropovich told Whitney, "and we will both become very famous." The fame of both of them ended up having to rest on prior accomplishments.)

Whitney's recovery was slow, and incomplete. That he was alive at all was considered by the people closest to him to be a testimonial to his ruggedness. From then on, though, his activities were severely circumscribed. Betsey herself was having spells of poor health; their regular New York and Long Island household staff of thirty (the figure did not include chauffeurs, gardeners, and the like) would presently be augmented by six full-time nurses. The Whitneys had moved out of their East Sixty-third Street town house in 1976, because a new subway line was being built beneath it. They bought a duplex apartment on Beekman Place to camp out in until the tunnel was finished, if ever it should be. The six Picassos Whitney had come into as his share of the Gertrude Stein collection were hung in his Beekman Place bedroom, but, spending as he did most of his days, and nights, on Long Island, he would rarely get a glimpse of them.

Now and then, during his lengthy convalescence, Whitney would go to New York and visit his office for an hour or two; usually, though, his associates would bring things to him at Greentree. They always hoped it would be most convenient for him if they could arrive at noon. It was characteristic of Jock that it embarrassed him to suggest that any of his people make the half-hour drive out to Long Island when they needed his eye or ear; but none of them objected. There were few restaurants in New York City where they could expect to find as fine a lunch. All in all, Greentree was as comfortable a private home to be in, whatever the state of one's health, as anyone could ask for. When a society reporter traipsed out there one day to write about the estate, Jock and Betsey were abashed because they feared she might inquire how many rooms their main house contained, and further abashed because they didn't know. (Depending on whether or not certain anterooms and walk-in closets were counted, a fairly accurate response would have been seventy-six.) Similarly, Jock had once been asked how many people lived on his estate. "I haven't the faintest idea," he had replied, and then out of curiosity had turned that stumper over to Sam Park, who, following some intensive research, had informed him—stressing that this was only a guess—that the answer was one hundred and twenty-nine.

During his recovery from the heart attack, Whitney once flew to Saratoga for the August races. An elevator had been installed in his house there to facilitate his getting about, but even so he felt so tired after landing that after a brief look at some of his horses he returned to Long Island without even entering the residence. He flew to Thomasville a couple of winters, but felt too weary to avail himself of most of its attractions. His legs were weak. When he ventured out quail shooting, he kept tripping over the underbrush, and that distressed his companions for several reasons: rattlesnakes had long lurked among the Georgia briars. Dove shooting was better. One went after doves sitting down, in a blind.

But the departures from Greentree would be rare. There would be a lot of time—too much time, for a man so long so vigorous. Watching daytime television would kill time, all right, but not very satisfyingly. For most of his adult life, Whitney had been hard pressed to squeeze into his waking hours all the things he wanted to do, or felt he had to do. Now there were hours to spare—hours for introspection, for wondering if he had made the most of the exceptional opportunities his exceptional assets had blessed him with; for wondering, too, how to dispose of those assets, not least among them the very house he was chafingly confined to. Greentree had to be regarded from any angle as one of the last great estates of its kind in private hands—as, indeed, was Jock himself perhaps one of the last of his uniquely endowed species.

Not long after the brutal assassination of Whitney's old friend Earl Mountbatten, Jock got to reminiscing one day about Lord Mountbatten's affection for and devotion to one of his big landed properties, and musing what might become of his own place. "What is the outlook for any member of the Whitney family to continue to occupy Greentree in the future?" Jock told a visitor. "Meager, if not hopeless. Not only would that not be in the American tradition, but the cost of maintaining this establishment, after inheritance taxes and all of that, would be all but insurmountable." He had already engaged the architect I. M. Pei to devise several possible destinies for the property—in public or private hands or both.

What had it all added up to? Here was a man who in a single year could and did give away more money than most people see in a lifetime

—six million dollars, say—and still live like a king. He had not been an especially inventive or creative man. Most of the institutions he faithfully and lavishly supported—hospitals, museums, universities—were existing ones; in his absence, they might have been sustained by other benefactors. The business enterprises that bore his name had made money but had hardly made history. His foundation was small and might not long outlast him. The newspaper that had meant the most to him of any of his enterprises was gone. The Republican President of the United States, for all that Whitney had done for his party for so many years, was a man Jock had only known in Hollywood as a movie actor. Apart from the pleasure Whitney's company had given to so many people in so many different walks of life, it seemed likely that he might best be remembered, when the time came for that sort of thing, as a symbol. He had epitomized, in a world of increasing egalitarianism, the vanishing patrician. If the extraordinarily affluent men and women of his era were ever to be judged by his behavior, history would treat them gently—at least those of them who, like Jock, had constantly cherished and epitomized the belief that traditions should be responsive to new ideas. For he had been a philanthropist in the very best sense of that word—a man who combined generosity (and self-indulgence) with fairness, decency, and, so important in his day and age, a genuine social conscience.

In the dark autumn days of Whitney's long and mainly sunny life, there would be a few moments of special pleasure. His Greentree Stable had had only two stakes-race winners in 1976, and none at all in 1977. Jock's long-time trainer, John Gaver, had taken ill, too, and had had to retire in 1978, with his son John, Jr., succeeding him. That year, five Greentree horses, all homebred at the Greentree Stud, had provided their owner with thirteen stakes trophies—led by the filly Late Bloomer, which as a four-year-old won six races in a row. For the first time in the stable's history, Greentree earned more than a million dollars in purses in 1978. (The winnings nonetheless fell considerably short of covering the cost of maintaining *that* enterprise.) In 1979, Greentree came up with another fairly late bloomer, the five-year-old gelding Bowl Game, on which the turfwriters bestowed the title of Grass Horse of the Year, and which won over half a million dollars in purses. In a touching anthropomorphic gesture, when the Jockeys' Agents Benevolent Association made Whitney their *Man* of that year, the printed program for their twenty-third annual dinner dance contained a full-page "Congratulations to Our Boss" advertisement that was signed by Bowl Game, Late Bloomer, and their stablemates Fuzzbuster, Buckaroo, and San Juan Hill. The hundred-and-fifty-dollar cost of that testimonial would eventually, of course, become a debit on their boss's racing ledger.

By then, Whitney did not feel up to going to tracks and watching his horses run. Occasionally, he could see his colors carried to victory on television. An incident that happened in the spring of 1980 was illustrative of both his latter-day concerns and the concern that people who had long been affiliated with him felt for him. He had a three-year-old named Prince Valiant, which for a time was regarded as a contender for the Kentucky Derby. The horse went into a slump and never even made it to the starting gate at Churchill Downs, but earlier in the season he won a couple of big races. One of these took place in Florida, and the event wasn't carried, up north, on either television or radio. A retired superintendent of the Greentree estate, Mike Malone, was living in Florida, and he knew how much it would mean to Whitney to follow that race at first hand. So Malone tuned it in on a local radio station in Florida, called up his ex-boss on Long Island, and held his telephone mouthpiece alongside the radio throughout the race while Whitney glued his ear to his own receiver. After the *Herald Tribune* lost its race for survival, its Paris counterpart had described Jock's effort to keep the paper going—an effort that had required regal spending—as "valiant." After that Florida race, one of Whitney's friends remarked, "Prince Valiant wasn't named for Jock, of course [he got its name because his sire was Stage Door Johnny and his dam Royal Folly], but when you stop to think about it Jock was certainly born a prince, and among all the adjectives one could grope for to apply to him, I can't think of many more appropriate than 'valiant.'"

INDEX